App and Website Accessibility Developments and Compliance Strategies

Yakup Akgül
Alanya Alaaddin Keykubat University, Turkey

A volume in the Advances in Web
Technologies and Engineering
(AWTE) Book Series

Published in the United States of America by
IGI Global
Engineering Science Reference (an imprint of IGI Global)
701 E. Chocolate Avenue
Hershey PA, USA 17033
Tel: 717-533-8845
Fax: 717-533-8661
E-mail: cust@igi-global.com
Web site: http://www.igi-global.com

Library of Congress Cataloging-in-Publication Data

Names: Akgul, Yakup, 1977- editor.
Title: App and website accessibility developments and compliance strategies
  / Yakup Akgül, editor.
Description: Hershey, PA : Engineering Science Reference, [2021] | Includes
  bibliographical references and index. | Summary: "This edited book
  reviews the importance of website usability and accessibility in this
  age of digitization and offers a look at research, government standards
  and technology improvements into the goal of making websites
  barrier-free for all"-- Provided by publisher.
Identifiers: LCCN 2020052344 (print) | LCCN 2020052345 (ebook) | ISBN
  9781799878483 (hardcover) | ISBN 9781799878490 (paperback) | ISBN
  9781799878506 (ebook)
Subjects: LCSH: Web site development. | Accessible Web sites for people
  with disabilities. | User-centered system design. | Computer
  software--Human factors.
Classification: LCC TK5105.888 .A59 2021 (print) | LCC TK5105.888 (ebook)
  | DDC 006.701/9--dc23
LC record available at https://lccn.loc.gov/2020052344
LC ebook record available at https://lccn.loc.gov/2020052345

This book is published in the IGI Global book series Advances in Web Technologies and Engineering (AWTE) (ISSN: 2328-2762; eISSN: 2328-2754)

British Cataloguing in Publication Data
A Cataloguing in Publication record for this book is available from the British Library.

All work contributed to this book is new, previously-unpublished material.
The views expressed in this book are those of the authors, but not necessarily of the publisher.

For electronic access to this publication, please contact: eresources@igi-global.com.

Advances in Web Technologies and Engineering (AWTE) Book Series

ISSN:2328-2762
EISSN:2328-2754

Editor-in-Chief: Ghazi I. Alkhatib, The Hashemite University, Jordan; David C. Rine, George Mason University, USA

MISSION

The **Advances in Web Technologies and Engineering (AWTE) Book Series** aims to provide a platform for research in the area of Information Technology (IT) concepts, tools, methodologies, and ethnography, in the contexts of global communication systems and Web engineered applications. Organizations are continuously overwhelmed by a variety of new information technologies, many are Web based. These new technologies are capitalizing on the widespread use of network and communication technologies for seamless integration of various issues in information and knowledge sharing within and among organizations. This emphasis on integrated approaches is unique to this book series and dictates cross platform and multidisciplinary strategy to research and practice.

The **Advances in Web Technologies and Engineering (AWTE) Book Series** seeks to create a stage where comprehensive publications are distributed for the objective of bettering and expanding the field of web systems, knowledge capture, and communication technologies. The series will provide researchers and practitioners with solutions for improving how technology is utilized for the purpose of a growing awareness of the importance of web applications and engineering.

COVERAGE

- IT education and training
- Knowledge structure, classification, and search algorithms or engines
- Information filtering and display adaptation techniques for wireless devices
- Radio Frequency Identification (RFID) research and applications in Web engineered systems
- Competitive/intelligent information systems
- Metrics-based performance measurement of IT-based and web-based organizations
- Web Systems Architectures, Including Distributed, Grid Computer, and Communication Systems Processing
- Data analytics for business and government organizations
- Integrated user profile, provisioning, and context-based processing
- Mobile, location-aware, and ubiquitous computing

IGI Global is currently accepting manuscripts for publication within this series. To submit a proposal for a volume in this series, please contact our Acquisition Editors at Acquisitions@igi-global.com or visit: http://www.igi-global.com/publish/.

Titles in this Series

For a list of additional titles in this series, please visit: http://www.igi-global.com/book-series/

IoT Protocols and Applications for Improving Industry, Environment, ad Society
Cristian González García (University of Oviedo, Spain) and Vicente García-Díaz (University of Oviedo, Spain)
Engineering Science Reference • © 2021 • 321pp • H/C (ISBN: 9781799864639) • US $245.00

Integration and Implementation of the Internet of Things Through Cloud Computing
Pradeep Tomar (Gautam Buddha University, India)
Engineering Science Reference • © 2021 • 357pp • H/C (ISBN: 9781799869818) • US $245.00

Design Innovation and Network Architecture for the Future Internet
Mohamed Boucadair (Orange S.A., France) and Christian Jacquenet (Orange S.A., France)
Engineering Science Reference • © 2021 • 478pp • H/C (ISBN: 9781799876465) • US $225.00

Challenges and Opportunities for the Convergence of IoT, Big Data, and Cloud Computing
Sathiyamoorthi Velayutham (Sona College of Technology, India)
Engineering Science Reference • © 2021 • 350pp • H/C (ISBN: 9781799831112) • US $215.00

Examining the Impact of Deep Learning and IoT on Multi-Industry Applications
Roshani Raut (Pimpri Chinchwad College of Engineering (PCCOE), Pune, India) and Albena Dimitrova Mihovska (CTIF Global Capsule (CGC), Denmark)
Engineering Science Reference • © 2021 • 304pp • H/C (ISBN: 9781799875116) • US $245.00

Result Page Generation for Web Searching Emerging Research and Opportunities
Mostafa Alli (Tsinghua University, China)
Engineering Science Reference • © 2021 • 126pp • H/C (ISBN: 9781799809616) • US $165.00

701 East Chocolate Avenue, Hershey, PA 17033, USA
Tel: 717-533-8845 x100 • Fax: 717-533-8661
E-Mail: cust@igi-global.com • www.igi-global.com

Table of Contents

Detailed Table of Contents

An organization's website is a gateway to its information, products, and services. As such, it should be a reflection of the needs of the clients that it serves. Unfortunately, website design and development is often driven by technology or organizational structure or business objectives, rather than user needs. Since higher educational institutions have started to use their websites as a means of recruiting students, an effective website design emerged as a critical factor in attracting students. The usability factor is an extremely important aspect in an individual website as it ensures the survival of each institution in digital environment. In addition to the importance of website usability, the COVID-19 virus significantly increased the importance of websites, especially university websites. Website users and designers accept usability as major criteria in developing websites. If any institution website has poor usability, it is difficult to use, and visitors may turn to other institutions' websites.

The study aims to reveal the most effective factors on the accessibility statistics of the Electronic Data Delivery System (EDDS) of The Central Bank of The Turkish Republic. Besides, another aim is to reveal the effect of the exchange rate on the access statistics of EDDS exchange rate data. For this purpose, a stepwise regression model was used to find the most effective factors on accessibility statistics. According to the results of stepwise regression analysis, it was revealed that 9 out of 26 variables significantly affected the EDDS access statistics. Engle-Granger cointegration test was chosen as the method to examine the relationship between exchange rate and EDDS access statistics. It has been revealed that there is a long-run equilibrium relationship between the EURO/TRY exchange rate and the access statistics of EDDS exchange rate data.

Chapter 3

Gonca Gokce Menekse Dalveren, Atilim University, Turkey
Serhat Peker, Izmir Bakırçay University, Turkey

This study aims to present an exploratory study about the accessibility and usability evaluation of digital library article pages. For this purpose, four widely known digital libraries (DLs), namely Science Direct, Institute of Electric and Electronic Engineering Xplore, Association for Computing Machinery, and SpringerLink, were examined. In the first stage, article web interfaces of these selected DLs were analyzed based on standard web guidelines using automatic evaluation tools to assess their accessibility. In the second stage, to evaluate the usability of these web interfaces, eye-tracking experiments with 30 participants were conducted. Obtained results of the analysis show that article pages of digital libraries are not of free of accessibility and usability problems. Overall, this study highlights accessibility and usability problems of digital library article interfaces, and these findings can provide the feedback to web developers in making their article pages more accessible and usable for their users.

Chapter 4

Pınar Onay Durdu, Kocaeli University, Turkey
Ömer Naci Soydemir, Kocaeli University, Turkey

Currently, providing accessible websites for all users is an essential requirement. There are various qualitative and quantitative evaluation methods to assure accessibility. Among these, the quantitative methods show the level of accessibility of the website using web accessibility metrics (WAM), which provide a way to understand, control, and improve these websites. This study was aimed to identify current trends and analyze WAMs through a systematic literature review. Therefore, 30 WAM studies that were published since 2008 were determined and investigated according to attributes defined for the metrics such as guideline set used by the metric, coupling level with the guidelines, type of evaluation, site complexity, and validation with the user. Fourteen recently proposed WAMs were determined since 2008. Recently proposed WAMs have begun to consider more elaborate issues such as rich internet applications, website complexity, usability, or user experience issues and implement some machine learning approaches for the metrics.

Chapter 5

Fernando Almeida, Polytechnic Institute of Gaya, Portugal
Nuno Bernardo, Polytechnic Institute of Gaya, Portugal
Rúben Lacerda, Polytechnic Institute of Gaya, Portugal

There is a huge proliferation of digital products on the market today for both large enterprises and small businesses. Most of these companies have experienced the development of software products for the mobile market and have been faced with the major challenge of capturing the customer's attention. There is a great focus on making a great first impact and providing the audience with the best possible digital experience. Accordingly, issues related to usability, accessibility, and user experience are extremely relevant. This chapter addresses how these practices can be used in practice by building an app that offers car cleaning services. Several approaches based on building app interfaces that increase user engagement and retention levels are explored and discussed.

Chapter 6

Zehra Altuntaş, Kocaeli University, Turkey
Pınar Onay Durdu, Kocaeli University, Turkey

In this chapter, a unified web accessibility assessment (UWAA) framework and its software has been proposed. UWAA framework was developed by considering Web Content Accessibility Guideline 2.0 to evaluate accessibility of web sites by integrating more than one evaluation approach. Achecker tool as an automated evaluation approach and barrier walkthrough (BW) as an expert-based evaluation approach were integrated in the UWAA framework. The framework also provides suggestions to recover from the problems determined to the evaluators. The websites of three universities were evaluated to determine the framework's accuracy and consistency. It was revealed that the results obtained from automated and expert-based evaluation methods were consistent and complementary with each other. Furthermore, it has been demonstrated that problems which cannot be determined by an automated tool but which can be detected by an expert can be identified by BW method.

Chapter 7

Yakup Akgül, Alanya Alaaddin Keykubat University, Turkey

Disabled people encounter many barriers while attempting to access the services on the web. E-commerce websites have been also intensively and widely used. The e-commerce market in Turkey will hit TL 400 billion by 2021. It also evaluates the accessibility of 10 popular Turkish e-commerce websites using five accessibility testing tools, namely Achecker, TAW, Eval Access, MAUVE, and FAE. This research has found that most accessibility guidelines are covered by A checker tool. Navigation, readability, input assistance, and timing are the common found accessibility problems while assessing the accessibility of the targeted websites.

Chapter 8

Aşkın Özdağoğlu, Dokuz Eylul University, Turkey

Murat Kemal Keleş, Keçiborlu Vocational School, Isparta University of Applied Sciences, Turkey

Barış Işıldak, Keçiborlu Vocational School, Isparta University of Applied Sciences, Turkey

Technological and social developments cause the birth and death rates to decrease. This has a direct effect on the increase in the rate of old age in the total population. In Turkey like in other countries, they face various problems in transportation in addition to education, health, justice, and social security. Therefore, the airline companies should provide some special services to elderly individuals in terms of accessibility and usability for their websites. This chapter aims to examine the accessibility of websites of airline companies for 65 and older individuals. Then, the second aim of this chapter is to determine the criteria for accessibility and alternatives. Then the next aim of this chapter is to determine the weights of these criteria and evaluate the alternatives with multi-criteria decision-making methods. The best airline company for airline website according to OWA, WASPAS, WSM, and WPM methods is Alternative 1.

Chapter 9

Fredrick Ishengoma, The University of Dodoma, Tanzania

For the past decade, the Tanzanian government has started implementing m-government initiatives. However, little is known about the factors surrounding m-government adoption in Tanzania. Consequently, some m-government services have been successfully adopted while others are still struggling (having a low level of adoption). In this chapter, the authors investigate critical success factors (CSFs) that favor the adoption of m-government services from a web analytics point of view. The results show that inspecting the web analytics data from multiple viewpoints and varying levels of detail, gives insights on the CSFs towards the adoption of m-government services. The findings suggest that perceived usefulness, user needs, and usability favor the adoption of one m-government service over the other. Moreover, factors like the loading time of the service, the number of requests, and bounce rate seem not to have an effect.

Chapter 10
Yakup Akgül, Alanya Alaaddin Keykubat University, Turkey

The website has become a crucial part of digitalization. In recent years, the airline sector has shifted to online platforms in order to expand its client base and provide consumers with timely information and services. Usability and accessibility are essential aspects of web quality that influence consumer acquisition and retention. As a result, the purpose of this study is to assess the quality of Turkish airline websites. The website is assessed based on its accessibility, usability, and readability utilizing online automated techniques. Finally, internet tools are used to assess the mobile-friendliness of websites. According to the findings, none of the Turkish airline websites meet the WCAG 2.0 accessibility criteria and have severe usability problems.

Preface

The book *App and Website Accessibility Developments and Compliance Strategies* provides theoretical and practical contributions on the role of accessible applications and websites in the development of accessible e-services. This is an area of utmost relevance in increasing the participation of all people in e-services activities, independent of their characteristics. Web accessibility is only an extreme instance, since we shall all be hampered by technology or the environment in the end. Web accessibility work is assisting us in addressing a variety of other topics, particularly those centered on user mobility. Work on physical disabilities and the Web, for example, is assisting in the resolution of usability issues with mobile technologies. The operational challenges of mobile engagement in moving surroundings are handled by adopting the same technology that is used to offset a physically handicapped user's tremors and jerky motions to the mobile Web. Similarly, accessibility and usability issues affect mobile Web access, making the Web as difficult to connect with for mainstream users as it is for visually impaired users. Again, ideas offered in the Web accessibility community three to four years ago are now being implemented on popular mobile devices. Indeed, we are all unique, which is a reality that is often overlooked. Improving our knowledge and understanding of the Web via research and innovation is a crucial step toward achieving Web accessibility. Web accessibility raises the vision of designers, programmers, and academics working tirelessly to make the World Wide Web (Web) accessible to people with disabilities. While this is somewhat correct, the truth is slightly different.

Web accessibility has always been viewed as a Web Design difficulty, and as a result, the majority of relevant publications are prescriptive instructions on how to accomplish Web accessibility. However, hundreds, if not thousands, of research scientists and research and development programmers in academia and industry are striving to improve our understanding of the present Web and to make advancements in the next Web more accessible. As a result, this book will focus on Web accessibility from a purely research standpoint. As the authoritative, foundational source on Web Accessibility from a highly research viewpoint, the book is primarily intended for academics, scientists, engineers, and postgraduate students. The disabled user serves as a reminder that Web accessibility is a truly personal experience, and that by understanding the flexibility and personalization required by disabled users, we can anticipate that this same flexibility and personalization will be required by all users at some point in the future. To comprehend the requirements of handicapped users, one must comprehend the needs of all people. Indeed, knowing the interaction of impaired users improves our knowledge of all users working in limited modalities, when the user is hampered by both the environment and technology. Web accessibility is a natural preliminary to greater Web usability and universal accessibility for this reason; it is also why mainstream human factors researchers take it seriously and recognize its cross-cutting advantages.

Acknowledgment

The editor would like to thank all people and organizations involved directly or indirectly in this project. First, my thanks to all the authors for their excellent contributions to increasing knowledge in an area that is still little explored in the literature. Second, I also grateful to all reviewers for their valuable suggestions. Lastly, I also grateful to IGI Global Publications for the opportunity to publish this book.

Yakup Akgül
Alanya Alaaddin Keykubat University, Turkey

Chapter 1
Importance and Usability of University Websites

Ersin Caglar
ⓘD https://orcid.org/0000-0002-2175-5141
European University of Lefke, Turkey

ABSTRACT

An organization's website is a gateway to its information, products, and services. As such, it should be a reflection of the needs of the clients that it serves. Unfortunately, website design and development is often driven by technology or organizational structure or business objectives, rather than user needs. Since higher educational institutions have started to use their websites as a means of recruiting students, an effective website design emerged as a critical factor in attracting students. The usability factor is an extremely important aspect in an individual website as it ensures the survival of each institution in digital environment. In addition to the importance of website usability, the COVID-19 virus significantly increased the importance of websites, especially university websites. Website users and designers accept usability as major criteria in developing websites. If any institution website has poor usability, it is difficult to use, and visitors may turn to other institutions' websites.

INTRODUCTION

At any time, education affects almost all of us, such as employees, students, parents and citizens. In this sense, education can be considered as a basic necessity like health care. Educational institutions are a large, complex, and changing industry with universities, private schools, and a small but very rapidly growing number of private for-profit educational institutions (Perna, 2020).

DOI: 10.4018/978-1-7998-7848-3.ch001

Growing demand of education improved accessibility and convenience, and the technology is changing the environment for education globally. In this dramatically changing environment, educational institutions are attempting to adapt purposes, structures, program while new institutions are emerging in response (Chauhan et. al., 2020). Changes and new developments are being fueled by accelerating advances in digital communication technologies that are sweeping the world. Significantly growing demand for education combined with these technical advances are in fact a critical pressure point for challenging the dominant assumptions and characteristics of existing traditionally organized educational institutions in the 21st century (Daniela et. al., 2018).

The recent developments such as artificial intelligence, cloud computing, and new applications of virtual reality to build simulated learning environments are predicted to have dramatic effects upon learning environments at all levels. In higher education industry, educational institutions are designing or develop new programs to take advantage of these emerging technologies (Quintero and Selwyn, 2018). At the same time, educational institutions are trying to market their programs to new or existing audiences in new ways. Corporations also have formed new alliances with universities to promote technology for education. Totally new models for educational institutions are also being developed to respond to the opportunities created by a worldwide market for education and new technologies (Dunn and Kennedy, 2019).

Shortly, after the commercialization of the web, the multimedia component of the web which is called the world wide web (WWW), experienced a phenomenal growth. Businesses, higher education institutions and individuals raced to place websites and content on the web as part of this growth (Ferris and Farrell, 2003). Like all other higher education institutions, universities are required to present and market their services on the internet. So, the web has become a crucial tool in communicating with the various constituencies of an institution such as prospective and current students, parents, academicians, employees and competitor universities. Because of these endless opportunities, the number of websites has continued to increase as well as the importance of website usability.

The rapidly changing environment, particularly the recent marked increase in public availability of information leads the global higher education system to become more marketed. In other words, the endless opportunities of the web, increasing number of websites and websites themselves open the door to the emerging competitors and new organizations that will compete directly for students, academicians, departments and prestige. The competition over the internet among a large number and different kinds of universities has introduced new phrases and developed new concepts since the needs, desires and expectations of students change in accordance with the internet (Morse, 2017).

Apart from competitive environment, COVID-19 created a highly competitive environment in today's conditions. So, university websites have become the most popular means for various purposes such as announcements, online courses, online exams and etc.… Due to the importance of websites, the needs and demands of users are also increasing dramatically (Burki, 2020).

In this competitive environment and COVID-19, website usability is an important concept for the universities as website users have become familiar with web and begun to expect more and more. Many websites offer similar facilities with poor usability, but the existing website users have becoming more demanding according to their needs and expectations. Website users prefer visiting websites, which are easy to use and operate and aesthetically appealing. So, the usability of a website plays a significant role to keep users online or determining the number of hits to that website.

GLOBALIZATION AND TECHNOLOGY

Technology is a driving factor in the development and process of globalization. The developments in the early 1990s in hardware, software and telecommunications have caused widespread improvements to access information. These opportunities have facilitated efficiency gains in all sectors of the communication. Growing technology provides the communication network that facilitates the expansion of services, ideas products, and resources among nations and people regardless of their geographical location. Upon creating effective and efficient channels to exchange information, technology has been the catalyst for global integration (Chareonwongsak, 2002, Schaeffer, 2003). Without internet connection, it would be impossible to transfer any information at negligible or minimum costs from one part of the world to another and this is the material condition which ensures globalization in various aspects like fashion, media, finance, production and culture. On the other hand, the production and dissemination of inventions and innovations have become much more global in scope than in the past (Qadri and Bhat, 2018).

Last decades, internet technology is the most significant technological innovation that plays a critical role in the development of globalization. It facilitated the expansion of the movement towards a global village through the creation of cheaper, faster and easier means of communication, provision of a vast pool of information, and expansion of e-commerce. So, internet has created a global audience (Schroeder, 2018)

The effects of internet technology on globalization have both positive and at the same time negative aspects. The positive effects of the internet on globalization contains the modernization and improvement in the business area on a worldwide. Any business improves their global competitiveness and productivity with more efficient electronic transaction and instant access to information. New communication technologies (ICT) and radically changing international political and regulatory environments reshaped the nature of management consulting where ICT took center stage for global management consulting firms. Now, the market is more competitive with consumers having vast variety of choices (Jungherr, 2019).

While Internet can have a positive impact on globalization, some negative aspects may also be possible. The interdependence and internet technological advancement have increased in some parts of the world, yet this is not applicable in the vast majority world and less developed and third world countries. Despite the growing globalization of the internet technology, the less developed or third world countries cannot benefit as much as those of the developed countries in economic as well as in political institutions (Fernández, 2020).

Internet Technology

In the last decade, technological and technical improvements increased the use electronic devices that are fast and cheap such as computers, smart phones and smart devices. Especially the internet has boomed in the number of users and amount of information that it makes available and the number of different programs you can use (Kusek, 2018). The internet is networked computers and a significant global tool for communication, content and commerce. It is a powerful tool for building relationships with all targets and competitors. Most traditional communications media including telephone, music, film, and television are being reshaped or redefined by the Internet. Newspapers, books and printed press have to adapt to websites (Curran et. al., 2016).

Internet is cheap, immediate and repeatable with appropriate technology that can be personalized. So, internet is an important environment to allow enterprises obtain the great benefits and increase user satisfaction. Because of these reasons, the millions of people have been using internet to search information, learn something and communicate. On the other hand, internet user population growth rapidly, because internet has endless opportunities such as 24/7 connection to communicate, unlimited content, easy to target multiple audiences, world-wide reach and quick finding and access to information (Hassan et. al, 2016, Agarwal and Shiju 2018).

The use of internet is growing each day. Figure 1 indicates the number of internet users and its rapid increase from 2005 to 2019. The easier access to computers, modernization of countries all around the world and an increased utilization of smart tools and devices have given people the opportunity to use the internet more frequently with more convenience. As shown in Figure 1, the total number of internet users 3.97 billion in 2019 all around the world, and going up from 3.74 billion in the previous year (Johnson, 2021).

Figure 1. The Growth of Internet Users in the World From 2005-2019
Source: *(Johnson, 2021)*

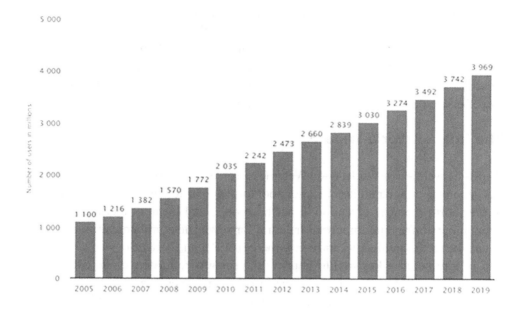

Internet technology is rapidly growing and changing while becoming a important and dominant factor in business, academia, and everyday life. This change began with news and advertisements, followed by entertainment and traditional businesses, such as financing, brokerage, retail sales and auctions. Now a days, new businesses and services are created on and for the internet. In terms of business, internet is a critical technologic tool and venue for conducting commerce. As a tool, it provides sellers and buyers nearly unlimited access to information of goods and services. As a venue, it eliminates the boundaries or obstacles of geography, time zones and in some cases, the need for a physical office. With its tremendous potential, Internet has become a common place for businesses and consumers to utilize a variety of transactions ranging from emails to actual online purchases (Soegoto and Rafi, 2018, Patro, 2021, Langley, 2021).

Universities are facing with increasing challenges caused by rapid changes in information technology and fast development of internet, severe financial constraints, and lingering institutional rigidities. At the same time, there are many more demands on higher education institutions to provide better and greater student access to education, better undergraduate programs, and increased productivity. To address all sets of issues, the higher education institutions are turning to up to date communication and information technologies that promise to increase access, improve the quality of tutoring, and control costs (Molero Jurado et. al., 2021). So, the proposed or usage aim of the internet as the preferred technology to raise productivity and improve lecture quality, increase access. At the same time, universities should use the internet as a tool to attract students. These educational institutions knew that parents and high school students use the internet as an initial tool to shop around for the best university. Hence, the goal of higher education institutions should be creating their web sites where they will present the academic programs and opportunities that they can offer via their web sites (Ruiz, 2021, Apuke and Iyendo, 2018).

The Role of World Wide Web

With the invention of World Wide Web's (Web or WWW) in the early 1990s, WWW has become a popular communication tool for many different kinds of information. In the short time after invention, it has become a vital mean of facilitating global communication and an important medium for scientific communication including but not limited to publishing and e-commerce (O'Regan, 2018). So, web is a popular part of internet as a key tool to improve the scientific, academic and educational competences of any university. E-education or e-learning programs and online access initiatives allow knowledge of these institutions to spread beyond geographical regions. Web can be used as a tool to attract students, scholars and funding from other places by spreading the prestige of these educational institutions all over the world. This has provoked competition between universities to achieve an advantageous visibility on the web and improve their position in search engine results (Pesce, 2017).

Website is some kind of place (location) on the web and is a collection of related web pages, images, videos and other digital assets. Websites have become the most useful tool or device that include information in a very short period of time for a huge amount of the world's population (Kumar, 2018). Figure 2 shows the exponential growth in the number of websites between the years of 1991-2019 (Armstrong, 2019).

The websites are rapidly changing the internet from a difficult-to-use device for academics and technicians to an easy-to-use device for finding information for businesses and consumers. This rapid change in the web technology has opened up an extraordinary range of opportunities for universities that aim to create and improve their communication with prospective students upon influencing the university selection decision. The huge popularity of the internet among college-bound youth has made the prospect of using institutional web sites as effective and even powerful communication vehicle (Ganiyu et. al., 2017).

Figure 2. Number of Web Sites All over the World
Source: (Armstrong, 2019)

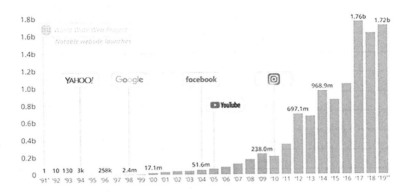

Competition Over Internet

The higher education industry is changing and experiencing dramatic growth with increasing competition. In addition, the COVID-19 virus also played a major role in this dramatic change. The advancements in technology have a very critical role in the efforts of universities in attracting new students. Apart from such changes, university population is drastically increasing all around the world as shown in Table 1 (Valero and Van Reenen, 2019, Uslu, 2018).

The increasing competition in the current global market has affected the education sector. Universities all around the world are competing for students and try to find effective ways to satisfy the needs of students (Cattaneo et. al., 20 17). Following the decreasing of the student's population, the universities gave more emphasis to market their services in order to attract more students. This increased the competition among the universities (Brankovic, 2018).

All around the world, higher education system has always considered itself competitive. The universities have always competed for students, research, athletic titles and prestige. In 2000's the rivalry intensified because of the increase in the number of universities and this upwards trend still continues (Hossain and Ahmed, 2020). But the competition reality was changed again after COVID-19. After COVID-19 the communication is not enough and the universities must use their websites for online education. Hence, the physical location of the university in not much more important rather than website (Marelli et. al., 2021).

Table 1. University population by countries

No	Country	No. of University
1	India	8.407
2	USA	5.758
3	Philippines	2.06
4	Argentina	1.705
5	Spain	1.415
6	Mexico	1.341
7	Bangladesh	1.268
8	Indonesia	1.236
9	Japan	1.223
10	Russia	1.108
11	France	1.062
12	China	1.054
13	İran	343
14	South Korea	322
15	Vietnam	209
16	Turkey	206
17	Egypt	173
18	Thailand	158

Source: (Valero and Van Reenen, 2019, Uslu, 2018)

In order to survive, universities need to be present and actively market their services on the internet. They should use internet to provide information and services to all staffs related with university. So, the university web sites should have specific sections that address the needs of each group such as potential students, enrolled students, employees, academicians, parents, competitors and all other stakeholders for any purposes such as communication, advertising, promotion, public relations, online course, exams etc. (McGrew et. al., 2019).

The Importance of University Websites

University website is much more popular tool for any university. However, with COVID-19, university websites have become even more important and indispensable device for create communication with the various constituencies of the university. With respect to their primary audiences, students, universities extensively utilize the web to create communication on both academic and non-academic endeavors (Yamada, 2021).

In the last decades, the ability of university web sites as an information provider for the interested public was somewhat mixed. Universities benefit from the advantages of web in providing university information such as basic statistical data, university history, admissions and scholarship information, library, and departmental information. So, websites of any university provide the technology and information necessary for today's students, academicians and others who are related with university to take full advantage of the services and academic offers of the university (Rezaeean, 2012).

The university website is a tool or device to create communication with students, faculty, alumni, visitors or who related with university. It is not only a cost efficient and timely way to communicate with various audiences. But also, a way for an institution to shape its image. Higher educations need to do everything within their power to keep positive attractive images within their various constituents, and one way to do this is to make use of the opportunities provided by the websites. On the other hand, universities use their websites as a marketing and public relations tool to reach prospective students and staff. Prospective students may likely apply to university if information about current students are more reliable and prominent on the website since they may see someone with similar goals who has made significant accomplishments or someone from their hometown or someone with similar interests. This kind of information may help to define an institution's image and differentiate it from other universities. At the same time, such a distinction is likely to help prospective faculty members who are pondering a job offer. They may see information regarding faculty research accomplishments or a faculty member's teaching awards (Mogaji, 2016, Almahamid, 2016).

In consideration with the aspects given above, a university website has different users like (Caglar and Mentes, 2012);

- Prospective students
- Parents
- Prospective faculty and staff
- Donors & Alumni
- Events

Because of different user types, a university website must offer different tools and services like web mail, blackboard (a virtual classroom tool), and student info (a student account and registration resource featuring on-line registration and transcript information, available course sections, and on-line grade accessibility). Besides these, university website should also offer quick links to the university catalog, admissions office, calendars, clubs and organizations, news, campus events, library databases, and a virtual campus tour can also be found on the university website (Caglar and Mentes, 2012).

Liu and Jones (2018) argue that any developed and modern university has to satisfy the following expectations on its web page:

- Course lists and timetables,
- Possibility to registration online (increase administrative efficiency)
- Payment procedures,
- Specific information,
- Course schedules and materials
- Academic calendar,
- Results, exams, application, registration,
- Online lectures.

Universities are trying to meet the expectations of different users by designing an appealing website to attract them. A study conducted by Student et. al., 2017 showed that universities have failed to meet the students' university search requirements. The research concluded that universities have not been clear or useful sources of information and need to improve their communication with students. The researcher warns the universities that students will not be patient with universities' websites since the statistics show that each month, 17.3 million kids and teens use the internet and spend only 8 seconds on a website to determine whether it contains what they are interested in (Chandra et. al., 2019).

Apart from the significance of university website, COVID-19 has changed everything. In terms of COVID-19, the role of university web site totally changes since websites are the only and most powerful tool to reach students and staff under COVID-19 curfew. Websites must contain all functionality of university such as payment issues, advertisement, announcement, online courses, exams etc. With the dramatically increase of website importance, universities should pay attention to their website design respectively (Yamada, 2021, Manzoor et. al., 2019).

WEBSITE DESIGN

The web user expectations have grown together with the development of web itself. As user become familiar with what they can find and how to find it, they have begun to expect more and fresh information from the web sites that they visit. Web users utilize the web in many ways so their needs and expectations may vary accordingly. For these purposes, it is difficult to design a web page for such scope. Consequently, designers need to understand issues such as why people visit a website and what they expect since these designers have to find new ways of meeting these expectations (Bocchi et. al., 2017).

Unless a website meets the expectation of the users, it will not meet the needs of the relevant organization. Development of website should be user-oriented by, evaluating the evolving design against user requirements. In the beginning, designer would be to find out the business objectives and goals, and to specify the intended contexts of use. These should drive an iterative process of design and evaluation, starting with partial mock-ups and moving to functional prototypes. The sustainable usability requires subsequent management and maintenance (Dzulfiqar et. al., 2018).

Universities began to use their websites as a mean to attract prospective students. Hence the universities need to be very careful about the profile that is projected through its website. The universities know that parents and high school students use the internet as a primary tool to shop around for the best college. A common concern of these universities should be whether websites are projecting their universities effectively. So, the aim of these university should be to effectively design and present their academic offerings and opportunities through their websites (Le and Vo, 2017).

Design Objectives and Goals

Universities were among the first organizations to create and design websites. In the earlier days, universities wanted simply to have a presence on the web. But today all universities have websites attempting to include a strong content combined with information about the university and their educational resources.

According to Lynch and Horton (2016), there are two phases in planning a website before design:

Phase One: Determination of the objectives and goals. The designers should determine what the organization wants to accomplish on the web. The sample objectives are as follows:

- To assist the prospective student in acquiring the information and resources necessary, leading to completion of an admissions application,
- To create a community for event followers,
- To provide prospective employees (staff and faculty) with job availability and employment information, leading to submit an employment application,
- To ensure further involvement of alumni with the university, including facilitating donations and endowments.

Phase Two: Identification of the target audience, website details, required technology, and an assessment of the results. The primary audiences are academic and general staff and students whereas the secondary audience comes from general public and other educational institutions.

University Website Design

The web is used for the dissemination device of information by many different public and private organizations as a source of information (Brügger, 2009). In the late 1999's, Nielsen (1999) conducted a research concluded that people do not use web for an 'experience' but rather they use for information. Similarly, Koman (1998) has reported that 2/3 of the web users are looking for specific information. Yet, the impact of a website's information architecture on the ability of a user to navigate that website is overlooked by many web-site designers, who tend to focus primarily on the site's 'look and feel'. The way that information is categorized, labeled and presented and how navigation and access are facilitated - the information architecture - determines not only whether users will and can find what they need, but also affects user satisfaction and influences return visits. This is not just a matter for traditional purveyors of information yet it also affects e-commerce sites. Recently, another research study illustrated that poorly designed web sites can cause the loss of 50% in potential sales when people cannot find what they are looking for, and that 40% of users do not return to a site when that first experience is negative (Manning et. al, 1998).

Results from researches of e-commerce websites offer insights to universities which operate in a competitive marketplace environment. Potential students may not login to a university site again if the needs or expectations are not met in the first visit, or information is difficult and frustrating to locate. In addition, the efficiency and effectiveness of current students and faculty member may be compromised when the information organization is not so intuitive that users can negotiate clear pathways. So, bad designed web site projects poor and bad image to everyone (Ghandour, 2015).

Designing a website is not a single project with static contents but it is rather a continuously process which needs long term technical management and editorial process. Almost all organizations try to define how viewers react to their websites and what attracts them. Experts believe that it is the content that brings users to a website. So, experts suggest that a more dynamic, valuable and up to date contents can attract more viewers. However, the challenge is that many website designers have not much knowledge or experience of user interface design and usability. Therefore, this kind of websites are wasting users' time and causing unnecessary traffic on the Internet (Lynch and Horton 2016).

In the development phase, any website should be examined through several design guidelines to success that the website can achieve the objectives and goals intended to be accomplished. In addition to these, any organization website is a passage to its information, products and services. It must be a reflection of the expectations of the users it serves. But design of website is always driven by technology, organizational structure or business objectives, except users' needs and expectation (Lynch and Horton 2016).

Everything within universities' website must have only one aim; attract their users to get action. Words are the most powerful advertise and marketing weapon that you have. Correct words will turn users into customers. But the wrong words will cause them to click away and never return back to website. Words are the entire foundation of any business. Services, product, website and marketing strategies all depend on words usage. Fancy animations don't do the work but the words do (Owoyele, 2017).

Design Problems

Regardless the functionality, design is the most important concept for any websites since it will increase the usability of websites. If website is simple, pure and basic, it will be more usable. But if website contains many animations, transitions or colorful images, it will not be usable for users (Astani, 2013).

1. **Splash screen usage:** A splash screen is an introductory screen, usually design with animation software that some websites run before displaying the home page. A splash screen consists of flashy images designed to jazz up the entry to a site or to create a certain mood for users entering the site. But almost all splash screens have a skip or ignore intro button to escape. Many website proponents claim that they are unnecessary and get in the way of the user experience (Nielsen and Loranger, 2006). According to Jennings (2004), splash screen usually takes a long time to download and for the most part they are worthless. Nielsen (2000) says bluntly, "Splash screens must die". The author contends that splash screens are annoying and ineffective, and users click off them as fast as they can.

2. **Horizontal scrolling:** Some websites are so broad-wide that they require users to scroll right to fully view their contents. When this occurs, many users will not make the additional effort required to scroll back and forth — especially horizontally — to view the rest of site. According to Johnson (2000), although users seem like will tolerate a little to moderate amount of downward scrolling, they really dislike having to scroll sideways and often simply will not. Gold (2003) also states that users should not be required to scroll right to fully view

site contents. It must be taken into account that whether or not scrolling is necessary depends on which screen resolution is used.

3. **Frequently Asked Questions (FAQ) or help:** Since users get lost on the web and have trouble finding the needed information and accomplishing their purposes. Possible support solution is to provide a FAQ or Help button on the website and this option must be visible. Van Duyne et al. (2003) stated that multiple links may be placed on your FAQ page, including one from the navigation bar to the FAQ page, labeled FAQ or Help. Lynch and Horton (2016) added that the inclusion of a FAQ option is ideal for any websites that are built to provide support and information and that a well-designed FAQ page can develop users' understanding of the information and services offered and reduce demands on your support staff.

4. **Navigation problem:** According to designers plan the objectives of a site, they need to keep in mind that many users have many difficulties as they search through a website (navigational problem) and they lost within the structure. Research stated that 58% of users will make at least two or more navigational problem while browsing information, and 66.8% concluded that users have problems in searching the information that they are looking for (Bernard, 2003). The simple navigation links should be present consistently on every site in the same location. A logical and successful website organization matches the users' need and will authorize them to make predictions about where to find information (Astani, 2013).

Design Guideline

The web has become a very popular place to publish information. A vast amount of information in website already exists and new information's are being created at a very rapid rate. Most of the sites on web repositories provide elements that allow users to interact with them. Thus, the website designers actually design user interfaces. The reproduction of websites with bad usability suggests that most of the designers of websites have not much knowledge of user interface design and usability engineering. This is an important problem that needs to solution because websites with bad design and usability waste user time discourage exploration and create a large amount of unnecessary traffic on the internet. On the other hand, it is important to build practical methodologies for designing usable website (Perdomo et. al., 2017).

There are a number of challenges in the design process of an effective university website. The information that it provides should be useful and easy to find. The site should be attractive and unique. The creation of a website that meets all of these criteria can be difficult, especially when designing the university website is only one in a list of a media specialist's responsibilities. These criteria are as follows (Perdomo et. al., 2017, Dzulfiqar et. al., 2018, Ganiyu et. al., 2017);

1. **Clearly state the goals of the site before you begin:** The first step to a more usable website is to understand the "who," "what," and "why" of the site. Who will come to the site, what will they do there, and why will they do it? Will visitors be parents looking for homework assignments or the academic calendar? Will they be students looking up assignments when they're sick? Will they be teachers looking for titles from the university library? Understanding the site's audience will help the designers make good decisions about how the site should be organized and laid out. It's easier to point visitors to the information that they need if you know what they're looking for. Having this information also will enable the designers to make better decisions about the areas of the site on which to spend the most time. For example, many university websites have pages with long lists of links to the external resources, but parents and teachers may simply need to access the academic calendar.

2. **Make pages easy to read but keep pages small:** Websites should be attractive, but they also must be easy on the eyes. This is a particularly common problem for university websites, since the designers of such sites often want to use bright colors for graphics, text, and background: colors that appeal to children's tastes. Children, however, aren't the only visitors to universities websites. In order to create a colorful but readable website, it's essential to use color combinations that contrast well.

The use of well-thought-out headings for paragraphs can make a site much easier to read. When reading text on any website, many people merely scan the headers first in order to decide if it's worth their time to read on. The use of meaningful headers can greatly simplify a visitor's search for information.

Recommendations for page size vary, but there's a consensus among usability researchers that smaller is better when it comes to creating a website. For university websites, small page size offers obvious advantages. Because university websites' users often have a wide variety of equipment, connection speed, and patience, it's vital to make sure that pages download quickly.

3. **Navigation:** Perhaps the most important rule of design and usability is to keep navigation predictable and consistent. This rule may seem obvious, but it's surprising how often sites employ different navigation methods from page to page. If navigation is consistent on every page, the users will be able to find information in a predictable manner from every area on the site.

Avoid using icons for navigation whenever possible. Many sites use icons with unclear meaning. An icon's purpose may be perfectly evident to the designer, but it might be difficult for a visitor to decipher. Linking text allows designers to incorporate a more meaningful explanation of where the link leads.

It's also important to pay attention to the number of clicks it takes users to find the information they need on the site. Revisit the goals outlined at the beginning of the design process: What are the users to the site doing? Try to limit the number of clicks it takes them to find what they're seeking.

4. **Design for accessibility:** A part of making sure that a university website is usable is about ensuring its useability for everyone, including people with disabilities. The web can offer physically challenged people a powerful tool to access information, but only if sites are designed with them in mind. A poorly designed site simply presents an immense obstacle. Designers can implement a number of simple ideas to create a more accessible site and break the obstacle.

5. **Be personal and easy to find:** Domain name selection must be simple that most people would think of if people were trying to find and one that is easy to remember. Manage the positioning on search engines. The visitor of website must feel like a member of a community. Where applicable, there should be an opportunity for interaction and communication. Be sure to make the privacy policy clear.

6. **Contact information:** Provide visitors with your full contact information. This contact information must contain the real post address. An organization that hides behind a post office box loses credibility. Design a page to add to the website called "about" and contains all of the following:
   a. A history
   b. A photograph
   c. A complete description
   d. Website objectives
   e. Name, address, phone number and email address

7. **Update and feedback:** Website user's expectation change quickly and users begin to expect that information on website would be the most current.

At many times, visitors will have questions with regard to your services and products. Design a website on your website called "feedback or frequently ask questions (FAQ)" and place some kind of complain or advice form on this page to enable the visitors to contact with you. It is very important that the answer would be given to these questions as quickly as possible. This kind of form will also enable you to gather testimonials and receive suggestions to assist of improving website, products or services.

8.   **Finally, think of the website as an online brochure:** Start with the information you would put in a brochure such as services, products, quality and price information. Now realize that designers can update this "brochure" much more easily than if it was printed with the latest prices, services or more.

WEBSITE USABILITY CONCEPT

The use experience on a website has been increasingly becoming a popular topic both for academia and organizations that use websites to advertise or market their products or services (Herhausen et. al., 2020). The website design is an important factor of users' online issues and revisit intentions (EL-firjani et. al., 2017).

Any website which has amazing design is not always as usable. The study by Rachwani et. al. (2020) indicated that services or products will be usable when a person can figure out what to do with them and when the person can tell what is going on. Substantially, any website may be visually appealing and contains all the resources that meet the site's objectives, but still be unusable. Because of such bad usability. Website users can encounter multiple problems when trying to acquire knowledge from a website and to use a website's functionalities. So, this is leading to dissatisfaction of users with websites and blockage in knowledge acquisition, online purchasing and other online issues (Fang and Holsapple, 2007).

The discussion on the components of "usable" website is still continuously. To a certain degree, usability concepts based on the purpose and target audience of a particular site. However, there is a general knowledge about that a usable website is consistent, accessible, appealing, clear, simple, navigable and forgiving of user blunders (Akgül, 2021).

Definition of Usability

Usability is defined in different terms by different authors. According to Issa and Isaias (2015), "usability is a measure of the ease with which a system can be learned and used, its safety, effectiveness and efficiency and the attitude of its users towards it." Zaphiris and Ellis (2001) defined web usability as "anyone using any kind of web browsing technology must be able to visit any site and get a full and complete understanding of the information, as well as have the full and complete ability to interact with the site if that is necessary." Shackel (2009) describes usability as "a technology's capability to be used easily and effectively by the specified range of users, given specified training and user support, to fulfill the specified range of tasks, within the specified range of environmental scenarios".

Another authors (Alonso-Ríos et. al., 2009) explain it as "an expression used to describe computer systems which are designed to be simple to use by untrained users, by means of self-explanatory or self-evident interaction between user and computer." Niederst and Robbins (2000) defines web site usability as "the extent to which a site can be used by a specified group of users to achieve specified goals with effectiveness, efficiency, and satisfaction in a specified context of use" based on the International Standards Organization (ISO). Apart from these definitions, another author defines usability with a short sentence; "easy to use" or "user friendly" (Perdomo et. al., 2017).

Why Is Usability Important?

In the early of 2000, a number of authors defined the concept of usability and its importance. As Nielsen (2000) explains usability rules of the web. Simply stated, if the customer can't find a product or service, then he or she will not buy it. According to this, usability concept is highly important concept of any website and whole website design. For e-commerce websites, Goldsborough (2005) explains that 28% of website transactions concluded that consumer failure and frustration, 60% of users who leave a web site in frustration say that they won't return to the site or patronize the company. If usability is ignored by the designer, then a business is likely to lose customers and miss out on profit opportunities, negatively impacting the cornerstones of any successful business (Perdomo et. al., 2017).

In other words, website usability is an indispensable concept for survival on the internet environment. If a website is not easy to use, people leave and do not come back. If the website fails to simple state what a company offers and what users can do on the site, people leave. If users lost on in website, they leave. If a website's information or animation is hard to read or doesn't reply users' key questions, they leave.

Factors That Effect Usability

Nowadays, the website has few guidelines that elaborate on how to design the site and present the content. However, the use of the web has rapidly continuous to grow. Businesses have identified that simply having a web presence no longer guarantees that an organization's site will attract visitors. So, industry and researchers have begun to research factors that affect usability, various aspects of website, web site design, and at different ways of evaluating website design in order to attract new users and to current users (Rusdi et. al., 2017).

Website usability is the indispensable concept of website design. Where a website has bad usability, it is highly possible that a possible user may turn to another websites. Moreover, usability is potentially complex and there are a wide range various factors that affect usability such as user characteristics, website domain (Luna-Nevarez and Hyman, 2012).

User Characteristics

Since web technology is now accessible to millions of users, many of them dependent on the characteristics of the individual user including age, gender, cultural background, personality, cognitive capabilities, and physical capabilities. Lee, Y., & Chen (2011) claimed that: "Any useful evaluation must take the psychology of the user into consideration. Given the psychological complexity of users, usability issues may be difficult to evaluate individually." Nikulchev et. al, (2020) argued that basic demographics (i.e., age, gender, and country) strongly influence perceptions of website usability. These basic demographics appear more important than computer experience, Internet experience, and frequency of internet access.

In terms of the specific influence of age, Nikulchev et. al (2020) asserted that since the number of older individuals with access to PC and the internet is significantly growing, the age-related deterioration of cognitive, visual and physical capabilities makes the design of usable computer systems particularly challenging. Other researchers found that users under the age of 30 tend to be more critical of amateurism on a site compared to those over the age of 37.3 years (van der Vaart et. al., 2019). Whitehead (2006) concluded that younger users have less tolerance towards the less usable sites with problems like, typos or broken links. According to this context, it is apparent that age-related characteristics of the user affect the usability respectively.

In a study on the gender of users, Nikulchev et. al (2020) concluded that females were more likely to agree with particular usability concepts than male participants. With cultural differences, the results concluded that Swiss participants were more negative than US participants and in terms of age differences; and the study found that older participants were more likely to provide negative comments than younger participants.

In terms of how usability concepts are affected by experience, Rzeszewski and Kotus (2019) claimed that users develop an understanding of usability based on the experiences that they have had with other systems, their job and/or what they do for a living, and the conditions under which they have become users. Bayraktar and Bayram (2018) also found that the previous experiences of users with the web influence their reactions towards the web sites. In particular, the study concluded that the more website experiences the user had, the more favorable their attitude toward a website would be.

Website Domain

The user characteristics is not only the important factor that affect usability in the evaluation of websites, but the domain of the site is also important. In other words, in assessing the usability concept, it is important to know the aim and basic functionality of the site: academic, commercial, government, non-profit etc. (Akgül, 2019). In the investigation of usability among different domains, Nagpal (2017) examined eleven categories of usability issues (information content, cognitive outcomes, enjoyment, privacy, user empowerment, visual experience, technical support, navigation, organization of information content, credibility, and impartiality) containing 42 core features across six domains;

- Financial
- Education
- Government
- E-commerce
- Medical
- Entertainment.

The study conducted by Nagpal (2017) explained that navigation was considered as the most important principles of website usability across all six domains. Additionally, the study stated that completeness and comprehensiveness of information was important in all but the e-commerce and entertainment domains; site technical features was important in all but the financial and entertainment domains; currency, timeliness and update was important among the financial, medical, and government domains; accuracy was important among the financial, medical, and government domains; and that readability, comprehension and clarity was important for the financial, education, and e-commerce domains. Furthermore, the research concluded that certain domains had unique requirements that have less importance in any of the other domains:

- Education domain required information reliability and reputation
- E-commerce demanded security and privacy and product and service concerns
- Entertainment required four unique families: visual design, engaging, information representation, and site accessibility and responsiveness.

An interesting side effect from the research was the conclusion explained that, users treated products and services as website features for the e-commerce domain. This mean that having impressive or great website features alone is not enough and users need better products and services from the company behind the website (Santiworarak and Choochaiwattana, 2018).

Other Usability Factor

The study by Williams (2020) argued that the first and second impression of a new user will most likely be important in making the user stay. The studies argue that the beauty of a website is an important factor in determining how it will be experienced and judged. The users may judge website to be similar based on the amount of complexity, legibility, and order, but they may like them based on their beauty.

- Complexity, ambiguous and complex of the website. Website must in contrast to being simple and clear.
- Legibility, legible of the website and appearance of the graphics, typography and layout.
- Order, ordered of the website. If the website has clear and distinctly structured so, beauty was indicated by how beautiful and appealing the person thought the page to be as opposed to how ugly it was.

Mistakes in Usability Design

The research conducted by Nong and Gainsbury (2020) listed the most important mistakes in website design as: frames usage, long pages, non-standard link colors, and overly long download times. According to another author (He, 2015), there are five possible problem areas that the website visitors experience: difficult site navigation; slow download times for graphics, documents, and applications; difficulty on finding information; multiple clicks to complete an objective; and a confusing home page.

Van Duyne (2007) presented the following problem areas as the misuse of screen real estate; content should account for at least half of a page's design, and preferably closer to 80 percent. Navigation should be kept below 20% of the space; not implementing cross-platform design. Pages should be designed to account for the lowest user's capabilities and to be accessible in as many browsers as possible and on as many platforms (e.g., Windows, Macintosh, Linux, etc.) as possible. Fast response or downloading time/speed are the most important design criterion for websites. Insufficient links are the basis for the web, but they should be used sparingly, not using style sheets allow for standardized design across an entire site. Improper use of frames can become a user's nightmare when applied improperly, in addition to creating problems with printing and bookmarking websites, not establishing credibility encourages users to return to the site. Printing the pages should be considered as a considerable number of users print websites in order to review them later. Not writing content for the web, the web is not a new type of printed media where publishers can simply duplicate their printed material, but a new media altogether that requires a whole new paradigm for displaying content; not accounting for international use and not accounting for accessibility issues that allow users with disabilities to view the pages. Leavitt and Shneiderman (2006) also explained that the following problem areas:

- Not designing "for the least common denominator," using features that not all browsers support;
- A common complaint about e-commerce transactions is that they are too slow
- A common design mistake is to assume that what shows up on your browser is what will show up on other people's browsers.

Increasing the Usability in University Websites

Usability concept is one of the indispensable factors in designing a website. Website users and designers accept usability concept as a common factor in improving website. Every user has different needs and expectations, so the website should provide a usable platform. Most of the problems occur from the fact that a designer builds a system from his point of view. Specialists, designers, and programmers work on solutions for the user but from their individual perspective (Nielsen, 2003). Therefore, designers should use a guideline to improve usability;

- Display space of the website must not be divided into small sections and users must not have to scroll left and right to read the content of the website because this will cause reading difficulty.
- A website must be accessible to users with different browser capabilities.
- A website must include no orphan pages. Every page must include at least one link-up to the home page and some indication of current page location, such as a site map or menu.
- The placement and content of the site map or menu must be consistent so that users can easily find them and define the targeted link and the information can be easily searched.
- There must be update information on the site and website must show the update time. Download time and speed must not exceed 15 seconds as users do not want to wait too long to download a file or access a page.
- Eliminate elements that look like web advertising as too many advertisements will irritate users (Chiew and Salim, 2003).

Usable university websites enable the users to get the most efficiency from the websites by increasing the level of user website interaction. Usability is an important concept for university websites as well since usable websites allow students to learn more effectively and attractively (İşman and İşbulan, 2010). So, a university website should;

- Provide students with registration information in order to enable them to either register online or handle the process of registration.
- Provide students with faculty information in order to enable them to choose their degrees and modules carefully.
- Provide instructor information to enable students to learn more about the lecturers that will be teaching and mentoring them (Mustafa and Al-Zoua'bi, 2008).

The research conducted by Alonso-Virgós et. al. (2019) states that, effective usability designs will provide appropriate contextual cues and navigational aids that support users' tasks. Contextual cues help web users to understand where they are, where they have been, and where they can go. So, navigational aids help users locate the information that they need. Research concludes that the elimination of graphical enhancements has limited effect on user perceptions. It appears that designers are spending more time to create the website while users are spending more time to download it, but there is a little benefit in terms of improved user perceptions.

Usability Measurement

In the beginning of 90's, different scientists have proposed different criteria to measure usability; Shackel (2009) identified speed effectiveness, error effectiveness, both in learnability flexibility and attitude as the major criteria affecting usability. Nielsen's (2006) five criteria of usability are learnability, efficiency of use, memorability, errors and satisfaction. Hix and Hartson (1993) related learnability, long term performance, retainability and long-term user satisfaction to usability. Rogers et. al., (2011) described usability in terms of throughput, learnability and attitude. Wixon and Wilson (1997) characterized usability by learnability, efficiency, memorability, error rates and satisfaction. Shneiderman and Plaisant (2010) cited usability criteria as time to learn, speed of performance, retention over time, rate of errors by users and subjective satisfaction. Constantine and Lockwood (1999) defined usability in terms of efficiency in use, learnability, rememberability, reliability in use and user satisfaction. These criteria will create today's website design tools.

The usability guidelines that Powell (2000) suggest for websites are; learnability, rememberability, efficiency of use, reliability in use and user satisfaction.

Relationship Between Usability and Trust

Another important criterion associated with the usability of a website is the trust that the user places on a site. The relationship between usability and trust is a very complex relationship. According to Seckler et. al. (2015), usability is a component that affects trust but Pengnate and Sarathy (2017) suggested that trust and usability are both the components of credibility.

It is debatable whether a usable site leads to trust formation or trust increases the usability of a website. According to Pengnate and Sarathy (2017), both are closely related to each other. Initial reputation of a site might lead to the first visit to the site. If the user finds the site usable, then there might be revisits. This increases the duration of relationship between the user and website, which enhances the user trust towards the website. On the other hand, a first time browsing of the site may encourage the user to revisit the site, if it is usable. A satisfied user spreads reputation of the site's leading to increase trust towards the website.

Figure 3 illustrated that usability and trust have direct relationship. Usability leads to trust the website. However, the trust of users improves usability (Pengnate and Sarathy 2017).

Figure 3. Relationship between trust and usability
Source: (Pengnate and Sarathy 2017)

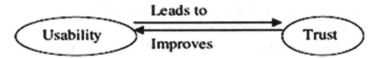

Usability Pyramid

Banati et. al (2006) argued that complete measure of usability cannot be achieved in a single step. It needs repeated iterations to evolve a usable website. Figure 4 presents the usability pyramid where each of these stages should be completed before moving on to the higher stage.

Figure 4. Usability pyramid
Source: (Banati 2006)

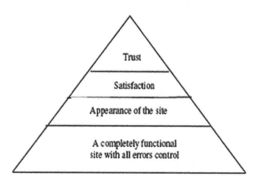

The pyramid is built on the key requirements of usable website. In order to consider a site as useable it should be completely functional with all links working with correct information and complete prevention and recovery of errors. Only when a site possesses such characteristics, then the attention should be diverted to the aesthetic appearance of the site. The look and feel of the site along with the ease of navigation contribute to improve the usability of the site to the next level. Moreover, a proper attention should be paid to the ease of learning to use and memorizing the workflow of the site. These all lead to a degree of work satisfaction. The focus of the next stage should therefore be to provide the user with an emotional satisfaction. However, the ultimate stage is to encourage the user to have complete faith in the website (Banati et. al, 2006).

Usability Metrics

Usability metrics are the measures of a particular aspect of a website that has an impact on usability. Whitehead (2006) stated that web site metrics originally grew out of traditional information technology disciplines that measured the timing of transactions and transactional components. Ivory et al. (2001) asserts that the use of the techniques in evaluating websites has traditionally focused clicking patterns traffic base analysis and time-based analysis provide data that the evaluator must interpret in order to identify usability problems. The authors contended that these methods are faulty in terms of evaluating the usability of a website because of the inconsistencies in tracing user behavior and delays inherent in the network of which the site is a part.

There are many kinds of proposed metrics. In performing quantitative usability testing, Manzoor (2019) and Ivory et al. (2001) stated the following website metrics as the most important in evaluating usability:

- Total words on a page
- Percentage of words that are body vs. display text
- Portion of body text that is emphasized
- Changes in text position from flush left
- Text areas highlighted with color, bordered regions, rules or lists
- Total links on a page
- Total bytes for the page as well as elements graphics and stylesheets
- Percentage of page bytes that are for graphics
- Total graphics on a page
- Total colors employed
- Total fonts employed

Usability Evaluation Methods

Usability concept is one of the common aspects that define the success of a website. It is important therefore to have various measurement methods to assess the usability of websites. The methods could be used to help website designers make their websites more usable (Chiew and Salim 2003).

Therefore, the evaluation of website usability is important. However, problems in getting usability results used more in development are basically due to the lack of usability of the usability evaluation methods and results. The precision of usability evaluation method itself will determine the accuracy of the evaluation. By using different evaluation methods, different results may be obtained for the usability of the same system (Nielsen, 2006). Website usability can be studied from different perspectives. Different website usability evaluation tools can be designed based on the different perspectives emphasized (Shum and McKnight 1997).

Various evaluation methods have been proposed to assess the usability of websites in order to suggest enhancements to the design of websites. Some methods are addressed towards experts, while others are directed towards the users. Such evaluation methods are (Mustafa and Al-Zoua'bi, 2008),

- Heuristics used by a group of experts with reference to established guidelines or design principles (Muller et. al., 1998),
- Prototyping based on designing a mock site that can be shown to users before the real site is launched. Users can also participate in focus user groups or

controlled laboratory sessions to provide usability feedback (Kantner and Rosenbaum, 1997),

- Checklists of usability items (Keevil, 1998),
- Cognitive walkthroughs involving one or a group of evaluators inspecting a user interface by going through a set of tasks to evaluate website understandability and ease of learning (Polson et. al, 1992),
- Questionnaires for extracting, recording, and collecting information to measure the user satisfaction with website usability (Perlman, 1998).

According to Mack (1994), the evaluation methods can be classified into 4 categories. The categories are:

- Automated; usability measures are computed by running a user specification through evaluation software.
- Empirical; usability is assessed by testing the interface with real users.
- Formal; using exact models and formulas to calculate usability measures.
- Informal; based on rules of thumb and the general skill, knowledge and experience of the evaluators.

Similarly, Benbunan-Fich (2001) categorized usability evaluation methods into 4 categories:

- Objective performance; measures the capability of the visitors using the website in terms of time taken to complete specific tasks through the system.
- Subjective user preferences; measures the users' preferences to the system by asking them to elicit their opinions or use a questionnaire for rating the system.
- Experimental; based on controlled experiments to test hypotheses about design and their impact on user performance and preferences.
- Direct observation; inspect and monitor the users' behavior while they are interacting with the system to detect usability problems.

Each method has its strengths and weaknesses. Website designers or developers need to select suitable evaluation methods based on certain factors including stage of design, novelty of project, number of expected users, criticality of the interface, cost of product and finances allocated for testing, time available, and experience of the design and evaluation team (Riihiaho, 2017).

REFERENCES

Agarwal, N., & Shiju, P. S. (2018). A Study on Content Generation for Internet Usage. *International Journal of Advanced Research and Development*, *3*(2), 1380–1382. doi:10.5281/zenodo.3764806

Akgül, Y. (2019). The accessibility, usability, quality and readability of Turkish state and local government websites an exploratory study. *International Journal of Electronic Government Research*, *15*(1), 62–81. doi:10.4018/IJEGR.2019010105

Akgül, Y. (2021). Accessibility, usability, quality performance, and readability evaluation of university websites of Turkey: A comparative study of state and private universities. *Universal Access in the Information Society*, *20*(1), 157–170. doi:10.100710209-020-00715-w

Almahamid, S. M., Tweiqat, A. F., & Almanaseer, M. S. (2016). University website quality characteristics and success: Lecturers' perspective. *International Journal of Business Information Systems*, *22*(1), 41–61. doi:10.1504/IJBIS.2016.075717

Alonso-Ríos, D., Vázquez-García, A., Mosqueira-Rey, E., & Moret-Bonillo, V. (2009). Usability: A critical analysis and a taxonomy. *International Journal of Human-Computer Interaction*, *26*(1), 53–74. doi:10.1080/10447310903025552

Alonso-Virgós, L., Espada, J. P., & Crespo, R. G. (2019). Analyzing compliance and application of usability guidelines and recommendations by web developers. *Computer Standards & Interfaces*, *64*, 117–132. doi:10.1016/j.csi.2019.01.004

Apuke, O. D., & Iyendo, T. O. (2018). University students' usage of the internet resources for research and learning: Forms of access and perceptions of utility. *Heliyon*, *4*(12), e01052. doi:10.1016/j.heliyon.2018.e01052 PMID:30582057

Armstrong, M. (2019). How Many Websites Are There? *Statistica*. https://www.statista.com/chart/19058/how-many-websites-are-there/

Astani, M. (2013). A decade of changes in university website design. *Issues in Information Systems*, *14*(1), 189–196.

Banati, H., Bedi, P., & Grover, P. S. (2006). Evaluating web usability from the user's perspective. *Journal of Computational Science*, *2*(4), 314–317. doi:10.3844/jcssp.2006.314.317

Bayraktar, D. M., & Bayram, S. (2018). Teachers' Website Design Experiences and Usability Test: The Case of Weebly. Com. *World Journal on Educational Technology: Current Issues*, *10*(4), 37–51. doi:10.18844/wjet.v10i4.3783

Benbunan-Fich, R. (2001). Using protocol analysis to evaluate the usability of a commercial web site. *Information & Management, 39*(2), 151–163. doi:10.1016/S0378-7206(01)00085-4

Bernard, M. (2003). *Criteria for optimal web design (designing for usability).* Academic Press.

Bocchi, E., De Cicco, L., Mellia, M., & Rossi, D. (2017). The web, the users, and the mos: Influence of http/2 on user experience. In *International Conference on Passive and Active Network Measurement* (pp. 47-59). Springer. 10.1007/978-3-319-54328-4_4

Brankovic, J., Ringel, L., & Werron, T. (2018). How rankings produce competition: The case of global university rankings. *Zeitschrift für Soziologie, 47*(4), 270–288. doi:10.1515/zfsoz-2018-0118

Brügger, N. (2009). Website history and the website as an object of study. *New Media & Society, 11*(1-2), 115–132. doi:10.1177/1461444808099574

Burki, T. K. (2020). COVID-19: Consequences for higher education. *The Lancet. Oncology, 21*(6), 758. doi:10.1016/S1470-2045(20)30287-4 PMID:32446322

Caglar, E., & Mentes, S. A. (2012). The usability of university websites–a study on European University of Lefke. *International Journal of Business Information Systems, 11*(1), 22–40. doi:10.1504/IJBIS.2012.048340

Cattaneo, M., Malighetti, P., Meoli, M., & Paleari, S. (2017). University spatial competition for students: The Italian case. *Regional Studies, 51*(5), 750–764. doi:10.1080/00343404.2015.1135240

Chandra, T., Hafni, L., Chandra, S., Purwati, A. A., & Chandra, J. (2019). The influence of service quality, university image on student satisfaction and student loyalty. *Benchmarking, 26*(5), 1533–1549. doi:10.1108/BIJ-07-2018-0212

Chareonwongsak, K. (2002). Globalization and technology: How will they change society? *Technology in Society, 24*(3), 191–206. doi:10.1016/S0160-791X(02)00004-0

Chauhan, S., Gupta, P., Palvia, S., & Jaiswal, M. (2020). Information technology transforming higher education: A meta-analytic review. *Journal of Information Technology Case and Application Research*, 1-33.

Chiew, T. K., & Salim, S. S. (2003). Webuse: Website usability evaluation tool. *Malaysian Journal of Computer Science, 16*(1), 47–57.

Constantine, L. L., & Lockwood, L. A. (1999). *Software for use: a practical guide to the models and methods of usage-centered design.* Pearson Education.

Curran, J., Fenton, N., & Freedman, D. (2016). *Misunderstanding the internet.* Routledge. doi:10.4324/9781315695624

Daniela, L., Visvizi, A., Gutiérrez-Braojos, C., & Lytras, M. D. (2018). Sustainable higher education and technology-enhanced learning (TEL). *Sustainability, 10*(11), 3883. doi:10.3390u10113883

Dunn, T. J., & Kennedy, M. (2019). Technology Enhanced Learning in higher education; motivations, engagement and academic achievement. *Computers & Education, 137*, 104–113. doi:10.1016/j.compedu.2019.04.004

Dzulfiqar, M. D., Khairani, D., & Wardhani, L. K. (2018). The Development of University Website using User Centered Design Method with ISO 9126 Standard. In *2018 6th International Conference on Cyber and IT Service Management (CITSM)* (pp. 1-4). IEEE.

Dzulfiqar, M. D., Khairani, D., & Wardhani, L. K. (2018). The Development of University Website using User Centered Design Method with ISO 9126 Standard. In *2018 6th International Conference on Cyber and IT Service Management (CITSM)* (pp. 1-4). IEEE.

El-Firjani, N. F., Elberkawi, E. K., & Maatuk, A. M. (2017). *Method For Website Usability Evaluation* (Doctoral dissertation). University of Benghazi.

Fang, X., & Holsapple, C. W. (2007). An empirical study of web site navigation structures' impacts on web site usability. *Decision Support Systems, 43*(2), 476–491. doi:10.1016/j.dss.2006.11.004

Fernández, D. P. (2020). Will the Internet fragment? Sovereignty, globalization and cyberspace. *Revista española de ciencia política*, (53), 195-200.

Ferris, C., & Farrell, J. (2003). What are web services? *Communications of the ACM, 46*(6), 31. doi:10.1145/777313.777335

Ganiyu, A. A., Mishra, A., Elijah, J., & Gana, U. M. (2017). The Importance of Usability of a Website. *IUP Journal of Information Technology, 13*(3).

Ghandour, A. (2015). Ecommerce website value model for SMEs. *International Journal of Electronic Commerce Studies, 6*(2), 203–222. doi:10.7903/ijecs.1403

Gold, M. (2003). *Making your website work-for your user.* Stanford Videos.

Goldsborough, R. (2005). Gauging the Success of Your Web Site. *Black Issues in Higher Education, 21*(24), 37.

Hassan, S., Din, I. U., Habbal, A., & Zakaria, N. H. (2016). A popularity based caching strategy for the future Internet. In 2016 ITU Kaleidoscope: ICTs for a Sustainable World (ITU WT) (pp. 1-8). IEEE. doi:10.1109/ITU-WT.2016.7805723

He, R. Y. (2015). Design and implementation of web based on Laravel framework. In *2014 International Conference on Computer Science and Electronic Technology (ICCSET 2014)* (pp. 301-304). Atlantis Press. 10.2991/iccset-14.2015.66

Herhausen, D., Miočević, D., Morgan, R. E., & Kleijnen, M. H. (2020). The digital marketing capabilities gap. *Industrial Marketing Management, 90*, 276–290. doi:10.1016/j.indmarman.2020.07.022

Hix, D., & Hartson, H. R. (1993). *Developing user interfaces: ensuring usability through product & process*. John Wiley & Sons, Inc.

Hossain, M. N., & Ahmed, S. Z. (2020). *Use of scholarly communication and citation-based metrics as a basis for university ranking in developing country perspective*. Global Knowledge, Memory and Communication. doi:10.1108/GKMC-09-2019-0112

Isman, A., & Isbulan, O. (2010). Usability level of distance education website (sakarya university sample). *Turkish Online Journal of Educational Technology-TOJET, 9*(1), 243–258.

Issa, T., & Isaias, P. (2015). Usability and human computer interaction (HCI). In *Sustainable design* (pp. 19–36). Springer. doi:10.1007/978-1-4471-6753-2_2

Ivory, M. Y., Sinha, R. R., & Hearst, M. A. (2001). Empirically validated web page design metrics. In *Proceedings of the SIGCHI conference on Human factors in computing systems* (pp. 53-60). 10.1145/365024.365035

Jennings, A. S. (2004). Son of Web Pages That Suck: Learn Good Design by Looking at Bad Design. *Technical Communication (Washington), 51*(3), 421–423.

Johnson, J. (2000). GUI Bloopers: Don'ts and Do's for Software Developers and Web Designers. San Francisco, CA: Morgan Kaufmann Publishers.

Johnson, J. (2021). Number of internet users worldwide from 2005 to 2019. *Statistica*. https://www.statista.com/statistics/273018/number-of-internet-users-worldwide/

Jungherr, A. (2019). Book Review: Social Theory after the Internet: Media, Technology and Globalization. SAGE Publications.

Kantner, L., & Rosenbaum, S. (1997). Usability studies of WWW sites: Heuristic evaluation vs. laboratory testing. In *Proceedings of the 15th annual international conference on Computer documentation* (pp. 153-160). 10.1145/263367.263388

Keevil, B. (1998). Measuring the usability index of your web site. In *Proceedings of the 16th annual international conference on Computer documentation* (pp. 271-277). 10.1145/296336.296394

Koman, R. (1998). The scent of information: Helping users find their way by making your site "smelly.". *Dr. Dobb's Journal, 5*(15), 1.

Kumar, A. (2018). *The World Wide Web. Web Technology*. Chapman and Hall/CRC.

Kusek, M. (2018). Internet of things: Today and tomorrow. In *2018 41st International Convention on Information and Communication Technology, Electronics and Microelectronics (MIPRO)* (pp. 335-338). IEEE.

Langley, D. J., van Doorn, J., Ng, I. C., Stieglitz, S., Lazovik, A., & Boonstra, A. (2021). The Internet of Everything: Smart things and their impact on business models. *Journal of Business Research, 122*, 853–863. doi:10.1016/j.jbusres.2019.12.035

Le, T. D., & Vo, H. (2017). Consumer attitude towards website advertising formats: A comparative study of banner, pop-up and in-line display advertisements. *International Journal of Internet Marketing and Advertising, 11*(3), 202–217. doi:10.1504/IJIMA.2017.085654

Leavitt, M. O., & Shneiderman, B. (2006). *Based web design & usability guidelines*. Health and Human Services Department.

Lee, Y., & Chen, A. N. (2011). Usability design and psychological ownership of a virtual world. *Journal of Management Information Systems, 28*(3), 269–308. doi:10.2753/MIS0742-1222280308

Liu, C. Y. A., & Jones, K. J. (2018). Determining the Student Services which Align with Undergraduate Student Expectations A Study of Student Perceptions and University Service Delivery. *Journal of Leadership and Management, 2*(12).

Luna-Nevarez, C., & Hyman, M. R. (2012). Common practices in destination website design. *Journal of Destination Marketing & Management, 1*(1-2), 94–106. doi:10.1016/j.jdmm.2012.08.002

Lynch, P. J., & Horton, S. (2016). *Web style guide: Foundations of user experience design*. Yale University Press.

Mack, R. L. (1994). *Executive Summary*. Usability Inspection Methods.

Manning, H., McCarthy, J., & Souza, R. (1998). *Why Most Web Sites Fail Interactive Technology Series, 3.7.* Forrester Research.

Manzoor, M., Hussain, W., Sohaib, O., Hussain, F. K., & Alkhalaf, S. (2019). Methodological investigation for enhancing the usability of university websites. *Journal of Ambient Intelligence and Humanized Computing, 10*(2), 531–549. doi:10.100712652-018-0686-6

Marelli, S., Castelnuovo, A., Somma, A., Castronovo, V., Mombelli, S., Bottoni, D., Leitner, C., Fossati, A., & Ferini-Strambi, L. (2021). Impact of COVID-19 lockdown on sleep quality in university students and administration staff. *Journal of Neurology, 268*(1), 8–15. doi:10.100700415-020-10056-6 PMID:32654065

McGrew, S., Smith, M., Breakstone, J., Ortega, T., & Wineburg, S. (2019). Improving university students' web savvy: An intervention study. *The British Journal of Educational Psychology, 89*(3), 485–500. doi:10.1111/bjep.12279 PMID:30993684

Mogaji, E. (2016). *University website design in international student recruitment: Some reflections. International marketing of higher education.* Palgrave Macmillan.

Molero Jurado, M., Martos Martínez, Á., Cardila Fernández, F., Barragán Martín, A. B., Pérez-Fuentes, M., Gázquez Linares, J. J., & Roales-Nieto, J. G. (2021). *Use of Internet and social networks by university students.* European Journal of Child Development, Education and Psychopathology., doi:10.30552/ejpad.v2i3.20

Morse, A. (2017). *The higher education market.* National Audit Office.

Muller, M. J., Matheson, L., Page, C., & Gallup, R. (1998). Methods & tools: participatory heuristic evaluation. *Interactions, 5*(5), 13-18.

Mustafa, S. H., & Al-Zoua'bi, L. F. (2008). Usability of the academic websites of Jordan's universities an evaluation study. In *Proceedings of the 9th International Arab Conference for Information Technology* (pp. 31-40). Academic Press.

Nagpal, R., Mehrotra, D., & Bhatia, P. K. (2017). *The state of art in website usability evaluation methods. In Design Solutions for User-Centric Information Systems.* IGI Global.

Niederst, J., & Robbins, J. N. (2001). *Web design in a nutshell: A desktop quick reference* (Vol. 2). O'Reilly Media, Inc.

Nielsen, J. (1999). User interface directions for the web. *Communications of the ACM, 42*(1), 65–72. doi:10.1145/291469.291470

Nielsen, J. (2000). Designing Web Usability: The Practice of Simplicity. Indianapolis, IN: New Riders Publishing.

Nielsen, J. (2003). *Persuasive Design: New Captology Book*. Jakob Nielsen's Alertbox.

Nielsen, J., & Loranger, H. (2006). *Prioritizing Web Usability: the practice of simplicity*. New Riders Publishing.

Nikulchev, E., Ilin, D., Silaeva, A., Kolyasnikov, P., Belov, V., Runtov, A., Pushkin, P., Laptev, N., Alexeenko, A., Magomedov, S., Kosenkov, A., Zakharov, I., Ismatullina, V., & Malykh, S. (2020). Digital Psychological Platform for Mass Web-Surveys. *Data, 5*(4), 95. doi:10.3390/data5040095

Nong, Z., & Gainsbury, S. (2020). Website design features: Exploring how social cues present in the online environment may impact risk taking. *Human Behavior and Emerging Technologies, 2*(1), 39–49. doi:10.1002/hbe2.136

O'Regan, G. (2018). *World Wide Web. In The Innovation in Computing Companion*. Springer. doi:10.1007/978-3-030-02619-6

Owoyele, S. (2017). *Website as a marketing communication tool*. Theseus.

Patro, C. S. (2021). *Internet-Enabled Business Models and Marketing Strategies. In Impact of Globalization and Advanced Technologies on Online Business Models*. IGI Global.

Pengnate, S. F., & Sarathy, R. (2017). An experimental investigation of the influence of website emotional design features on trust in unfamiliar online vendors. *Computers in Human Behavior, 67*, 49–60. doi:10.1016/j.chb.2016.10.018

Perdomo, E. G., Cardozo, M. T., Perdomo, C. C., & Serrezuela, R. R. (2017). A Review of the User Based Web Design: Usability and Information Architecture. *International Journal of Applied Engineering Research: IJAER, 12*(21), 11685–11690.

Perlman, G. (1998). *Web-based user interface evaluation with questionnaires*. Academic Press.

Perna, L. W. (2020). Higher Education: Handbook of Theory and Research. Springer.

Pesce, M. (2017, April). The Web-Wide World. *Proceedings of the 26th International Conference on World Wide Web*. 10.1145/3038912.3050770

Polson, P. G., Lewis, C., Rieman, J., & Wharton, C. (1992). Cognitive walkthroughs: A method for theory-based evaluation of user interfaces. *International Journal of Man-Machine Studies, 36*(5), 741–773. doi:10.1016/0020-7373(92)90039-N

Powell, T. A. (2000). *The complete reference: Web design.* Osborne, McGraw-Hill.

Qadri, B., & Bhat, M. (2018). Interface between globalization and technology. *Asian J. Manag. Sci, 7*(3), 1–6.

Quintero, L. J. C., & Selwyn, N. (2018). More than tools? Making sense of the ongoing digitizations of higher education. *International Journal of Educational Technology in Higher Education,* (15), 26.

Rachwani, J., Tamis-LeMonda, C. S., Lockman, J. J., Karasik, L. B., & Adolph, K. E. (2020). Learning the designed actions of everyday objects. *Journal of Experimental Psychology. General, 149*(1), 67–78. doi:10.1037/xge0000631 PMID:31219298

Rezaeean, A., Bairamzadeh, S., & Bolhari, A. (2012). The importance of Website Innovation on Students' Satisfaction of University Websites. *World Applied Sciences Journal, 18*(8), 1023–1029.

Riihiaho, S. (2017). *Usability testing. The Wiley Handbook of Human Computer Interaction Set.*

Rogers, Y., Sharp, H., & Preece, J. (2011). *Interaction design: Beyond human-computer interaction.* John Wiley & Sons.

Ruiz, N. V. (2021). How to Use the Internet for University Work. *Aularia: Revista Digital de Comunicación, 10*(1), 131–136.

Rusdi, R., Sahari, N., & Noor, S. (2017). Usability guidelines for elderly website interface. *Asia-Pacific Journal of Information Technology and Multimedia, 6*(2), 109–122. doi:10.17576/apjitm-2017-0602-10

Rzeszewski, M., & Kotus, J. (2019). Usability and usefulness of internet mapping platforms in participatory spatial planning. *Applied Geography (Sevenoaks, England), 103,* 56–69. doi:10.1016/j.apgeog.2019.01.001

Santiworarak, L., & Choochaiwattana, W. (2018). A Case Study of Usability Design Principle in Responsive e-Commerce Web Application. *International Journal of e-Education, e-Business, e- Management Learning, 8*(3).

Schaeffer, R. K. (2003). Globalization and technology. *Phi Kappa Phi Forum, 83*(4), 30-34.

Schroeder, R. (2018). *Social theory after the internet: Media, technology and globalization.* UCL Press. doi:10.2307/j.ctt20krxdr

Seckler, M., Heinz, S., Forde, S., Tuch, A. N., & Opwis, K. (2015). Trust and distrust on the web: User experiences and website characteristics. *Computers in Human Behavior, 45*, 39–50. doi:10.1016/j.chb.2014.11.064

Shackel, B. (2009). Usability–Context, framework, definition, design and evaluation. *Interacting with Computers, 21*(5-6), 339–346. doi:10.1016/j.intcom.2009.04.007

Shneiderman, B., & Plaisant, C. (2010). *Designing the user interface: Strategies for effective human-computer interaction.* Pearson Education India.

Shum, S. B., & McKnight, C. (1997). World Wide Web usability: Introduction to this special issue. *International Journal of Human-Computer Studies, 47*(1), 1–4. doi:10.1006/ijhc.1997.0132

Soegoto, E. S., & Rafi, M. S. F. (2018). Internet role in improving business transaction. *IOP Conference Series. Materials Science and Engineering, 407*(1), 012059. doi:10.1088/1757-899X/407/1/012059

Student, R., Kendall, K., & Day, L. (2017). Being a refugee university student: A collaborative auto-ethnography. *Journal of Refugee Studies, 30*(4), 580–604.

Uslu, B. (2018). Dünya Üniversiteler Sıralaması: Genişletilen Gösterge Setine Göre Sıralamada Oluşan Farklılıklar. *Journal of Higher Education & Science/ Yükseköğretim ve Bilim Dergisi, 12*(3).

Valero, A., & Van Reenen, J. (2019). The economic impact of universities: Evidence from across the globe. *Economics of Education Review, 68*, 53–67. doi:10.1016/j.econedurev.2018.09.001

van der Vaart, R., van Driel, D., Pronk, K., Paulussen, S., Te Boekhorst, S., Rosmalen, J. G., & Evers, A. W. (2019). The role of age, education, and digital health literacy in the usability of Internet-based cognitive behavioral therapy for chronic pain: Mixed methods study. *JMIR Formative Research, 3*(4), e12883. doi:10.2196/12883 PMID:31750839

Van Duyne, D. K., Landay, J. A., & Hong, J. I. (2003). The Design of Sites: Patterns, Principles and Processes for Crafting a Customer-Centered Web Experience. Boston, MA: Addison-Wesley.

Van Duyne, D. K., Landay, J. A., & Hong, J. I. (2007). *The design of sites: Patterns for creating winning web sites.* Prentice Hall Professional.

Whitehead, C. C. (2006). Evaluating web page and web site usability. *Proceedings of the 44th annual Southeast regional conference*, 788-789. 10.1145/1185448.1185637

Williams, P. (2020). *Methods to test website usability. In Learning Disabilities and e-Information*. Emerald Publishing Limited. doi:10.1108/9781789731514

Wixon, D., & Wilson, C. (1997). The usability engineering framework for product design and evaluation. In Handbook of human-computer interaction (pp. 653-688). North-Holland. doi:10.1016/B978-044481862-1.50093-5

Yamada, T. (2021). On the Spectrum of Communication: Locating the Use of New Media in the 2020 COVID-19 Emergency Response. In Handbook of Research on New Media Applications in Public Relations and Advertising (pp. 422-432). IGI Global.

Zaphiris, P., & Ellis, R. D. (2001). Website usability and content accessibility of the top USA universities. *Proceedings of WebNet 2001 Conference*.

Chapter 2
A Statistical Analysis for the Accessibility of Electronic Data Delivery System of the Central Bank of the Turkish Republic

Yakup Ari
(iD) https://orcid.org/0000-0002-5666-5365
Alanya Alaaddin Keykubat University, Turkey

ABSTRACT

The study aims to reveal the most effective factors on the accessibility statistics of the Electronic Data Delivery System (EDDS) of The Central Bank of The Turkish Republic. Besides, another aim is to reveal the effect of the exchange rate on the access statistics of EDDS exchange rate data. For this purpose, a stepwise regression model was used to find the most effective factors on accessibility statistics. According to the results of stepwise regression analysis, it was revealed that 9 out of 26 variables significantly affected the EDDS access statistics. Engle-Granger cointegration test was chosen as the method to examine the relationship between exchange rate and EDDS access statistics. It has been revealed that there is a long-run equilibrium relationship between the EURO/TRY exchange rate and the access statistics of EDDS exchange rate data.

DOI: 10.4018/978-1-7998-7848-3.ch002

INTRODUCTION

Today, the main factor that causes the rapid development of information and communication technologies is the expansion of the internet network and its widespread use. In addition, developments in internet speed have facilitated the access of web-based information and increased the variety of information requested over the internet. Public and state institutions have also followed this development to the extent of their possibilities. In today's information-oriented societies, people want to access information from anywhere, anytime within seconds. Therefore, websites serve as a source of information for people. For example, websites are mainly geared towards end-users. Because it is often thought that the current or future consumers of an organization use the organization's official websites as the main place where they can get information about the products. Today, concerning organizational web content and design, public opinion is taken into account as well as potential employees when creating specific content. Official websites of corporations provide an opportunity to present internal and external information to the public and provide an opportunity for the organization to share and communicate its organizational culture and the values attached to them, its practices, principles and philosophies, and strategies. Official websites should be designed with a professional eye and be rich and relevant in terms of content, under the field they provide products and/or services. Public institutions are obliged to present all kinds of information related to the institution to which they are affiliated, which are not objectionable to be disclosed to the public and which are required to be disclosed by relevant laws, in an easily accessible, understandable, accurate, up-to-date and easily readable form. The content of the sites can vary greatly according to the characteristics of the institutions. Some websites may consist of several information pages, while others may be in the form of a large portal with many interactive services. In this context, internet speed and accessibility gain importance. Especially in the fields of trade, finance, and economy, where speed and knowledge are very important factors, this importance is increasing even more. Website accessibility is expressed as the ability of all target users to access the website, use the website and understand the content of the website. In other words, websites should have a design and content that will appeal not only to a specific audience, but also to different user groups such as the disabled and the elderly. Unlike the private sector, any public institution is generally the only institution in the service sector it is related to. For this reason, it is the only authorized authority that anyone who wants to get service in that field can apply. It is essential that the services provided are accessible to the entire society. As a matter of fact, the most important expectation is to ensure that the entire society has access to the services offered through internet sites (KAMiS, 2021). Internet speed, internet security and internet accessibility are prior topics in the economy and financial markets where accurate and fast information is important. It is clear that access to data emerging in the banking and finance sector has high costs. In this case, it is one of the difficulties of instant access to information for ordinary people who are not in the banking and finance sector. In terms of financial literacy, which is an important topic of today, it has become important to reach the data emerging in the economy and financial markets. Because, especially in developing economies, the public needs to reach the emerging data and information in order to be a part of the capital markets. Therefore, internet access and data provision over the internet are important concepts.

According to data from 2019, compared to the individual Internet use rate of Turkey's population is 74% has an important place among the developing countries (World Bank, 2020). But, the Speedtest Global Index shows that Turkey has 58th ranked for mobile internet speed and 112th for fixed broadband speed in the world (Speedtest, 2020). This situation points out that Turkey has not many problems in terms of internet access, but Turkey should progress in terms of internet infrastructure. Access speed is as important as internet accessibility for the economy and financial markets. In this context, the Central Bank of the Republic of Turkey (CBRT) has established an Electronic Data Delivery System (EDDS) for the economy and financial

Table 1. The Main Topics Covered in EDDS

Topics in EDDS	
Number of Registered Users	Financial Statistics
Number of Total Visits	Surveys
Number of Unique Visitors	CBRT Balance Sheet Data
User and Visit Statistics	Payment Systems and Emission
Exchange Rates	Price Indices
Market Statistics	Gold Statistics
Financial Accounts	Production Statistics
Balance of Payments International Investment Position	Housing and Construction Statistics
External Debts	Tourism Statistics
Foreign Trade Statistics	Employment Statistics
Interest Rates	Public Finance
Deposits and Participation Funds Subject to Required Reserves	Bank for International Settlements (BIS Comparative Country Statistics
Money and Banking Statistics	Archive
Weekly Securities Statistics	Total

data distribution and accessible by anyone. In this system, micro and macro data are shared under many headings that are given in Table 1 (EVDS, 2020).

One can speak of a possible physical relationship – physical response to impact – between a human being as a living being and a machine as an inanimate being. However, there is a very close relationship and interaction between human and computer. While this interaction directs people's attitudes and behaviors, it also enables computers to be equipped with more user-friendly applications, to gain the ability to learn, and to become "intelligent". People are exposed to a longer-term association with computers and other information tools, they try to improve their information literacy, they start to trust such tools more and they realize how important information is (Gülseçen, 2020).

From the information's importance of view, the data presented in EDDS is the subject of this study to reveal the reasons that affect the accessibility of information and data. The titles given above were accepted as variables and the factors affecting the total internet access were revealed with various statistical analyzes. As a result, the flow of the chapter is organized as follows; After the introduction part, there is a short literature review. Then, the utilized methodology is introduced in the third section. The findings obtained from the analysis are given in the fourth section under three subsections. The last section is structured where the results are summarized, and a short discussion is made.

BRIEF LITERATURE REVIEW

There are many studies on the quality and accessibility of websites. However, in this literature review, only studies on government websites are briefly mentioned. Because there are very few studies on the usage statistics of websites. Therefore, in this section, studies on web accessibility of public institutions in the literature are briefly mentioned.

Two of the most important studies on the accessibility and performance of government websites in Turkey can be listed as follows. First, Akgül and Vatansever (2016) evaluated 25 Turkish state official websites using many different automation tools. According to the results obtained, it has been determined that government websites have critical accessibility violations and problems. Almost all the websites evaluated failed to meet the minimum accessibility requirements for people with disabilities. Second, Akgül (2019) investigated the accessibility and performance of websites of the state and local level e-government in the Turkish Republic. He collected data by examining 77 state and 247 local e-government sites. In conclusion, it is observed that there are many mistakes in the accessibility, usability, quality, and readability of Turkish government websites. Akgül (2021) examines features such as accessibility, usability, quality performance, and readability of institutions' websites in Turkey. In this study, it was concluded that the websites of private and public universities do not meet the WCAG 2.0 accessibility criteria. These results show poor usability, quality performance and readability, highlighting the need for Turkish universities to devote more resources to develop their own operations.

In the study of Durmuş and Çağıltay (2012), 33 public institutions' websites in Turkey were evaluated through content analysis, and interviews were held with the people responsible for the website design of eight public institutions. As a result of these studies, the problems encountered while using the electronic services of the evaluated public institutions and the causes of these problems were determined. In another study, Alır et al. (2007) evaluated the home page of the websites of 24 Public Institutions (16 Ministries and eight General Directorates) in terms of 30 criteria under eight categories. According to the research findings, while public web pages mostly meet the specified criteria in terms of general features, they show significant deficiencies in service delivery, technical features, and interactive services.

The study conducted by İsmailova and İnal (2016), it was aimed to determine the accessibility and quality of the ministry websites in Kyrgyzstan, Azerbaijan, Kazakhstan, and Turkey. Sixteen websites for each country were tested using online automation tools Pingdom and AChecker. In terms of quality of use, state websites of the Republic of Azerbaijan have higher speed, fewer broken connections, and higher performance scores. This is followed by the websites of the Republic of Kyrgyzstan, the Republic of Turkey, and the Republic of Kazakhstan. In addition to websites, Turkey has become a country where approximately 60% of government services can be accessed through mobile applications.

In another study by Akgül (2016) the quality of the e-government websites of Turkey is measured via web diagnostic tools online. 51 government websites are analyzed by testing their existing design with the help of online tools. The aim of the analysis is to understand their deviations from the standards and to evaluate their performance with respect to the parameters considered by the tool. The results show that the design of e-government websites should be more effective and user-friendly to increase their accessibility.

Studies in the literature are mostly on the accessibility and performance of corporate websites. There are not many studies on website usage statistics. Access to data can be cited as the reason for this. In addition, general internet statistics for Turkey can be accessed via BTK – INTERNET (2021).

METHODOLOGY

Stepwise Regression

In this study, stepwise methods are examined. Before discussing the application of the method, the multiple regression model is as follows

$$Y_{ti} = \beta_0 + \beta_1 X_{1ti} + \beta_2 X_{2ti} + \ldots + \beta_k X_{kti} + u_{tij} \; for \, i = 1, 2, \ldots, n \, and \, j = 1, 2, \ldots, k$$

$$(3.1)$$

where $\beta_0, \beta_1, \ldots \beta_k \in \mathbb{R}$, Y_{ti} is dependent variable, X_{tij} are independent variables and u_{tij} is independent and identically distributed error term.

The forward selection method is desired to find the most appropriate regression model by adding one independent variable each time. The backward selection method is the opposite of the forward selection method. The model starts with all independent variables. In the stepwise selection method, both the forward selection and backward selection methods are used simultaneously. In the forward selection method, the variable selection process starts with the equation in which only the constant term is present in the model, and the variables are added to the model one by one. The first independent variable considered to be included in the model is the variable with the highest correlation with the dependent variable. At the same time, this variable is the variable with the highest F statistic with the dependent variable Y. If the calculated F statistic is significant at the α significance level, this variable is included in the model and the forward selection method continues. As a result of the test, if this variable is not included in the model, the selection process ends. The stepwise selection method consists of editing the forward selection method. The argument previously added to the model is re-evaluated with partial F statistics. An independent variable previously added to the model can be removed from the model in later steps. In this method, the aim is to select the variables that are not related to each other and that affect the dependent variable the most after determining the independent variables that can affect the dependent variable Y theoretically (Montgomery et al., 2001; Kayaalp et al., 2015).

The most important benefit of the selection method is that it provides a solution to the multicollinearity problem. When the relationships are insignificant, the model remains as variable as the independent variables that have a significant relationship (Keller et al., 1990; Mendenhall & Sincich, 1996; Myers, 1990). In addition to the benefits of this method, there are many criticisms of the step-by-step regression process. There are even calls to stop using the method altogether. Statisticians point out several disadvantages of the approach, including inaccurate results, an inherent bias in the process itself, and the necessity of significant computing power to develop complex regression models through iteration. According to Smith (2018), stepwise regression is less effective as the number of potential explanatory variables increases. The stepwise regression method cannot solve the problems that may occur especially in Big Data with too many explanatory variables. Big Data exacerbates the failures of step-by-step regression. One can read the paper of Flom (2018) to reach the detailed discussions on stepwise regression.

Engle-Granger Cointegration

In this section, the methodological way in the study of Arı (2021) is followed exactly. According to this study, the concept of stationarity and Engle-Granger cointegration analysis are briefly as follows: The concept of stationarity; it is defined as the time series data fluctuates around a zero mean and this fluctuation variance remains constant especially over time. Granger and Newbold (1974) discussed in their studies that non-stationary time series produce standard errors with deviation in the long run and therefore variables should have a stationary structure.

According to the cointegration analysis, which investigates whether the time series that are not stationary at the level move together in the long run, it would not be appropriate to take the differences of these variables if the nonstationary series are cointegrated. Since the variables have a trend moving together, taking their difference will eliminate this common trend. Accordingly, there will be no spurious regression in the analyzes made with the level values of the series that are cointegrated and in other words, move together in the long run.

It is Engle and Granger (1987) who brought the cointegration relationship between the series to the literature. According to the two-stage Engel-Granger method, the error terms are obtained by estimating the model with the help of the Ordinary Least Squares (OLS) method in the first stage. In the second step, unit root test is performed on the error terms obtained. As a result, if the error terms are stationary, there is cointegration. The fact that the error terms have unit roots indicates that there is no cointegration relationship between the series in question. Although the Engel-Granger method is simple to apply, when more than two variables are in question, the number of cointegration will increase with the number of variables, so it cannot give healthy results and the results may change in different normalizations. In conclusion, Engle and Granger (1987) cointegration approach is used to reveal the long-run relationship between the two variables. According to the test, variables are assumed to be stationary at the same level. Both variables should have first-order stationarity, likely both variables should be I(1). Let Y_t and X_t be I(1) series which means that Y_t

and X_t are not stationary at the level, but the first difference of the series are stationary. The regression model using Y_t and X_t series is as follows

$$Y_t = a_0 + a_1 X_t + u_t \tag{4.1}$$

where $a_0, a_1 \in \mathbb{R}$ and u_t is error term. If u_t is I(0) or $\Delta \hat{u}_t = \rho_1 \hat{u}_{t-1} + \sum_{i=0}^{p} \zeta_i \Delta \hat{u}_{t-i} + z_t$ where $|\rho_1| < 1$ then Y_t and X_t are cointegrated.

If the series are cointegrated, there is at least one causal relationship between the series. For the series to be cointegrated, they must be stationary. The differencing process is applied to ensure stationarity. However, applying the differencing process causes a loss of long-run information. Therefore, these imbalances are tried to be eliminated by using the error correction model. If there is a long-run relationship between series, an error correction model, which is used to determine the short-run relationship, shows a deviation period from a long-run equilibrium. The following error correction model (ECM) is utilized to determine the possible causality relationship between the cointegrated series and to determine the direction.

$$\Delta Y_t = \theta_0 + \sum_{i=0}^{p} \theta_{1i} \Delta Y_{t-i} + \sum_{i=0}^{q} \theta_{2i} \Delta X_{t-i} + \theta_3 \hat{u}_{t-1} + \varepsilon_t \tag{4.2}$$

where θ_0 is a constant parameter, θ_3 is error correction parameter or adjustment parameter and $-1 < \theta_3 < 0$ and $\hat{u}_{t-1}$ is equilibrium error term or error correction term where $\hat{u}_{t-1} = Y_{t-1} - a_0 - a_1 X_{t-1}$.

The special case of ECM is

$$\Delta Y_t = \theta_0 + \theta_1 \Delta Y_{t-1} + \theta_2 \Delta X_{t-1} + \theta_3 \hat{u}_{t-1} + \varepsilon_t \tag{4.3}$$

ECM describes how Y and X behave in the short run consistent with a long run cointegrating relationship.

RESULTS AND FINDINGS

The Stepwise Regression Results

In this study, the factors that affect the total number of clicks are determined utilizing the numbers of internet access for the topics given in Table 1. For this purpose, monthly data for the 2018-07 and 2020-11 periods were applied. Jamovi and Gretl software programs, which are open source and free, were used for the analysis (The Jamovi Project, 2021; R Core Team, 2021; Fox& Weisberg., 2020; Baiocchi & Distaso, 2003). The most convenient factors were determined with the stepwise regression method.

In the first stepwise regression model, it is found that the factors that most affect the total number of Internet accesses are Exchange Rates, Weekly Securities Statistics, Surveys, Price Indices, Financial Statistics, Housing and Construction Statistics, Deposits and Participation Funds Subject to Required Reserves, Number of Total Visits paras and BIS Comparative Country Statistics. Among the variables mentioned, it was found that the most affecting factor to the total number of access is the number of access to exchange rates data. The parameter estimation of stepwise regression - 1 for the dependent variable "the total number of Internet accesses" is given in the Table 2. According to the results obtained from the stepwise regression model, a 1% change in access for Exchange Rates causes a 0.2759% change in "the total number of Internet accesses". In other words, the Exchange Rates Access elasticity of "the total number of Internet accesses" is 0.2759%. This situation shows that Exchange Rates is the most interesting issue for EDDS access. In addition, it is understood that the number of entries to the expectation surveys is the second biggest topic that affects the total number of Internet access.

The model fit measures, diagnostic test results of the model and the variables excluded from the model are given in Appendix A from Table 7 through Table 10. According to the model fit measures values, the explanatory power of the model is 99.5% and the adjusted r-square value is 99.2%, which is a very high value. The diagnostic test results at Appendix A in Table 8 show that the model does not have heteroskedasticity, autocorrelation, multicollinearity, model specification error, structural break and parameters instability. Moreover, the residuals are normally distributed.

Table 2. The parameter estimation of stepwise regression - 1 for the dependent variable "the total number of Internet accesses"

Model - 1 Coefficients - Total Number of Access					
Predictor	Estimate	SE	t	p	Stand. Estimate
Intercept	2.8419	0.55365	5.13	<.001	
Exchange Rates	0.2759	0.01749	15.77	<.001	0.3821
Weekly Securities Statistics	0.1437	0.02245	6.4	<.001	0.233
Surveys	0.1795	0.02967	6.05	<.001	0.2025
Price Indices	0.0682	0.02505	2.72	0.014	0.095
Financial Statistics	0.0763	0.01234	6.19	<.001	0.1654
Housing and Construction Statistics	0.0524	0.02262	2.32	0.032	0.0802
Deposits and Participation Funds Subject to Required Reserves	0.0467	0.01434	3.25	0.004	0.0951
Number of Total Visits	0.1686	0.05272	3.2	0.005	0.0923
BIS Comparative Country Statistics	0.0238	0.00971	2.45	0.024	0.07

Based on the first model results, USD / TRY and EURO / TRY spot exchange rates were also added to the independent variable pool to reveal the factors affecting the number of entries for the exchange rate. The stepwise regression analysis was performed in logarithmic form to determine the factors affecting the total number of access to exchange rates data. The results showed that the only factor affecting the total number of access to exchange rates data was the EURO / TRY exchange rate variable. The coefficient of the EURO / TRY exchange rate in the stepwise regression model indicates that a 1% change in EURO / TRY exchange rate causes a 3.81% change in "the total number of Exchange Rates accesses".

Table 3. The parameter estimation of stepwise regression - 2 for the dependent variable "the total number of Exchange Rates Access"

Model – 2 Coefficients - Exchange_Rates				p	Stand. Estimate
Predictor	Estimate	SE	t		
Intercept	7.73	1.357	5.7	<.001	
EURO / TRY	3.81	0.701	5.44	<.001	0.723

The model fit measures, diagnostic test results of the model and the variables excluded from the model are given in Appendix B from Table 11 through Table 13. In addition to high adjusted R-squared, the model satisfies all diagnostics test. Cointegration analysis is performed to understand whether the regression model built on these two variables is spurious. In this way, short and long run relationships between variables are revealed.

The Engle-Granger Cointegration Results

Before starting the cointegration analysis, the stationarity levels of the variables should be examined. Because the Engle-Granger cointegration approach assumes that the variables are stationary at first difference. The stationarity of the variables, in other words, whether they contain a unit root or not, is checked with the Augmented Dickey-Fuller (ADF) test of which results are given in Table 4. ADF Unit Root Test indicates that the mentioned variables are stationary at the first difference level. So, they are I(1). Furthermore, the Engle-Granger cointegration analysis can be applied

Table 4. ADF Unit Root Test Results for Exchange Rates and EURO/TRY

ADF Equation		At Level		At First Difference	
		ER	**EURO**	**d(ER)**	**d(EURO)**
With Constant	t-Stat	-2.0711	-0.356	-6.9471	-4.3517
	Prob.	0.257	0.9038	0	0.0021
With Constant & Trend	t-Stat	-3.0542	-1.2324	-6.8946	-4.7749
	Prob.	0.1363	0.8837	0	0.0037
Without Constant & Trend	t-Stat	0.4588	1.7929	-6.9682	-4.3711
	Prob.	0.8072	0.9796	0	0.0001

The long-run equilibrium model which is estimated in the previous section using stepwise regression is as follows.

$$\ln ER_t = 7.73 + 3.81 \ln EURO_t + u_t \tag{5.1}$$

where ER and EURO are exchange rates access and EURO/TRY foreign exchange rates respectively and u_t denotes the error terms. The parameter statistics of the long-run equilibrium equation are available in Table 3. The stationarity test result of the error terms (residuals) obtained from this equation is given in Table 5.

Table 5. ADF Unit Root Test Results for Error Terms (residuals) obtained from long-run equation

ADF Equation		At Level
		Error Terms (residuals)
With Constant	t-Statistic	-4.12024
	Prob.	0.003519
With Constant & Trend	t-Statistic	-4.109
	Prob.	0.01622
Without Constant & Trend	t-Statistic	-4.19687
	Prob.	0.0001537

When the stationarity of the error terms obtained from Equation 5.1 is tested with the ADF Unit Root Test, it is seen that the error terms are stationary at the level. Therefore, it is concluded that exchange rates access and EURO/TRY foreign exchange rates are cointegrated and there is a statistically significant long-run equilibrium relationship.

The Error Correction Model (ECM) is estimated to examine the short-run relationship between variables. The coefficient of the Error Correction Term (ECT) in this model shows whether the short-run relationship between the variables is significant. The estimated Error Correction Model coefficients are given in table 6.

$$\Delta \ln ER_t = 0.061 + 0.063\Delta \ln ER_{t-1} - 0.067\Delta \ln EURO_{t-1} - 0.738\hat{u}_{t-1} + \varepsilon_t$$
$$(5.2)$$

where $\hat{u}_{t-1}$ is error correction term that is obtained by

$$\hat{u}_t = \ln ER_t - 7.73 + 3.81\ln EURO_t.$$

The error correction parameter or adjustment parameter that is statistically significant is equal to -0.738. It means that the long-run equilibrium between exchange rates access and EURO/TRY foreign exchange rates is re-balanced in (1/0.738) month which is approximately 1.35 month.

Table 6. The Parameter Estimation of the Error Correction Model for $\Delta \ln ER_t$

Error Correction Model Coefficients - $\Delta \ln ER_t$				
Predictor	**Estimate**	**SE**	**t**	**p**
const	0.061	0.111	0.550	0.587
$\Delta \ln ER_{t-1}$	0.063	0.220	0.285	0.777
$\Delta \ln EURO_{t-1}$	−0.670	1.916	−0.349	0.729
Δu_{t-1} (ECT)	−0.738	0.267	−2.76	0.011

where Δ is a difference operator. One can write the ECM equation as following

CONCLUSION

In this study, the factors that affect the total number of clicks are determined utilizing the numbers of internet access for the topics mentioned in the Electronic Data Delivery System of Central Bank of the Republic of Turkey. For this purpose, monthly data for the 2018-07 and 2020-11 periods were used and the most suitable factors were determined with the stepwise regression method. In the first stage, it is found that the factors that most affect the total number of Internet accesses are Exchange Rates, Weekly Securities Statistics, Surveys, Price Indices, Financial Statistics, Housing and Construction Statistics, Deposits and Participation Funds Subject to Required Reserves, Number of Total Visits paras and BIS Comparative Country Statistics. Among the variables mentioned, it was found that the most affecting factor to the total number of access is the number of access to exchange rates data. In the second stage of the analysis, stepwise regression analysis was performed in logarithmic form to determine the factors affecting the total number of access to exchange rates data. However, the variables USD / TRY and EURO / TRY exchange rate were also added to this analysis. The results showed that the only factor affecting the total number of access to exchange rates data was the EURO / TRY exchange rate variable.

Then, in the third stage, Engle-Granger cointegration test was applied with the Error Correction Model (ECM) for the analysis of the long and short-term relationship between the total number of access to exchange rates data and the EURO / TRY exchange rate variable.

The results showed that there is a statistically significant long-run relationship between the total number of access to exchange rates data in EDDS and the EURO / TRY exchange rate variables. Likewise, statistically significant results were found in ECM, which shows short-run relationships. According to the results of ECM analysis, the deterioration in the long-run equilibrium relationship between the variables comes to balance again in about 1.35 periods.

In the diagnostics tests made for the aforementioned analyzes, it was seen that no statistical assumptions were violated. The sample size can be said to be the biggest limitation of this study. When the number of variables is high, a high degree of freedom occurs and consequently, there is not enough data left for the use of multivariate models. Therefore, the factors affecting the total number of access variables found in the first stage have been neglected.

REFERENCES

Akgül, Y. (2016). Quality evaluation of E-government websites of Turkey. *11th Iberian Conference on Information Systems and Technologies (CISTI) Proceedings*, 1-7. 10.1109/CISTI.2016.7521567

Akgül, Y. (2019). The Accessibility. Usability. Quality and Readability of Turkish State and Local Government Websites an Exploratory Study. *International Journal of Electronic Government Research*, *15*(1), 62–81. doi:10.4018/IJEGR.2019010105

Akgül, Y. (2021). Accessibility, usability, quality performance, and readability evaluation of university websites of Turkey: A comparative study of state and private universities. *Universal Access in the Information Society*, *20*(1), 157–170. doi:10.100710209-020-00715-w

Akgül, Y., & Vatansever, K. (2016). Web Accessibility Evaluation of Government Websites for People with Disabilities in Turkey. *Journal of Advanced Management Science*, *4*(3), 201–210. doi:10.12720/joams.4.3.201-210

Alır, G., Soydal, İ., & Öztürk, Ö. (2007). Türkiye'de E-devlet Uygulamaları Kapsamında Kamu Kurumlarına Ait Web Sayfalarının Değerlendirilmesi. In S. Kurbanoğlu, Y. Tonta, & U. Al (Eds.), Değişen Dünyada Bilgi Yönetimi Sempozyumu Proceedings. Academic Press.

Arı, Y. (2021). Engle-Granger Cointegration Analysis Between GARCH-Type Volatilities of Gold and Silver Returns. *Alanya Akademik Bakış*, *5*(2), 589-618. Retrieved from https://dergipark.org.tr/tr/pub/alanyaakademik/issue/62638/838284

Baiocchi, G., & Distaso, W. (2003). *GRETL: Econometric software for the GNU generation.* JSTOR.

BTK Internet. (2021). https://internet.btk.gov.tr/istatistikler

Durmus, S., & Cagiltay, K. (2012). Kamu Kurumu Web Siteleri ve Kullanılabilirlik. In M. Z. Sobacı & M. Yıldız (Eds.), *E-Devlet Kamu Yönetimi ve Teknoloji İlişkisinde Güncel Gelişmeler* (pp. 293–322). Nobel Akademik Yayıncılık.

Engle, R., & Granger, J. (1987). Co-Integration and Error Correction: Representation. Estimation. and Testing. *Econometrica, 55*(2), 251–276. doi:10.2307/1913236

EVDS. (2020). All Series in Electronic Data Delivery System. *TCMB EVDS.* Retrieved from https://evds2.tcmb.gov.tr/index.php?/evds/serieMarket

Flom, P. (2018, December 11). *Stopping stepwise: Why stepwise selection is bad and what you should use instead.* Medium. Retrieved from https://towardsdatascience.com/stopping-stepwise-why-stepwise-selection-is-bad-and-what-you-should-use-instead-90818b3f52df

Fox, J., & Weisberg, S. (2020). *car: Companion to Applied Regression* [R package]. Retrieved from https://cran.r-project.org/package=car

Gulsecen, S. (2020). İnsan ve Bilgisayar. In S. Gülseçen, K. Rızvanoğlu, N. Tosun, & E. Akadal (Eds.), *İnsan Bilgisayar Etkileşimi: Araştırma ve Uygulamalar.* Istanbul University Press., doi:10.26650/B/ET07.2020.012.01

Ismailova, R., & Inal, Y. (2016). Web Site Accessibility and Quality in Use: A Comparative Study of Government Web Sites in Kyrgyzstan, Azerbaijan, Kazakhstan and Turkey. *Universal Access in the Information Society*, 1–10.

KAMİS. (2021, February 12). *Dijital Akademi.* https://dijitalakademi.bilgem.tubitak.gov.tr/kamis

Kayaalp, G., Çelik Güney, M., & Cebeci, Z. (2015). Çoklu Doğrusal Regresyon Modelinde Değişken Seçiminin Zootekniye Uygulanışı. *Çukurova Üniversitesi Ziraat Fakültesi Dergisi, 30*(1), 1-8. Retrieved from https://dergipark.org.tr/tr/pub/cuzfd/issue/23798/253617

Keller, G., Warrack, B., & Bartel, H. (1990). *Statistics for Management and Economics. A System Approach* (2nd ed.). Wadsworth Publishing Company.

Mendenhall, W., & Sincich, T. (1996) A Second Course in Statistics: Regression Analysis (5th ed.). Simon and Schuster.

Montgomery, D. C., Peck, E. A., & Vining, G. G. (2001). *Introduction to Linear Regression Analysis* (3rd ed.). John Wiley & Sons.

Myers, R. H. (1990). *Classical and Modern Regression with Applications* (2nd ed.). PWS-Kent Publishers.

R Core Team. (2021). *R: A Language and environment for statistical computing (Version 4.0)* [Computer software]. Retrieved from https://cran.r-project.org

Smith, G. (2018). Step away from stepwise. *Journal of Big Data*, *5*(1), 32. doi:10.118640537-018-0143-6

Speedtest. (2020). *Monthly comparisons of internet speeds from around the world.* Speedtest Global Index. Retrieved from https://www.speedtest.net/global-index

The jamovi project (2021). *jamovi (Version 1.8)* [Computer Software]. Retrieved from https://www.jamovi.org

World Bank. (2020). Individuals using the Internet (%of Population). In *World Development Indicators*. The World Bank Group. Retrieved from: https://data. worldbank.org/indicator/IT.NET.USER.ZS

APPENDIX A

The Output of Stepwise Regression - 1 for the dependent variable "the total number of Internet accesses"

Table 7. Model Fit Measures

Model Fit Measures			Overall Model Test							
Model	R	R²	Adj R²	AIC	BIC	RMSE	F	df1	df2	p
1	0.997	0.995	0.992	-86	-70.9	0.0376	390	9	19	< .001

Table 8. Diagnostics Tests

Test	Null Hypothesis	Test Statistic	p-Value
White's test for heteroskedasticity	heteroskedasticity not present	LM = 27.1035	P(Chi-square (18) > 27.1035) = 0.0770745
Breusch-Pagan test for heteroskedasticity	heteroskedasticity not present	LM = 9.19616	P(Chi-square(9) > 9.19616) = 0.419368
Test for normality of residual	error is normally distributed	Chi-square(2) = 0.293928	0.863325
RESET test for specification	specification is adequate	F(1, 18) = 2.88622	P(F(1, 18) > 2.88622) = 0.106558
Chow test for structural break at observation 2019	no structural break	F(10, 9) = 2.05865	P(F(10, 9) > 2.05865) = 0.146108
LM test for autocorrelation	no autocorrelation	LMF = 0.374946	P(F(12, 7) > 0.374946) = 0.934932
CUSUM test for parameter stability	no change in parameters	Harvey-Collier t(18) = -0.668198	P(t(18) > -0.668198) = 0.512485

Table 9. Diagnostics Tests for Collinearity

Collinearity Statistics	VIF	Tolerance
Variables		
Exchange_Rates	2.07	0.482
Weekly_Securities_Statistics	4.68	0.214
Surveys	3.95	0.253
Price_Indices	4.3	0.233
Financial_Statistics	2.52	0.396
Housing_and_Construction_Statistics	4.23	0.237
Deposits_and_Participation_Funds_Subject_to_Required_Reserves	3.02	0.331
Number_of_Total_Visits	2.94	0.34
BIS_Comparative_Country_Statistics	2.89	0.346

Table 10. Excluded Variables in the stepwise regression - 1

Variables	Beta In	t	sig	Partial Correlation	Collinearity Statistics
Number of Registered Users	.002	.041	.968	.010	.097
Number of Unique Visitors	.019	.557	.585	.130	.264
Financial Accounts	-.066	-1.590	.129	-.351	.151
Balance of Payments International Investment Position	-.039	-.740	.469	-.172	.102
External Debts	-.011	-.344	.735	-.081	.280
Foreign Trade Statistics	-.090	-1.939	.068	-.416	.114
Interest Rates	-.004	-.107	.916	-.025	.273
Money and Banking Statistics	-.026	-.481	.636	-.113	.101
CBRT Balance Sheet Data	-.035	-.933	.363	-.215	.200
Payment Systems and Emission	.013	.494	.627	.116	.415
Gold Statistics	-.025	-.521	.609	-.122	.129
Production Statistics	-.014	-.327	.748	-.077	.165
Tourism Statistics	-.002	-.077	.939	-.018	.502
Employment Statistics	-.016	-.554	.587	-.129	.365
Public Finance	.057	1.430	.170	.319	.172
Archive	-.023	-.693	.497	-.161	.264
Market Statistics	.040[i]	.730	.475	.170	.097

APPENDIX B

The Output of Stepwise Regression - 1 for the dependent variable "the total number of Exchange Rate accesses"

Table 11. Model Fit Measures

Model Fit Measures			Overall Model Test							
Model	R	R²	Adjusted R²	AIC	BIC	RMSE	F	df1	df2	p
1	0.723	0.522	0.505	47	51.1	0.491	29.5	1	27	< .001

Table 12. Diagnostics Tests

Test	Null Hypothesis	Test Statistic	p-Value
White's test for heteroskedasticity	heteroskedasticity not present	LM = 1.5141	P(Chi-square(2) > 1.5141) = 0.469047
Breusch-Pagan test for heteroskedasticity	heteroskedasticity not present	LM = 0.000141475	P(Chi-square(1) > 0.000141475) = 0.99051
Test for normality of residual	error is normally distributed	Chi-square(2) = 0.53514	0.380989
RAMSEY RESET test for specification	specification is adequate	F(1, 26) = 2.11955	P(F(1, 26) > 2.11955) = 0.1574
Chow test for structural break at observation 2019	no structural break	F(2, 25) = 0.731774	P(F(2, 25) > 0.731774) = 0.491077
Breusch-Godfrey LM test for autocorrelation	no autocorrelation	LMF = 0.821173	P(F(12, 15) > 0.821173) = 0.629695
CUSUM test for parameter stability	no change in parameters	Harvey-Collier t(26) = 1.66721	P(t(26) > 1.66721) = 0.107474

Table 13. Excluded Variables in the stepwise regression - 2

Variables	Beta In	t	Sig.	Partial Cor	VIF
USD/TRY	-.918	-1.238	.227	-.236	31.698
Number of Registered Users	.112	.615	.544	.120	1.827
Number of Total Visits	-.351	-1.903	.068	-.350	2.109
Number of Unique Visitors	-.281	-1.841	.077	-.340	1.432
Market Statistics	-.202	-.916	.368	-.177	2.728
Financial Accounts	-.002	-.011	.992	-.002	2.717
Balance of Payments International Investment Position	.036	.180	.858	.035	2.143
External Debts	.137	.740	.466	.144	1.904
Foreign Trade Statistics	-.040	-.207	.838	-.041	2.060
Interest Rates	.123	.897	.378	.173	1.052
Deposits and Participation Funds Subject to Required Reserves	-.110	-.623	.539	-.121	1.733
Money and Banking Statistics	.109	.526	.603	.103	2.380
Weekly Securities Statistics	-.103	-.722	.477	-.140	1.133
Financial Statistics	.170	1.126	.271	.216	1.309
Surveys	.258	1.461	.156	.275	1.844
CBRT Balance Sheet Data	-.064	-.319	.752	-.062	2.171
Payment Systems and Emission	-.161	-1.044	.306	-.201	1.345
Price Indices	-.058	-.390	.700	-.076	1.220
Gold Statistics	-.134	-.921	.365	-.178	1.184
Production Statistics	.109	.538	.595	.105	2.270
Housing and Construction Statistics	-.109	-.741	.465	-.144	1.206
Tourism Statistics	.025	.159	.875	.031	1.323
Employment Statistics	.261	1.454	.158	.274	1.900
Public Finance	.053	.309	.760	.061	1.589
BIS Comparative Country Statistics	-.080	-.388	.701	-.076	2.317
Archive	-.056	-.290	.774	-.057	2.024
Housing	-.093	-.631	.534	-.123	1.189

Chapter 3

Accessibility and Usability Evaluation of Digital Library Article Pages

Gonca Gokce Menekse Dalveren
iD https://orcid.org/0000-0002-8649-1909
Atilim University, Turkey

Serhat Peker
Izmir Bakırçay University, Turkey

ABSTRACT

This study aims to present an exploratory study about the accessibility and usability evaluation of digital library article pages. For this purpose, four widely known digital libraries (DLs), namely Science Direct, Institute of Electric and Electronic Engineering Xplore, Association for Computing Machinery, and SpringerLink, were examined. In the first stage, article web interfaces of these selected DLs were analyzed based on standard web guidelines using automatic evaluation tools to assess their accessibility. In the second stage, to evaluate the usability of these web interfaces, eye-tracking experiments with 30 participants were conducted. Obtained results of the analysis show that article pages of digital libraries are not of free of accessibility and usability problems. Overall, this study highlights accessibility and usability problems of digital library article interfaces, and these findings can provide the feedback to web developers in making their article pages more accessible and usable for their users.

DOI: 10.4018/978-1-7998-7848-3.ch003

INTRODUCTION

Digital libraries (DLs) have emerged as a consequence of the advances in Information and Communications Technology (ICT). A DL serves a collection of documents in well-organized digital version to improve the access of user communities to information (Borgman, 1999). The explosive growth of the Internet has led to a flood of books, journals, and any types of research articles in electronic form. This abundance of digital resources such as journal issues, book chapters and conference proceedings in today's academy has put academic DLs into a critical position for research activities. With the increased availability of such massive amounts of electronic research materials, DLs present a platform for students, academicians, and researchers. In this context, most higher education institutions subscribe to academic DLs such as IEEE Xplore Digital Library and ACM Digital Library in order to get access their digital resources.

The highly usage of DLs removes the barriers to information access and enables many users accessing various academic materials simultaneously as well. Due to their importance in accessing research documents, numerous research efforts been made on DLs in the last two decades. In this context, service quality is one of the important practices and research areas in academic DLs (Zhang, 2010). Providing high quality service delivery to users plays a very crucial role in encouraging them to use DL services, and thereby it is a key factor in the success of a DL.

The major indicators that impact the quality of a DL are accessibility and usability (Bertot, Snead, Jaeger, & McClure, 2006; Saracevic, 2004). Accessibility can be defined as "the ability of a product, service, environment or equipment to be used by a large range of people with very different capabilities" (ISO, 2008). In this sense, interfaces should be designed based on the corresponding universal accessibility practices so that all potential users can have equal access and effectively utilize their digital resources on the same level. Another important characteristic for the success of DLs is usability. The International Organization for Standardization (ISO) defines usability as "the level of effectiveness, efficiency and satisfaction a certain group of users, of a product or environment, accomplishes for a specific purpose in a certain context of use" (International Organization for Standardization, 1998). When a website is hard to use, this may prevent users to visit that website again in the future (Matera, Rizzo, & Carughi, 2006). Therefore, it is important to make sure that websites are well designed so that users can easily interact with them and perform tasks on them successfully (Yan & Guo, 2010).

Academic DLs should be accessible to all users, with or without disabilities and have usable interfaces as well. Both factors are relatively essential for DLs to deliver high quality of services to their main targeted users. Hence, to ensure high level quality in academic DLs, it is crucial to evaluate both accessibility and usability of them. The usability of DL user interfaces has been investigated in the literature (Fuhr et al., 2007; Jabeen, Qinjian, Yihan, Jabeen, & Imran, 2017; Jeng, 2006; Joo & Lee, 2011; Quijano-Solís & Novelo-Peña, 2005; Tsakonas & Papatheodorou, 2008; Xie, 2008). However, such attention is distinctly lacking when it comes to accessibility evaluation of DLs. Very few studies have investigated accessibility issues in DLs, and this limits the understanding of the current challenges in utilizing their services faced by all users. Further, related to usability assessment of DLs, prior studies have employed many conventional usability testing methods such as user tests, observation, heuristic evaluation, participant feedback elicitation via questionnaire. However, eye-tracking method, which is recently a widely used technique in usability analysis has not been used in the past studies on usability evaluation of DLs. Indeed, this method is very effective in detecting usability problems in web interfaces by providing objective and quantitative data about users' visual attention (Buscher, Cutrell, & Morris, 2009; Ehmke & Wilson, 2007).

This main purpose of study is fulfilling these existing gaps in the literature by examining the accessibility and usability of article web pages of selected widely used academic DLs. This study considers the following DLs: Science Direct, Institute of Electric and Electronic Engineering (IEEE) Xplore, Association for Computing Machinery (ACM) and SpringerLink. For the usability evaluation of these academic DLs, this research employs eye-tracking method by conducting controlled lab experiments and uses automated tools to assess the compliance of them with corresponding accessibility guidelines and standards. This present study is the first detailed research that explores both accessibility and usability levels of four popular academic DLs and it offers suggestions to improve the overall quality of DLs by highlighting critical problems related to accessibility and usability. These recommendations and the findings of the study may be helpful for policy makers in the development of accessible and usable DLs.

METHODOLOGY

In order to gather data for the accessibility and usability assessment of the digital library article pages, different tools and techniques were employed. For the accessibility analysis, a set of automatic evaluation tools were used, while eye tracking experiment method was used for the usability evaluation of the corresponding web interfaces. Quantitative data obtained from the automated tools and eye tracking technique provided assessment of the accessibility and usability of websites/pages.

To evaluate the selected digital libraries in terms of accessibility and usability, article URLs were identified for each digital library and these are listed in Table 1.

Table 1. List of selected article pages for each digital library evaluated

Digital Library	Article URLs
ACM	https://dl.acm.org/doi/10.5555/3040226.3040228
Elsevier	https://www.sciencedirect.com/science/article/pii/S1071581916000215
IEEE Xplore	https://ieeexplore.ieee.org/document/7281117
SpringerLink	https://link.springer.com/article/10.1007/s10209-016-0511-y

Stages and instruments for both accessibility and usability evaluation were detailed separately in the following sub-sections.

Accessibility Evaluation

For accessibility assessment of selected digital libraries' article pages, we used three automated tools: AChecker, WAVE tool, and aXe. These automated tools are widely used ones for the evaluation of accessibility and their effectiveness has previously been validated in several research studies on different application areas.

AChecker Tool

AChecker (Gay & Li, 2010) is an open-source tool which is available at https://achecker.ca/checker/index.php. This instrument enables users to automatically test accessibility of web interfaces based on certain guidelines such as WCAG 1.0 and WCAG 2.0. After performing accessibility analysis for a website, the user interface of this tool is presented in Figure 1.

As shown in Figure 1, accessibility-related problems are listed in three basic categories: (i) known problems, i.e. the accessibility barriers that have been identified with certainty, (ii) likely problems, and (iii) potential problems. Likely problems and potential problems are probable ones and requires further manual assessment to determine if they are really accessibility barriers. This study test selected user interfaces for accessibility defects using WCAG 2.0 guideline under all levels of conformance, namely, A, AA and AAA with Known (KP), Likely (LP) and Potential (PP) problems.

WAVE Tool

WAVE (Kasday, 2000) is an automated accessibility tool which evaluates if a web interface is universally accessible to people with and without disabilities. It performs an accessibility analysis based on the certain success criteria of WCAG 2 guideline and list the evaluation results in terms of errors, contrast errors, alerts, features, structural Elements, and ARIA.

This tool has a browser extension which enables testing within web browser of the user. Figure 2 shows the screenshot related to the summary accessibility results of this tool's Chrome extension.

This study used Chrome extension of this tool and accessibility analysis results were investigated using detected errors, contrast errors and alerts.

Figure 1. The user interface of AChecker tool

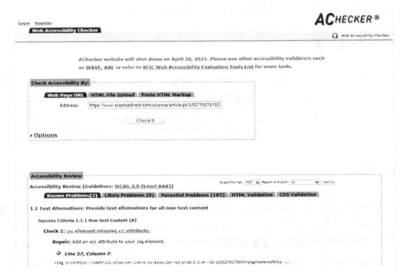

aXe Tool

The aXe is an open-source automated testing tool which validates web applications to identify the common accessibility problems. It presents the results as violations and needs review. Violations which indicate the number of problems based on standard web guidelines are provided in four categories: Minor, Moderate, Serious, and Critical. On the other hand, the needs review shows the issues which require for accessibility expert to review them. This tool runs as an extension within web browsers such Chrome, Firefox, or Edge. This study used Chrome extension of this tool and a snapshot of Chrome extension is shown in Figure 3.

Figure 2. The user interface of WAVE chrome extension

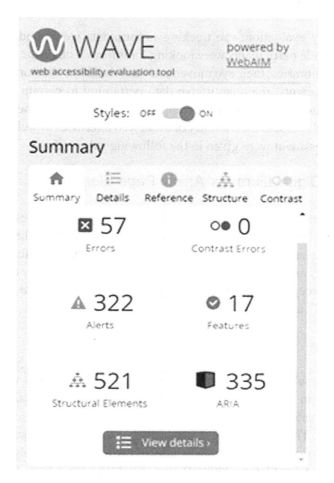

Figure 3. The user interface of aXe chrome extension

Usability Evaluation

For the usability evaluation, eye tracking experiments were conducted. In these experiments, while participants were looking for information on the article pages of selected digital libraries, their eye movements and fixation behavior were recorded. After the experiments, the quantitative data pertaining to certain eye movement variables were analyzed to explore participants' interaction with the corresponding article pages and to assess the usability of these web interfaces as well. All processes of usability assessment were given in the following sub-sections.

Selection of Digital Libraries' Article Page Elements

The first step to evaluating usability of the digital library article pages is to determine a set of elements, so that the participants look for these elements on the corresponding web interfaces. It has been paid attention that these components are found throughout the digital library article pages and are frequently used or needed by the visitors. For this purpose, three components have been determined as "Journal Name", "PDF/ Download PDF", and "References".

Participants

In this study 30 subjects voluntarily participated. Verbal consent was taken from all participants in accordance with the Declaration of Helsinki. All statistical analyzes were made based on the experimental data of the 30 participants (16 men and 14 women). This sample size is generally considered sufficient for qualitative and exploratory eye tracking studies conducted with comparatively small number participants (Wedel & Pieters, 2008). Participants' ages range from 19 to 26, with an average of 22.07 (SD = 1.82). All participants had normal vision or vision corrected by wearing glasses or contact lenses. Moreover, they are all right-handed and have left-to-right reading behavior like the Western system.

Data Collection Instruments

The experiments were carried out in Atılım University SimLab in a quiet room. The experimental tools in this room consisted of a Tobii X60 eye tracker with a screen resolution of 1366-768 pixels, a desktop computer and an 18.5 inch LED monitor. All these devices were interconnected. The sampling frequency of the eye tracker is 60 Hz and the accuracy level is 0.5 degrees. In addition, Tobii Studio Software was used for presenting the stimuli, calibrating the eye tracker, recording eye movement data of participant and analyzing eye movement behaviors, and creating descriptive statistics.

Experimental Design and Data Collection Process

Before the experiments, a pilot experiment was conducted with five subjects to evaluate the experimental environment and settings and, essentially, to decide how long each web page should be displayed, with the structure and content identical to the real experiments.

Real experiments involved a series of stages. First, the participants were informed about the experimental process and eye tracker. Then, then verbal informed consent obtained from the participants for voluntarily participation in the study. Participants were seated in front of the computer screen and their sitting positions were arranged to be centered at a distance of 70 cm in front of the monitor. Consistent monitor brightness and ambient light were provided, and participants were informed to keeo looking to the screen throughout the experiment. The eye tracking device was placed below of the monitor and a calibration process was completed to confirm that the eye tracking device correctly recorded the eye movements.

After the calibration process ensure accurate level, the relevant web pages were presented to the attention of the participants. While the participants tried to find the desired web page elements in each web page, their eye tracking behaviors were recorded by the software. Because of the average time that participants spent viewing the web pages in the pilot study, four digital library webpages were automatically displayed for 20 seconds for each menu item. In this way, watching times longer than 20 seconds can cause participants to become bored, visually tired and lose concentration. In addition, in order to avoid any possible bias in the results, digital library webpages were presented to the users in four different combinations in the experiments. Before each web page appears on the screen, a red circle is presented on a white background image for 3 seconds so that the participants do not focus on different points of the web pages, and the webpage element that participants are asked to find is indicated in this circle. Thus, the attention of the participants was drawn to the same place.

Eye Tracking Measures and Data Analysis

The level of attention was assessed using variables related to data based on eye movement data of areas of interest (AOI) previously identified. In all areas of research, AOIs are used to correlate eye movement measurements with parts of the stimulus presented and are individually defined to identify the most relevant parts of stimuli [30]. In this study, AOI's were identified during the experimental design phase. Tobii Studio Software allows researchers to define AOI's to use these areas for analysis. AOI's are small sections and geometric areas of a web page that correspond to certain content (Figure 4). To analyze eye movements, AOI's were defined for each web page menu component before experiments. Defined AOI's are as follows: "Journal Name", "PDF", and "References". Figure 1 shows the webpage components AOIs determined on the ACM digital library webpage. These AOI's were numbered during the experimental design phase and the analyzes were made by examining the eye movements in these AOI's. The fixation counts and durations of the participants were monitored during the display of the web page components. In eye tracking studies, fixation means that a participant's eye pauses at a particular AOI for more than a specified time.

Figure 4. AOI definitions for Elsevier digital library article page (A: Journal Name, B: PDF, C: References)

Three common eye movement variables created by Tobii Studio Software were used to assess the interest of the participants in each AOI. These are the fixation count (FC), time to first fixation (TFF) and total fixation duration (TFD). FC is the fixation number on a given AOI. The higher an AOI's FC, the more attractive it is to the viewer. TFF is the time from the beginning of a stimulus screen to the participant's first fixation on AOI. If AOI's TFF is short, this indicates that the region is very noticeable. TFD is the duration of all visits within a given AOI, and the longer TFD in a given AOI indicates that the more time is spent for that area.

The data of these eye movement variables were preprocessed for analysis, followed by statistical analysis using the SPSS software package for Windows (version 22; IBM Corporation, New York, USA). A series of repeated measures analysis of variance (RM-ANOVA) (for the within-subject factor) tests were conducted on the eye movement data of all participants for each participant to assess the effect of locations on visual attention given to web page elements. Given the significant ANOVA results, Bonferroni post hoc tests were used to investigate paired comparisons of differences and .05 alpha level was used for statistical analysis. In addition, heat maps were created with Tobii Studio Software in this study. Heat maps in eye tracking studies show the qualitative impression of the users' gaze distribution. A heat map is created by collecting gaze positions and determining focused areas during the observation period. Using heat maps created from the eye movements of the participants, the eye movement behaviors of the participants on the web pages were examined.

RESULTS

Accessibility Analysis

AChecker Tool

Table 2 repots the AChecker evaluation results of corresponding digital libraries' article pages in terms of WCAG 2.0 guideline. The results are given under three basic conformance levels, namely, A, AA and AAA for each problem type (known problems (KP), Likely problems (LP) and Potential problems (PP)) separately.

Table 2. Problem types by AChecker tool report

DL	Level A			Level AA			Level AAA			Total
	KP	LP	PP	KP	LP	PP	KP	LP	PP	
Elsevier	2	0	151	0	0	20	0	0	12	185
SpringerLink	1	0	226	16	1	39	0	0	13	296
ACM	1	0	151	7	0	15	0	0	10	184
IEEE Xplore	0	0	187	2	0	8	0	0	5	202

As shown in Table 2, the highest rate of problems (83%) in digital libraries' article pages are related to accessibility issues at conformance level A, whereas 12% and 5% of observed problems were at conformance levels AA and AAA, respectively. Moreover, results indicate that ACM and Elsevier have the lowest total number of errors (184 and 185, respectively), while the highest total number of errors were observed in SpringerLink article web page (296 errors).

AChecker detected 29 known problems which are classified as important. Web developers need to take immediate action to remove these barriers. Table 3 shows the frequency of identified known problems along with corresponding success criteria.

As seen in Table 3, most of the identified known problems are related to success criterion 1.4.4 "Resize text". The other violated success criteria were 1.1.1 "Non-text Content", 2.4.2 "Page Titled", 3.3.2 "Labels or Instructions" and 4.1.1 "Parsing". For each of these success criteria, exactly one known problem was observed by different article page of digital libraries.

Table 3. Frequency of known problems among DL article pages with WCAG success criteria

Success Criteria	Frequency of Appearance			
	Elsevier	SpringerLink	ACM	IEEE Xplore
1.1.1 Non-text Content (A)	1			
1.4.4 Resize text (AA)		16	7	2
2.4.2 Page Titled (A)			1	
3.3.2 Labels or Instructions (A)	1			
4.1.1 Parsing (A)		1		

WAVE Tool

Accessibility evaluation results of digital libraries' article pages by the WAVE tool are given in Table 4.

Table 4. Accessibility report of WAVE tool

DL	Errors	Contrast Errors	Alerts
Elsevier	0	0	18
SpringerLink	3	0	15
ACM	14	6	160
IEEE Xplore	9	3	6

As shown in Table 4, the number of errors, contrast errors and alerts were reported for each digital library interface. Among the digital library interfaces, ACM has the highest of errors, contrast errors and alerts, and IEEE Xplore follows it with 14 errors and 6 contrast errors. On the other hand, the article page of Elsevier does not have any errors or contrast errors, and it has only 18 alerts.

The different error types identified by WAVE, their frequency, their related WCAG 2 success criteria with corresponding conformance levels are reported in Table 5.

As seen in Table 5, there are 10 types of errors and contrast errors identified by WAVE tool. Very low contrast error was the most frequent error type identified, with 9 instances across all digital library article interfaces. This error type is related to success criterion 1.4.3 "Contrast". Empty link with 7 instances was the second most frequent error type observed. Further, results show that most of the errors identified by WAVE tool are related to both success criterion 1.1.1 "Non-text Content" and

2.4.4 "Link Purpose" (11 instances for both separately). The results in Table 5 also indicate that article page of ACM violated 8 different error types. Article pages of IEEE Xplore and Springer had 4 and 2 different types of errors, respectively.

Table 5. Frequency of error types with their related WCAG 2 Success Criteria

Type of Error	Success Criteria
Spacer image missing alternative text	1.1.1 Non-text Content (Level A)
Empty button	1.1.1 Non-text Content (Level A) 2.4.4 Link Purpose (In Context) (Level A)
Missing alternative text	1.1.1 Non-text Content (Level A)
Missing form label	1.1.1 Non-text Content (Level A) 1.3.1 Info and Relationships (Level A) 2.4.6 Headings and Labels (Level AA) 3.3.2 Labels or Instructions (Level A)
Multiple form labels	1.1.1 Non-text Content (Level A) 1.3.1 Info and Relationships (Level A) 2.4.6 Headings and Labels (Level AA) 3.3.2 Labels or Instructions (Level A)
Empty heading	1.3.1 Info and Relationships (Level A) 2.4.1 Bypass Blocks (Level A) 2.4.6 Headings and Labels (Level AA)
Empty link	2.4.4 Link Purpose (In Context) (Level A)
Broken ARIA reference	1.3.1 Info and Relationships (Level A) 4.1.2 Name, Role, Value (Level A)
Broken ARIA menu	2.1.1 Keyboard (Level A) 4.1.2 Name, Role, Value (Level A)
Very low contrast	1.4.3 Contrast (Minimum) (Level AA)

aXe Tool

The aXe tool results of digital libraries' article pages are shown in Table 6. The results were presented as the violations (given as Minor, Moderate, Serious, or Critical) and needs review.

As seen in Table 6, the highest number of violations was found in the interface of IEEE Xplore, with the instances of 39. ACM's article page follows it with 28 errors and 50 needs review. ACM's interface also had the highest number of critical violations with the instances of 7. On the other hand, the lowest number of violations was found in the interface of SpringerLink. Similarly, Elsevier's article page had the minimal number of needs review with only 2 instances. We can conclude that total violations are higher in the interfaces of IEEE Xplore and ACM than in the ones of Elsevier and SpringerLink.

Table 6. Result of aXe tool

DL	Violations					Needs Review
	Critical	**Serious**	**Moderate**	**Minor**	**Total**	
Elsevier	0	1	4	1	6	2
SpringerLink	2	0	3	0	5	4
ACM	7	10	10	1	28	50
IEEE Xplore	1	11	27	0	39	4

Usability Analysis

Usability evaluation results are presented using different gaze-related measures which are based on quantitative eye-tracking data. The averages of FC, TFD and TFF measurements for the AOI's of each of the four digital library web pages are shown in the figures below. Figures 5 and 6 show which web page element has the highest FC count and TVD. IEEE for the "Journal Name" and "PDF" web page AOI's, ACM for the "References" web page AOI, has the highest FC. This shows which web page element is the most attractive area and which areas are the least popular.

Figure 5. Distribution of FC in three areas of interest of digital libraries

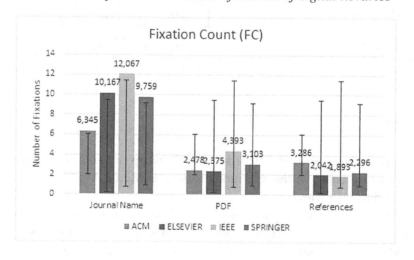

Figure 6. Distribution of TFD in three areas of interest of digital libraries

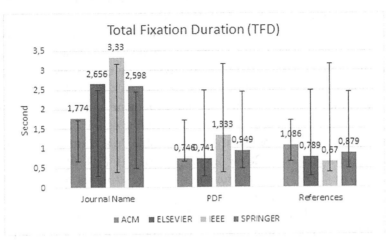

The results of the TFF values (Figure 7) of the AOI's of the digital library web pages revealed that ACM has the highest TFF value for "Journal Name" web page element. On the other hand, Elsevier has the highest for the "PDF" and "References" web page elements. This result suggested that "Journal Name" web page element of ACM and "PDF" and "References" web page elements of Elsevier were noticed in more time compared to other digital libraries, and therefore they were less noticeable.

Figure 7. Distribution of time until the first fixation in three areas of interest of digital libraries

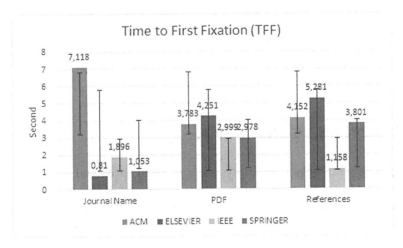

To determine whether digital library article web pages had a significant impact on the attention captured by each AOI, RM-ANOVAs were performed on the eye tracking data for each of the three AOI identified. In the post-hoc comparisons column in Table 7, the relevant assumptions were confirmed and the results of the post hoc tests reflecting a significant difference are given. The results revealed significant differences among four digital libraries for all three web page elements. Regarding the TFF scale, the "Journal Name" web page element of the digital library web pages $(F (519.254) = 22.056, p <.001)$ and "References" $(F (126.036) = 6.826, p <.001)$, web page elements are specified in the Table. In addition, the results for the TFD measurement are $(F (9.528) = 4.570, p <.001)$, $(F (2.430) = 7.997, p <.001)$ and $(F (0.891) = 4.299, p <.001)$ for the web page "Journal Name", "PDF" and "References" menu components, respectively. This has shown a significant effect on the visual interest. In addition, the results for the FC measurement also showed a significant effect on the visual interest shown in the web page menu item "Journal Name" $(F (184.514) = 6.338, p <.001)$, "PDF" $(F (43.200) = 8.760, p <.001)$ and "References" $(F (14.407) = 7.936, p <.001)$.

Table 7. Test results showing the impact of web page elements on visual attention

AOI	Measure	F	Post-hoc Comparisons [a]
Journal Name	TFF	22.056	Elsevier<ACM, IEEE<ACM, Springer<ACM
	TFD	4.570	ACM<IEEE
	FC	6.338	ACM<Elsevier, ACM<IEEE
PDF	TFD	7.997	ACM<IEEE, Elsevier<IEEE, Springer<IEEE
	FC	8.760	ACM<IEEE, Elsevier<IEEE
References	TFF	6.826	IEEE<ACM, IEEE<Elsevier, IEEE<Springer
	TFD	4.299	IEEE<ACM
	FC	7.936	Elsevier<ACM, IEEE<ACM, Springer<ACM

[a]< statistically significant
$p < .001$

DISCUSSION AND CONCLUSION

Assessing accessibility and usability is very useful to extend the knowledge of the current state of the digital library article pages and reveal the needs of users. Therefore, in this study the accessibility problems of these pages were examined with automatic assessment tools. Based on the findings of this study the highest rate of problems (83%) in digital libraries' article pages are related to accessibility issues at conformance level A. Also, for the levels AA and AAA observed problems were at 12% and 5% conformance levels. According to the results of AChecker highest number of errors observed in SpringerLink digital library article page with 296 errors. Also, results reveal that there are other important issues that web developers need to take action. Digital library article pages were assessed with the tool WAVE and the number of errors and their frequencies were identified. Based on the results, ACM has the highest errors, contrast errors and alerts. The violation states were examined with the tool Axe and according to the results the highest number of violations occurred for the IEEE Xplore and ACM digital library article page.

In this study usability assessments of digital library article pages performed based on different gaze-related measures which were gathered from eye-tracking data. These measures are the averages of FC, TFD and TFF measurements for the defined AOI's of each digital library web pages. Based on the results of FC and TVD it possible to say which parts of a web page is more attractive. Accordingly, for the "Journal Name" and "PDF" web page elements designed more eye catching in IEEE Xplore digital library wen page. The "References" web page element is more attractive in ACM digital library web page. On the other hand, TFF represents the time spent to reach on a specific area. Hence, higher TFF indicates less attractive web page elements. The results of this study shows that the "Journal Name" web page element of ACM and "PDF" and "References" web page elements of Elsevier takes more to be noticed. The findings of this study show that each digital library article pages have its specific powerful and weak points which can be used to comply with guidelines for designing web pages in a better way. The information obtained from this study provides information to the developers about the problems that exist on the web pages and shows the accessibility level of their web pages. Thus, recurring accessibility and usability faults are identified and possible solutions can be derived to solve these problems. The following suggestions can be given to better design web pages based on the results of this study.

- Headers can be presented for all content.
- For the non-text web page elements text alternatives can be given.
- Color contrasts and brightness can be controlled.
- Size and position of important information can be controlled.
- Distance between the web page elements can be controlled.
- Necessary information and web content can be presented modest to make it accessible.

In this study the current situation of the accessibility and usability states of four digital library article pages were presented. Therefore, web page developers and designers should consider the results of accessibility and usability assessment results of web pages and give attention to the important points to accomplish web accessibility and usability in an improved way. As a future work, similar study can be conducted in different fields with higher number of participants to evaluate more web pages and web page elements for increasing the accuracy of the results.

ACKNOWLEDGMENT

The authors would like to thank to Dr. Yavuz İnal for his valuable support and contribution throughout the research.

REFERENCES

Bertot, J. C., Snead, J. T., Jaeger, P. T., & McClure, C. R. (2006). *Functionality, usability, and accessibility: Iterative user-centered evaluation strategies for digital libraries*. Performance Measurement and Metrics. doi:10.1108/14678040610654828

Borgman, C. L. (1999). What are digital libraries? Competing visions. *Information Processing & Management*. Advance online publication. doi:10.1016/S0306-4573(98)00059-4

Buscher, G., Cutrell, E., & Morris, M. R. (2009). What do you see when you're surfing? Using eye tracking to predict salient regions of web pages. *Conference on Human Factors in Computing Systems - Proceedings*. 10.1145/1518701.1518705

Ehmke, C., & Wilson, S. (2007). Identifying web usability problems from eye-tracking data. *People and Computers XXI HCI.But Not as We Know It - Proceedings of HCI 2007: The 21st British HCI Group Annual Conference*. 10.14236/ewic/HCI2007.12

Fuhr, N., Tsakonas, G., Aalberg, T., Agosti, M., Hansen, P., Kapidakis, S., Klas, C.-P., Kovács, L., Landoni, M., Micsik, A., Papatheodorou, C., Peters, C., & Sølvberg, I. (2007). Evaluation of digital libraries. *International Journal on Digital Libraries*, *8*(1), 21–38. Advance online publication. doi:10.100700799-007-0011-z

Gay, G., & Li, C. Q. (2010). AChecker: Open, interactive, customizable, web accessibility checking. *W4A 2010 - International Cross Disciplinary Conference on Web Accessibility Raleigh 2010*. 10.1145/1805986.1806019

International Organization for Standardization. (1998). *ISO 9241-11: Ergonomic requirements for office work with visual display terminals (VDTs) - part 11: guidance on usability*. International Organization for Standardization. doi:10.1038j. mp.4001776

ISO. (2008). Ergonomics of human-system interaction — Part 171 : Guidance on software accessibility. *International Organization.*

Jabeen, M., Qinjian, Y., Yihan, Z., Jabeen, M., & Imran, M. (2017). *Usability study of digital libraries: An analysis of user perception, satisfaction, challenges, and opportunities at university libraries of Nanjing*. Library Collections, Acquisition and Technical Services. doi:10.1080/14649055.2017.1331654

Jeng, J. (2006). Usability of the digital library: An evaluation model. *College & Research Libraries News.*

Joo, S., & Lee, J. Y. (2011). Measuring the usability of academic digital libraries: Instrument development and validation. *The Electronic Library*, *29*(4), 523–537. Advance online publication. doi:10.1108/02640471111156777

Kasday, L. R. (2000). A tool to evaluate universal web accessibility. *Proceedings of the Conference on Universal Usability*. 10.1145/355460.355559

Matera, M., Rizzo, F., & Carughi, G. T. (2006). Web usability: Principles and evaluation methods. Web Engineering. doi:10.1007/3-540-28218-1_5

Quijano-Solís, Á., & Novelo-Peña, R. (2005). Evaluating a monolingual multinational digital library by using usability: An exploratory approach from a developing country. *The International Information & Library Review*, *37*(4), 329–336. Advance online publication. doi:10.1080/10572317.2005.10762690

Saracevic, T. (2004). How were digital libraries evaluated? *DELOS WP7 Workshop on the Evaluation of Digital Libraries.*

Tsakonas, G., & Papatheodorou, C. (2008). Exploring usefulness and usability in the evaluation of open access digital libraries. *Information Processing & Management*, *44*(3), 1234–1250. Advance online publication. doi:10.1016/j.ipm.2007.07.008

Wedel, M., & Pieters, R. (2008). Eye Tracking for Visual Marketing. *Foundations and Trends® in Marketing, 1*(4), 231–320. doi:10.1561/1700000011

Xie, H. I. (2008). Users' evaluation of digital libraries (DLs): Their uses, their criteria, and their assessment. *Information Processing & Management*, *44*(3), 1346–1373. Advance online publication. doi:10.1016/j.ipm.2007.10.003

Yan, P., & Guo, J. (2010). The research of web usability design. *2010 The 2nd International Conference on Computer and Automation Engineering, ICCAE 2010.* 10.1109/ICCAE.2010.5451619

Zhang, Y. (2010). Developing a holistic model for digital library evaluation. *Journal of the American Society for Information Science and Technology*, *61*(1), 88–110. Advance online publication. doi:10.1002/asi.21220

Chapter 4

A Systematic Review of Web Accessibility Metrics

Pınar Onay Durdu
Kocaeli University, Turkey

Ömer Naci Soydemir
Kocaeli University, Turkey

ABSTRACT

Currently, providing accessible websites for all users is an essential requirement. There are various qualitative and quantitative evaluation methods to assure accessibility. Among these, the quantitative methods show the level of accessibility of the website using web accessibility metrics (WAM), which provide a way to understand, control, and improve these websites. This study was aimed to identify current trends and analyze WAMs through a systematic literature review. Therefore, 30 WAM studies that were published since 2008 were determined and investigated according to attributes defined for the metrics such as guideline set used by the metric, coupling level with the guidelines, type of evaluation, site complexity, and validation with the user. Fourteen recently proposed WAMs were determined since 2008. Recently proposed WAMs have begun to consider more elaborate issues such as rich internet applications, website complexity, usability, or user experience issues and implement some machine learning approaches for the metrics.

DOI: 10.4018/978-1-7998-7848-3.ch004

INTRODUCTION

Currently web sites have become a main dissemination mechanism of information and services. People do most of their daily transactions through the web sites. On the other hand, 15% of world's population is estimated to be disabled by World Health Organization (Chan & Zoellick, 2011). In addition, the aging of the population would affect to increase the numbers because elderly people begin to have problems in vision or their cognitive skills. Therefore, the audiences of websites are various people with different abilities or disabilities (Masri & Luján-Mora, 2011). Thus, providing inclusive and accessible websites for all people is necessary.

Since web sites have become indispensable, some countries make use of general guidelines such as WCAG (Web Content Accessibility Guidelines) 1.0 (W3.org, 1999) or 2.0 (W3.org, 2008) or some rules or regulations such as ISO 9241-20 (ISO, 2008) or Section 508 (US Access Board, 2000) to make the web contents more accessible. Recently, WCAG 3.0 (W3C, 2021) was publicized as a working draft but WCAG 2.0 [3] is still used as a general guideline for accessibility evaluations by developers, designers, etc. to provide a certain level of accessibility for all users.

There are various evaluation methods to assure web accessibility in the literature and these methods can be categorized as qualitative and quantitative methods in general (Masri & Luján-Mora, 2011). Qualitative methods are used to investigate a website's compliance to guidelines by the use of automatic tools (Zaphiris & Ellis, 2001) or to some heuristics by experts manually (Brajnik, 2011). Other than these two analytical methods, user testing conducted with people with disabilities is an empirical method which reveals accessibility problems more accurately (Masri & Luján-Mora, 2011). Many recent research (Akgül, 2021; Alajarmeh, 2021; Baeza-Yates, 2020) also focuses on website accessibility evaluations as well. On the other hand, quantitative methods show the level of accessibility of the website by the use of accessibility metrics which have been proposed in the literature (Freire et al., 2008). These metric-based methods are important to help understand products, processes, and control and improve them in software development (Fenton & Bieman, 2014). In terms of accessibility, metrics are useful for increasing accessibility of existing products and identifying accessibility problems in a product in the development process. Various studies (Sullivan & Matson, 2000) have been carried out on metric definition and application of these metrics in measuring web accessibility .

There are several studies (Hackett et al., 2003; Sirithumgul et al., 2009a; Vigo et al., 2007) that propose WAMs (Web Accessibility Metrics) and these are very valuable for developers and researchers studying in this domain. There are some reviews on WAMs in the literature. Freire et al. (2008) and Brajnik and Vigo (2011) report WAMs which were proposed until 2011. Vigo et al. (2007) also offers a comprehensive list of metrics in their work, where they proposed a framework for comparing WAMs. In a recent study, Brajnik and Vigo (2019) updated the information on accessibility metrics proposed until 2018.

Above mentioned review studies were generally conducted as traditional reviews. Alternatively, within the scope of this study, it is aimed to identify current trends and analyze WAMs via a systematic literature review (SLR) (Kitchenham & Charters, 2007). This study is implemented as a secondary study based on evidence-based software engineering (Kitchenham et al., 2004) and involves gathering the primary studies especially on WAMs. The scope of the SLR is determined to be started from 2008 which is the year of publication of WCAG 2.0. The aim is to provide a complete picture of WAMs by revealing the trends in WAMs, characteristics of these metrics, how they were developed and validated. The results are believed to provide insight to the researchers who are studying or would like to study on WAMs and to evaluators who would like to use these metrics for their assessments.

BACKGROUND

Web Accessibility and Accessibility Guidelines

Websites are public platforms used to present information. They are currently used by diverse categories of user groups including disabled or people with some special needs. Any web site can be considered as accessible when all individuals who has or has not any disability can access and use them effectively (Slatin & Rush, 2003). W3C (WAI, 2005, p.) provides a parallel definition for web accessibility as people with disabilities can use the web as well as "perceive, understand, navigate, interact and contribute to the Web".

There are other various definitions for web accessibility. For instance Arch (2009) considers web accessibility as a part of usability. Some other definitions extend the target of accessibility to older people (Thatcher et al., 2006) or to other context such as mobile (Yesilada et al., 2013). Thus it can be said that there is not a commonly agreed upon only definition for web accessibility but the definition of W3C (WAI, 2005) is commonly agreed definition among the software professionals in the field (Yesilada et al., 2012).

Many current websites contain accessibility barriers that make it difficult for people to access the information they are looking for (WAI, 2005). In order to ensure equal access and equal opportunity for all people, the Web Accessibility Initiative (WAI) (W3C, n.d) established by the World Wide Web Consortium (W3C) (W3C, n.d.), has developed the Web Accessibility Content Guidelines (WCAG). In 1999 W3C published the first version of its guideline as WCAG 1.0 (W3C, 1999) and updated it as WCAG 2.0 (W3C, 2008) in 2008. Currently WCAG 3.0 (W3C, 2021) is available as a working draft on WAI's web page. WCAG 3.0 can be considered as a successor of WCAG guidelines and extends its predecessors by incorporating content UAAG 2.0 (User Agent Accessibility Guidelines) and ATAG 2.0 (Authoring Tool Accessibility Guidelines). In addition, WCAG 3.0 includes additional tests and different scoring mechanics. On the other hand, WCAG 2.0 is still expected to be used as the main guideline by some organizations (W3C, 2021).

WAI (W3C, 2008) has defined four principles in WCAG 2.0 guidelines for making web content accessible. These principles can be listed as being perceivable, operable, understandable, and robust for any web content. Under these 12 guidelines determined for the principles, there are 61 testable success criteria which can be used for conformance testing. In addition, three levels of conformance are defined as A (lowest – 25 criteria), AA (13 criteria) and AAA (highest – 23 criteria) to meet the needs of different groups and situations.

Apart from the WAI's guidelines ISO 9241 (ISO, 2021, p. 92) series provides ergonomic guidance that contributes to accessibility of interactive systems to meet the needs of users. Accessibility focused design activities defined in these series provide a basis for identifying user accessibility needs and deriving user requirements specific to accessibility. In addition, the Section 508 standards was established by The US Access Board to implement the law and provide the requirements for accessibility. Section 508 requires e-government web sites to be accessible to all people regardless of having any disabilities (US EPA, 2013).

Accessibility Evaluation Methods

With the aim of developing accessible web sites, accessibility evaluations should be conducted continuously both during the development process as well as after their release. Web accessibility evaluation covers the assessment of a web site whether it can be used by its users (Harper & Yesilada, 2008) in addition to its conformance to accessibility standards as well. There are various web site accessibility evaluation methods and there are various categorizations for these methods. Brajnik (Brajnik, 2008b) provides a detailed taxonomy based on the purpose, type of input information used, and type of results and then summarized the most typical evaluation methods in categories of automated tests, conformance reviews, screening techniques, subjective assessments barrier walkthrough, and user testing. On the other hand, Abascal at al. (2019) classifies them into three main categories as manual inspection, automated testing, and user testing.

Automated testing can be conducted by software tools that check the compliance of a website according to the guidelines. These software tools also can be grouped into two groups. The first group includes tools such as SortSite (2021) and AChecker (2021) that evaluate the conformance to guidelines such as WCAG or Section 508.

Second group includes tools that evaluate specific issues such as Contrast Checker (2017) which tests color contrast.

Manual inspection is the review and evaluation of the website by an expert according to the accessibility guidelines (Brajnik, 2008a). These inspections can be supported by some assistive technologies such as screen readers. Barrier Walkthrough (Brajnik, 2011) which is similar to heuristic evaluation in usability evaluations can be given as an example for this type of evaluation method. This method can be used throughout the whole development process of a web site, but it requires a subjective human judgement and therefore can take a lot of time.

User testing methods can be considered as an informal empirical usability tests based on individual users conducting with a set of tasks (Abascal et al., 2019). Test users provide their feedback by surveys, interviews or etc, and their behavior and interactions are analyzed by experts. Although it is a more reliable evaluation method that derives results from the real experiences of disabled users, such user tests are quite time consuming and expensive.

Evaluation methods generally are conducted by following three major steps (Brajnik & Lomuscio, 2007): i) Collecting web pages by a web crawler. ii) Inspection of web pages by an automated tool, an expert or a user. iii) Analyzing the results to determine accessibility problems. There are several issues to be considered during these steps. For instance, current web sites have a huge number of pages, and it is not possible to crawl and inspect all the pages. Therefore, many sampling methods are implemented to reduce the cost of accessibility evaluation. Some of the sampling methods proposed can be summarized as ad hoc, uniform random, random walk, and stratified sampling methods (Zhang et al., 2015). In ad hoc sampling some predefined pages such as homepage, contact page, etc. are used (WAB Cluster, 2006). In random-based methods each page has the same probability of being selected (Henzinger et al., 2000). In stratified sampling, clustering web pages by their error profiles and then selecting samples from each cluster is implemented (King et al., 2005). Brajnik et al. (2007) compared 13 of the sampling methods and reported that stratified sampling methods are the best for especially for WCAG conformance although they are the most expensive ones. Appropriate sampling approach should be selected in line with the purpose of the evaluation.

Another concern is related with Rich Internet Applications (RIAs) since the evolution of Web 2.0 applications which includes more interactive navigation of dynamic web contents (Gibson, 2007). Evaluating RIAs without considering their dynamic components provides an erroneous perception of accessibility (Fernandes et al., 2013). Because accessibility evaluation tools available generally check the accessibility of static traditional web pages according to the general accessibility guidelines like WCAG (Doush et al., 2013; N. Fernandes et al., 2013). WAI developed WAI-ARIA (Accessible Rich Internet Applications) (W3C, 2020) specifications to help in evaluating the dynamic content and advanced user interface controls developed with HTML, JavaScript, and related technologies. There is a need to run-time testing of RIAs.

While analyzing the results of conformance testing approaches, it is generally the case that a web site is conformant to guidelines at an adequate level of accessibility, it still may not be sufficient for the users or the vice versa (Aizpurua et al., 2016). In addition, these results generally do not inform the evaluators to distinguish the major problems from minor ones (Brajnik, 2008b). This is due to the problem that evaluation methods other than user testing do not consider usability or user experience of the real users.

Web Accessibility Metrics (WAMs)

There is a growing interest in defining metrics for measuring web accessibility since the release of WCAG 1.0 in 1999. Accessibility evaluation methods provide results that report the conformance levels of a web site according to guidelines. For instance, WCAG 2.0 has three levels of conformance which are A, AA, and AAA. However, this approach is not precise enough because it defines both web sites as level A, when both comply with all level A criteria while one of them also comply some of the level AA criteria (Vigo et al., 2007). Rather than having this type of accept/reject approach while determining accessibility, defining quantitative metrics would provide more precise measurement scale for the comparison of two or more web sites and enable to track quality improvement in the quality assurance process. The quantitative metrics are calculated based on a two-step process which is summarized by Song et al. (2017) as first step focusing on the investigation of barriers and their different properties which are gathered during the inspection of web pages and the second step involving aggregating the results with weighting of checkpoints.

Metrics provides a way to understand, control and improve all software products and processes (Fenton & Bieman, 2014). Important characteristics of software metrics were defined as being simple to understand and precisely defined, objective, cost effective and informative (Daskalantonakis, 1992). In terms of web site accessibility, metrics are also useful in increasing the accessibility of existing products and identifying accessibility problems in a product in the development process and should also have these characteristics as well.

WAMs (web accessibility metrics) are defined in three categories which were totally automatic, totally manual and hybrid metrics (Vigo & Brajnik, 2011). Automatic metrics depend on the results of automatic evaluation tools; while manual metrics are based on human judgements on accessibility defects and experts determine a value according to their judgements and finally hybrid metrics use the data which are produced by tools and interpreted and graded by humans. All categories have their own advantages and disadvantages. Automatic metrics are fast and easy and since no human intervention is required; their results are more reliable and can be implemented for the mass number of evaluations. On the other hand, they inherit the limitations of the automatic assessment tools that they depend on. The accuracy of these tools are considered to be low (Brajnik, 2004). Likewise, the reliability and validity of manual metrics are not optimal, and they are also considered to be expensive since they require expert judgement. Hybrid metrics tries to match the bests of two approaches. Zeng (2004) and Freire et al. (2008) defined main features to compare accessibility metrics as; guideline set, type of evaluation, site complexity consideration, automated tool support, barrier coefficients, validation with users, and use in large scale. These features were also used as good accessibility attributes to good metrics. In addition, these features also provide a guideline for project managers and developers to decide on the metric more appropriate for their Web development project (2008)

There are several proposed web site accessibility metrics since 2000 (Freire et al., 2008) and many of the initial ones are mainly based on WCAG 1.0 (1999) guideline since they are proposed until before the publication of WCAG 2.0 in 2008. These metrics generally use the number of barriers or problems determined in a web page, number of potential barriers, some coefficient for barrier weights, the number of pages evaluated, and the number of tests carried out as variables in their formula.

For instance one of the initial accessibility metric also known as failure rate (FR) (Sullivan & Matson, 2000) depends on the ratio between the number of actual and potential problems in a page. Web pages are evaluated by using eight of the priority 1 checkpoints of WCAG 1.0 and then accessibility value is calculated as a failure rate which is proportional to total number of failures in a web page to total number of potential barriers. The web sites are classified in four levels as highly accessible, mostly accessible, partly accessible, and inaccessible. This metric does not include any weighing coefficients for the detected barriers or does not consider web site complexity. Therefore, it can be said that FR provides a way to measure how good accessibility features were provided by the developers (Vigo & Brajnik, 2011).

Some other metrics implement some coefficients for barrier weights. Gonzales et al. (2003) proposed KAI (Kit for the Accessibility to the Internet) as metric for visually impaired users by implementing barrier coefficients. First a global ratio is calculated based on the determined accessibility problems and potential problems based on barriers. Then this ratio is multiplied by weighting coefficients based on the percentage of blindness. In addition, Web Quality Evaluation Method (Olsina & Rossi, 2002). Provides a normalized overall accessibility value.

Another metric web accessibility barrier (WAB) (Parmanto & Zeng, 2005a) implement weights as the inverse of the priority of each WCAG checkpoints. In addition, this metric also considers the complexity of a website i.e., total number of pages that a site contains. Web pages are evaluated based on 25 checkpoints of WCAG 1.0. A web site that has a WAB score calculated greater than 5.5 is accepted to have serious accessibility problems – while a score close or equal to 0 show best results.

Aggregation formula, which is an another important metric, is defined by UWEM (Unified Web Evaluation Methodology) project (WAB Cluster, 2006). This metric also implements potential problems and weighting of barriers. Moreover, in this metric the use of user-derived coefficients for barriers weights are used. They use 0.05 for the weighing value of all barriers. The score for the metric is calculated between values 0 and 1 and the score close to 0 is considered as best accessibility level as in WAB.

Bühler et al. (2006) proposed A3 – improved aggregation formula as an extension to UWEM metric. They considered the complexity of web pages, severity of a user group of each barrier. They also implemented 0.05 for the weighing value of all barriers.

Different from the previous metrics, Web Accessibility Quality Metric (WAQM) (Vigo et al., 2007) also considers problems identified as warnings by evaluation tools. The weighing coefficients are determined experimentally as 0.8 for priority 1, 0.16 for priority 2, and 0.04 for priority 3. The scores of this metric ranges from 0 to 100, where the score of 100 represents accessible sites.

Related Works

The studies, which include accessibility evaluations and accessibility metric proposals, are very valuable for developers and researchers studying in this field. When previous studies are examined, it is seen that studies that are conducted by following a systematic review methodology generally focus on general accessibility evaluation studies in certain application areas. There are some review studies that also focus on WAMs (web accessibility metrics) but they can be considered as narrative reviews rather than systematic literature reviews.

Sanchez-Gordon and Luján-Mora (2018) focuses their systematic literature review study on the accessibility of major online course (MOOC) platforms while Akram and Sulaiman (2017) focus on general accessibility issues on university and government websites in Saudi Arabia. In addition, the findings of another systematic review study focus on measures for electronic communication accessibility for users with cognitive disabilities (Borg et al., 2015).

On the other hand, in Freire et al.'s study (2008) various WAMs proposed are listed and are compared according to their attributes defined by Zeng (2004). These metrics are listed as guideline set used by the metric, coupling level with the guidelines, type of evaluation, site complexity, type of barrier weights coefficients, default coefficients, validation with user, automated tool support and use in large scale. As a result of the study, they cannot make any conclusion on a metric that would be more effective in general case.

Vigo and Brajnik (2011) present a comprehensive list of WAMs in their study, where they suggest a framework for comparing WAMs. Their framework includes a set of properties for the quality of metrics as validity, reliability, sensitivity, adequacy and complexity. They compared seven proposed accessibility metrics according to these criteria in four different scenarios and concluded that web accessibility quantitative metric (WAQM) (Vigo et al., 2007) and web accessibility barrier (WAB) (Parmanto & Zeng, 2005a) are the highest quality metrics. In 2019, Brajnik and Vigo (2019) reported on more recent WAMs proposed from 2011 to 2018. These newer metrics use new kinds of data like human judgement or questionnaires to support data from automated tools, so reliability and validity issues of the initial metrics are addressed.

METHODOLOGY

The goal of a systematic literature review (SLR) can be listed as "to summarize the existing evidence concerning a treatment or a technology; to identify any gaps in the current research to suggest further investigation areas and to provide a background for positioning new research activities" (Kitchenham & Charters, 2007). This method can be summarized as giving a general idea about a particular research and giving information about the amount, type, and results of the studies in that area. The procedure determined by Kitchenham at al. (2004) was applied for the review process in this study. It was conducted in four phases namely, determination of boundaries, execution of searches, selection of studies, and analysis and reporting as depicted in Figure 1.

Figure 1. Research design

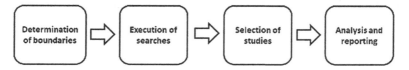

85

Determination of Boundaries

In the first phase of the study, the boundaries of the study were set to determine the scope. Therefore, research questions, search keywords and inclusion and exclusion were determined.

Research Questions

Following research questions were determined to reveal the current situation regarding WAMs (web accessibility metrics) for the last decade.

1. What is the general information distribution of WAM studies in the literature?
2. What are the implemented or mentioned metrics in the studies since 2008?
3. What are the recently proposed metrics in the studies since 2008?
    a. What are the characteristics of those recent metrics?
    b. How were these metrics developed in terms of source and methodology?
    c. How were they validated?

Search Keywords

In line with the purpose of the study and research questions, keywords to be used in searches are defined as "web/website accessibility", "web/website accessibility evaluation" and "metrics" to find primary studies. It is important to consider usability, accessibility and quality criteria for selecting primary sources (Thompson et al., 2003). All these search keywords were combined by using the Boolean operators of "OR, AND", so that a study that focuses on both accessibility evaluation and accessibility metrics would be retrieved.

Execution of Searches

In the execution of search phase, searches were conducted according to search keywords and strings which were determined in previous phase. Searches were conducted in several databases including Web of Science (WoS), Science Direct (Elsevier), IEEExplore Library, ACM Digital Library. These databases were selected since they publish peer reviewed research in the field of information systems. At the end of the initial searches, 148 studies were determined.

Inclusion and Exclusion Criteria

Criteria were defined to select and review studies for the review. Studies were excluded if they did not meet the following criteria:

- Articles which were written in other languages in English
- Articles which were accessible only to abstracts
- Articles which were published in other than journals, conference proceedings or book chapters such as thesis or industry reports.
- Articles which only mention about WAM rather than proposing or at least implementing a metric for the evaluation of web site accessibility

In addition to above mentioned criteria that could be controlled by just looking at the title and abstract of the studies, quality assessment was also implemented for the studies to be included in the review. For the quality assessment, screening approach determined by Ekman (2004) were used. In this approach there are 10 quality assessment items. When an article completely complies with the item then the maximum score 2 is assigned while it complies partly then the score 1 is assigned and the score of 0 is assigned to any item if the article does not comply at all. A total quality score of 17-20 implies quality rating A, a score of 11-16 implies quality rating B and a score of 10 or less implies quality rating C. All the studies included based on the inclusion and exclusion criteria complied with the quality score of above 10 so none of the studies were determined to be excluded based on the quality assessment.

Selection of the Studies

The studies were selected based on the predefined inclusion and exclusion criteria and then 20 studies were left. Before the final stage, forward snowballing technique (Wohlin, 2014), was used to support the systematic review stages. This method provides not to miss and access to more relevant studies by using references and citations of a study (Sanchez-Gordon & Luján-Mora, 2018). However, snowballing can not only look up reference lists and citations, but also complement the work with a systematic way of looking at the cited locations and where the article is cited. Google Scholar was used to access these papers. As a result, 10 more papers were identified after the implementation of this method. In the scope of this study, total of 30 studies were determined by following a systematic literature review procedure. The number of studies determined in the first round and the number of left studies at the end of all stages can be seen in Table 1.

Table 1. Number of studies gathered from databases and the number of studies included in the study.

Database	# of Studies Gathered From Databases	# of Studies Included
Web of Science (WoS)	61	3
Science Direct	41	2
IEEE-xplore	74	0
ACM	62	15
Google Scholar (Forward snowballing)	70	10
Total	148	30

Analysis and Reporting

All the selected papers determined according to the predetermined systematic search were investigated in this phase. Both authors reviewed and analyzed all the studies according to the determined research criteria. An investigation form was used by both authors to extract common data from the studies. Extracted data from each researcher were compared and disagreements were discussed and resolved by consensus in meetings. The data were synthesized by identifying common themes emanating from the findings reported in each of the paper reviewed in this study.

RESULTS

Detailed findings of the review of these studies based on the research questions determined are presented in the following three subsections which are general trends of WAM studies, recently proposed WAMs and their characteristics, and implemented/mentioned WAMs in the studies.

General Trends of WAM Studies

According to the results of this systematic review, 30 WAM studies published since 2008 are gathered. The list of the studies with their references can be seen in Table 5 in Appendix 1 as coded sources [S] to be mentioned in text. The scope distribution of these studies was categorized as proposal and implementation (P&I, N=13), review and implementation (R&I, N=2), just implementation (I, N=14), and just review (R, N=1). The yearly distribution of total number of WAM studies and number of WAM proposal studies can be seen in Figure 2. Most studies on

WAMs were published in the years 2014 and 2015, with 5 studies each. There were 14 WAM proposal studies since 2008 and more proposal studies were published especially in 2015 with three studies. On the other hand, in 2012, 2013 and 2016, there were no WAM proposal studies.

Figure 2. Distribution of WAM related studies over years

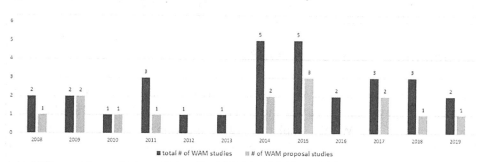

WAM studies were gathered from various databases and that distribution can be seen in Table 2. Half of the studies (N=15) were gathered from the ACM database while many studies (N=10) were collected by the forward snowballing approach from Google Scholar. The distribution of WAM proposal studies was in proportion to these numbers as many of the studies were accessed through ACM (N=8) or forward snowballing (N=6). None of the studies were accessed through Web of Science or Science Direct databases.

Table 2. Database Distribution of WAM related studies

Database	# of WAM Studies	# of WAM Proposal Studies
Web of Science (WoS)	3	-
Science Direct	2	-
ACM	15	8
Google Scholar (Forward snowballing)	10	6
Total	30	14

Most of the WAM studies were published in conference proceedings (N=19) while some of them were published in journals (N=10) and only one of them was a book chapter. Similar to that distribution, 10 WAM proposal studies were published in conference proceedings while four of them were published in journals. The subjects of these conferences or journals were generally human-computer interaction, web, or Internet in general, and accessibility. On the other hand, one of the studies was including just the review of WAMs while the rest involved the implementation of one or more WAMs (N=15).

Implemented / Mentioned WAMs

The studies investigated in the scope of this study were either implemented a WAM for accessibility evaluation of a website or at least mentioned it in detail as a literature review. Some of the WAMs implemented or mentioned were proposed before 2008 but they were still used as fundamental reference in accessibility evaluation studies investigated in the scope of this study as can be seen in Table 3. Twenty-four different WAMs were either implemented or mentioned in studies since 2008. Among these, mostly mentioned WAMs were WAB (Web Accessibility Barrier) (Parmanto & Zeng, 2005) (N=16), UWEM: Unified Web Evaluation Methodology -Aggregation formula – (WAB Cluster, 2006) (N=13), and Failure Rate (Sullivan & Matson, 2000) (N=12) while mostly implemented WAMs were WAB: Web Accessibility Barrier (Parmanto & Zeng, 2005) (N=7), WAQM: Web Accessibility Quality Metric (Vigo et al., 2007) (N=5) and UWEM: Unified Web Evaluation Methodology -Aggregation formula – (WAB Cluster, 2006) (N=4) and descriptive metrics (conservative, optimistic and strict rates) (Lopes et al., 2010) (N=4).

Table 3. Implemented/mentioned WAMs in the investigated studies

WAMs and References	Implemented Source ID	Mentioned Source ID	Total Number
Failure Rate (Sullivan & Matson, 2000)	[S1], [S8]	[S3], [S5], [S13], [S18], [S20], [S23], [S24], [S25], [S26], [S30]	12
KAI - Metric for blind users (Kit for the Accessibility to the Internet) (González et al., 2003)	[S1], [S8]	[S13], [S30]	4
WAB: Web Accessibility Barrier (Parmanto & Zeng, 2005)	[S1], [S7], [S8], [S11], [S14], [S15], [S22]	[S3], [S4], [S13], [S18], [S20], [S23], [S24], [S25], [S30]	16
OAM: Overall Accessibilty Metric (Bailey & Burd, 2005)	-	[S30]	1

continues on following page

Table 3. Continued

WAMs and References	Implemented Source ID	Mentioned Source ID	Total Number
Navigability and listenability metric for blind users (Fukuda et al., 2005)	-	[S30]	1
UWEM: Unified Web Evaluation Methodology -Aggregation formula – (WAB Cluster, 2006)	[S1], [S8], [S14], [S22]	[S3], [S4], [S5], [S13], [S20], [S23], [S25], [S26], [S30]	13
A3: Improved Aggregation formula (Bühler et al., 2006)	[S1], [S3], [S8]	[S3], [S18], [S26], [S30]	7
Page Measure (Bailey & Burd, 2007)	[S8]	[S30]	2
WAQM: Web Accessibility Quality Metric (Vigo et al., 2007)	[S1], [S8], [S20], [S21], [S25]	[S13], [S23], [S26], [S30]	9
SAMBA: Semi-Automatic Method for Measuring Barriers of Accessibility (Brajnik & Lomuscio, 2007)		[S24]	1
WIE: Web Interaction Environments (Lopes & Carriço, 2008)	[S2], [S8]	[S13], [S30]	4
WAB* (Ana Belén Martínez et al., 2009)	[S4], [S22]	-	2
T¹ (Sirithumgul et al., 2009)	[S3]	-	1
Descriptive metrics: conservative rate, optimistic rate and strict rate (Lopes et al., 2010)	[S5], [S9], [S10], [S19]	-	4
EXaminator Metric Web@X (J. Fernandes & Benavidez, 2011)	[S6]	[S30]	2
M_{HEUA}: Heuristic Evaluation with Usability and Accessibility Metric (Dias et al., 2014)	[S12]	-	1
AAEM: Accessibility Assistance Evaluation Metric (Gohin & Vinod, 2014)	[S13]	-	1
Simple metrics for each method (automatic, expert, user-based evaluations) (Medina et al., 2015)	[S16]	-	1
WABS: A Web Accessibility Barrier Severity Metric (Abu-Addous et al., 2015)	[S17], [S24]	-	2
FONA: Focus Navigation Assessment (Watanabe et al., 2015)	[S18]	-	1
WAEM: Web Accessibility Experience Metric (Shuyi Song et al., 2017)	[S23]	[S26]	2
OPS-WAQM: Optimal Sampling Web Accessibility Quality Metric (Zhang et al., 2017)	[S25], [S27], [S28]	[S30]	4
RA-WAEM: Reliability Aware Web Accessibility Experience Metric (Song et al., 2018a)	[S26], [S28]	[S30]	3
MAI: Mexican Accessibility Index (Ochoa & Crovi, 2019)	[S29]	[S30]	2

The distribution of implemented WAMs are presented in Figure 3. Few of the recently proposed WAMs were mentioned or used in more than two or three studies. For instance, Lopes et al.'s (2010) descriptive metrics were implemented in four studies ([S5], [S9], [S10], [S19]) and OPS-WAQM (Optimal Sampling Web Accessibility Quality Metric) (Zhang et al., 2017) were implemented in three studies ([S25], [S27], [S28]). However, it is seen that these studies contain co-authors. Therefore, it can be said that none of the recently proposed WAMs were used as a fundamental reference for any other study.

Figure 3. Distribution of WAMs implemented in studies

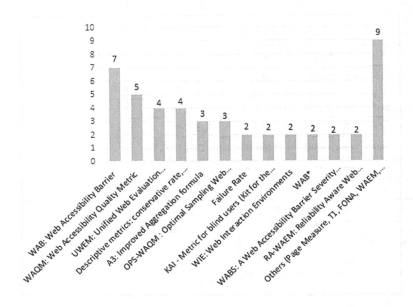

Recently Proposed WAMs

There were 14 WAMs proposed since 2008. General characteristics and how these metrics were developed and validated as well as their distinguishing characteristics are presented in this section. In addition, Zeng (2004) defined the attributes for the metrics as follows; guideline set used by the metric, coupling level with the guidelines, type of evaluation, site complexity, type of barrier weights coefficients, default coefficients, validation with user, automated tool support and use in large scale. All the WAMs were investigated according to these attributes and the results are presented in Table 4. On the other hand, the formula of the WAMs is not presented in the scope of this study since metrics formula used different variable symbols. Therefore, original studies should be consulted for the details of the formulas.

Most of the proposed metrics used the WCAGs as a guideline set for accessibility conformance except [S18] and [S25]. Until 2014, WCAG 1.0 was the main guideline set while only the WAM T1 was proposed in [S3] can be tailored to WCAG 2.0. WCAG 2.0 was first started to be used in MHEUA [S12] and AAEM [S13]. In addition, in [S25] Web accessibility standard of China (YD/T1761-2012) was used as a guideline set for the accessibility evaluation. Almost all the proposed WAMs used WCAG priorities as barrier coefficients and they implemented weighting coefficients for metrics based on priority.

In [S18] WAI-ARIA was used as guideline since the proposed WAM, Fona, focused on Rich Internet Applications since current web sites includes more interactive interfaces that requires different evaluation approaches rather than static web sites. Although Fona's evaluation approach only focuses on one accessibility requirement it enables monitoring how Focus Navigation and ARIA requirements were implemented in large number of web pages.

Some of the proposed WAMs also considered usability or user experience other than just accessibility perspective. [S2] and [S12] considered usability of websites [S23] and [S26] considered user experience. WIE [S2] was proposed as modelling framework to assess universal usability on the Web and includes a quantification approach for the accessibility in its scope. On the other hand, MHEUA [S12] has a different approach from all other WAMs and it aggregated the issues about usability and accessibility in a questionnaire based instrument consisted of 93 requirements categorized according to Nielsen's (1994) usability heuristics. WAEM [23] was proposed as a first WAM that considered the experience of people with disabilities. The metric included the partial user experience orders (PUEXO), which was defined as pairwise UX comparisons of users between different websites. In addition, since the experience of people was a subjective issue, a machine learning model was implemented for the metric to provide a more analytical solution. Afterwards RA-WAEM [23] which was based on WAEM [23] also considered the user experience of people with disabilities and implemented optimization algorithm based on Expectation Maximization to determine the objectivity of the severity of accessibility barriers reliably.

Most of the proposed WAMs generally depends on the automated checks based on some automated tools such as EvalAccess, AChecker or some developed tools specific to the metrics. However, recently in some proposed WAMs, human judgements or manual evaluations were also considered as in [S3], [S12], [S16], [S23], [S26], and [S29]. These manual evaluations were not generally conducted by usability or accessibility experts. Only in [S29], experts were mentioned explicitly as they were involved for the weighting stage of the accessibility assessment. In [23] and [26] experts were involved with other disabled users. but in many of the studies the importance of the level of expertise was also emphasized. In [S3], experts were involved in finding possible barriers in the assessed web sited according to barrier walkthrough method. In addition, studies [S3] mentioned about the effect of the level of the expertise of the assessors.

Many of the WAMs considers the characteristics of general users regardless of any disability type. However, some of the WAMs focuses some disability types explicitly such as [S3], [S13], [S23] and [S26].

WAMs generally proposed to quantitatively evaluate the accessibility level of websites, however the scope of the some proposed WAMs were different. For instance, the goal of WABS [17] was to determine barriers severity rather than not website evaluation. This metric was more concerned about revealing the persistent barriers that limit the accessibility based on their severity rather than total conformance to priority levels. Likewise, the scope of OPS-WAQM [S25] was to define a sampling method optimized for Web Accessibility Quantitative Metric (WAQM) to determine the web pages to be investigated for the accessibility assessment. In this method, a minimal sampling error model was proposed by using greedy algorithm to approximately solve the optimization problem to determine the sample numbers in different layers of the website.

Earlier proposed WAMs, were based either on UWEM (Unified Web Evaluation Metholodogy) (WAB Cluster, 2006) such as [S2], [S4] and [S5] or WAB (Parmanto & Zeng, 2005) such as [S3] and [S4]. T1 which was proposed in [S3] adopted barriers from Barrier Walkthrough (Brajnik, 2011) and adopted WAB metric which considered each violated checkpoint to be one barrier type. The calculated metric provided a single value which was normalized in the range of [0,1] representing the accessibility of a web page. WAB*, proposed in [S4] was also based on WAB metric with extensions gathered from the UWEM metric. It had all WAB checkpoints in addition to eleven automatic checkpoints from the UWEM metric. Three descriptive metrics based on UWEM were proposed in [S5] and these were conservative, optimistic, and strict rates. Conservative rate represented the warnings based on failures as defined in failure rate (Sullivan & Matson, 2000) while optimistic rate represented warnings interpreted as passed and strict rate represented warnings based on actual failures. All these rates were aggregated into a final score representing the accessibility quality of a web page.

Almost all the investigated WAM studies except [S16] proposed metrics for the accessibility evaluation of general websites. In [S16] metrics to be used in web-based map applications were proposed. Different metrics were proposed for each accessibility evaluation methods of expert, automatic or user-based evaluations.

Website complexity was begun to be considered in especially in the more recently proposed WAMs. Few of the proposed WAMs also reported about the validation with users. For instance, only, [S16], [S23] and [S26] included end-user evaluations. Finally, almost all the proposed WAMs were also implemented in large scale evaluation experiments except MHEUA proposed in [S12]. Implementations were conducted with the web sites on various domains such as bank websites, municipality web sites, governmental websites or map websites.

CONCLUSION

Within the scope of this study, 30 Web Accessibility Metric (WAM) studies published since 2008 were investigated through systematic literature review method to identify current trends and analyze WAMs. During the research process, Kitchenham et al's (2009) proposed review framework was implemented. It was conducted in four phases namely, determination of boundaries, execution of searches, selection of studies, and analysis and reporting. It was believed that the result of this study would provide insight to the researchers who are studying or would like to study on WAMs and to evaluators who would like to use these metrics for their assessments.

According to the results, it was revealed that the studies were frequently published in conference proceedings. Mostly mentioned WAMs were WAB (Web Accessibility Barrier) (Parmanto & Zeng, 2005), UWEM: Unified Web Evaluation Methodology -Aggregation formula – (WAB Cluster, 2006), and Failure Rate (Sullivan & Matson, 2000) while mostly implemented WAMs were WAB: Web Accessibility Barrier (Parmanto & Zeng, 2005), WAQM: Web Accessibility Quality Metric (Vigo et al., 2007), UWEM: Unified Web Evaluation Methodology -Aggregation formula – (WAB Cluster, 2006) and descriptive metrics (conservative, optimistic and strict rates) (Lopes et al., 2010).

There were 14 WAMs proposed since 2008 and many of them were proposed in the last five years. The general characteristics oof these WAMs can be listed as follows:

- Most of the proposed metrics used the WCAGs as a guideline for accessibility compliance set.
- Almost all the proposed WAMs used WCAG priorities as barrier coefficients and they implemented weighting coefficients for metrics based on priority.
- Recently proposed WAMs also considered usability or user experience perspectives.
- Many of the WAMs considers the characteristics of general users regardless of any disability type.
- Website complexity was begun to be considered in especially in the more recently proposed WAMs.

Table 4. Attributes of recently proposed WAMs

Source ID	Name of the Metric	Type of Evaluation	Automated Tool Support	Guideline Set	Barrier Coefficients	Weighting Coefficients of Metrics	Default Coefficients	Web Site Complexity	Validation With Users	Use in Large Scale
[S2]	WIE: Web Interaction Environments	Automated	Jtidy	WCAG 1.0	WCAG priorities	Equal	if a checkpoint c passes than it is 1, and is 0 otherwise	No	No	Yes
[S3]	T^1	Automated / Manual	EvalAccess	WCAG 1.0 but can be tailored to WCAG 2.0	Vision and hearing-impaired	Priority	adopted WAB weighting (inverse priority of checkpoint): W2=W1/2 W3=W1/3	No	No	Yes
[S4]	WAB*: A Quantitative Metric Based on WAB	Automated	Iris	WCAG 1.0	WCAG priorities	Priority	1/priority	Yes	No	Yes
[S5]	Descriptive metrics: Conservative, optimistic and strict rates	Automated	Developed tool	WCAG 1.0	No	NA	NONE	Yes	No	Yes
[S6]	eXaminator	Automated	Developed tool	WCAG 1.0	WCAG priorities	Priority	Priority 1 =10 Priority 2= 8 Priority 3 = 6	Yes	No	Yes
[S12]	M_{HEUA}	Manual	None	WCAG 2.0	No	NA	NONE	No	No	No.
[S13]	AAEM: Accessibility Assistance Evaluation Metric	Automated	Achecker	WCAG1.0, WCAG 2.0, Section508, HTML, CSS, BITV, Stanca Act	WCAG priorities	Priority	1/priority	Yes	No	Yes

continues on following page

Table 4. Continued

Source ID	Name of the Metric	Type of Evaluation	Automated Tool Support	Guideline Set	Barrier Coefficients	Weighting Coefficients of Metrics	Default Coefficients	Web Site Complexity	Validation With Users	Use in Large Scale
[S16]	Simple metrics for each method	Automated, Expert, User	AChecker, Total Validator, CynthiaSays, TAW, AccessMonitor	WCAG 2.0	None	None	NA	No	Yes	Yes
[S17]	WABS: A Web Accessibility Barrier Severity Metric	Automated	Achecker	WCAG 2.0	WCAG priorities	Priority	Priority "A"=0.8, "AA"=0.16, "AAA"=0.04	Yes	No	Yes
[S18]	Fona: Focus Navigation Assessment	Automated	Developed tool	WAI-ARIA	None	None	NA	No	No	Yes
[S23]	WAEM: Web Accessibility Experience Metric	Manual	None	WCAG 2.0	WCAG priorities	Priority	optimal checkpoint weights from Partial User Experience Order	Yes	Yes	Yes
[S25]	OPS-WAQM: Optimized for Web Accessibility Quantitative Metric	Automated	NA	Web accessibility standard of China (YD/T1761-2012)	Web accessibility standard of China (YD/T1761-2012)	Priority	Priority of checkpoints	Yes	No	Yes
[S26]	RA-WAEM: Reliability Aware Web Accessibility Experience Metric	Manual	None	WCAG 2.0	WCAG priorities	Priority	optimal checkpoint weights from Partial User Experience Order	Yes	Yes	Yes
[S29]	MAI: Mexican Accessibility Index	Automated/Manual	TAW	WCAG 2.0	Priority	Expert judgements	NA	No	No	Yes

LIMITATIONS AND FUTURE WORK

One of the most important limitations of this type of studies is reliability. For this purpose, the study was carried out with a repetitive process. The researchers examined the studies on their own, and then they gathered their findings and reached a consensus. Thus, bias that might be based on a single examiner was tried to be prevented.

Another limitation is the possibility of missing some relevant studies. However, to prevent this, many of the scientific databases where publications are indexed on this subject were included in the study and finally, related studies from Google Scholar were also gathered by forward snowballing method.

REFERENCES

Abascal, J., Arrue, M., & Valencia, X. (2019). Tools for web accessibility evaluation. In *Web Accessibility* (pp. 479–503). Springer. doi:10.1007/978-1-4471-7440-0_26

Abu-Addous, H. Y., Jali, M. Z., & Basir, N. (2017). Quantitative metric for ranking web accessibility barriers based on their severity. *Journal of Information and Communication Technology*, *16*(1), 81–102.

Abu-Addous, H. Y. M., Jali, W. A. W. A. B. S. M., & Basir, N. (2015). WABS: Web Accessibility Barrier Severity Metric. *Proceedings of the 5 Th International Conference on Computing and Informatics, ICOCI 2015*, 481–487.

AChecker. (2021). *IDI Web Accessibility Checker: Web Accessibility Checker*. https://achecker.ca/checker/index.php

Aizpurua, A., Harper, S., & Vigo, M. (2016). Exploring the relationship between web accessibility and user experience. *International Journal of Human-Computer Studies*, *91*, 13–23. doi:10.1016/j.ijhcs.2016.03.008

Akgül, Y. (2021). Accessibility, usability, quality performance, and readability evaluation of university websites of Turkey: A comparative study of state and private universities. *Universal Access in the Information Society*, *20*(1), 157–170. doi:10.100710209-020-00715-w

Akram, M., & Sulaiman, R. B. (2017). A systematic literature review to determine the web accessibility issues in Saudi Arabian university and government websites for disable people. *International Journal of Advanced Computer Science and Applications*, *8*(6). Advance online publication. doi:10.14569/IJACSA.2017.080642

Alajarmeh, N. (2021). Evaluating the accessibility of public health websites: An exploratory cross-country study. *Universal Access in the Information Society*, 1–19. PMID:33526996

Arch, A. (2009). Web accessibility for older users: Successes and opportunities (keynote). *Proceedings of the 2009 International Cross-Disciplinary Conference on Web Accessibililty (W4A)*, 1–6. 10.1145/1535654.1535655

Baeza-Yates, R. (2020). Bias on the web and beyond: an accessibility point of view. In *Proceedings of the 17th International Web for All Conference* (pp. 1-1). Academic Press.

Bailey, J., & Burd, E. (2005). Tree-map visualisation for web accessibility. *29th Annual International Computer Software and Applications Conference (COMPSAC'05)*, *1*, 275–280. 10.1109/COMPSAC.2005.161

Bailey, J., & Burd, E. (2007). Towards more mature web maintenance practices for accessibility. *2007 9th IEEE International Workshop on Web Site Evolution*, 81–87.

Borg, J., Lantz, A., & Gulliksen, J. (2015). Accessibility to electronic communication for people with cognitive disabilities: A systematic search and review of empirical evidence. *Universal Access in the Information Society*, *14*(4), 547–562. doi:10.100710209-014-0351-6

Brajnik, G. (2004). Comparing accessibility evaluation tools: A method for tool effectiveness. *Universal Access in the Information Society*, *3*(3), 252–263. doi:10.100710209-004-0105-y

Brajnik, G. (2008a). A comparative test of web accessibility evaluation methods. *Proceedings of the 10th International ACM SIGACCESS Conference on Computers and Accessibility*, 113–120. 10.1145/1414471.1414494

Brajnik, G. (2008b). Beyond conformance: The role of accessibility evaluation methods. *International Conference on Web Information Systems Engineering*, 63–80. 10.1007/978-3-540-85200-1_9

Brajnik, G. (2011). *Barrier walkthrough*. https://users.dimi.uniud.it/~giorgio.brajnik/projects/bw/bw.html

Brajnik, G., & Lomuscio, R. (2007). SAMBA: A semi-automatic method for measuring barriers of accessibility. *Proceedings of the 9th International ACM SIGACCESS Conference on Computers and Accessibility*, 43–50. 10.1145/1296843.1296853

Brajnik, G., Mulas, A., & Pitton, C. (2007). Effects of sampling methods on web accessibility evaluations. *Proceedings of the 9th International ACM SIGACCESS Conference on Computers and Accessibility*, 59–66. 10.1145/1296843.1296855

Brajnik, G., & Vigo, M. (2019). *Automatic Web Accessibility Metrics-Where We Were and Where We Went*. Academic Press.

Bühler, C., Heck, H., Perlick, O., Nietzio, A., & Ulltveit-Moe, N. (2006). Interpreting results from large scale automatic evaluation of web accessibility. *International Conference on Computers for Handicapped Persons*, 184–191. 10.1007/11788713_28

Chan, M., & Zoellick, R. B. (2011). *World report on disability*. WHO. https://www.who.int/disabilities/world_report/2011/report/en/

Cluster, W. A. B. (2006). *UWEM1.0 released (Unified Web-Accessibility Evaluation Methodology)* [Text]. Shaping Europe's Digital Future - European Commission. https://ec.europa.eu/digital-single-market/en/news/uwem10-released-unified-web-accessibility-evaluation-methodology

Contrast Checker. (2017). *WCAG Contrast Checker*. Contrast Checker. https://contrastchecker.com/

Costa, D., Carriço, L., & Duarte, C. (2015). The differences in accessibility of tv and desktop web applications from the perspective of automated evaluation. *Procedia Computer Science*, *67*, 388–396. doi:10.1016/j.procs.2015.09.283

Daskalantonakis, M. K. (1992). A practical view of software measurement and implementation experiences within Motorola. *IEEE Transactions on Software Engineering*, *18*(11), 998–1010. doi:10.1109/32.177369

Dias, A. L., de Mattos Fortes, R. P., & Masiero, P. C. (2014). HEUA: A Heuristic Evaluation with Usability and Accessibility requirements to assess Web systems. *Proceedings of the 11th Web for All Conference*, 1–4. 10.1145/2596695.2596706

Doush, I. A., Alkhateeb, F., Al Maghayreh, E., & Al-Betar, M. A. (2013). The design of RIA accessibility evaluation tool. *Advances in Engineering Software*, *57*, 1–7. doi:10.1016/j.advengsoft.2012.11.004

Ekman, B. (2004). Community-based health insurance in low-income countries: A systematic review of the evidence. *Health Policy and Planning*, *19*(5), 249–270. doi:10.1093/heapol/czh031 PMID:15310661

Fenton, N., & Bieman, J. (2014). *Software metrics: A rigorous and practical approach.* CRC press. doi:10.1201/b17461

Fernandes, J., & Benavidez, C. (2011). A zero in echecker equals a 10 in examinator: A comparison between two metrics by their scores. *W3C Symposium on Website Accessibility Metrics, 8.*

Fernandes, N., Batista, A. S., Costa, D., Duarte, C., & Carriço, L. (2013). Three web accessibility evaluation perspectives for RIA. *Proceedings of the 10th International Cross-Disciplinary Conference on Web Accessibility*, 1–9. 10.1145/2461121.2461122

Fernandes, N., & Carriço, L. (2012). A macroscopic Web accessibility evaluation at different processing phases. *Proceedings of the International Cross-Disciplinary Conference on Web Accessibility*, 1–4. 10.1145/2207016.2207025

Fernandes, N., Kaklanis, N., Votis, K., Tzovaras, D., & Carriço, L. (2014). An analysis of personalized web accessibility. *Proceedings of the 11th Web for All Conference*, 1–10.

Freire, A. P., Fortes, R. P., Turine, M. A., & Paiva, D. M. (2008). An evaluation of web accessibility metrics based on their attributes. *Proceedings of the 26th Annual ACM International Conference on Design of Communication*, 73–80. 10.1145/1456536.1456551

Fukuda, K., Saito, S., Takagi, H., & Asakawa, C. (2005). Proposing new metrics to evaluate web usability for the blind. *CHI'05 Extended Abstracts on Human Factors in Computing Systems*, 1387–1390.

Gibson, B. (2007). Enabling an accessible web 2.0. *Proceedings of the 2007 International Cross-Disciplinary Conference on Web Accessibility (W4A)*, 1–6.

Gohin, B., & Vinod, V. (2014). AAEM: Accessibility assistance evaluation metric. *Int. Rev. Comput. Softw*, *9*(5), 872–882.

González, J., Macías, M., Rodríguez, R., & Sánchez, F. (2003). Accessibility metrics of web pages for blind end-users. *International Conference on Web Engineering*, 374–383. 10.1007/3-540-45068-8_68

Hackett, S., Parmanto, B., & Zeng, X. (2003). Accessibility of Internet websites through time. *ACM SIGACCESS Accessibility and Computing*, *77–78*(77-78), 32–39. doi:10.1145/1029014.1028638

Harper, S., & Yesilada, Y. (2008). *Web accessibility: A foundation for research.* Springer. doi:10.1007/978-1-84800-050-6

Henzinger, M. R., Heydon, A., Mitzenmacher, M., & Najork, M. (2000). On near-uniform URL sampling. *Computer Networks*, *33*(1–6), 295–308. doi:10.1016/S1389-1286(00)00055-4

ISO. (2008). *ISO 9241-20:2008(en), Ergonomics of human-system interaction—Part 20: Accessibility guidelines for information/communication technology (ICT) equipment and services.* ISO 9241-20:2008(En), Ergonomics of Human-System Interaction — Part 20: Accessibility Guidelines for Information/Communication Technology (ICT) Equipment and Services. https://www.iso.org/obp/ui/#iso:std:iso:9241:-20:ed-1:v1:en:en/

ISO. (2021). *ISO/DIS 9241-20(en), Ergonomics of human-system interaction—Part 20: An ergonomic approach to accessibility within the ISO 9241 series.* https://www.iso.org/obp/ui#iso:std:iso:9241:-20:dis:ed-2:v1:en

Kamoun, F., & Almourad, M. B. (2014). Accessibility as an integral factor in e-government web site evaluation: The case of Dubai e-government. *Information Technology & People*, *27*(2), 208–228. doi:10.1108/ITP-07-2013-0130

King, M., Thatcher, J. W., Bronstad, P. M., & Easton, R. (2005). Managing usability for people with disabilities in a large web presence. *IBM Systems Journal*, *44*(3), 519–535. doi:10.1147j.443.0519

Kitchenham, B., Brereton, O. P., Budgen, D., Turner, M., Bailey, J., & Linkman, S. (2009). Systematic literature reviews in software engineering–a systematic literature review. *Information and Software Technology*, *51*(1), 7–15. doi:10.1016/j.infsof.2008.09.009

Kitchenham, B. A., & Charters, S. (2007). *Guidelines for performing Systematic Literature Reviews in Software Engineering (EBSE 2007-001)* [Keele University and Durham University Joint Report]. Keele University and Durham University. https://www.bibsonomy.org/bibtex/aed0229656ada843d3e3f24e5e5c9eb9

Kitchenham, B. A., Dyba, T., & Jorgensen, M. (2004). Evidence-based software engineering. *Proceedings. 26th International Conference on Software Engineering*, 273–281.

Lopes, R., & Carriço, L. (2008). The impact of accessibility assessment in macro scale universal usability studies of the web. *Proceedings of the 2008 International Cross-Disciplinary Conference on Web Accessibility (W4A)*, 5–14. 10.1145/1368044.1368048

Lopes, R., Gomes, D., & Carriço, L. (2010). Web not for all: A large scale study of web accessibility. *Proceedings of the 2010 International Cross Disciplinary Conference on Web Accessibility (W4A)*, 1–4. 10.1145/1805986.1806001

Lorca, P., De Andrés, J., & Martínez, A. B. (2016). Does Web accessibility differ among banks? *World Wide Web (Bussum)*, *19*(3), 351–373. doi:10.100711280-014-0314-0

Martínez, A. B., De Andrés, J., & García, J. (2014). Determinants of the Web accessibility of European banks. *Information Processing & Management*, *50*(1), 69–86. doi:10.1016/j.ipm.2013.08.001

Martínez, A. B., Juan, A. A., Álvarez, D., & del Carmen, S. M. (2009). WAB*: A quantitative metric based on WAB. *International Conference on Web Engineering*, 485–488. 10.1007/978-3-642-02818-2_44

Masri, F., & Luján-Mora, S. (2011). A combined agile methodology for the evaluation of web accessibility. *IADIS International Conference Interfaces and Human Computer Interaction (IHCI 2011)*, 423–428.

Medina, J. L., Cagnin, M. I., & Paiva, D. M. B. (2015). Evaluation of web accessibility on the maps domain. *Proceedings of the 30th Annual ACM Symposium on Applied Computing*, 157–162. 10.1145/2695664.2695771

Nielsen, J. (1994). *Usability engineering*. Morgan Kaufmann.

Ochoa, R. L., & Crovi, D. M. (2019). Evaluation of accessibility in Mexican cybermedia. *Universal Access in the Information Society*, *18*(2), 413–422. doi:10.100710209-018-0613-9

Olsina, L., & Rossi, G. (2002). Measuring Web application quality with WebQEM. *IEEE MultiMedia*, *9*(4), 20–29. doi:10.1109/MMUL.2002.1041945

Parmanto, B., & Zeng, X. (2005). Metric for web accessibility evaluation. *Journal of the American Society for Information Science and Technology*, *56*(13), 1394–1404. doi:10.1002/asi.20233

Sanchez-Gordon, S., & Luján-Mora, S. (2018). Research challenges in accessible MOOCs: A systematic literature review 2008–2016. *Universal Access in the Information Society*, *17*(4), 775–789. doi:10.100710209-017-0531-2

Sirithumgul, P., Suchato, A., & Punyabukkana, P. (2009). Quantitative evaluation for web accessibility with respect to disabled groups. *Proceedings of the 2009 International Cross-Disciplinary Conference on Web Accessibililty (W4A)*, 136–141. 10.1145/1535654.1535687

Slatin, J. M., & Rush, S. (2003). *Maximum accessibility: Making your web site more usable for everyone*. Addison-Wesley Professional.

Song, S., Bu, J., Wang, Y., Yu, Z., Artmeier, A., Dai, L., & Wang, C. (2018b). Web accessibility evaluation in a crowdsourcing-based system with expertise-based decision strategy. In *Proceedings of the Internet of Accessible Things* (pp. 1–4). 10.1145/3192714.3192827

Song, S., Bu, J., Artmeier, A., Shi, K., Wang, Y., Yu, Z., & Wang, C. (2018c). Crowdsourcing-based web accessibility evaluation with golden maximum likelihood inference. *Proceedings of the ACM on Human-Computer Interaction, 2*(CSCW), 1–21. 10.1145/3274432

Song, S., Bu, J., Shen, C., Artmeier, A., Yu, Z., & Zhou, Q. (2018a). Reliability aware web accessibility experience metric. In *Proceedings of the Internet of Accessible Things* (pp. 1–4). Academic Press.

Song, S., Wang, C., Li, L., Yu, Z., Lin, X., & Bu, J. (2017). WAEM: A web accessibility evaluation metric based on partial user experience order. *Proceedings of the 14th Web for All Conference on The Future of Accessible Work*, 1–4. 10.1145/3058555.3058576

SortSite. (2021). *Website Error Checker: Accessibility & Link Checker—SortSite*. https://www.powermapper.com/products/sortsite/

Sullivan, T., & Matson, R. (2000). Barriers to use: Usability and content accessibility on the Web's most popular sites. *Proceedings on the 2000 Conference on Universal Usability*, 139–144. 10.1145/355460.355549

Thatcher, J., Lauke, P. H., Waddell, C., Henry, S. L., Lawson, B., Lawson, B., Heilmann, C., Burks, M. R., Regan, B., & Rutter, R. (2006). *Web accessibility: Web standards and regulatory compliance*. Apress.

Thompson, T., Burgstahler, S., & Comden, D. (2003). Research on web accessibility in higher education. *Journal of Information Technology and Disabilities, 9*(2).

US Access Board. (2000). *U.S. Access Board—Revised 508 Standards and 255 Guidelines*. https://www.access-board.gov/ict/

US EPA. O. (2013, September 26). *What is Section 508?* [Overviews and Factsheets]. US EPA. https://www.epa.gov/accessibility/what-section-508

Vigo, M., Arrue, M., Brajnik, G., Lomuscio, R., & Abascal, J. (2007). Quantitative metrics for measuring web accessibility. *Proceedings of the 2007 International Cross-Disciplinary Conference on Web Accessibility (W4A)*, 99–107. 10.1145/1243441.1243465

Vigo, M., & Brajnik, G. (2011). Automatic web accessibility metrics: Where we are and where we can go. *Interacting with Computers*, *23*(2), 137–155. doi:10.1016/j.intcom.2011.01.001

W3C. (1999). *Web Content Accessibility Guidelines 1.0*. https://www.w3.org/TR/WCAG10/

W3C. (2008). *Web Content Accessibility Guidelines (WCAG) 2.0*. https://www.w3.org/TR/WCAG20/

W3C. (2020). *WAI-ARIA Overview*. Web Accessibility Initiative (WAI). https://www.w3.org/WAI/standards-guidelines/aria/

W3C. (2021, January 21). *Web Content Accessibility Guidelines (WCAG) 3.0*. https://www.w3.org/TR/wcag-3.0/

W3C. (n.d.a). *Web Accessibility Initaitive*. Web Accessibility Initiative (WAI). Retrieved May 8, 2021, from https://www.w3.org/WAI/

W3C. (n.d.b). *World Wide Web Consortium (W3C)*. https://www.w3.org/

W3.org. (1999). *Web Content Accessibility Guidelines 1.0*. https://www.w3.org/TR/WAI-WEBCONTENT/

W3.org. (2008). *Web Content Accessibility Guidelines (WCAG) 2.0*. https://www.w3.org/TR/WCAG20/WAI. W. (2005). *Introduction to Web Accessibility*. Web Accessibility Initiative (WAI). https://www.w3.org/WAI/fundamentals/accessibility-intro/

Watanabe, W. M., Dias, A. L., & Fortes, R. P. D. M. (2015). Fona: Quantitative metric to measure focus navigation on rich internet applications. *ACM Transactions on the Web*, *9*(4), 1–28. doi:10.1145/2812812

Wohlin, C. (2014). Guidelines for snowballing in systematic literature studies and a replication in software engineering. *Proceedings of the 18th International Conference on Evaluation and Assessment in Software Engineering*, 1–10. 10.1145/2601248.2601268

Yesilada, Y., Brajnik, G., Vigo, M., & Harper, S. (2012). Understanding web accessibility and its drivers. *Proceedings of the International Cross-Disciplinary Conference on Web Accessibility*, 1–9.

Yesilada, Y., Chuter, A., & Henry, S. L. (2013). Shared web experiences: Barriers common to mobile device users and people with disabilities. *W3C Web Accessibility Initiative*. Http://Www. W3. Org/WAI

Zaphiris, P., & Ellis, R. D. (2001). *Website usability and content accessibility of the top USA universities*. WebNet 2001 Conference, Orlando, FL. https://ktisis.cut.ac.cy/handle/10488/5263

Zeng, X. (2004). Evaluation and enhancement of web content accessibility for persons with disabilities (Doctoral Dissertation, University of Pittsburgh, 2004). *Dissertation Abstracts International, 65*(8), 8.

Zhang, M., Wang, C., Bu, J., Li, L., & Yu, Z. (2017). An optimal sampling method for web accessibility quantitative metric and its online extension. *Internet Research, 27*(5), 1190–1208. doi:10.1108/IntR-07-2016-0205

Zhang, M., Wang, C., Bu, J., Yu, Z., Lu, Y., Zhang, R., & Chen, C. (2015). An optimal sampling method for web accessibility quantitative metric. *Proceedings of the 12th Web for All Conference*, 1–4. 10.1145/2745555.2746663

ADDITIONAL READING

Brajnik, G. (2008). A comparative test of web accessibility evaluation methods. In *Proceedings of the 10th international ACM SIGACCESS Conference on Computers and Accessibility* (pp. 113-120). 10.1145/1414471.1414494

Doush, I. A., Alkhateeb, F., Al Maghayreh, E., & Al-Betar, M. A. (2013). The design of RIA accessibility evaluation tool. *Advances in Engineering Software, 57*, 1–7. doi:10.1016/j.advengsoft.2012.11.004

Freire, A. P., Fortes, R. P., Turine, M. A., & Paiva, D. M. (2008). An evaluation of web accessibility metrics based on their attributes. *Proceedings of the 26th Annual ACM International Conference on Design of Communication*, 73–80. 10.1145/1456536.1456551

Ismailova, R. (2017). Web site accessibility, usability and security: A survey of government web sites in Kyrgyz Republic. *Universal Access in the Information Society, 16*(1), 257–264. doi:10.100710209-015-0446-8

Vigo, M., & Brajnik, G. (2011). Automatic web accessibility metrics: Where we are and where we can go. *Interacting with Computers, 23*(2), 137–155. doi:10.1016/j.intcom.2011.01.001

Yesilada, Y., Brajnik, G., Vigo, M., & Harper, S. (2012). Understanding web accessibility and its drivers. *Proceedings of the International Cross-Disciplinary Conference on Web Accessibility*, 1–9.

KEY TERMS AND DEFINITIONS

Automated Accessibility Evaluation: Automated accessibility assessment is an assessment by use of software programs or online services that help determine whether a website complies with certain web accessibility rules or standards.

Barrier: Any condition that prevents user from reaching his/her goals on a website.

Manual Evaluation: It is the review and evaluation of the website by an expert according to the rules of the accessibility directive.

Systematic Literature Review (SLR): SLR is an approach that aims to summarize a research topic systematically to identify any gaps in the current research and to provide a background for new research activities.

Web Accessibility: Web accessibility means that the entire target audience can access, use, and understand the web application.

Web Accessibility Metric: Metric that help to indicate the accessibility level of websites.

Web Content Accessibility Guidelines (WCAG): Guidelines defined by Web Accessibility Initiative that defines the accessibility criteria that a website should comply with.

APPENDIX

Table 5. The list of the reviewed studies

Source ID	Authors/Year	Scope	Publication Type
[S1]	(Freire et al., 2008)	R & I	Conf
[S2]	(Lopes & Carriço, 2008)	P & I	Conf
[S3]	(Sirithumgul et al., 2009)	P & I	Conf
[S4]	(Martínez et al., 2009)	P & I	Conf
[S5]	(Lopes et al., 2010)	P & I	Conf
[S6]	(Fernandes & Benavidez, 2011)	P & I	Conf
[S7]	(Masri & Luján-Mora, 2011)	I	Conf
[S8]	(Vigo & Brajnik, 2011)	R & I	Journal
[S9]	(Fernandes & Carriço, 2012)	I	Conf
[S10]	(Fernandes et al., 2013)	I	Conf
[S11]	(Kamoun & Almourad, 2014)	I	Journal
[S12]	(Dias et al., 2014)	P & I	Conf
[S13]	(Gohin & Vinod, 2014)	P & I	Journal
[S14]	(Martínez et al., 2014)	I	Journal
[S15]	(Fernandes et al., 2014)	I	Conf
[S16]	(Medina et al., 2015)	P & I	Conf
[S17]	(Abu-Addous et al., 2015)	P & I	Conf
[S18]	(Watanabe et al., 2015)	P & I	Journal
[S19]	(Costa et al., 2015)	I	Conf
[S20]	(Zhang et al., 2015)	I	Conf
[S21]	(Aizpurua et al., 2016)	I	Journal
[S22]	(Lorca et al., 2016)	I	Journal
[S23]	(Shuyi Song et al., 2017)	P & I	Conf
[S24]	(Abu-Addous et al., 2017)	I	Journal
[S25]	(Zhang et al., 2017)	P & I	Journal
[S26]	(Song, et al., 2018a)	P & I	Conf
[S27]	(Song et al., 2018b)	I	Conf
[S28]	(Song et al., 2018c)	I	Conf
[S29]	(Ochoa & Crovi, 2019)	P & I	Journal
[S30]	(Brajnik & Vigo, 2019)	R	Book Chapter

Chapter 5

Practical Approach for Apps Design in Compliance With Accessibility, Usability, and User Experience

Fernando Almeida
iD https://orcid.org/0000-0002-6758-4843
Polytechnic Institute of Gaya, Portugal

Nuno Bernardo
Polytechnic Institute of Gaya, Portugal

Rúben Lacerda
Polytechnic Institute of Gaya, Portugal

ABSTRACT

There is a huge proliferation of digital products on the market today for both large enterprises and small businesses. Most of these companies have experienced the development of software products for the mobile market and have been faced with the major challenge of capturing the customer's attention. There is a great focus on making a great first impact and providing the audience with the best possible digital experience. Accordingly, issues related to usability, accessibility, and user experience are extremely relevant. This chapter addresses how these practices can be used in practice by building an app that offers car cleaning services. Several approaches based on building app interfaces that increase user engagement and retention levels are explored and discussed.

DOI: 10.4018/978-1-7998-7848-3.ch005

INTRODUCTION

The technological evolution and the appearance of mobile devices required the development of interfaces to optimize the interaction between man and machine. According to Joo (2017), interaction design has as its focus the user's interaction and, in this sense, explores the factors that affect this interaction, namely the social and cultural context. Whittaker (2013) advocates that knowing how to identify user needs and how to improve user interactions with the system are the key points for interaction design. This view necessarily has practical implications. The designer assumes a key role in the conception of how the user will send, receive, and respond, that is, interact with the information contained in the app.

Several authors suggest some fundamental principles for the development of a project in the interaction design field. Schnall et al. (2016) highlight the importance of user focus. Therefore, to develop an app it is necessary to consider the target audience and how the app can help them. In this context, it is essential to understand the user's interests, the tasks they have to perform, and the goals they have to fulfill within their limits. Camburn et al. (2017) point out that the development of new apps should have innovative ideas and prototypes as a starting point. According to this perspective, design solutions are born by brainstorming ideas that are then tested using prototypes. It should be noted that the prototype does not represent the final state of the solution, but a possible solution with an evolution that encourages the emergence of new solutions that must be tested until the final solution is reached. Finally, Karmokar et al. (2016) point out that design is influenced by several areas such as engineering, psychology, ergonomics, architecture, among others. In this way, the design process of an app should involve multidisciplinary teams. Furthermore, interaction design requires constant user participation, because only then is it possible to obtain an app that meets the user's needs (Lopes et al., 2018).

Interaction design includes simultaneously the concepts of usability and accessibility (Godoi & Valentim, 2019; Langdon et al., 2014; Lazar et al., 2015). However, these terms are often confused, used incorrectly and undifferentiated. In practice, they are distinct concepts with different purposes. According to Shackel (2009), usability seeks to make the access experience clearer and easier for anyone. Therefore, the user should find what he or she is looking for easily, in the shortest time possible, and with satisfaction. While the concept of accessibility seeks to make the app more accessible to people with some kind of special need so that all users can have the same access experience, regardless of their condition (Petrie et al., 2015). We still find apps that despite having accessible information or the features programmed by the developer, do not have easy access. It is then clear the importance of an accessible website, promoting inclusion and expanding the possibilities of access by anyone with a positive navigation experience.

Taking usability and accessibility into account when designing an app is a key strategy for an app's success in the market (Nowak, 2020; Xiao, 2019). However, in recent years a new complementary concept has emerged that focuses on the users' perspective. User Experience (UX) seeks to gain a deep understanding of users and how they interact with a digital product. Sinha & Fukey (2020) state that its focus is on understanding user behavior through which it seeks to identify what they need and value. Baylé (2018) states that UX promotes improving the quality of user interaction and perception of the products and services offered by the company. Morville (2004) points out that UX should add value through: (i) the information should be useful and satisfy a need; (ii) usable through the ease of use; (iii) desirable through evoking emotion and appreciation; (iv) findable in the sense that the content should be easily located and navigable; (v) the content should also be accessible to people with disabilities; and (vi) credible considering both the content of the information and the way it is displayed.

This chapter intends to address the relationship between the themes of usability, accessibility, and user experience. In the first phase, it aims to understand this phenomenon and distinguish these three concepts that are fundamental in the development of an app. However, the main innovative and differentiating element of this study is its focus on the practical component, namely on how these three concepts can be materialized in the construction of an app. The scenario considered the development of an app that provides car-washing services anywhere (e.g., home, work, shopping, doctor, and beach). This market need arises due to changes in consumer habits and changes in the economic environment variables, demographic, legislative, social, economic, or political, which cause changes in consumer buying habits and generate new business opportunities. This service is mainly aimed at people who feel the need to manage their time and, therefore, do not have time to do these activities in their daily lives. The way the app was developed and the strategic approaches in the development of each interface are explored. It is intended, therefore, to realize that in the development of an app interface several strategic options have a strong impact on the user experience that is offered to the user.

The chapter is organized as follows: In an initial phase, a theoretical background on the topics of usability, accessibility, and user experience is performed. Next, the objectives of this study and the methodological approach are presented. After that, several solutions and recommendations for the construction of mobile solutions are presented. Finally, future research directions are presented, and the conclusions of this study are summarized.

BACKGROUND

The Concept of Usability

Usability looks at a set of rules and best practices that evaluate how users learn and use a product to achieve their goals (Shackel, 2009). Dreheeb & Fabil (2016) further add that usability also evaluates user satisfaction during this process. To obtain the necessary information, a variety of methods can be used by gathering feedback from users regarding a system. Usability is integrated within the larger domain of quality and search for effectiveness and efficiency of system operation. In this regard, it is important to distinguish between effectiveness and efficiency. To be effective is to do the right things with the least number of errors, while to be efficient is to do things correctly with the least amount of effort (Peacock, 2011).

One of the first ways to evaluate usability was presented in the publication of the ISO/IEC 9126:1991 standard. In this document, usability was referenced for the first time as a quality characteristic (ISO, 1991). This standard established that usability should be evaluated considering a set of attributes that highlight the effort required to use a software product. This evaluation should be individual and involve a large set of users. In this standard, usability was presented according to three characteristics (Al-Kilidar et al., 2005): (i) understandability, the ability of a software product to enable the user to understand whether the product is suitable and how it can be used to accomplish specific tasks under a given condition of use; (ii) learnability, the ability of a software product to enable the user to learn how to use it; and (iii) operability, the ability of the software to enable the user to control and operate it. Other standards emerged later, like ISO 9241:1998, which broadened the scope of usability by involving the user in this process. According to this standard, usability now also includes the ability of a software product to be used by specific users to achieve specific goals related to effectiveness (e.g., the accuracy and completeness with which users achieve specific goals), efficiency (e.g., the resources that must be expended for the intended goals to be achieved), and satisfaction (e.g., the way in which users find the use of the product acceptable). This standard has since been replaced by ISO/IEC 25010, which defines quality models for the use of software products. According to this standard, the quality of use of software should be evidenced by eight characteristics (ISO, 2011): functional suitability, performance, compatibility, usability, reliability, security, maintainability, and portability.

Another form of usability measurement was proposed by Nielsen in 1993, in which five attributes are presented (Nielsen, 1993):

- Learnability - measures how easily and quickly users learn to use a system and perform tasks with it;

- Efficiency - measures how quickly users can perform tasks after learning to use a given interface;
- Memorability - measures how easily users return to use a given interface successfully after a period of absence;
- Errors - determines how many errors are made by users, the severity of those errors, and the ease with which those errors can be overcome by users;
- Satisfaction - measures the level of satisfaction with an interface, namely whether it allows for a pleasant and intuitive interaction.

The approach followed by Nielsen (1993) adopts heuristics in the process of usability analysis. Heuristics can be seen as rules that are based on good practices in interface design and establish a set of guidelines to avoid usability issues. Ssemugabi & de Villiers (2010) refer that usability evaluation by heuristics is a non-empirical, quick, and easy form of evaluation. This type of evaluation is performed by experts and in classifying the problems found according to a certain model. There are essentially two problems associated with this approach. De Kock et al. (2009) note that adopting heuristics is not an empirical method that involves system users, who should be the ones that ultimately decide on the usability of a software product. Gonzalez-Holland et al. (2017) add that this evaluation is subjective as each evaluator will have a different personal technique in their evaluation which will lead to different results.

Cognitive exploration is another alternative and it is a technique by inspection used to identify usability issues (Kushniruk & Patel, 2004). It is task-oriented and performed by experts who take the role of users, following a protocol determined by several steps. The main objective of this technique is to verify how easy it is to use a system. This technique is essentially used in the context of software development teams, in which the main objective is to verify how easy it is to use a system.

Prototyping and the emergence of agile development methodologies is another approach that has gained strong market relevance in recent years. This approach has a low cost and can be quickly implemented at any stage of the project (Tanvir et al., 2017). Another alternative is the creation of focus groups complementing with questionnaires and/or interviews. This technique can also be used at any stage of project development and is useful for discovering user needs (Rose et al., 2005). Finally, automatic evaluation tools that collect information and identify potential problems of a software product are also emerging. Two classes of tools emerge in this domain: those that try to predict the use of the software product and those that assess compliance with standards and guidelines (Norman & Panizzi, 2006).

The Concept of Accessibility

When we approach the design of digital interfaces, accessibility is related to the possibility that is given to the individual to receive information made available in a clear way. According to Batty (2009), accessibility works as a condition to obtain security and autonomy in accessing a service. Therefore, and contextualizing it to web accessibility, it corresponds to the ability of any individual (e.g., people with disabilities, elderly, reduced capacities) to receive, understand, navigate, and interact with web contents (Lima et al., 2012).

Nowadays the two concepts of usability and accessibility are related. This has enabled people with special needs to be part of the target audience for most web pages. Schmutz et al. (2017) state that by making a webpage accessible for users with special needs, we are simultaneously improving usability for all users. Note that a key relationship between the two concepts lies in the importance given to the ease of use of a web page. By building a web page based on the principles of accessibility, we are also ensuring that all users benefit from it.

To build a web page it is indispensable to follow a set of standards. W3C is an international community that develops free standards to ensure the long-term growth of the Internet. A W3C standard is a specification or a set of guidelines achieved after consultation between members of the organization and the general public (Daoust, 2020). W3C (2017) refers to the existence of three types of users with special needs:

- Users with hearing problems - two subgroups emerge: the first encompasses cases of mild and moderate deafness, while the second refers to cases of profound deafness;
- Users with cognitive and neurological problems - this type of problem can affect any part of the nervous system. It can influence the ability to see, hear, move, speak, or understand information;
- Users with vision problems - these can also be grouped into two categories: cases of partial vision loss, or cases of substantial and incorrigible vision. Other associated limitations may include low sensitivity to color distinction (e.g., daltonic individuals) or a high level of sensitivity to color brightness.

The W3C has released the Web Content Accessibility Guidelines (WCAG) which provides a set of guidelines on accessibility for content available on the Internet (WCAG, 2020). It presents recommendations for making content accessible to users, especially those with special needs. It has three levels of recommendations (WCAG, 2020):

- Level A (high priority) - content developers need to meet these requirements, otherwise the content cannot be accessed;
- Level AA (medium priority) - content developers must meet these requirements, otherwise users will have difficulty accessing the content;
- Level AAA (low priority) - content developers can satisfy these requirements, as it will make it easier to access the content.

In applying these recommendations, it becomes relevant to adopt four principles that should be applied to website components, navigation, and information architecture (Firth, 2019). The contents should be perceivable. To this end, there should be alternative descriptions of the images, videos, captions, etc. With these measures, the content will not be being conveyed in a single way which makes it noticeable to an audience that would have previously been unable to access it. Content must also be operable, in which all users can perform the various operations without access barriers. The content must also be understandable through clear and objective writing and by avoiding specific expressions. Finally, it must be robust and able to be used with the aid of assistive technologies (e.g., making the site navigable by keyboard for a person with motor disabilities).

The Emergence of User Experience (UX)

With the development of new technologies, users are not only looking to get a task done but also to have a pleasant experience. In this sense, usability is no longer sufficient to define the quality of a software and achieve user acceptance. Tio et al. (2019) state that UX is holistic encompassing all details about the interaction between users and the product, from the perception of how the product works, but also the needs and expectations in any context. UX addresses human needs beyond the instrumental and creates a holistic interaction. Furthermore, Persada (2018) advocates that UX is focused on checking the importance of emotions as consequences, antecedents of product use, and checking ways to emphasize the experience produced by interactive products.

One of the first works in the UX domain was developed by Morville (2004) who presents the UX honeycomb. This model structures the components of UX in seven hexagons: useful, usable, findable, valuable, desirable, accessible, and credible. This was a fundamental reference for the advancement of UX and for developers to realize that exclusively analyzing usability is not enough for the development of digital interactions.

Other works have followed. It is worth mentioning the study developed by Minge & Thüring (2018), who propose a UX evaluation approach involving pragmatic and hedonic aspects. Pragmatic aspects are related to task accomplishment, while hedonic aspects are related to emotions. In this sense, UX is a broader concept than usability. The hedonic aspects contribute directly to a positive experience, while the pragmatic aspects facilitate the achievement of goals.

It is unequivocally possible to conclude that all companies offer a UX to their users. The difference is whether the UX is planned to be relevant or not. Studies by Badran & Al-Haddad (2018) and Fabricant (2013) make it evident that user perception is the key to success. For example, by adopting a relevance scale, the user can evaluate whether a digital product is useful, has differentiated value, or is enjoyable to use.

UX encompasses all user interactions with the company, its products, services, and processes. Buley (2013) mentions that UX considers several factors such as: (i) the feelings and emotions provoked in users since the experience is personal; (ii) the channel, product or service that represent the context in which the experience is lived; and (iii) the evolution of the experience over time. These guidelines allow UX to be taken to several business areas in different segments and, most importantly, place the user at the center of the company's actions. A study conducted by Almeida & Monteiro (2017) highlights that this new positioning of the user is key to building UX web experiences.

UX has essentially been used in the context of web experience development. Even before mobile devices, user experience was already a decisive factor in the use of products and interfaces in general. Understanding this experience is important for companies because it contributes directly to a more positive view of the product or services offered by the company. However, with the growth of the mobile market, user experience has become even more complex and important for brands, since it guides all the points of contact of the target audience with the brand (Yu & Huang, 2020). The mobile device market, as well as the context in which they are used, determines unique and specific requirements in user experience design. Some specific characteristics of mobile device interaction emerge. Mobile users interact with their devices at crucial moments and for short periods. Therefore, their experiences need to be personalized, efficient, and enjoyable to keep the user engaged (Sun & May, 2014).

MAIN FOCUS OF THE CHAPTER

This chapter aims to address how the principles of usability, accessibility and UX can from a practical perspective be adopted in the development of a mobile application. We considered the development of a native Android app (i.e., Carewash) that provides car-washing services, namely car cleaning services. The Carewash app has two types of users: the customer and the employee. It enables its customers to make their reservations more easily and effectively. To do this, simply download the app and install it on an Android smartphone. The user will be required to register and log in. After the login is successfully executed, the customer will have access to all features of the app, such as adding, editing, and deleting vehicles, adding and managing reservations, and customizing his/her profile. The employee has access to the list with his daily services. By selecting a service, the employee has access to all the detailed information of the respective reservation. To start the service, it is only necessary to press the "start" button that informs the employee of the booking address based on the customer's location via Google Maps. Upon arrival at the user's destination, the employee notifies the customer of his/her arrival. To terminate the service, the employee simply presses the "finish" button, and the service will be removed from the list of services.

The WCAG 2.0 framework was used in analyzing the accessibility practices implemented in the Carewash app. As Valle & Connor (2019) note, accessibility involves a wide range of disabilities such as speech, visual, hearing, physical, cognitive, learning, and neurological disabilities. While the guidelines offered by WCAG 2.0 cover a wide diversity of issues, they cannot fully address the needs of person with all types, degrees, and combinations of disabilities. These guidelines also have the benefit of making interfaces more usable by older individuals with changing abilities due to aging and often also help improve usability for all users.

A large number of techniques considered in the WCAG 2.0 framework are equally applicable and relevant for interface design in mobile applications. Nevertheless, WCAG 2.0 has defined a set of guidelines for mobile-specific interface design that can be applied to mobile web applications, hybrid, and web-native applications (WCAG, 2015). These recommendations recognize two situations. From one perspective, most usability-related issues apply to both web and mobile interfaces; on the other hand, mobile devices present specific issues different from a web access from a desktop or laptop environment.

In analyzing usability and UX, the framework proposed by kashfi et al. (2019) was considered in which it is argued that user experience is a set of disciplines comprising usability and other areas (e.g., interface design, interface design, information architecture, etc.). Kashfi et al. (2019) argue that the user interaction design process should involve both pragmatic and hedonic components. This referential was complemented by the approach proposed by Ananjeva et al. (2020) in which it is proposed that UX development should be integrated with agile methodologies, namely in user stories. Therefore, and in the analysis of the interfaces developed in the Carewash app, user stories were considered that simultaneously express the needs of users in the dual perspective of UX and accessibility. A total of 12 user stories were considered as presented in Table 1.

Table 1. User stories

ID	Actors	Description
US1	Customer and Employee	Access to the app is reserved for holders of access credentials.
US2	Customer	The app must allow the registration of new users.
US3	Customer	The customer should check the personal data stored in the app and ensure that it is GDPR compliant.
US4	Customer	The client must have permission to include new vehicles. The same client can have more than one associated vehicle.
US5	Customer	All operations performed in the app must be directly accessible from the dashboard.
US6	Customer	The customer must have information about the pricing applied to each vehicle segment.
US7	Customer	The app should obtain the customer's GPS location and also allow for manual editing considering the company's geographic areas of intervention.
US8	Customer	The customer must indicate the date and time of his reservation.
US9	Customer	The app should enable various payment methods to be chosen by the customer.
US10	Employee	The employee must have access to his or her personal data and information about his/her rating resulting from the customers' evaluation of the services provided.
US11	Employee	The employee must have access to the list of services that are assigned to him/her.
US12	Employee	The employee must have a description of the services provided by the client considering the service's location and telephone contact.

Source: authors

SOLUTIONS AND RECOMMENDATIONS

Login and Register

WCAG 2.0 provides a set of recommendations developed by W3C for the purpose of making web content more accessible. These standards were extended in 2015 to also address the challenges of accessibility in the context of mobile devices (WCAG, 2015). These standards were adopted in the development of the Carewash app. Figure 1 (window A) shows the app login; Figure 1 (window B) shows the same window converted to black and white; Figure 1 (window C) shows the user registration interface. We highlight the implementation of the following guidelines:

- Small screen size - the amount of information that is displayed in each window has been minimized. Furthermore, a responsive design has been adopted that adjusts to the screen size of each device;
- Zoom/Magnification - the user can control from their device's accessibility settings the size of the font and buttons in the window. Both elements are resized according to the user's preferences;
- Contrast - mobile devices are used in very diverse environments that present numerous lighting challenges. In this sense, the app uses high contrast colors that make it easy to use against the light. Additionally, and for colorblind users, a black-white interface with high contrast is used as recommended by Tuchkov (2018);
- Screen orientation - the app can be used in either landscape or portrait orientation of the screen;
- Consistent layout - the components that are repeated on multiple pages as it appears with the header are consistent across the various windows. Moreover, the interaction form and colors are consistent across all windows.

A determining factor in the construction of the interface is that the interaction of users with a web and mobile application is necessarily different. While it is true that this asymmetry has been reversed in recent years with the increase in the screen size of mobile devices and the emergence of laptops with touchscreens, the user experience is necessarily different. This situation is addressed by Hoober (2017) who explores how users interact with their mobile phone and in which he identified six types of interaction (i.e., cradled, hold and touch, two hands - landscape, one hand - first order, one hand - second order, and two hands - portrait). The form of interaction depends both on the type of user but also on where that content is accessed.

In Figure 1 (window A), the recommendation of Masha (2019) was adopted, in which it is advocated the existence of a quick access to the "forgot password?" functionality. Since this app will be used only occasionally, this feature is even more relevant. In fact, rarely used passwords are forgotten, and retrieving them has to be a quick process.

A very fast and intuitive registration process was implemented in the app (Figure 1, window C). It only requested information about the user's name, email, and password. We avoided requesting other information (e.g., taxpayer, mobile phone) that are not essential in this case. The principle advocated by Ji et al. (2018) in which if users want to get more benefits by providing additional information, they can do so by editing their profile was followed. Furthermore, this approach allows conforming to the minimization principles enshrined in the GDPR. The minimization principle states that the data to be processed must be adequate, relevant, and limited to what is required by the purposes determining the processing (Crutzen et al.,

2019). According to this principle, personal data should only be processed if the purpose of the processing cannot be reasonably achieved by other means. It follows from this same principle that only data necessary for the intended purpose should be processed and not any other. If it turns out that excessive data is requested, the processing becomes unlawful.

Figure 1. Login and register windows
Source: authors

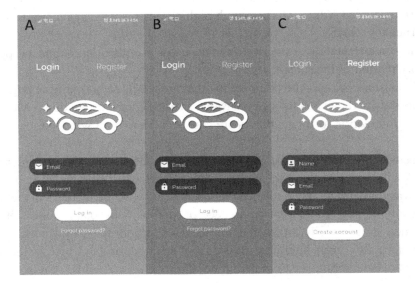

Dashboard

Figure 2 (window A) shows the dashboard window with the respective menu features; while Figure 2 (window B) lists the prices of the services considering the vehicle segment. In the presentation of the various buttons in the menu, enough distance between them was considered to give greater visibility and avoid conflicts between buttons due to touch. Two recommendations provided in WCAG (2015) were considered, namely:

- It has been ensured that all buttons are larger than 9mm*9mm in size;
- It has been ensured that all buttons are surrounded by a small amount of inactive space.

The buttons have been positioned to be easily reached when the device is used in different positions. WCAG (2015) reports that mobile developers often tend to favor one-handed use. However, this can lead to accessibility issues for other users, hence it is important to ensure flexible use.

One identifiable best practice is that on smartphones larger buttons should be considered. On smartphones, we deal with interactive screens via touchscreen technology. While on desktop computers we are used to the precision of the mouse, on the mobile side our tool is almost always the finger.

Finally, a determining factor in the use of this app is prior knowledge of the cost of each service. This information should be made available to the user in a transparent way. Therefore, and in the interface construction of Figure 2 (window B), the prices of the three types of services (i.e., inside, outside, inside and outside) are presented for all vehicle segments. According to Gilbert (2019), this approach also contributes to increasing user trust in the app, which is fundamental to the commercial success of an app.

Figure 2. Dashboard windows
Source: authors

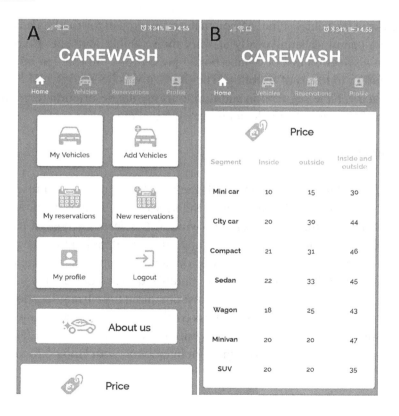

Customer's Profile

Figure 3 shows the user profile interface. The interface in Figure 3 (window A) allows the user to consult and edit his profile data; while Figure 3 (window B) enables the user to add new vehicles. A user can have more than one vehicle associated with his/her profile.

WCAG 2 (2015) recommends that when building interfaces, special attention should be paid to distinguishing the various types of objects, namely those that trigger actions in the system. In this sense, the buttons are highlighted in a distinct color that allows them to be distinguished from the text boxes that are used for the presentation of content and status information. An alternative name was also defined in each button and text box to support the adoption of screen readers, such as COBRA, Hal, and JAWS (Deshmukh et al., 2018).

One of the big points of difference between mobile apps and mobile websites is that apps allow users to stay logged in longer. This offers benefits in terms of convenience and personalization, derived from their information, behaviors, and transaction history. However, from the reverse perspective, it is important that the user explicitly has the possibility to logout as is implemented in Figure 3 (window A).

One of the difficulties that the user may experience when adding new vehicles is the selection of the vehicle type. Although the referential of the road code is adopted, not all users can always univocally identify their vehicle segment. Therefore, the adoption of a selection box or combo box to present this information might not be a good solution in terms of usability. Therefore, it was decided to add an allusive image of each vehicle segment in addition to its textual description (e.g., mini car, city car, compact, etc.). Both elements are used together.

Reservations

Figure 4 shows three windows in which the workflow process of a reservation is presented. In window A the location of the service is selected; window B shows the date and time of the reservation; and window C selects the type of payment.

The construction of these interfaces took into consideration that the process of typing on mobile devices is not as easy as on laptop computers. As Babich (2016) advocates, the need for typing should be minimized to avoid user errors. In Figure 4 (window A) the user has two possibilities: obtaining his current location through his device's GPS, and including an address considering that the company's services only cover three municipalities (i.e., Matosinhos, Porto, and V.N.Gaia. The address can be dynamically set by the user through interaction with Google Maps.

Figure 3. Customer's profile windows
Source: authors

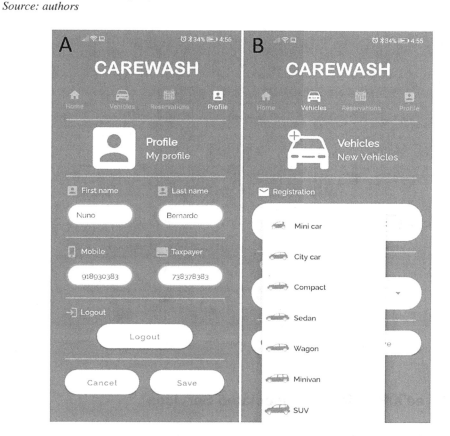

In Figure 4 (window B) a calendar is provided for date selection. The recommendation of Minhas (2019) was followed in which date selection is done via a touchscreen using a calendar. This selection method helps the user understand the various date possibilities available. The time selection considers the availability of employees against previously made reservations. Therefore, non-available time slots are identified as unavailable.

Payment for the service is made in Figure 4 (window C). Three payment methods are available: MBWay, Credit Card, and Bank Transfer. The payment method selected by the user is highlighted with a fill color. When paying, the user has access to the booking details. Access to this information at the time of payment is important to increase the transparency of the process.

Figure 4. Reservations windows
Source: authors

Employee's Profile and Associated Services

The employee is another user of this app. The employee should be able to access his/her profile and see the daily services associated with him/her. Figure 5 (window A) shows the employee profile; Figure 5 (window B) presents the services assigned to the employee; and Figure 5 (window C) provides the details of a service. The employee profile also shows the total rating that results from the average score of all services performed by the employee.

The service list screen is built to provide the user with an intuitive journey that allows them to focus on the priority tasks that need to be done, as well as providing content that meets their expectations. Only the navigation and the primary content are visible in the default configuration, with the secondary content being hidden. This was achieved, since window B shows a summary of each service, while window C shows the details of this service (e.g., customer address, mobile phone). This approach is in line with the recommendation of McKenna (2018) who highlights that an overload of data makes it difficult for your user to have a good experience.

Figure 5. Employee's profile and associated services windows
Source: authors

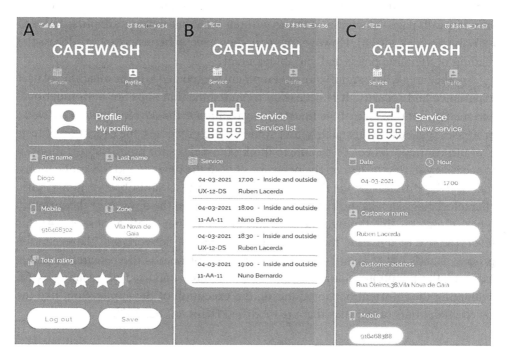

FUTURE RESEARCH DIRECTIONS

Several research areas are emerging in the fields of usability, accessibility and UX design. One of the essential aspects is to consider that UX design is an interdisciplinary field and, therefore, involves knowledge from several disciplines. Interface design is a fundamental area in software engineering since a poor user experience leads to loss of empathy. These challenges take on a different perspective in mobile development fields.

Mobile First is a concept that has become more prevalent in the market (Tran, 2019; Xia, 2017). The initial focus of architecture and development shifts to mobile devices. In this logic of thinking, the entire execution of the process is reversed. Instead of starting the information architecture for the desktop, its architecture is designed for mobile. This new paradigm makes rethink the implementation process of a digital project (e.g., design, content, images, video, programming, etc.).

One of the difficulties in building immersive apps is the speed at which pages load. Therefore, one of the areas of research is the development of Accelerated Mobile Pages (AMP) technology that allows to significantly increase the loading speed of a page. Normally, the loading speed of a site always depends on the size and quantity of files. Therefore, the AMP framework aims to minimize the total size of a web page. The entire website will not load, but rather a simplified part of it (Wibowo et al., 2018). However, new models have to be proposed to address the loading of dynamic pages and variable content.

Another area where significant development is expected is in the matching of user experience and security. It is necessary to guarantee that apps are both functional and secure. For this, one of the lines of investigation is the development of software processes that ensure this quality, and among these processes, the execution of tests is of utmost importance. To be able to think of test cases for mobile applications, it is necessary to first reflect on the behavior of both the devices and the applications. Identify the differences for the common intrusion tests and observe the specific characteristics, such as the vulnerabilities coming from the devices or the different types of attacks, like through the Internet, through other applications, etc. At this level, the use of dynamic methods by monitoring the network and the execution process stands out (Elsantil. 2020). Also worthy of note is the research line that explores the adoption of forensic methods that are supported on techniques for evaluating the information stored during the execution of the application, like the saved credentials or the files that are modified (Kim & Lee, 2020).

CONCLUSION

Interfaces are the main communication channel between the software and the user. An interface that is not well planned can compromise the success of a project. Users want a user experience that is pleasant and simple, and that they do not intend to read manuals or instructions to complete some task, much less call a support line to ask questions. Developing experiences that create affectivity in users is one of the most important differentiations in the competitive market. The level of user experience will depend on the user's expectations and the business goal. Developing for mobile is a challenge that has several limitations and particularities. Although mobile devices share elements required on the web, there are several differences to take into account for mobile success. The mobile experience needs to find new ways for users to interact with information, understanding the context of its use, because in comparison to the desktop, mobile has a greater variety of contexts and environments.

The main function of mobile design is to establish visual hierarchies, where emphasis is placed on the most important parts, so the user understands the message through a consistent organization of information. Another key element is the search for contrast. Contrast emphasizes and differentiates various types of information, using elements to augment the information, and allow the user to interpret. Screen size is another element that must be considered when designing an interface. Design is the first impression of the experience that the user will get. A good design gives the user high expectations about the product, and a bad design lowers the user's expectations. The system should be as simple as possible to allow the user to interact intuitively. Identical actions should have identical results; the same terminology should be used in all menus, in dialog windows, and in contextual aids. Performance is another key factor. Users want to access information quickly. It is necessary to balance functionality with simplicity. On the other hand, it is necessary to consider various constraints, like screen size, among others.

In this work, practices in interface design are addressed to increase the usability, accessibility and UX of an app. The study essentially offers practical contributions by allowing the identification of approaches that allow increasing the consistency of information, button arrangements, organization of information with a focus on priority tasks, reversible actions, collection of information from the user's location, etc. These practices can be applied in several scenarios and allow offering a better user experience to the user considering the particularities of a mobile interface, namely in the form and context of its use.

REFERENCES

Al-Kilidar, H., Cox, K., & Kitchenham, B. (2005). The use and usefulness of the ISO/IEC 9126 quality standard. *Proceedings of the 2005 International Symposium on Empirical Software Engineering*, 1-7. 10.1109/ISESE.2005.1541821

Almeida, F., & Monteiro, J. A. (2017). Approaches and Principles for UX Web Experiences. *International Journal of Information Technology and Web Engineering*, *12*(2), 49–65. doi:10.4018/IJITWE.2017040103

Ananjeva, A., Persson, J. S., & Bruun, A. (2020). Integrating UX work with agile development through user stories: An action research study in a small software company. *Journal of Systems and Software*, *170*, 1–10. doi:10.1016/j.jss.2020.110785

Babich, N. (2016). *Mobile Form Usability*. Retrieved from https://uxplanet.org/mobile-form-usability-2279f672917d

Badran, O., & Al-Haddad, S. (2018). The impact of software user experience on customer satisfaction. *Journal of Management Information and Decision Sciences*, *21*(1), 1–20.

Batty, M. (2009). Accessibility: In search of a unified theory. *Environment and Planning. B, Planning & Design*, *36*(2), 191–194. doi:10.1068/b3602ed

Baylé, M. (2018). *Experience Design: a new discipline?* Retrieved from https://uxdesign.cc/experience-design-a-new-discipline-e62db76d5ed1

Buley, L. (2013). *The User Experience Team of One: A Research and Design Survival Guide*. Rosenfeld Media.

Camburn, B., Viswanathan, V., Linsey, J., Anderson, D., Jensen, D., Crawford, R., Otto, K., & Wood, K. (2017). Design prototyping methods: State of the art in strategies, techniques, and guidelines. *Design Science*, *3*, e13. doi:10.1017/dsj.2017.10

Crutzen, R., Peters, G. J., & Mondschein, C. (2019). Why and how we should care about the General Data Protection Regulation. *Psychology & Health*, *34*(11), 1347–1357. doi:10.1080/08870446.2019.1606222 PMID:31111730

Daoust, F. (2020). Update from the World Wide Web Consortium (WC3). *SMPTE Motion Imaging Journal*, *129*(8), 80–83. doi:10.5594/JMI.2020.3001776

De Kock, E., Van Biljon, J., & Pretorius, M. (2009). Usability evaluation methods: Mind the gaps. *Proceedings of the 2009 Annual Conference of the South African Institute of Computer Scientists and Information Technologists*, 122-131. 10.1145/1632149.1632166

Deshmukh, M., Phatak, D., & Save, B. (2018). User Experience for Person with Disabilities. *International Journal of Computers and Applications*, *180*(44), 6–11. doi:10.5120/ijca2018917141

Dreheeb, A. E., & Fabil, N. B. (2016). Impact of System Quality on Users' Satisfaction in Continuation of the Use of e-Learning System. *International Journal of e-Education, e-Business, e- Management Learning*, *6*(1), 13–20.

Elsantil, Y. (2020). User Perceptions of the Security of Mobile Applications. *International Journal of E-Services and Mobile Applications*, *12*(4), 24–41. doi:10.4018/IJESMA.2020100102

Fabricant, R. (2013). *Scaling Your UX Strategy*. Retrieved from https://hbr.org/2013/01/scaling-your-ux-strategy

Firth, A. (2019). *Practical Web Inclusion and Accessibility: A Comprehensive Guide to Access Needs*. Apress. doi:10.1007/978-1-4842-5452-3

Gilbert, R. M. (2019). *Inclusive Design for a Digital World: Designing with Accessibility in Mind*. Apress. doi:10.1007/978-1-4842-5016-7

Godoi, T. X., & Valentim, N. M. (2019). Towards an Integrated Evaluation of Usability, User Experience and Accessibility in Assistive Technologies. *Proceedings of the XVIII Brazilian Symposium on Software Quality*, 234-239. 10.1145/3364641.3364669

Gonzalez-Holland, E., Whitmer, D., Moralez, L., & Mouloua, M. (2017). Examination of the Use of Nielsen's 10 Usability Heuristics & Outlooks for the Future. *Proceedings of the Human Factors and Ergonomics Society Annual Meeting*, *61*(1), 1472–1475. doi:10.1177/1541931213601853

Hoober, S. (2017). *Design for Fingers, Touch, and People, Part 1*. Retrieved from https://www.uxmatters.com/mt/archives/2017/03/design-for-fingers-touch-and-people-part-1.php

ISO. (1991). *ISO/IEC 9126:1991 Software engineering - Product quality*. Retrieved from https://www.iso.org/standard/16722.html

ISO. (2011). *ISO/IEC 25010:2011 Systems and software engineering — Systems and software Quality Requirements and Evaluation (SQuaRE) - System and software quality models*. Retrieved from https://www.iso.org/standard/35733.html

Ji, H., Yun, Y., Lee, S., Kim, K., & Lim, H. (2018). An adaptable UI/UX considering user's cognitive and behavior information in distributed environment. *Cluster Computing*, *21*(1), 1045–1058. doi:10.100710586-017-0999-9

Joo, H. (2017). A Study on Understanding of UI and UX, and Understanding of Design According to User Interface Change. *International Journal of Applied Engineering Research: IJAER*, *12*(20), 9931–9935.

Karmokar, S., Singh, H., & Tan, F. B. (2016). Using Multidisciplinary Design Principles to Improve the Website Design Process. *Pacific Asia Journal of the Association for Information Systems*, *8*(3), 17–28. doi:10.17705/1pais.08302

Kashfi, P., Feldt, R., & Nilsson, A. (2019). Integrating UX principles and practices into software development organizations: A case study of influencing events. *Journal of Systems and Software*, *154*, 37–58. doi:10.1016/j.jss.2019.03.066

Kim, D., & Lee, S. (2020). Study of identifying and managing the potential evidence for effective Android forensics. *Forensic Science International: Digital Investigation*, *33*, 1–18.

Kushniruk, A. W., & Patel, V. L. (2004). Cognitive and usability engineering methods for the evaluation of clinical information systems. *Journal of Biomedical Informatics*, *37*(1), 56–76. doi:10.1016/j.jbi.2004.01.003 PMID:15016386

Lazar, J., Goldstein, D. F., & Taylor, A. (2015). *Ensuring Digital Accessibility through Process and Policy*. Morgan Kaufmann.

Lima, J. F., Caran, G. M., Molinaro, L. F., & Garrossini, D. F. (2012). Analysis of Accessibility Initiatives Applied to the Web. *Procedia Technology*, *5*, 319–326. doi:10.1016/j.protcy.2012.09.035

Longdon, P. M., Lazar, J., & Heylighen, A. (2014). *Inclusive Designing: Joining Usability, Accessibility, and Inclusion*. Springer. doi:10.1007/978-3-319-05095-9

Lopes, A., Valentim, N., Moraes, B., Zilse, R., & Conte, T. (2018). Applying user-centered techniques to analyze and design a mobile application. *Journal of Software Engineering Research and Development*, *6*(5), 1–23. doi:10.118640411-018-0049-1

Masha, S. (2019). *UX Guide: Password Reset User Flow*. Retrieved from https://blog.prototypr.io/ux-guide-password-reset-user-flow-bfa35a16e527

McKenna, B. (2018). *Data overload is not about human limitations; it's about design failure*. Retrieved from https://uxdesign.cc/data-overload-is-a-design-problem-bcdb76e3cd6c

Minge, M., & Thüring, M. (2018). Hedonic and pragmatic halo effects at early stages of User Experience. *International Journal of Human-Computer Studies*, *109*, 13–25. doi:10.1016/j.ijhcs.2017.07.007

Minhas, S. (2019). *How to Design a Perfect Date Picker Control?* Retrieved from https://uxplanet.org/how-to-design-a-perfect-date-picker-control-7f47d1290c3a

Morville, P. (2004). *User Experience Design*. Retrieved from http://semanticstudios.com/user_experience_design/

Nielsen, J. (1993). *Usability Engineering*. Academic Press. doi:10.1016/B978-0-08-052029-2.50007-3

Norman, K. L., & Panizzi, E. (2006). Levels of automation and user participation in usability testing. *Interacting with Computers*, *18*(2), 246–264. doi:10.1016/j.intcom.2005.06.002

Nowak, M. (2020). *Why Usability and Accessibility Matter in App Development*. Retrieved from https://www.nomtek.com/blog/usability-accessibility

Peacock, M. (2011). *Why its more important to have an Effective Website than an Efficient Website*. Retrieved from https://wp-agency.co.uk/why-its-more-important-to-be-effective-than-efficient/

Persada, A. (2018). Emotional Design on User Experience-based Development System. *Proceedings of the 2018 International Conference on Electrical Engineering and Computer Science (ICECOS)*, 1-6. 10.1109/ICECOS.2018.8605199

Petrie, H. L., Savva, A., & Power, C. (2015). Towards a unified definition of web accessibility. *Proceedings of the 12th Web for All Conference*, 1-13. 10.1145/2745555.2746653

Rose, A. F., Schnipper, J. L., Park, E. R., Poon, E. G., Li, Q., & Middleton, B. (2005). Using qualitative studies to improve the usability of an EMR. *Journal of Biomedical Informatics*, *38*(1), 51–60. doi:10.1016/j.jbi.2004.11.006 PMID:15694885

Schmutz, S., Sonderegger, A., & Sauer, J. (2017). Implementing Recommendations From Web Accessibility Guidelines: A Comparative Study of Nondisabled Users and Users With Visual Impairments. *Human Factors*, *49*(6), 956–972. doi:10.1177/0018720817708397 PMID:28467134

Schnall, R., Rojas, M., Bakken, S., Brown, W., Carballo-Dieguez, A., Carry, M., Gelaude, D., Mosley, J. P., & Travers, J. (2016). A user-centered model for designing consumer mobile health (mHealth) applications (apps). *Journal of Biomedical Informatics*, *60*, 243–251. doi:10.1016/j.jbi.2016.02.002 PMID:26903153

Shackel, B. (2009). Usability – Context, framework, definition, design and evaluation. *Interacting with Computers*, *21*(5-6), 339–346. doi:10.1016/j.intcom.2009.04.007

Sinha, M., & Fukey, L. N. (2020). Web user Experience and Consumer behaviour: The Influence of Colour, Usability and Aesthetics on the Consumer Buying behaviour. *Test Engineering and Management*, *82*, 16592–16600.

Ssemugabi, S., & de Villiers, M. R. (2010). Effectiveness of heuristic evaluation in usability evaluation of e-learning applications in higher education. *South African Computer Journal*, *45*, 26–39. doi:10.18489acj.v45i0.37

Sun, X., & May, A. J. (2014). Design of the User Experience for Personalized Mobile Services. *International Journal of Human-Computer Interaction*, *5*(2), 21–39.

Tanvir, S., Safdar, M., Tufail, H., & Qamar, U. (2017). Merging Prototyping with Agile Software Development Methodology. *Proceedings of the International Conference on Engineering, Computing & Information Technology*, 50-54.

Tio, E., Torkildson, M., Su, D., Toussaint, H., Bhargava, A., & Shaikh, D. (2019). Measuring Holistic User Experience: Keeping an Eye on What Matters Most to Users. *Proceedings of the 21st International Conference on Human-Computer Interaction with Mobile Devices and Services (MobileHCI '19)*, 1-4. 10.1145/3338286.3344425

Tran, T. H. (2019). *What does mobile-first design mean for digital designers?* Retrieved from https://www.invisionapp.com/inside-design/mobile-first-design/

Tuchkov, I. (2018). *Color blindness: how to design an accessible user interface.* Retrieved from https://uxdesign.cc/color-blindness-in-user-interfaces-66c27331b858

Valle, J. W., & Connor, D. J. (2019). *Rethinking Disability: A Disability Studies Approach to Inclusive Practices.* Routledge. doi:10.4324/9781315111209

W3C. (2017). *Diverse Abilities and Barriers.* Retrieved from https://www.w3.org/WAI/people-use-web/abilities-barriers/

WCAG. (2015). *Mobile Accessibility: How WCAG 2.0 and Other W3C/WAI Guidelines Apply to Mobile.* Retrieved from https://www.w3.org/TR/mobile-accessibility-mapping/

WCAG. (2020). *Web Content Accessibility Guidelines (WCAG) Overview.* Retrieved from https://www.w3.org/WAI/standards-guidelines/wcag/

Whittaker, S. (2013). *Interaction Design: What we know and what we need to know.* Retrieved from https://interactions.acm.org/archive/view/july-august-2013/interaction-design

Wibowo, A., Aryotejo, G., & Mufadhol, M. (2018). Accelerated Mobile Pages from JavaScript as Accelerator Tool for Web Service on E-Commerce in the E-Business. *Iranian Journal of Electrical and Computer Engineering*, 8(4), 2399–2405. doi:10.11591/ijece.v8i4.pp2399-2405

Xia, V. (2017). *What is Mobile First Design? Why It's Important & How To Make It?* Retrieved from https://medium.com/@Vincentxia77/what-is-mobile-first-design-why-its-important-how-to-make-it-7d3cf2e29d00

Xiao, L. (2019). *What designers need to know about mobile accessibility.* Retrieved from https://uxplanet.org/what-designers-need-to-know-about-mobile-accessibility-9f6360f53f38

Yu, N., & Huang, Y. T. (2020). Important Factors Affecting User Experience Design and Satisfaction of a Mobile Health App - A Case Study of Daily Yoga App. *International Journal of Environmental Research and Public Health*, 17(19), 1–16. doi:10.3390/ijerph17196967 PMID:32977635

ADDITIONAL READING

Ataei, M., Degbelo, A., & Kray, C. (2018). Privacy theory in practice: Designing a user interface for managing location privacy on mobile devices. *Journal of Location Based Services*, *12*(3-4), 141–178. doi:10.1080/17489725.2018.1511839

Bollini, L. (2017). Beautiful interfaces. From user experience to user interface design. *The Design Journal*, *20*(sup1), 89–101. doi:10.1080/14606925.2017.1352649

Johnson, J. (2020). *Designing with the Mind in Mind: Simple Guide to Understanding User Interface Design Guidelines*. Morgan Kaufmann.

MacKenzie, I. S. (2012). *Human-Computer Interaction: An Empirical Research Perspective*. Morgan Kaufmann.

Mohamed, M. A., Chakraborty, J., & Dehlinger, J. (2017). Trading off usability and security in user interface design through mental models. *Behaviour & Information Technology*, *36*(5), 493–516. doi:10.1080/0144929X.2016.1262897

Oulasvirta, A., & Abowd, G. D. (2016). User Interface Design in the 21st Century. *Computer*, *49*(7), 11–13. doi:10.1109/MC.2016.201

Sarsam, S. M., & Al-Samarrale, H. (2018). A First Look at the Effectiveness of Personality Dimensions in Promoting Users' Satisfaction With the System. *SAGE Open*, *8*(2), 1–12. doi:10.1177/2158244018769125

Shamat, N. A., Sulaiman, S., & Sinpang, J. S. (2017). A Systematic Literature Review on User Interface Design for Web Applications. *Journal of Telecommunication. Electronic and Computer Engineering*, *9*(3-4), 57–61.

Tidwell, J., Brewer, C., & Valencia, A. (2020). *Designing Interfaces: Patterns for Effective Interaction Design*. O'Reilly Media.

Tillman, B., Tillman, P., Rose, R. R., & Woodson, W. E. (2016). *Human Factors and Ergonomics Design Handbook*. McGraw-Hill Education.

Wilson, C. (2013). *User Interface Inspection Methods: A User-Centered Design Method*. Morgan Kaufmann.

KEY TERMS AND DEFINITIONS

Accelerated Mobile Pages (AMP): Technology to significantly increase web page loading in the mobile environment.

General Data Protection Regulation (EU GDPR): European diploma (EU 2016/679) establishing the rules relating to the protection, processing, and free movement of personal data of natural persons in all member countries of the European Union.

Global Positioning System (GPS): Satellite positioning system that lets a mobile device know its physical location in outdoor environments.

Heuristic: Inspection technique that helps identify usability problems in an interface. In this inspection, usability experts examine and judge whether each element of the interface conforms to usability principles (heuristics).

MBWay: Payment solution that allows a user to purchase online and in physical stores, generate MB NET virtual cards, send, request money, and split the account, and even use and withdraw money via their smartphone, in a proprietary app, or in their bank's channels.

User Experience: Encompasses all aspects of the end user's interaction with the company, its services, and its products.

User Interface: Analyzes how a person interacts with a software application or a physical device.

W3C: Consortium that regulates web standards.

Web Content Accessibility Guidelines (WCAG): Provides a set of recommendations that are intended to make web content accessible to all users, particularly those with special needs.

Chapter 6
Unified Website Accessibility Assessment Framework

Zehra Altuntaş
Kocaeli University, Turkey

Pınar Onay Durdu
Kocaeli University, Turkey

ABSTRACT

In this chapter, a unified web accessibility assessment (UWAA) framework and its software has been proposed. UWAA framework was developed by considering Web Content Accessibility Guideline 2.0 to evaluate accessibility of web sites by integrating more than one evaluation approach. Achecker tool as an automated evaluation approach and barrier walkthrough (BW) as an expert-based evaluation approach were integrated in the UWAA framework. The framework also provides suggestions to recover from the problems determined to the evaluators. The websites of three universities were evaluated to determine the framework's accuracy and consistency. It was revealed that the results obtained from automated and expert-based evaluation methods were consistent and complementary with each other. Furthermore, it has been demonstrated that problems which cannot be determined by an automated tool but which can be detected by an expert can be identified by BW method.

INTRODUCTION

According to the Global Digital report (2019) published in January 2019, over 7 billion people live worldwide and there are approximately 4.39 billion Internet users. Compared to January 2018 data, it was observed that the number of Internet

DOI: 10.4018/978-1-7998-7848-3.ch006

users increased by 366 million (approximately 9%) in a year. Besides, according to Internet live statistics, there are currently more than 1.7 billion websites, and this number is increasing every day (W3C, 2020).

Websites become main mechanism to disseminate information to a variety of audiences for a wide spectrum of organizations from commercial to governmental. Since they operate in all aspects of daily life, people have begun to meet many of their needs by them. Therefore, the importance that organizations place on their websites to sustain their existence is also growing.

Websites are public platforms that are used to present and access to information at the same time. It is used by all user groups, including those with special needs (Shneiderman, 2000). As a result, websites need to be designed to be understandable and accessible to everyone (Henry et al., 2014). At this point, the concept of "universal design" emerges (Zaphiris & Ellis, 2001). Universal design is a very broad concept that includes the concepts of accessibility and usability (Iwarsson & Staahl, 2003; Mcguire et al., 2006). It is defined as providing web pages that all people regardless of having any disability or being old can easily access ("KAMİS," 2019; Laux, 1998).

Although usability and accessibility are the two terms that are closely related, they are not the same. Usability is expressed as the effectiveness, efficiency, and user satisfaction of a product within the context and objectives set by a specific user group (ISO, 2019). Even if usability implies accessibility, it does not correspond exactly to accessibility (W3C_WAI, 2016). On the other hand, Web Accessibility Initiative (WAI) defines accessibility as people with disabilities can perceive, understand, navigate, and interact with the Web and contribute to the Web (W3C_WAI, 2019). Although accessibility primarily focuses on users with disabilities according to this definition, it also aims to be useful for all users. It is sometimes considered as a subset of usability (Henry, 2002; Ma & Zaphiris, 2003). However, to put it together, both are complementary design philosophies and implement methods and techniques of each other (Alexander, 2006).

Web Accessibility Initiative (2019) defines web accessibility as "people can perceive, understand, navigate, and interact with the Web and contribute to the Web". World Wide Web Consortium (W3C) has developed Web Content Accessibility Guidelines (WCAG) for ensuring web site accessibility. Three versions of these guidelines were developed up until now and these are WCAG 1.0 (W3C, 1999), WCAG 2.0 (W3C, 2008) and WCAG 2.1 (W3C, 2018). Apart from these general guidelines, many countries have made web accessibility mandatory with regulations such as ISO 9241-20 (ISO, 2008) or Section 508 (US Access Board, 2000).

There are several approaches to evaluate the accessibility of websites. These are automated evaluation, expert based / manual evaluation, user tests and some hybrid approaches. Automated evaluation is an evaluation carried out with software tools (W3, 2016) that check websites with respect to accessibility guidelines. Expert based (manual) evaluation is a method in which web pages are evaluated in terms of some accessibility criteria by experts (Brajnik, 2008). User tests involves real users, and the evaluation takes place while they are interacting with the websites.

It is known that automated evaluation approaches alone are not sufficient to evaluate the accessibility of a web page so hybrid methods in which automated and manual evaluation are carried out together are suggested to be used (Acosta-Vargas, et al., 2018b). Although that issue is accepted in the literature the use of hybrid evaluation approaches is not many. The lack of frameworks or tools to enable evaluators to make hybrid assessments is believed to be one of the reasons for this. Therefore, within the scope of this study, a Unified Web Accessibility Assessment (UWAA) Framework and its software application was developed by considering Web Content Accessibility Guideline 2.0 to evaluate the accessibility of websites. Automated and expert-based evaluation approaches are integrated in the scope of UWAA framework. Achecker tool (2011) is used as an automated evaluation method, and Barrier Walkthrough (BW) method (Brajnik, 2011) is used as an expert-based evaluation method. In UWAA framework software application, the evaluation results from both evaluation methods can be reported separately or they can be presented in a unified way by matching them according to the WCAG 2.0. In addition, corrective suggestions are offered to the evaluators to overcome the detected accessibility problems.

Accessibility assessments of three university websites were conducted using the UWAA framework and its software. The findings of automated and expert-based evaluation methods were compared, and the reports gathered were analyzed. As a result of this accessibility assessment, it was observed that the data obtained from automated and expert based assessments were consistent and complementary with each other. It has been revealed that the issues that automated evaluation tool cannot control can be determined by the BW method. Finally, the developed software application not only provides comprehensive and detailed reporting of the errors to the evaluators, but also offers solutions from a single interface.

The rest of the article is structured as follows: Next section discusses background of the study. Section 3 presents the research design used in the study as well as the details of the proposed UWAA framework and its software application. This is followed by the Section 4, which reports the findings of the assessment of the accessibility of the three university websites conducted using the UWAA Framework and its software application. Finally, Section 5 presents conclusions and future work for this study.

BACKGROUND

Accessibility and Accessibility Guidelines

Accessibility has several definitions in the literature. Web Accessibility Initiative (WAI) defines web accessibility as being perceivable, understandable and easily used by people with disabilities (W3C_WAI, 2019). However, some definitions extend the target of accessibility to older people (Thatcher et al., 2006) other than disabled while others relate it to all users (Arch, 2009). Some others extend it to different context of use such as mobile (Yesilada et al., 2013). Moreover, some definitions also consider accessibility as usability (ISO, 2008) or at least a part of usability (Arch, 2009). Thus, it can be said that there is not a commonly agreed upon only definition for web accessibility. Due to having various definitions of the accessibility in the literature Yesilada et al. (2012) conducted a survey study that examined how people dealing with website accessibility defined it. Among 300 participants, 45% of them agreed with the WAI's definition.

Many websites used today have accessibility barriers that make it difficult for people to access the information they are looking for (W3C_WAI, 2019). To ensure equal access and equal opportunity for all people, the Web Accessibility Initiative (WAI) (WAI, 2018), established by W3C (W3C, n.d.), has developed the Web Content Accessibility Guidelines (WCAG), which has three versions up until now.

In addition to WCAG, WAI also developed other accessibility guidelines such as Authoring Tool Accessibility Guideline (ATAG) (W3C_WAI, 2005a) and User Agent Accessibility Guidelines (UAAG) (W3C_WAI, 2005b). ATAG defines how to make authoring tools accessible so that people with disabilities can create web content that conforms to WCAG while UAAG defines how to make user agents, such as browsers, browser extensions, media players, readers and other applications that render web content accessible to people with disabilities. Furthermore, some regulations such as ISO 9241-20 (ISO, 2008) or Section 508 (US Access Board, 2000) are accepted mandatory to ensure web accessibility in many countries (Cojocar & Guran, 2013; Hashemian, 2011).

WAI has defined four principles in its guidelines for making web content accessible. These principles can be listed as perceivable, operable, understandable and robust. For each principle, a set of guidelines and testable success criteria are provided has been determined (W3C, 2008). WCAG 2.0 has defined 61 success criteria to test these guidelines. These criteria are divided into three levels of conformance which are A (25 criteria), AA (13 criteria), and AAA (23 criteria). Level A means that website conforms to guideline items at minimum level, while AA is an extension of level A and AAA is an extension of level AA.

Accessibility Evaluation Methods

Many studies have been conducted to evaluate the accessibility of websites since the mid 90's. In these studies, the compatibility of the websites with the WCAGs has been checked by various evaluation methods. There are different methods used to evaluate web accessibility. These are automated evaluation, expert based / manual evaluation, user tests and hybrid methods.

Automated evaluation is an evaluation carried out with software tools (W3, 2016) which are developed to assess websites compliance with accessibility rules or standards. Accessibility assessment tools are divided into two groups (Al-Khalifa, 2012). First group tools evaluate websites according to general guidelines such as WCAG such as SortSite (PowerMapper, 2015) or AChecker (Achecker, 2011). The second group tools evaluate specific issues examined by web accessibility guidelines such as Contrast Controller (Acart Communications, 2017), which tests color contrast.

Expert based (manual) evaluation is a method in which web pages are evaluated in terms of some accessibility criteria by experts (Brajnik, 2008). This examination can also be done using assistive technologies (e.g. screen reading program) if required. This method is time consuming since it requires subjective judgment of an expert when conducting some tasks on the web page. For example; the Barrier Walkthrough (BW) (Brajnik, 2011) is a manual evaluation method which is similar to heuristics evaluation in usability (Yesilada et al., 2009).

User tests are often informal usability tests conducted with disabled users while performing a series of individual tasks. It is an evaluation method that results from the real experiences of disabled users. However, such user tests are also quite time consuming and expensive.

Among these methods automated evaluation requires the least time but it is known that conducting evaluation with only one method is not sufficient to evaluate the accessibility of a web page (Acosta-Vargas, et al., 2018a; Acosta-Vargas, et al., 2018b) . There are studies showing that accessibility tools give different results in accessibility assessments (Al-Khalifa, 2012; Ismail et al., 2019). Therefore, applying a hybrid approach that implements more than one method together would provide more elaborated evaluation.

Barrier Walkthrough

Barrier Walkthrough (BW) (Brajnik, 2011) is an expert-based evaluation approach which is similar to heuristics evaluation in usability studies. The evaluation is conducted with regard to defined barriers that prevent use. The main philosophy of this method is that it is better to start from known problems rather than using general design guidelines for testing and evaluation.

In BW, barrier is any condition that prevents the user from moving towards reaching a goal when the user is a disabled person.

A barrier is described in terms of the category of user regarding the type of disability, the type of assistive technology being used, the failure mode, that is the activity/ task that is hindered and how it is hindered, and which features in the page raise the barrier (Brajnik, 2011, p. 7)

Barriers were driven by interpreting known accessibility principles and guidelines in the context of general circumstances. The points need to be considered carefully are defining the relevant user categories, defining goals with respect to those user categories to ensure the relevant pages are tested, checking the barriers on those relevant pages and finally determining the severity of each barrier.

There are 9 different user categories defined in the BW method. These are listed as visually impaired, low-vision, deaf, color-blind, motor impaired users and users who have cognitive disabilities, users of browsers where JavaScript is disabled, users with photosensitive epilepsy and search engines. User goals are defined as usage scenarios in which users want to achieve while using the website. Possible barriers that may hinder the goal of the user are listed in the method and an expert conducts the evaluation by checking these barriers while carrying out the given scenario. Expert also rates severity of each barrier by assigning scores from 1 to 3 according to its impact, frequency, and severity.

Related Works

Accessibility Evaluation Methods

When the accessibility assessment studies of the websites are examined; it is seen that some studies were conducted by using different evaluation methods, some of them used the combination of more than one evaluation method or conducted by more than one automated evaluation tools. When the literature is examined, it is determined that the number of studies that used the automated tools is quite higher than expert-based evaluation studies. Examples of studies involving such different evaluation approaches are given in Table 1.

Table 1. Website Accessibility Evaluation Studies

Study	Region of Study	Evaluation Method	Automated Assessment Tool	Guideline
(Zaphiris & Ellis, 2001)	USA	• Automated	• Bobby • Lift	WCAG 1.0
(Thompson et al., 2003)	USA	• Automated	• Bobby	WCAG 1.0
(Kane et al., 2007)	Several countries • Australia • UK • USA • Netherlands • France • Switzerland	• Expert Based • Automated	• WebXACT / Bobby • Cynthia • Functional Accessibility Evaluator (FAE) • WebInSight	WCAG 1.0 Section508
(Harper & DeWaters, 2008)	USA	• Automated	• Watchfire • Bobby	• WCAG 1.0
(Aziz et al., 2010)	Malaysia	• Automated	• EvalAccess 2.0	WCAG 1.0
(Hashemian, 2011)	Finland	• Automated	• TAW Standalone (version 3.08)	WCAG 1.0
(Cojocar & Guran, 2013)	Romania	• Automated	• SortSite 5	
(Adepoju & Shehu, 2014)	Nigeria	• Automated	• AChecker • Hera • Wave	WCAG 1.0 WCAG 2.0
(Windriyani et al., 2014)	Indonesia	• Automated	• TAW	WCAG 2.0
(Ahmi & Mohamad, 2015)	Malaysia	• Automated	•AChecker -Wave	WCAG 2.0 Section508
(Kesswani & Kumar, 2016)	Several countries •England • Russia • China • Germany • India	• Automated	• Hera • Test de accessibilidad Web (TAW) • Firefox Accessibility Evaluation Toolbar	WCAG 2.0
(Alahmadi & Drew, 2017)	Several countries • Oceania • Arabia	• Automated	• AChecker	WCAG 2.0
(Acosta-Vargas et al., 2016)	Several countries • North America • Latin America • Europe • Asia • Africa • Oceania	• Automated	• TAW • Examinator	WCAG 2.0

continues on following page

Table 1. Continued

Study	Region of Study	Evaluation Method	Automated Assessment Tool	Guideline
(Kamal et al., 2016)	Jordan	• Automated	• AChecker • Cryptzone Cynthia Says • Functional Accessibility Evaluator (FAE) • HERA • Wave WebAIM • TAW	WCAG 1.0 WCAG 2.0
(Ismailova & Kimsanova, 2017)	Kirghizistan	• Automated	• EvalAccess 2.0	WCAG 1.0
(Akgül, 2017)	Turkey	• Automated	• Achecker	WCAG 1.0
(Kurt, 2017)	Turkey	• Automated	• Achecker	WCAG 2.0
(Yerlikaya & Onay Durdu, 2017)	Turkey	•	• SortSite	WCAG 2.0
(Acosta-Vargas, et al., 2018a)	Latin America	• Automated	• AChecker • Web Accessibility Checker • AccessMonitor • eXaminator • TAW • Tenon	WCAG 2.0
(Ismailova & Inal, 2018)	Several countries • Azerbaijan • Kazakhstan • Kyrgyzstan • Turkey	• Automated	• Achecker	WCAG 2.0
(Ismail & Kuppusamy, 2018)	India	• Automated	• AChecker • Webpage Analyzer • Wave	WCAG 2.0
(Król & Zdonek, 2020)	Poland	• Automated • Cognitive walkthrough • Survey	• WAVE • Utilitia • Lighthouse • Functional Accessibility Evaluator (FAE) • Opera Mobile Emulator	WCAG 2.0
(Eusébio et al., 2020)	Portugal	• Automated	• AccessMonitor • TAW	WCAG 2.0
(Acosta-Vargas et al., 2020)	Ecuador	• Survey-based	None	WCAG 2.0
(Teixeira et al., 2021)	Portugal	• Automated	• AccessMonitor • TAW	WCAG 2.0

In the studies exemplified in the Table 1, the accessibility assessments of the websites operating in one or more countries were conducted. Some of these evaluations (Akgül, 2017; Alahmadi & Drew, 2016; Aziz et al., 2010; Cojocar & Guran, 2013; Hashemian, 2011; Ismailova & Inal, 2018; Ismailova & Kimsanova, 2017; Kurt, 2017; Windriyani et al., 2014; Yerlikaya & Onay Durdu, 2017) were done using a single automated tool while some of them (Acosta-Vargas et al., 2018a, 2016; Adepoju & Shehu, 2014a; Ahmi & Mohamad, 2015; Eusébio et al., 2020; Harper & DeWaters, 2008; Ismail & Kuppusamy, 2018a; Kamal et al., 2016a; Kesswani & Kumar, 2016; Król & Zdonek, 2020; Teixeira et al., 2021; Zaphiris & Ellis, 2001a) reported the use of more than one automated tools. The evaluation of the websites with more than one tool also provided comparison of the automatic evaluation tools used. Thus, the accuracy and effectiveness of the tools were analyzed. It is seen that the "Achecker" automated evaluation tool, which also provides a web service, was preferred in many of the these studies (Acosta-Vargas, et al., 2018a; Adepoju & Shehu, 2014; Ahmi & Mohamad, 2015; Akgül, 2017; Alahmadi & Drew, 2016; Ismail & Kuppusamy, 2018; Ismailova & Inal, 2018; Kamal et al., 2016; Kurt, 2017). In the studies examined, there are also some hybrid studies (Kane et al., 2007; Thompson et al., 2003) in which expert-based evaluation was applied together with automated evaluation tools. In addition there are some recent studies (Acosta-Vargas et al., 2020; Król & Zdonek, 2020) that implement some questionnaire based evaluation approach.

While examining the studies conducted with expert-based evaluation method, the studies specifically related to the Barrier Walkthrough (BW) method were focused. In Table 2, there are examples of studies using BW as an accessibility evaluation method.

Yesilada et.al (2009) conducted an accessibility evaluation study in which BW was used as a method and they compared the assessment results of 19 expert and 51 non-expert evaluators to reveal whether expertise played role in this evaluation method. The study reported that expert evaluators conducted more detailed evaluation in shorter time with respect to non-experts.

In a study conducted using the BW method (Brajnik et al., 2009) a web accessibility assessment was conducted for elderly users. A new barrier set for elderly users was created by combining motor impaired and low vision users' barriers defined in the BW method. The evaluation was conducted by 19 experts and 49 non-experts. In a follow up study (Brajnik et al., 2011), 19 experts and 57 non-experts again conducted web accessibility assessment with the same barriers defined for elderly users. As a result of these evaluations, it was concluded that the barriers defined for elderly users were appropriate and the BW method was reliable method for the evaluation of web accessibility. Moreover, expert evaluators spent less time for the evaluation in this study, too but non-experts determined nearly the same number as expert evaluators.

Table 2. Website Accessibility Evaluation Studies using Barrier Walkthrough

Study	User Type	Evaluation Method	The Number of Participants
(Yesilada et al., 2009)	• Users with low vision • Visually impaired users • Motor disabled users • Mobile users	• only BW	70
(Brajnik et al., 2009)	• Old users	• only BW	68
(Brajnik et al., 2011)	• Users with motor impairment • Users with visual impairment	• only BW	76
(Braga et al., 2014)	• Old users	• only BW	2
(Acosta-Vargas, et al., 2018b)	• General user	• BW • Automated Evaluation Tools (Wave, Koa11y, Taw, Examinator)	Not mentioned.

In another study (Braga et al., 2014), web accessibility of an online banking site was conducted by BW method. Evaluation was conducted by one expert and one non-expert for elderly users. Evaluators reported the numbers of barriers as well as their criticality while they come across while conducting defined tasks for the evaluation.

In a more recent study, Acosta-Vargas et al.(2018b) conducted a hybrid evaluation study in which automated tool and BW methods were used together. They evaluated 45 university web sites in Latin America and based on their results, they concluded that automated tools alone are not sufficient and reliable in accessibility assessments. Therefore, they emphasized the use of expert-based evaluation methods such as BW as well.

Accessibility Evaluation Frameworks or Tools

Previously there were some accessibility evaluation frameworks or tools developed by integrating more than one accessibility evaluation approaches and various guidelines. It is aimed for evaluators to perform accessibility assessments from a single platform with these frameworks. The details of some former accessibility evaluation frameworks can be seen in Table 3.

Abascal et al. (2004) developed an automated accessibility evaluation tool, called as EvalIris, that allowed to easily update or modify accessibility guidelines due to its XML structure. The tool was compliant with WCAG 1.0. EvalIris first examined the mark-up of the Web page by dividing it into its HTML components. It then evaluates the accessibility of each component via the developed web service. Accessibility problems of the evaluated web site were presented as a report as a result in the tool.

Table 3. Studies including accessibility evaluation frameworks or tools

Study	Features of the Application	Compatible Guideline
(Abascal et al., 2004)	An application tool that allows to update / change accessibility guides	WCAG 1.0
(Nietzio et al., 2008)	An accessibility application that combines different assessment methods	WCAG 1.0
(Fernandes et al., 2011)	A tool that allows different environments (such as command line, scanner) to take advantage of the same evaluation procedures	WCAG 2.0

The Unified Web Evaluation Methodology (UWEM) (Nietzio et al., 2008) was developed by European expert organizations and offers evaluation method or procedure to evaluate websites according to WCAG 1.0 conformance. In the framework, a scenario was selected from among the evaluation options offered as expert-based, automatic or as a component of both depending on the needs of the organizations that want to perform the evaluation. In addition, the framework provided a clear sampling scheme, several reporting options, including score cards and other instruments to present the results of evaluations.

Another evaluation framework (Fernandes et al., 2011), which was called QualWeb, was developed to perform Web accessibly evaluations in different environments such that the Command Line environment in which the evaluations were performed to the original HTML document, and in the Browser environment, in which evaluation was targeted at the transformed version of the HTML document. Thus, accessibility assessment was made possible for these two different environments. The framework had an architecture which was compliant with WCAG 2.0.

UNIFIED WEBSITE ACCESSIBILITY ASSESSMENT (UWAA) FRAMEWORK

Within the scope of this study, a Unified Web Accessibility Assessment (UWAA) Framework and its software application was developed by integrating automated and expert-based evaluation approaches for website accessibility evaluation. The design and development phases of the Unified Website Accessibility Assessment (UWAA) Framework are shown in Figure 1. During the literature review phase, the guidelines used for evaluating web accessibility, various accessibility evaluation approaches and studies were examined. The details of this review were presented in previous sections. In the second phase which was the design of the accessibility assessment framework, accessibility assessment approaches were determined, and the basis of the framework was formulated based on the findings of the literature review phase. The next phase was the development of the UWAA Framework software in which the architectural design of the software as well as its implementation was finalized. In the evaluation phase, which is the last phase, the proposed framework was used in the accessibility assessment of the websites and the results obtained from the assessment were reported.

Figure 1. Research design

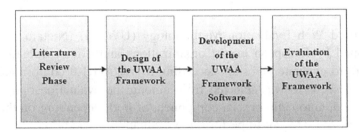

Design of the UWAA Framework

In order to design and develop the Unified Web Accessibility Assessment (UWAA) Framework and its software application, various automated evaluation tools listed on WAI's website (W3, 2016) were examined. The AChecker (AChecker, 2011) automated assessment tool has been determined to be integrated in the framework from the tools listed because it controls websites' accessibility in accordance with WCAG 2.0 guidelines and offers a free web service infrastructure for compliance checking. In addition, based on the literature review it was seen that it was also used in many studies (Acosta-Vargas, Acosta, et al., 2018b; Adepoju & Shehu, 2014; Ahmi & Mohamad, 2015.; Akgül, 2017; Alahmadi & Drew, 2017; Ismail & Kuppusamy, 2018; Ismailova & Inal, 2018; Kamal et al., 2016; Kurt, 2017). For the expert-based evaluation, the Barrier Walkthrough (BW) (Brajnik, 2011) method was integrated in the study. The BW method has been chosen because it is based on the interpretation of accessibility guidelines in the context of general scenarios for certain types of users and includes controls that are important to specified disabled users and provides solutions for the accessibility problems. Although 9 different types of disabled users are defined in the BW method, 3 types of disabled users, which are only related to visual impairments, were included in the UWAA framework proposed in the study. This study has focused on the visually impaired users (visually impaired, low vision and color blind users) due to the high number of people with visual impairments worldwide (Bourne et al., 2017). UWAA framework design that integrated Achecker as an automated method and BW as an expert-based method can be seen in Figure 2.

Figure 2. Unified Web Accessibility Assessment (UWAA) framework design

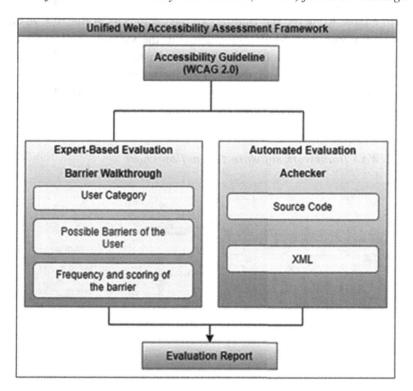

By using the two approaches together within this UWAA framework, it was aimed to highlight the positive aspects and advantages while reducing the weaknesses of different assessment approaches. In addition, it was aimed to present a more detailed evaluation result, to increase the accuracy of the data, and to give the user the opportunity to make detailed and objective analysis. Integration of the BW method as the expert-based evaluation method would provide to identify the controls that cannot be analyzed in most of the automated evaluation tools so the accessibility evaluation capacity would increase.

Components and System Architecture
of UWAA Framework Software

The requirements of the system and its components were analyzed to implement the UWAA framework software. The process flow of the software can be seen in Figure 3. There are two types of users, the administrator, and the evaluator, were defined in the system. Administrator should define the web site to be assessed in the system and the tasks that will be used by the evaluators during the evaluation process. The evaluations can be done by one or more evaluators in the system so the system will enable to merge the findings of the evaluators at the end. In addition, the assessment period should also be defined in the system. Evaluators can both run an automated evaluation and conduct a manual assessment by BW method steps defined in the system. At the end, they can get the results separately or they can get integrated. Finally, it is ensured that the evaluators are provided with suggestions for the actions to be taken to prevent accessibility problems detected.

Figure 3. UWAA framework software system flow chart

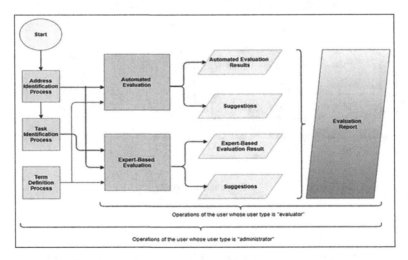

Multiple and different technologies were used for the development of the software. System interfaces that enable users to evaluate were developed with HTML, ColdFusion, JavaScript and CSS. MSSQL database management system was used for database operations. System architecture of UWAA Framework software can be seen in Figure 4.

Figure 4. UWAA framework system architecture

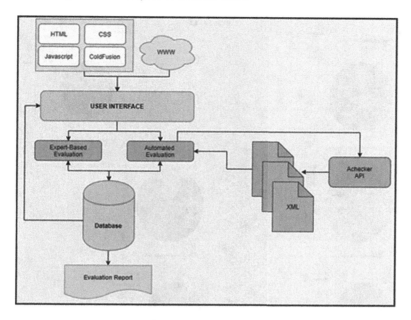

The framework consists of two main components which are for AChecker based automated evaluation and BW-based expert evaluation the automated evaluation component integrated the web service (API) provided by the AChecker automated assessment tool. The XML data communication standard was used to exchange data from the API application of the Achecker. The results gathered from AChecker are analyzed on the developed system and are recorded in the relevant tables in the system database.

In the scope of the UWAA Framework software, required interfaces and infrastructure were created to define the website address, the tasks and the barrier type to be needed for the implementation of BW method. Thus, an evaluator can implement the BW method through the framework software. An evaluator can manually assess the website according to the controls provided by the system and records the frequency and severity of the problems. The results obtained from both evaluation methods are matched according to WCAG 2.0 accessibility guideline. In addition to the list of problems determined, their possible solutions can also be provided to the evaluators through an evaluation report delivered by the application. An example interface for evaluation report can be seen in Figure 5. All the information regarding WCAG 2.0 and BW method were defined in the database of the system both in English and Turkish so the software supports both languages.

Figure 5. Sample interface for the report page of the UWAA Framework software

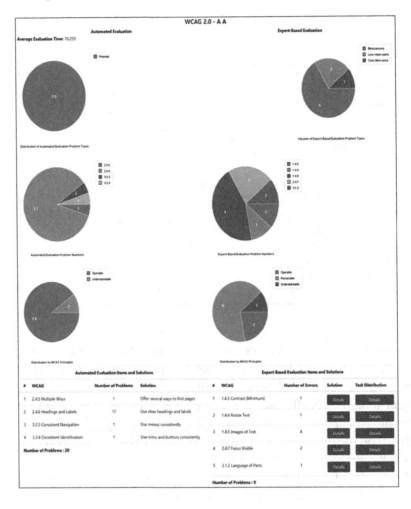

UWAA Framework Evaluation

With the aim of examining the use of the UWAA framework and software for accessibility assessments of websites, three websites were identified, and accessibility assessments were carried out. Three different university websites have been selected to be evaluated according to increasing number of accessibility problems (Yerlikaya & Onay Durdu, 2017). The websites were sorted according to the increasing accessibility problems and divided into 3 categories as the sites containing few, medium and many errors and a random example from each category was selected as can be seen in Table 4.

Table 4. University websites that were determined for the UWAA framework evaluation

#	University Code	Error Range
1	U1	0-15
2	U2	16-25
3	U3	26-35

Three basic tasks that can be performed on a university website which do not require any authorization were determined for the implementation of BW method to conduct this evaluation. These tasks were as follows

Task 1: Go to the Student Affairs Information System login page.
Task 2: View the academic calendar.
Task 3: Go to the University library web page.

Evaluations were conducted for the three types of disabilities (visually impaired, low vision and color-blind users) defined in the system. BW-based expert evaluation was conducted by a single evaluator. In the BW evaluation, "NV Access" (NV Access, 2020) screen reader program, which is one of the assistive technologies used by the visually impaired users, was used while performing the necessary controls.

RESULTS

Automated and expert-based accessibility assessments of 3 university websites were conducted through the UWAA Framework software developed within the scope of the study. The results obtained are examined under six sub-headings as follows, the total number of accessibility problems of the universities, the distribution of accessibility problems according to WCAG accessibility levels and BW user types, detailed distribution of accessibility problems according to accessibility guidelines, detailed distribution of accessibility problems according to accessibility principles, detailed distribution of accessibility problems according to BW user types and suggestions to fix the determined accessibility problems.

Total Number of Accessibility Problems of the Universities

According to the evaluation results gathered with automated and BW based expert evaluation components of the UWAA framework, total number of accessibility problems of universities are presented in Figure 6. The highest accessibility problems including all A, AA and AAA levels were determined on U2's web site with 849 problems and the lowest on U1's web site with 305 problems by the automated evaluation. On the other hand, according to BW based expert evaluation U3 has the highest number or problems (181) while U1 has the lowest number (74).

Figure 6. Total number of accessibility problems gathered with automated and expert based evaluation components of the UWAA framework

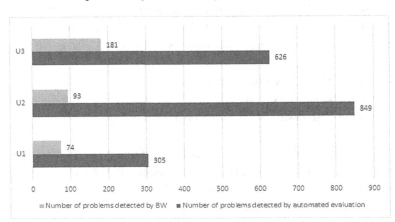

The Distribution of the Number of Accessibility Problems According to WCAG Levels and BW User Types

The distribution of accessibility problems of the three university websites evaluated according to the accessibility levels is presented in Figure 7. With this analysis, it is aimed to examine the status of websites on accessibility in detail in terms of three levels of the guidelines (WCAG-A, WCAG-AA and WCAG-AAA). When the distribution of problems according to the WCAG 2.0 accessibility guideline levels was examined, it was seen that the problems were more concentrated in the "WCAG-A" accessibility level in both automated and BW evaluation. Level A contains items that a website must meet at a minimum in terms of accessibility. Thus, it has been determined that the three university websites have critical inadequacies in accessibility.

The distribution of the accessibility problems of each university along with the tasks and the types of users was analyzed. Thus, it was aimed to determine that the tasks performed with the BW method revealed more problems for each user type for each university. When Figure 8 was examined; it could be seen that U3 had most problems for visually impaired users while U2 had most problems for low-vision users for the task 1 which required to go to student affairs information system login page. In contrast, U1 and U3 had the same number of problems for color-blind users for this task. For Task-2, which required viewing the academic calendar, U3 website contained more problems for the visually impaired users while both U2 and U3 websites had the same number of problems for low-vision users. Furthermore, U1 website had more problems for color blind users. For Task-3, which required to go to the library web page, U3 website had more problems for visually impaired users. On the other hand, U2 website had more problems for users with low vision. Compared to other websites, more problems were detected on the U1 website for color blind users.

Figure 7. The distribution of accessibility problems according to WCAG levels

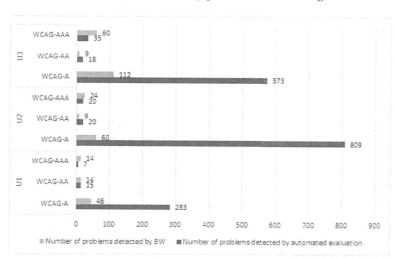

The Detailed Distribution of Accessibility Problems According to Accessibility Guidelines

In the scope of the accessibility evaluation, the accessibility problems of the web pages were also analyzed according to the accessibility guidelines. The distribution of problems revealed by both automated evaluation and BW according to WCAG is given separately in Table 5. The most common problems determined with both evaluation methods on these three university websites were WCAG-1.1.1 non-text content, WCAG-1.3.1 information and relationships, WCAG-1.4.1 use of color, WCAG-2.4.1 bypass blocks, WCAG-1.4.3 contrast and WCAG-2.4.10 section headings show intensity in the control items.

Figure 8. The distribution of accessibility problems according to BW user types

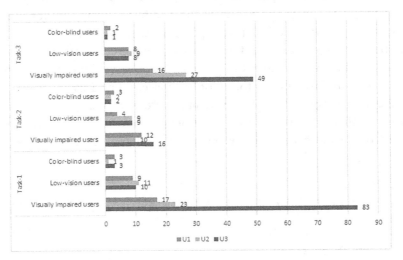

Table 5. The distribution of accessibility problems according to accessibility principles

WCAG #	WCAG Definition	U1		U2		U3	
		AE	BWE	AE	BWE	AE	BWE
WCAG-1.1.1	Non-text Content	4	7	3	8	71	29
WCAG-1.2.1	Audio-only and Video-only (Pre-recorded)	-	-	-	-	-	1
WCAG-1.2.2	Captions (Pre-recorded)	-	-	-	-	-	1
WCAG-1.2.3	Audio Description or Media Alternative (Pre-recorded)	-	-	-	-	-	1
WCAG-1.3.1	Information and Relationships	3	4	5	5	8	4
WCAG-1.3.2	Meaningful Sequence	-	-	-	2	-	3
WCAG-1.3.3	Sensory Characteristics	1	-	1	-	2	-
WCAG-1.4.1	Use of Colour	4	6	59	5	96	15
WCAG-2.1.1	Keyboard	-	7	8	10	38	20
WCAG-2.1.2	No Keyboard Trap	-	3	-	3	-	4
WCAG-2.2.2	Pause, Stop, Hide	-	3	-	6	-	6
WCAG-2.3.1	Three Flashes or Below	-	-	8	-	38	-
WCAG-2.4.1	Bypass Blocks	2	6	2	7	3	4
WCAG-2.4.2	Page Titled	1	2	1	1	1	-
WCAG-2.4.3	Focus Order	-	-	-	-	-	1
WCAG-2.4.4	Link Purpose (In Context)	268	-	722	4	304	16
WCAG-3.1.1	Language of Page	-	3	-	1	-	1

continues on following page

Table 5. Continued

WCAG #	WCAG Definition	U1		U2		U3	
		AE	BWE	AE	BWE	AE	BWE
WCAG-3.3.1	Error Identification	-	-	-	-	2	-
WCAG-3.3.2	Labels or Instructions	-	-	-	-	10	-
WCAG-4.1.2	Name, Role, Value	-	5	-	8	-	6
WCAG-1.2.4	Captions (Live)	-	-	-	-	-	1
WCAG-1.2.5	Audio Description (Pre-recorded)	-	-	-	-	-	1
WCAG-1.4.3	Contrast (Minimum)	-	3	-	1	-	3
WCAG-1.4.4	Resize Text	-	2	-	1	-	1
WCAG-1.4.5	Images of Text	-	3	-	4	-	1
WCAG-2.4.5	Multiple Ways	1	-	1	-	2	-
WCAG-2.4.6	Headings and Labels	11	-	17	-	4	-
WCAG-2.4.7	Focus Visible	-	3	-	2	-	1
WCAG-3.1.2	Language of Parts	1	3	-	1	-	1
WCAG-3.2.3	Consistent Navigation	1	-	1	-	4	-
WCAG-3.2.4	Consistent Identification	1	-	1	-	2	-
WCAG-3.3.3	Error Suggestion	-	-	-	-	2	-
WCAG-3.3.4	Error Prevention (Legal, Financial, Data)	-	-	-	-	4	-
WCAG-1.2.7	Extended Audio description (Pre-recorded)	-	-	-	-	-	1
WCAG-1.2.8	Media Alternative (Pre-recorded)	-	-	-	-	-	1
WCAG-1.2.9	Audio Only (Live)	-	-	-	-	-	1
WCAG-1.4.6	Contrast (Enhanced)	2	3	15	1	25	3
WCAG-2.1.3	Keyboard (No Exception)	-	7	-	10	-	20
WCAG-2.4.10	Section Headings	1	4	1	9	2	18
WCAG-2.4.8	Location	1	-	1	-	2	-
WCAG-2.4.9	Link Purpose (Link Only)	-	-	-	4	-	16
WCAG-3.1.3	Unusual words	1	-	1	-	2	-
WCAG-3.1.4	Abbreviations	2	-	2	-	4	-
	Total Problems	305	74	849	93	626	181

The Distribution of the Number of Accessibility Problems According to Accessibility Principles

There are four principles defined for making web content accessible in WCAG. These principles are listed as perceivable, operable, understandable and robust. Figure 9 presents the distribution of the number of accessibility problems according to these four accessibility principles. The principle that the most problems were detected was the principle of being "operable" whereas the principle that the least problems were detected was being "robust" for all three universities.

Figure 9. The distribution of accessibility problems according to accessibility principles

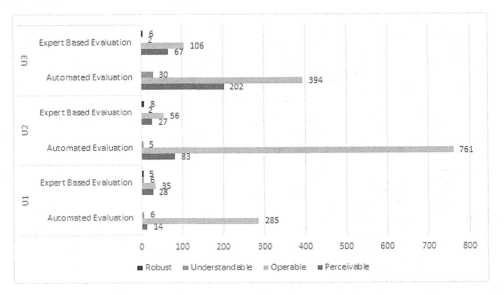

The Detailed Distribution of Accessibility Problems According to BW User Types

The accessibility problems which were determined by BW method are examined in detail according to the user types and the controlled BW items. Table 6 presents the barriers that are important for visually impaired users and the total frequency of problems related to these items on each of the university websites. As a result of the evaluation, the control items where the most problems were detected for the visually impaired users were as follows; VI-11 mouse events, VI-1 rich images

156

lacking equivalent text, VI-12 opaque objects, VI-14 too many links, and VI-6 image maps with no text.

Barriers checked for low-vision (LV) users and their frequencies on these university websites are listed in Table 7. Mostly detected control items were LV-8 having too many links and LV-10 having no keyboard shortcuts.

Table 6. The detailed distribution of accessibility problems according to visually impaired (VI) user type

#	Control	U1	U2	U3	Total
VI-1	Rich images lacking equivalent text	3	3	9	15
VI-2	Video with no captions			1	1
VI-3	Color is necessary		2	10	12
VI-4	Inaccessible frames			5	5
VI-5	Moving content	1	3	3	7
VI-6	Image maps with no text		2	10	12
VI-7	Functional images lacking text		2		2
VI-8	Generic links		2	8	10
VI-9	Ambiguous links		2	8	10
VI-	Dynamic menus in JavaScript	3	3	4	10
VI-11	Mouse events	2	3	15	20
VI-12	Opaque objects	3	1	10	14
VI-13	keyboard traps	3	3	4	10
VI-14	Too many links	2	4	8	14
VI-15	Forms with no LABEL tags	3	2	1	6
VI-16	Forms that are badly linearized			1	1
VI-17	Page without titles	2	1		3
VI-18	Frame without title		1	1	2
VI-19	Language markup	3	1	1	5
VI-20	No page headings	1	1	1	3
VI-21	Images used as titles	1	1		2
VI-22	No keyboard shortcuts		3	6	9
VI-23	Skip links not implemented	3	3	2	8
VI-24	Window without browser controls	1			1

Table 7. The detailed distribution of accessibility problems according to low-vision (LV) user type

#	Control	U1	U2	U3	Total
LV-1	Rich images that are badly positioned		2	2	4
LV-2	Rich images included in the page background	1		1	2
LV-3	Color is necessary	2	1	3	6
LV-4	Insufficient visual contrast	1		1	2
LV-5	Moving content	2	3	3	8
LV-6	Functional images lacking text	1			1
LV-7	Dynamic menus in JavaScript	2	4	1	7
LV-8	Too many links	1	4	9	14
LV-9	Images used as titles	1	1	1	3
LV-10	No keyboard shortcuts		3	6	9
LV-11	Text cannot be resized	1	1		2
LV-12	Inflexible page layout	1		1	2
LV-13	Skip links not implemented	3	3	1	7
LV-14	Window without browser controls	1			1

Finally, barriers for color-blind users and their frequencies on these university websites are listed in Table 8. Control item "CB-1 color is necessary" was detected more than "CB-2 insufficient visual contrast" especially on U1 website.

Table 8. The detailed distribution of accessibility problems according to color-blind (CB) user type

#	Control	U1	U2	U3	Total
CB-1	Color is necessary	4	2	2	8
CB-2	Insufficient visual contrast	2	1	2	5

Suggestions to Fix the Determined Accessibility Problems

The frequent accessibility problems determined by both methods were generally related to WCAG items of non-textual content, information, and relations, use of color, passing of blocks, contrast (increased) and section headings. Suggestions to fix these problems were provided from BW method as can be seen in Table 9. Main suggestions can be summarized as providing textual alternatives of the contents, information and their elations should be provided to be understandable by disabled users, attention should be given to use of color and contrast, provide better organizations by reducing the number of links or using appropriate section headings.

Table 9. Suggestions to fix the determined accessibility problems regarding WCAG items, visually impaired (VI), low vision (LV) and color-blind (CB) users' problems

Item #	Fix Suggestions
WCAG-1.1.1	Textual alternatives of the content used on the website should be given
WCAG-1.3.1	Page structure should be designed in such a way that disabled users can understand and use
WCAG-1.4.1	Attention should be paid to the use of colors to distinguish the contents or understand them correctly.
WCAG-2.4.1	It should be enabled that repeated content can be bypassed
WCAG-1.4.3	Text and visual elements should have appropriate contrast values
WCAG-2.4.10	Section headers should be used to organize the content
VI-1	Add an equivalent textual description to the image
VI-6	Add a textual description of the destination of each clickable region.
VI-11	Use also logical event handlers ("onfocus", "onkeypress", ...) in addition to mouse-oriented ones.
VI-12	Make sure the object is accessible (for example, follow the Flash guidelines); or remove it.
VI-14	Reduce the number of links in the page. If this is not possible then organize them properly into groups. Implement the groups with proper tags
LV-8	Reduce the number of links in the page. If this is not possible then organize them properly into groups. Implement the groups with proper tags
LV-10	For the controls which are repeated on many pages and when, from the users' perspective it is worthwhile to learn keyboard shortcuts for such controls
CB-1	Use redundant means to distinguish between two information items.
CB-2	Remove any background image or change them so that they could never interfere with perception and interpretation of the foreground content.

CONCLUSION

This study proposes the Unified Web Accessibility Assessment (UWAA) Framework which integrates more than one accessibility evaluation approach to conduct website accessibility assessments, and which provides suggestions to the determined problems. Besides, its supporting software that enables evaluators to conduct their assessments and to gather accessibility reports is developed. The UWAA framework integrates AChecker tool as automated evaluation component and Barrier Walkthrough (BW) method as expert-based assessment method. Consequently, it supports evaluators to conduct more comprehensive accessibility assessments conveniently since it highlights the advantages and reduces the weaknesses of both methods. The software enables the evaluators to conduct both type of evaluation on single software platform and provides them accessibility evaluation reports and correction suggestions. With the developed software, the evaluation results of both methods are matched with WCAG 2.0. Thus, it is possible to compare and analyze the results obtained from both methods. Previously there was not any supporting software for the implementation of BW method. It is believed that these features of the framework would provide convenience to evaluators. Furthermore, the framework and its software also support both English and Turkish.

The UWAA framework and its supporting software was used to evaluate the accessibility of three universities' websites and gathered accessibility evaluation results were reported and analyzed in detail in the study as well. Determined accessibility evaluation results especially the BW results were in line with the previous study (Yerlikaya & Onay Durdu, 2017). The frequent accessibility problems determined by both methods were generally related to WCAG 2.0 items of non-textual content, information, and relations, use of color, passing of blocks, contrast (increased) and section headings. Therefore, it was seen that both methods were complementary to each other and provided richer analysis. When the determined accessibility problems were analyzed with respect to accessibility principles it was seen that the problems were generally related to operability principle. The proposed UWAA framework provides more detailed analysis as well as recovery suggestion than previously proposed frameworks (Fernandes et al., 2011). Furthermore, it has been demonstrated that problems which cannot be determined by the automated evaluation tool, but which can be detected by an expert can also be identified by BW method.

LIMITATIONS AND FUTURE WORKS

There were several constraints and limitations to be mentioned on the study. The major limitation of the study was that the developed software mainly depends on the AChecker web service for its automated evaluation component. It will be a great advantage to design and integrate an application specific automated evaluation module in the future studies to overcome this limitation.

Another limitation of the study was related with the implementation of only three user types determined by the BW since it has nine user types. These three user types which were related with visual impairments were selected primarily since these were the most common disability types. However, it is necessary to include all user types in the framework in future studies to ensure that the UWAA framework reaches a significant level in accessibility assessment.

Moreover, the evaluation of the UWAA framework was conducted by only one evaluator. Evaluation with more than one expert should be provided. Thus, the deficiencies of the developed framework can be detected more easily. Besides, the use of UWAA framework could be used for the evaluation of other types of websites other than university web sites.

REFERENCES

Abascal, J., Arrue, M., Fajardo, I., Garay, N., & Tomás, J. (2004). The use of guidelines to automatically verify Web accessibility. *Universal Access in the Information Society*, *3*(1), 71–79. doi:10.100710209-003-0069-3

Acart Communications. (2017). *WCAG Contrast Checker*. https://contrastchecker.com/

AccessN. V. (2020). *NV Access*. https://www.nvaccess.org/

Achecker. (2011). *IDI Web Accessibility Checker: Web Accessibility Checker*. https://achecker.ca/checker/index.php

Acosta-Vargas, P., Acosta, T., & Luján-Mora, S. (2018a). Challenges to assess accessibility in Higher Education websites: A Comparative study of Latin America Universities. *IEEE Access: Practical Innovations, Open Solutions*, *6*, 36500–36508. doi:10.1109/ACCESS.2018.2848978

Acosta-Vargas, P., Hidalgo, P., Acosta-Vargas, G., Gonzalez, M., Guaña-Moya, J., & Salvador-Acosta, B. (2020). Challenges and improvements in website accessibility for health services. *International Conference on Intelligent Human Systems Integration*, 875-881. 10.1007/978-3-030-39512-4_134

Acosta-Vargas, P., Luján-Mora, S., Acosta, T., & Salvador-Ullauri, L. (2018b). Toward a combined method for evaluation of web accessibility. *International Conference on Information Theoretic Security*, 602-613. 10.1007/978-3-319-73450-7_57

Acosta-Vargas, P., Luján-Mora, S., & Salvador-Ullauri, L. (2016). Evaluation of the web accessibility of higher-education websites. *15th International Conference on Information Technology Based Higher Education and Training (ITHET)*, 1-6. 10.1109/ITHET.2016.7760703

Adepoju, S. A., & Shehu, I. S. (2014b). Usability evaluation of academic websites using automated tools. *2014 3rd International Conference on User Science and Engineering (i-USEr)*, 186-191. 10.1109/IUSER.2014.7002700

Ahmi, A., & Mohamad, R. (2015). Web accessibility of the Malaysian public university websites. *International Conference on E-Commerce (ICoEC) 2015.*

Akgül, Y. (2017). The most violated WCAG 1.0 guidelines by the developers of university websites in Turkey. *2017 12th Iberian Conference on Information Systems and Technologies (CISTI)*, 1-7.

Al-Khalifa, H. S. (2012a). *WCAG 2.0 Semi-automatic Accessibility Evaluation System: Design.* Academic Press.

Alahmadi, T., & Drew, S. (2016). An evaluation of the accessibility of top-ranking university websites: Accessibility rates from 2005 to 2015. *DEANZ Biennial Conference*, 224-233.

Alahmadi, T., & Drew, S. (2017). An evaluation of the accessibility of top-ranking university websites: Accessibility rates from 2005 to 2015. *Journal of Open, Flexible, and Distance Learning*, *21*(1), 7–24.

Alexender, D. (2006). Usability and accessibility: Best friends or worst enemies. *Proceedings of the 13th VALA Biennial Conference and Exhibition.*

Arch, A. (2009). Web accessibility for older users: Successes and opportunities (keynote). *Proceedings of the 2009 International Cross-Disciplinary Conference on Web Accessibility (W4A)*, 1-6. 10.1145/1535654.1535655

Aziz, M. A., Isa, W. A. R. W. M., & Nordin, N. (2010). Assessing the accessibility and usability of Malaysia Higher Education Website. *International Conference on User Science and Engineering (i-USEr)*, 203-208. 10.1109/IUSER.2010.5716752

Bourne, R. R. A., Flaxman, S. R., Braithwaite, T., Cicinelli, M. V., Das, A., Jonas, J. B., Keeffe, J., Kempen, J. H., Leasher, J., Limburg, H., Naidoo, K., Pesudovs, K., Resnikoff, S., Silvester, A., Stevens, G. A., Tahhan, N., Wong, T. Y., Taylor, H. R., Bourne, R., ... Zheng, Y. (2017). Magnitude, temporal trends, and projections of the global prevalence of blindness and distance and near vision impairment: A systematic review and meta-analysis. *The Lancet. Global Health*, *5*(9), e888–e897. doi:10.1016/S2214-109X(17)30293-0 PMID:28779882

Braga, H., Pereira, L. S., Ferreira, S. B. L., & Da Silveira, D. S. (2014). Applying the barrier walkthrough method: Going beyond the automatic evaluation of accessibility. *Procedia Computer Science*, *27*, 471–480. doi:10.1016/j.procs.2014.02.051

Brajnik, G. (2008). A comparative test of web accessibility evaluation methods. *Proceedings of the 10th international ACM SIGACCESS conference on Computers and accessibility*, 113-120. 10.1145/1414471.1414494

Brajnik, G. (2011). *Barrier walkthrough*. https://users.dimi.uniud.it/~giorgio.brajnik/projects/bw/bw.html

Brajnik, G., Yesilada, Y., & Harper, S. (2009). Guideline aggregation: Web accessibility evaluation for older users. *Proceedings of the 2009 International Cross-Disciplinary Conference on Web Accessibility (W4A)*, 127-135. 10.1145/1535654.1535686

Brajnik, G., Yesilada, Y., & Harper, S. (2011). Web accessibility guideline aggregation for older users and its validation. *Universal Access in the Information Society*, *10*(4), 403–423. doi:10.100710209-011-0220-5

Cojocar, G. S., & Guran, A. M. (2013). Evaluation of Romanian Academic Websites Accessibility: A Case Study. *Studia Universitatis Babes-Bolyai. Informatica*, *58*(4).

Digital 2019: Global Internet Use Accelerates. (2019). *We Are Social*. https://wearesocial.com/blog/2019/01/digital-2019-global-internet-use-accelerates

Eusébio, C., Silveiro, A., & Teixeira, L. (2020). Website accessibility of travel agents: An evaluation using web diagnostic tools. *Journal of Accessibility and Design for All*, *10*(2), 180–208.

Fernandes, N., Lopes, R., & Carriço, L. (2011). An architecture for multiple web accessibility evaluation environments. *International Conference on Universal Access in Human-Computer Interaction*, 206-214. 10.1007/978-3-642-21672-5_23

Harper, K. A., & DeWaters, J. (2008). A quest for website accessibility in higher education institutions. *The Internet and Higher Education*, *11*(3-4), 160–164. doi:10.1016/j.iheduc.2008.06.007

Hashemian, B. J. (2011). Analyzing web accessibility in Finnish higher education. *ACM SIGACCESS Accessibility and Computing*, *101*(101), 8–16. doi:10.1145/2047473.2047475

Henry, S. L. (2002). Another–ability: Accessibility primer for usability specialists. *UPA 2002, the Usability Professionals' Association Annual Conference*.

Henry, S. L., Abou-Zahra, S., & Brewer, J. (2014). The role of accessibility in a universal web. *Proceedings of the 11th Web for all Conference*, 1-4. 10.1145/2596695.2596719

Ismail, A., & Kuppusamy, K. S. (2018a). Accessibility of Indian universities' homepages: An exploratory study. *Journal of King Saud University-Computer and Information Sciences, 30*(2), 268–278. doi:10.1016/j.jksuci.2016.06.006

Ismail, A., Kuppusamy, K. S., & Paiva, S. (2019). Accessibility analysis of higher education institution websites of Portugal. *Universal Access in the Information Society,* ●●●, 1–16. doi:10.100710209-019-00653-2

Ismailova, R., & Inal, Y. (2018). Accessibility evaluation of top university websites: A comparative study of Kyrgyzstan, Azerbaijan, Kazakhstan, and Turkey. *Universal Access in the Information Society, 17*(2), 437–445. doi:10.100710209-017-0541-0

Ismailova, R., & Kimsanova, G. (2017). Universities of the Kyrgyz Republic on the Web: Accessibility and usability. *Universal Access in the Information Society, 16*(4), 1017–1025. doi:10.100710209-016-0481-0

ISO. (2008). *ISO 9241-20. (2008), Ergonomics of human-system interaction—Part 20: Accessibility guidelines for information/communication technology (ICT) equipment and services.* https://www.iso.org/obp/ui/#iso:std:iso:9241:-20:ed-1:v1:en:en/

ISO. (2019). *ISO 9241-210. (2019). Ergonomics of Human-System Interaction — Part 210: Human-Centred Design for Interactive Systems.* https://www.iso.org/cms/render/live/en/sites/isoorg/contents/data/standard/07/75/77520.html

Iwarsson, S., & Staahl, A. (2003). Accessibility, usability, and universal design—Positioning and definition of concepts describing person-environment relationships. *Disability and Rehabilitation, 25*(2), 57–66. doi:10.1080/dre.25.2.57.66 PMID:12554380

Kamal, I. W., Alsmadi, I. M., Wahsheh, H. A., & Al-Kabi, M. N. (2016a). Evaluating web accessibility metrics for Jordanian universities. *International Journal of Advanced Computer Science and Applications, 7*(7), 113–122.

KAMİS. (n.d.). *Erişilebilirlik nedir?* https://kamis.gov.tr/erisebilirlik-nedir/

Kane, S. K., Shulman, J. A., Shockley, T. J., & Ladner, R. E. (2007). A web accessibility report card for top international university web sites. *Proceedings of the 2007 international cross-disciplinary conference on Web accessibility (W4A),* 148-156. 10.1145/1243441.1243472

Kesswani, N., & Kumar, S. (2016). Accessibility analysis of websites of educational institutions. *Perspectives in Science, 8*, 210–212. doi:10.1016/j.pisc.2016.04.031

Król, K., & Zdonek, D. (2020). Local Government Website Accessibility—Evidence from Poland. *Administrative Sciences, 10*(2), 22. doi:10.3390/admsci10020022

Kurt, S. (2017a). Accessibility of Turkish university Web sites. *Universal Access in the Information Society, 16*(2), 505–515. doi:10.100710209-016-0468-x

Laux, L. (1998). Designing Web pages and applications for people with disabilities. Human Factors and Web Development, 87-95.

Ma, H.-Y. T., & Zaphiris, P. (2003). *The usability and content accessibility of the e-government in the UK*. Lawrence Erlbaum.

Mcguire, J. M., Scott, S. S., & Shaw, S. F. (2006). Universal design and its applications in educational environments. *Remedial and Special Education, 27*(3), 166–175. doi:10.1177/07419325060270030501

Nietzio, A., Strobbe, C., & Velleman, E. (2008). The unified Web evaluation methodology (UWEM) 1.2 for WCAG 1.0. *International Conference on Computers for Handicapped Persons*, 394-401. 10.1007/978-3-540-70540-6_57

PowerMapper. (2015). *Website Error Checker: Accessibility & Link Checker—SortSite*. https://www.powermapper.com/products/sortsite/

Shneiderman, B. (2000). Universal Usability. *Communications of the ACM, 43*(5), 84–91. doi:10.1145/332833.332843

Teixeira, P., Eusébio, C., & Teixeira, L. (2021). How diverse is hotel website accessibility? A study in the central region of Portugal using web diagnostic tools. *Tourism and Hospitality Research*, 14673584211022796.

Thatcher, J., Lauke, P. H., Waddell, C., Henry, S. L., Lawson, B., Lawson, B., Heilmann, C., Burks, M. R., Regan, B., & Rutter, R. (2006). *Web accessibility: Web standards and regulatory compliance*. Apress.

Thompson, T., Burgstahler, S., & Comden, D. (2003). Research on web accessibility in higher education. *Journal of Information Technology and Disabilities, 9*(2).

US Access Board. (2000). *Section 508 Standards—United States Access Board*. Section 508 Standards for Electronic and Information Technology. https://www.access-board.gov/guidelines-and-standards/communications-and-it/about-the-section-508-standards/section-508-standards

W3. (2016). *Web Accessibility Evaluation Tools List*. https://www.w3.org/WAI/ER/tools/

W3C. (1999). *Web Content Accessibility Guidelines 1.0*. https://www.w3.org/TR/WCAG10/

W3C. (2008). *Web Content Accessibility Guidelines (WCAG) 2.0.* https://www. w3.org/TR/WCAG20/

W3C. (2018). *Web Content Accessibility Guidelines (WCAG) 2.1.* https://www. w3.org/TR/WCAG21/

W3C. (2020). *Internet Live Stats—Internet Usage & Social Media Statistics.* https:// www.internetlivestats.com/

W3C. (n.d.). *World Wide Web Consortium (W3C).* https://www.w3.org/

W3C_WAI. (2005a). *Authoring Tool Accessibility Guidelines (ATAG) Overview.* Web Accessibility Initiative (WAI). https://www.w3.org/WAI/standards-guidelines/atag/

W3C_WAI. (2005b). *User Agent Accessibility Guidelines (UAAG) Overview.* Web Accessibility Initiative (WAI). https://www.w3.org/WAI/standards-guidelines/uaag/

W3C_WAI. (2016). *Accessibility, Usability, and Inclusion. Accessibility, Usability, and Inclusion, Web Accessibility Initiative (WAI).* https://www.w3.org/WAI/ fundamentals/accessibility-usability-inclusion/

W3C_WAI. (2019a). *Introduction to Web Accessibility.* https://www.w3.org/WAI/ fundamentals/accessibility-intro/

WAI. (n.d.). *Web Accessibility Initiative (WAI).* https://www.w3.org/WAI/

Windriyani, P., Ferdiana, R., & Najib, W. (2014). Accessibility evaluation using WCAG 2.0 guidelines webometrics-based assessment criteria (case study: Sebelas Maret University). *2014 International Conference on ICT for Smart Society (ICISS),* 305-311. 10.1109/ICTSS.2014.7013192

Yerlikaya, Z., & Onay Durdu, P. (2017). Evaluation of Accessibility of University Websites: A Case from Turkey. *International Conference on Human-Computer Interaction,* 663-668. 10.1007/978-3-319-58753-0_94

Yesilada, Y., Brajnik, G., & Harper, S. (2009). How much does expertise matter? A barrier walkthrough study with experts and non-experts. *Proceedings of the 11th International ACM SIGACCESS Conference on computers and accessibility,* 203-210.

Yesilada, Y., Brajnik, G., Vigo, M., & Harper, S. (2012). Understanding web accessibility and its drivers. *Proceedings of the international cross-disciplinary conference on web accessibility,* 1-9.

Yesilada, Y., Chuter, A., & Henry, S. L. (2013). *Shared web experiences: Barriers common to mobile device users and people with disabilities.* http://www.w3.org/WAI

Zaphiris, P., & Ellis, R. D. (2001). Website usability and content accessibility of the top USA universities. *Proceedings of WebNet 2001 World Conference on the WWW and Internet (WebNet)*, 1380-1385.

ADDITIONAL READING

Abascal, J., Arrue, M., Fajardo, I., Garay, N., & Tomás, J. (2004). The use of guidelines to automatically verify Web accessibility. *Universal Access in the Information Society*, *3*(1), 71–79. doi:10.100710209-003-0069-3

Braga, H., Pereira, L. S., Ferreira, S. B. L., & Da Silveira, D. S. (2014). Applying the barrier walkthrough method: Going beyond the automatic evaluation of accessibility. *Procedia Computer Science*, *27*, 471–480. doi:10.1016/j.procs.2014.02.051

Brajnik, G. (2008). A comparative test of web accessibility evaluation methods. *Proceedings of the 10th International ACM SIGACCESS Conference on Computers and Accessibility*, 113–120. 10.1145/1414471.1414494

Brajnik, G. (2011). *Barrier walkthrough*. https://users.dimi.uniud.it/~giorgio.brajnik/projects/bw/bw.html

Fernandes, N., Lopes, R., & Carriço, L. (2011). An architecture for multiple web accessibility evaluation environments. *International Conference on Universal Access in Human-Computer Interaction*, 206–214. 10.1007/978-3-642-21672-5_23

Harper, K. A., & DeWaters, J. (2008). A quest for website accessibility in higher education institutions. *The Internet and Higher Education*, *11*(3–4), 160–164. doi:10.1016/j.iheduc.2008.06.007

Nietzio, A., Strobbe, C., & Velleman, E. (2008). The unified Web evaluation methodology (UWEM) 1.2 for WCAG 1.0. *International Conference on Computers for Handicapped Persons*, 394–401. 10.1007/978-3-540-70540-6_57

Yesilada, Y., Brajnik, G., & Harper, S. (2009). How much does expertise matter? A barrier walkthrough study with experts and non-experts. *Proceedings of the 11th International ACM SIGACCESS Conference on Computers and Accessibility*, 203–210.

Yesilada, Y., Brajnik, G., Vigo, M., & Harper, S. (2012). Understanding web accessibility and its drivers. *Proceedings of the International Cross-Disciplinary Conference on Web Accessibility*, 1–9.

Yesilada, Y., Chuter, A., & Henry, S. L. (2013). Shared web experiences: Barriers common to mobile device users and people with disabilities. *W3C Web Accessibility Initiative.* Http://Www. W3. Org/WAI

KEY TERMS AND DEFINITIONS

Automated Accessibility Evaluation: Automated evaluation is an evaluation carried out with software tools which are developed to assess websites compliance with accessibility rules or standards.

Barrier: Any condition that prevents user from reaching his/her goals on a website.

Barrier Walkthrough: An expert-based accessibility evaluation method similar to heuristic evaluation and that uses barriers defined for disabled people for evaluation.

Expert-Based Accessibility Evaluation: Expert-based (manual) evaluation is a method in which web pages are evaluated in terms of some accessibility criteria by experts.

User Tests: Accessibility evaluations which are conducted with disabled users while performing a series of individual tasks on a website.

Web Content Accessibility Guidelines (WCAG): General guideline that defines the accessibility criteria that a website should comply with.

Website Accessibility: The quality of being perceived, understood, and easily used by all people.

Chapter 7
Accessibility Evaluation of Turkish E-Commerce Websites

Yakup Akgül

 https://orcid.org/0000-0001-5344-4359
Alanya Alaaddin Keykubat University, Turkey

ABSTRACT

Disabled people encounter many barriers while attempting to access the services on the web. E-commerce websites have been also intensively and widely used. The e-commerce market in Turkey will hit TL 400 billion by 2021. It also evaluates the accessibility of 10 popular Turkish e-commerce websites using five accessibility testing tools, namely Achecker, TAW, Eval Access, MAUVE, and FAE. This research has found that most accessibility guidelines are covered by A checker tool. Navigation, readability, input assistance, and timing are the common found accessibility problems while assessing the accessibility of the targeted websites.

INTRODUCTION

An e-commerce website is the central way an e-retailer communicates with their online consumers. E-retailer seeks to provide positive online purchasing experiences for online consumers of all ages. A website design encourages or discourages a consumer's online purchasing intentions (Cyr et al., 2015). In the context of business-to-consumer (B2C) e-commerce, website design features have different effects on forming consumers' trust and distrust (Ou and Sia, 2010). In particular, B2C websites those are accessible content, information and easy to navigate influences consumer trust to buy online and must appeal to consumers (Cyr, 2013; Éthier et al., 2008). However, online shopping websites need to be accessible to all consumers of all

DOI: 10.4018/978-1-7998-7848-3.ch007

ages, including those with disabilities. For-example, nowadays dynamic websites content (CSS—Cascading Style Sheets, Flash and JavaScript, etc.) are used in most of the e-commerce websites to provide a good visual presentation to attract or retain consumer.

Though, these dynamic webpages are inaccessible to disabled people, such as visual impaired person, since screen readers are not adept of handling it. Many researchers such as (King et al., 2004; Power and Jürgensen, 2010) have revealed dynamic contents using Flash animation, JavaScript, and graphic links etc. is a threat to web accessibility. The inability to shop online because of such interfaces increases web inaccessibility of e-commerce websites for people with disabilities. People with disabilities have limitations for going shopping, which put them at inconvenience because of their physical handicap. However, Internet has opened new possibilities of online shopping. In particular, disabled people can gain a sense of emotional stability by online shopping. However, if e-commerce websites are inaccessible, consumers with disabilities do not have the equal access they are guaranteed by law. Many online consumers may have various types of disabilities, such as sensory (hearing and vision), motor (limited use of hands) and cognitive (language and learning disabilities) impairments. An accessible web site can utilize all of assistive technologies such as screen readers, voice recognition, alternative pointing devices, alternate keyboards, and the website displays (Lazar et al., 2004). Even though these technologies can help people with disabilities, webpage navigation, conveying image and flash-based content are some of the serious issues for people with disabilities. Web accessibility is an important element in the design of e-commerce websites (Lazar and Sears, 2006; Sohaib and Kang, 2013). Therefore, there is a serious need of web accessibility in B2C e-commerce websites for user of all ages and in particular for people with disabilities such as sensory (hearing and vision), motor (limited use of hands) and cognitive (language and learning disabilities) impairments.

The combination of technology and people in human computer interaction is a vital part of modern society that enables a wide range of economic benefits. In particular, the emerging growth of business-to-consumer (B2C) e-commerce allows everyone to put up his or her own business online, locally or globally. Lazar and Sears (2006), the authors discussed that web accessibility should receive attention in e-commerce websites. The B2C website provides the consumers with instant online access to products without physical barriers. In order to get the most out of revenue from online trade, businesses must focus on an accessible B2C e-commerce website, which should also give a real and convenient shopping experience for consumers of all ages. In particular, people with disabilities, such as color blindness.

Because of the Internet availability, online shops provide consumer the ease of buying and selling products. However, the required web technological infrastructure is either insufficient or does not exist in terms of web accessibility guidelines. For that reason, the Web Content Accessibility Guidelines (WCAG 2.0) developed by the World Wide Web Consortium (W3C) help to make the website accessible for users of all ages and with disabilities such as colour blindness, deaf users, and age related vision problems. Therefore, the purpose of this study is to evaluate Turkish B2C e-commerce website accessibility for consumers with disabilities in particular.

Human-computer interaction is growing more popular and widespread these days; technology has made it simple to communicate with others via gadgets. In addition, the internet makes it easier to obtain information, communicate, read a book or the news, get a job, or even start a new business. Accessing the internet is not difficult for most people, but it is for those with impairments. Understanding user needs and preferences is one of the most important factors in boosting customer happiness and attracting customers, including handicapped individuals, by providing them with helpful and useful approaches. These approaches must be able to dynamically scale to the users' talents, skills, and requirements. Web accessibility seeks to enable handicapped individuals to use the internet in the same way that everyone else. It is unavoidable for every organization to adopt such tactics in order to keep up with its peers.

Many technologies have been created to assess the accessibility of online pages. These tools provide assessment reports that are intended to assist in the detection of problems and the provision of warnings in order to create an accessible website. The Internet has become a need for all users, regardless of skill. As a result, solutions have been developed to assist persons with specific requirements in using the internet. Websites of all types are required to be accessible, and they will be considered accessible if they fulfill web accessibility standards and regulations. This section covers the tools that handicapped people use to access the Internet. It also looks at the methods that are commonly used to determine how accessible the internet is. It also examines a variety of current research on web accessibility, as well as their results and conclusions.

ACCESSIBILITY TOOLS USED TO HELP DISABLED USERS

Despite the fact that handicapped individuals encounter several obstacles when accessing the internet, there are numerous ways in which their access to the internet could be improved. Browsers that don't enable expanding text or displaying photos without an alternate text, for example, are among the most prevalent issues that prevent people from using the internet (Paciello, 2000). Furthermore, colors have been employed to attract surfers, however this is a disadvantage for colorblind users, who are considered disabled, because putting text on a colored backdrop might cause problems for individuals who have trouble detecting colors (W3C, 2016).

Assistive technologies and adaptive strategies are the two main approaches for interacting with the web. The former refers to any hardware or software can improve disable users while interacting with the web. It includes screen readers, magnifiers and voice recognition. The latter includes the techniques which disabled users use while surfing the internet. These techniques are meant to help and improve the interaction of disabled users and the web such as mouse speed control, increasing text size or turning on captions (W3C, 2016a).

In reality, style sheets provide a helpful service to the colorblind by allowing them to substitute their own style sheets for the original style sheets, which takes very little effort. A handful of websites also employ high or low contrast to make navigation easier (W3C, 2016b).

The visually impaired have used a variety of adaptive technologies, such as a big display that allows them to magnify text. Fonts may be shown using screen expanding software and browsers like Internet Explorer. In addition to these technologies, some operating systems, such as Windows, allow you to raise the size of your text. Furthermore, there is a technique known as screen magnification, which was created to magnify the web so that those who have trouble focusing may read more readily (Paciello, 2000). Even modern technology like mobile phones and tablets include accessibility features that make it easier for individuals with disabilities to use the phone or the Internet. Some of the more widely utilized technologies are briefly described below to show some of the techniques that have been used by the impaired while accessing the web. The webpage is interpreted by a screen reader using voice synthesis. This has a distinct advantage: when it encounters a picture on the site, it reads an alternate text if one is available. Many people who have impaired vision or blindness have utilized it.

Furthermore, speech browsers, screen augmentation software, and text browsers such as Lynx are also popular methods to access the internet (Paciello, 2000). A screen reader can deliver information in two ways: through voice or through Braille. A screen reader converts on-screen information into speech that may be heard through speakers using a Text-To-Speech (TTS) engine. A TTS might be a software application that comes with the screen reader or a hardware device that connects to the computer.

Screen readers can also provide information in Braille in addition to spoken feedback. This necessitates the use of an external hardware device known as a refreshable Braille display. One or more rows of cells make up a refreshable Braille display. Every cell may be framed as a Braille character, which is a sequence of dots with a pattern similar to domino dots. The Braille letters on the presentation change when the data on the PC screen changes, providing refreshable data specifically from the PC. There are many screen readers available, including JAWS from Freedom Scientific, Window Eyes from GW Micro, or Thunder from Screenreader.net (AFB,

2015). A lot of programs and technologies, such as JAWS, are not free to use. Screen readers, on the other hand, are already included in most mobile operating systems. The navigation of the screen reader is the sole distinction between desktop and mobile accessibility testing. Where mobile screen readers may be connected using a Bluetooth keyboard or even specialized finger movements, keyboard shortcuts are necessary for desktop navigation (W3C, 2016c). Another method is to utilize a special browser that can distinguish the structure of your page, to the extent that it has one, and communicate the information to the user in a meaningful way (AFB, 2015a).

The screen magnification system enlarges text and images on a computer screen, and this is the final approach. It's stored in the computer's memory and works like a magnifying glass, traveling over a page, following the cursor, and magnifying the area around it. A client puts the pointer on the screen's segment to be magnified or has the cursor move organically across over and down a magnified page at a predefined pace using a mouse or console instructions. Screen magnification can be used in combination with screen readers (Gowases, et al., 2011). MAGic is a screen magnification and screen reading solution for low vision and visually impaired computer users.

MAGic can help users work more efficiently with business applications, documents, email, navigating the Internet, and engaging in social networking (Anon, 2015).

Nevertheless, proper web accessibility design guidelines were not presented to Retinitis Pigmentosa (RP) patients. Therefore, it can be concluded that visually impaired users are less beneficial from the web than the normal users (Kim et al., 2016). It can be seen that although different tools have been developed, some of the disabled users may not be able to utilize it due to their inability.

TOOLS USED FOR WEB ACCESSIBILITY EVALUATION

In general, there are a large variety of tools available for assessing web pages. Automatic tools such as Bobby and the W3C HTML Validation Tool are more in-depth. Manual evaluation methods based on comparing the web with accessibility standards are also available (W3C, 2016). However, automated methods have significant drawbacks in that they are not always capable of identifying all of the challenges that handicapped users may have, whereas manual evaluation is subjective and error-prone (Al-Khalifa 2012; W3C, 2016). This section will go over the necessity of using accessibility tools and look at a few different accessibility assessment tools.

A number of accessibility principles, such as the Web Content Accessibility Guidelines (WCAG), can assist designers in creating an accessible web page. In fact, all of the guidelines have checkpoints that help designers choose where an aid should be used (W3C, 2016d). Reports are also provided by assessment tools, which show the outcome of any evaluation, and some of them provide a grade to the website. The World Wide Web Consortium (W3C) categorized these tools into three categories: general, targeted, and services (W3C, 2016e). Some programs can also check for ALT text in images and ensure that HTML and links are correct.

To assess the accessibility of websites, a variety of professional tools are available. These tools are often used by Web developers. Some have been around for almost a decade (Kirchner, 2002). Some of the most popular automatic accessibility evaluation tools are AChecker (2016), 508 Checker (2016), Evaluera (2016), AccessMonitor (2016), Access Lint (2016), Cynthia Says (2016), SortSite (2016),WAVE —Web Accessibility Evaluation Tool (2016), Eval Access 2.0 (2016) and some others with similar features. These tools apply algorithms to analyse and detect accessibility errors in Web code.

There is a variety of tools that may be used to determine if a web page is accessible, and the W3C has suggested a few of them. Achecker is a semi-automated internet tool. It analyzes HTML pages using the BITV 1.0 standard. It is not possible for it to analyze all of the recommendations automatically. It generates three categories of errors: known, likely, and possible. It follows the worldwide accessibility criteria WCGA1.0 and WCGA2.0 (Elkabani et al., 2015; W3C, 2016f). WAVE is a collection of tools that are supposed to help with online accessibility testing by visualizing accessibility problems on the target page. It produces colored outcomes. Errors are indicated by the color yellow. It neither provides repair outcomes nor displays the guidelines that have been implemented (Elkabani et al., 2015; W3C, 2016f). TAW is a free utility that comes in two languages: English and Spanish. It evaluates the proposed website against the Web Content Accessibility Guidelines (WCAG). Elkabani et al., 2015; W3C, 2015) create three sorts of outcomes: issues, warnings, and not reviewed (Elkabani et al., 2015; W3C, 2016f). Cynthia claims that software is one of the publicly accessible tools that may be used to put up a certain web page that complies with W3C standards. This gives you the option of deciding on the level of accessibility for visually impaired people. Human judgment is also necessary, because some accessibility criteria cannot be established by automated methods alone (Akgül and Vatansever, 2016).

MAUVE (Multiguideline Accessibility Usability Validation Environment) is an accessibility testing environment. Its goal is to check both HTML and CSS, and it can even validate dynamic pages using plugins for specific browsers (W3C, 2016f). Furthermore, EvalAccess is an online accessibility evaluation tool that uses the W3C's WCAG 1.0 to automatically assess the accessibility of web sites (Aizpurua et al., 2011). The Functional Accessibility Evaluation (FAE) evaluates a website's compliance with the WCAG 2.0 Level A and AA criteria. It also includes a comprehensive report on the tests (W3C, 2016f).

RELATED WORK OF WEB ACCESSIBILITY EVALUATION

The importance of online accessibility standards in e-commerce has long been recognized (Bernard and Makienko, 2011; Sohaib and Kang, 2012). "As public and private organizations increasingly rely on web-based technologies for online commerce, information, and service delivery, they must develop policies to ensure that all users have complete access to web content" (Ou and Sia, 2010), and proposes a web accessibility model to benefit all public organizations and private businesses. As noted in Park and Ban (2010), "e-commerce sites lose up to 50% of potential online sales because users cannot find what they want". In Maswera et al., (2005), the authors analysed usability and accessibility errors of African e-commerce websites compared to Europe using an automated tools. In Maswera et al., (2009), the authors recommend putting their own accessibility guidelines for African countries to ensure accessibility for all users.

During their Web interaction, blind individuals frequently feel dissatisfaction. Five such difficulties were identified by Lazar et al. (2007): uncertainty caused by page layout and screen reader feedback; conflict between screen reader and program; poorly designed and/or labelled forms; and no inclusion of alternate language in photos. as well as issues with unclear hyperlinks, inaccessible PDF, and screen reader malfunctions.

In the study by Power et al. (2012), it was discovered that the WCAG 2.0 covered "50.4 percent of the issues faced by users." "16.7 percent of websites adopted strategies specified in WCAG 2.0, however the techniques did not fix the difficulties," according to the research. As a result, following the W3C–WCAG standards alone is insufficient to ensure accessibility (Power et al., 2012). Furthermore, because automatic evaluation tools only verify guidelines using HTML tags (Takagi et al., 2003), they were ineffective as a stand-alone tool for doing a full accessibility and usability assessment.

All evaluation approaches are thought to have strengths and limitations; nevertheless, using various integrated methods for identifying accessibility and usability problems impacting blind people, as outlined by Mankoff et al.,(2005) we may identify a maximum set of difficulties. Another important aspect that regard ensuring accessibility and usability in Web interaction by blind users is the appropriate functioning of the screen reader software.

Because of its application in Web interaction, screen readers are considered a helpful technology created for blind people. The program is capable of deciphering HTML code and reading it aloud (with a synthesized voice). The interaction may be done with either a regular keyboard or a Braille keyboard. The W3C–WCAG 2.0 has particular requirements for this technology; nevertheless, it only ensures "technical readability," i.e., if screen readers work. The standards do not specify if a website is "accessible" to blind users, that is, whether blind people can use it successfully (Di Blas et al., 2004).

According to the majority of research, websites adhere to the WCAG 2.0 guidelines at a minimum. However, other studies show that individuals with disabilities in a particular location continue to encounter barriers to inclusion in society alongside those without disabilities (Akgül and Vatansever, 2016). A lot of studies have looked at web accessibility in various ways, using a variety of techniques to assess web accessibility. The guidelines for accessibility are compiled and utilized in the evaluation. The major focus of this research was on evaluating e-government websites. In Saudi Arabia and Oman, the website's progress was reviewed. One of the assessment techniques was the United Nations e-government phases model. During the research period, eight Saudi ministries did not have an internet presence. Only 13 Saudi ministries have an internet presence, according to the report (Abanumy et al., 2005). They conducted a five-stage assessment. The selected websites were tested at each level, with the findings failing to satisfy accessibility norms and requirements. Bobby, a well-known commercial online tool, was also utilized by the writers to evaluate the websites. The process of evaluating these government websites, (13 from Saudi Arabia and 14 ministries' sites from Oman), showed that none of these websites conform to all priority1 checkpoints, which means that one or more groups will find it difficult to access information on these websites (Abanumy et al., 2005).

With other elements like as content, navigation, and speed, accessibility is regarded one of the success determinants for E-business. For virtual market needs, it has been a crucial success element (Hernández et al., 2009). It has also been linked to other important aspects in the development of successful e-commerce websites (Rababah and Masoud, 2010).

Studies have repeatedly found accessibility issues in a range of fields, including education sites (Akgül, 2017; Akgül, 2021; Fichten et al., 2009), corporate sites (Cappel and Huang, 2007; Gilbertson and Machin, 2012; Loiacono et al., 2009), e-commerce sites (Bose and Jürgensen, 2014; Gonçalves et al., 2018; Harrison and Petrie, 2007; Hasan and Morris, 2017; Isa et al., 2011; Lazar et al., 2012; Sohaib and Kang, 2017), the airline industry (Gutierrez et al., 2005), MOOCs (Akgül, 2018; Akgül, 2018a), banking websites (Akgül, 2018; Akgül, 2018b) and, of course, e-government sites at the national, state, and local levels (Akgül and Vatansever, 2016; Akgül, 2019; Akgül, 2016; Akgül, 2016a; Akgül, 2015; Al-Khalifa, 2012, Galvez and Youngblood, 2016; Olalere and Lazar, 2011; Youngblood and Mackiewicz, 2012; Youngblood and Youngblood, 2013; Yu and Parmanto, 2011).

Despite the fact that e-commerce is rapidly increasing, it is clear from recent research that measuring the accessibility of Turkish e-commerce has not been explored or studied. Turkey's e-commerce sector, for example, is expected to reach

$11.5 billion by 2019. In addition, while evaluating the accessibility of e-commerce websites, a variety of automated techniques should be utilized to provide more trustworthy findings. Therefore this study utilised a number of popular accessibility automated accessibility tools.

RESEARCH METHODOLOGY

Questionnaires, behavioral observation tools, and online accessibility evaluation automation tools are some of the techniques that may be used to assess the accessibility of a website. The structural and content evaluations are among them. This study evaluated the accessibility of e-commerce websites in Turkey using a variety of free accessibility evaluation tools. AChecker, TAW, SortSite, Multiguideline accessibility and usability validation environment (MAUVE), and Functional Assessment Evaluation 2.0 are the technologies that were used (FAE). This many tools are used to provide more accurate findings and expose more accessibility problems. Each tool looks at the website in question using a set of criteria. Table 1 compares various tools in terms of how they handle submission methods and the accessibility guidelines referenced.

Homepages of the Turkish e-commerce websites have been tested. MİGROS SANAL MARKET, HEPSİBURADA, SAHİBİNDEN, GİTTİGİDİYOR, YEMEKSEPETİ, ETSTUR, TRENDYOL, GRUPANYA, N11, and LETGO have all been identified as prominent Turkish e-commerce websites. Before the testing, a variety of procedures were followed. These websites were examined for their functioning, size, and resemblance. There are other Turkish e-commerce websites have been excluded due to the limit of this study or there may some parts under contractions or has a limited size.

RESULTS AND ANALYSIS

While testing the accessibility of the targeted websites in each tool, a number of issues, warnings, and errors were discovered. The outcomes are shown in Table 1. The term "AChecker" refers to the number of "known issues" discovered during automated testing. Such well-known accessibility issues are expected to be resolved. The existence of "Likely Problems" and "Potential Errors" has been revealed. Further research has been conducted to determine whether sorts of accessibility issues exist on the ten websites. HEPSİBURADA and YEMEKSEPETİ sites for which the tool displayed the error message as the tool was restricted by the robot.txt for analyzing.

Table 1. Accessibility tools and accessibility issues for each website

Tool	Criteria	1	2	3	4	5	6	7	8	9	10
Achecker	Known Problems	0	0	0	16	52	363	26	364	8	2
	Likely Problems	0	0	0	4	0	0	0	0	0	0
	Potential Problems	26	5	110	476	238	492	942	689	1347	7
TAW	Problems	1171	N/A	37	184	N/A	151	147	161	112	
	Warning	296	N/A	105	273	N/A	220	266	256	340	
	Not Reviewed	17	N/A	15	18	N/A	16	17	16	17	
SortSite	Level A	0	24	15	27	11	25	5	10	21	0
	Level AA	1	7	3	7	2	6	2	2	5	1
	Level AAA	0	3	1	4	3	4	1	1	3	0
MAUVE	Errors	242	138	108	47665	15	16	18	20	19	15
	Warnings	409	58	1	12738	2	3	2	4	2	2
FAE	Violations	6	22	9	23	11	26	11	10		12
	Warnings	4	5	1	5	2	3	4	3		3
	Manual checks	33	34	28	33	32	35	35	30		30
	Passed	23	11	14	18	23	18	19	10		22

Note: MİGROS SANAL MARKET=1, HEPSİBURADA=2, SAHİBİNDEN=3, GİTTİGİDİYOR=4, YEMEKSEPETİ=5, ETSTUR=6, TRENDYOL=7, GRUPANYA=8, N11=9, LETGO=10

Achecker has also automatically detected navigation, readability, and input help. Because it looks to be difficult, navigation has been noted as a common accessibility difficulty. Users are not always given a clear indicator (Orji, 2010). In addition, recognized or potential accessibility issues include the absence of suitable labels and instructions on data entry forms, as well as difficulties navigating when confronted with new or inconsistent terminology. Achecker is one of the top accessibility tools. According to a research done by Akgül (2021).

The offered reason for their assertion (Akgül, 2021) was that most accessibility standards are addressed by the Achecker tool. Despite the lack of professional evaluation, the results obtained using "Achecker" in this study are valuable. The TAW tool has identified a number of accessibility issues and warnings. The major accessibility requirements of perceivable, operable, and understandable should be either updated or evaluated depending on TAW findings for all three websites. For example, if the web page headers are not properly organized, screen readers will be unable to accurately recognize and interpret these headings. Some portions, on the other hand, passed the assessment tests since they correctly identified every online connection. In addition, the assessment test looked at the pages to see if they were useable when scripts or applets were not supported or turned off, and this page passed. SortSite also provides intriguing and useful findings, with the targeted websites scoring nearly identically in terms of issues and warnings discovered. Labels and instructions on data entry forms that are more suitable might be seen as warnings for the targeted websites. In the case of visually challenged individuals, it's particularly critical that the emphasis has enough contrast and can be clearly identified. MAUVE discovered a slew of problems and warnings. The findings are mostly for visually challenged people, with improved contrast between text and backdrop colors possible. A major accessibility issue with carousels and slideshows is a lack of controls, which, together with color contrast and alt text difficulties, is a widespread accessibility issue. The three websites targeted by FAE also yielded similar findings. It performed better in terms of timeliness, however it was noted that loading time should be taken into account because it appeared to be an issue while evaluating government websites (Al-Khalifa, 2012).

GENERAL REMARKS, RECOMMENDATIONS AND LIMITATIONS

Designers should consult extensively and examine the various elements that will assist them in creating genuinely accessible web pages in order to create an accessible web. Despite the numerous challenges that disabled users are likely to encounter when using the targeted websites, designers should be able to offer web pages to all users without difficulty. The notion of flexibility is the most crucial component of creating an accessible website in this regard. Designing for different sorts of browsers is one factor that designers should think about (Akgül and Vatansever, 2016; Akgül, 2021). Because Flash and Adobe Acrobat are less accessible than HTML, the latter is suggested (Orji, 2010). Although there are a range of impairments that affect web accessibility (Akgül and Vatansever, 2016; Akgül, 2021), adopting web standards is the best approach to develop an accessible web. There are criteria that make pages accessible for the visually impaired, according to the official accessibility guidelines, such as relying on language rather than just on colours, "providing equivalent alternatives to auditory and visual content" (W3C, 2016g), using markup and style sheets, and designing for device-independence. This has been highly recommended for web accessibility (Semaan et al., 2013). When all of the formal standards are followed, online pages should become considerably more accessible (W3C, 2016g). Other ways to increase accessibility include eliminating tiny text and providing an alternate text for each image on the page, as discovered while testing the targeted websites. These would encourage active involvement and should not offer significant challenges to designers, given the rapid rate of progress in this field. Furthermore, utilizing and arranging lists and tables is a key component of making online pages easier to access. Due to the fact that visually impaired people cannot read as quickly as those who are completely sighted, auto-refreshing is not suggested. Furthermore, the language level should be intelligible, and the site navigation should be simple to navigate between pages (Paciello, 2000). In this study, as well as previous studies such as (Akgül, 2019), navigation was identified as one of the most significant accessibility difficulties. Keeping websites simple is a fundamental need for excellent design (Nielsen, 1999). Headings, colors, and links are actually among the most important factors that designers should consider. Making headers more visible can make a big difference for visually impaired people. Because the latter is a barrier to the visually impaired, fully identifying every links is preferable than just saying "click here." (W3C, 2016c). Colors have a detrimental impact on color-blind people, despite their primary function of enhancing online sites. There are a few flaws in this study. For starters, it uses solely automated tools, despite the fact that five were utilized. It is not always possible to discover accessibility problems automatically. For a compensative review, it's best to enlist the help of an expert. Secondly. Because there are so many Turkish e-commerce websites, the results cannot be generalized. This research sought to look into 10 well-known ones. A number of the study's conclusions might lead to more research. For the same website, differing findings from different accessibility tools may be worth investigating to justify these disparities. The influence of e-commerce websites' accessibility difficulties on consumers' decisions might provide more useful information.

CONCLUSION

A variety of technologies that aid handicapped users have been covered, along with brief examinations of the techniques that are commonly used to assess the Web's accessibility. The study's objectives were reviewed in order to determine the accessibility of chosen Turkish e-commerce websites. In this study, five different accessibility tools were used. The findings reveal that the targeted websites have a variety of accessibility problems. This research also indicated that Achecker covers the majority of accessibility standards. Furthermore, while evaluating the accessibility of the targeted websites, navigation, readability, input help, and timeliness are the most commonly discovered accessibility issues. These difficulties are likely to be encountered by handicapped users. This document also includes a series of suggestions based on the study's findings. Expert participation is recommended for additional study and a compensatory evaluation. Furthermore, because there are numerous Turkish e-commerce websites and this study is confined to 10 e-commerce websites, the results obtained cannot be generalized. For the same website, different findings from different accessibility tools may be worth investigating to justify these disparities.

REFERENCES

Abanumy, A., Al-Badi, A., & Mayhew, P. (2005). e-Government Website accessibility: In-depth evaluation of Saudi Arabia and Oman. *The Electronic. Journal of E-Government*, *3*(3), 99–106.

Access Monitor. (2016). https://www.acessibilidade.gov.pt/accessmonitor/

Accesslint. (2016). http://accesslint.com

AChecker web accessibility checker. (2016). http://achecker.ca

AFB.org. (2015). *Screen Magnification Systems—Browse by Category—American Foundation*. Author.

AFB.org. (2015a). *The Visually Impaired Web User's Technology—American Foundation for the Blind*. https://www.afb.org/info/accessibility/creating-accessible-websites/the-users-technology/235

Aizpurua, A., Arrue, M., Vigo, M., & Abascal, J. (2011). Validating the effectiveness of EvalAccess when deploying WCAG 2.0 tests. *Universal Access in the Information Society*, *10*(4), 425–441.

Akgül, Y. (2015). Web content accessibility of municipal web sites in Turkey. In *European Conference on Digital Government* (p. 1). Academic Conferences International Limited.

Akgül, Y. (2016). Quality evaluation of E-government websites of Turkey. In *2016 11th Iberian conference on information systems and technologies (CISTI)* (pp. 1-7). IEEE.

Akgül, Y. (2016a). Web site accessibility, quality and vulnerability assessment: A survey of government web sites in the Turkish republic. *Journal of Information Systems Engineering & Management*, *1*(4), 50.

Akgül, Y. (2017). The most violated WCAG 1.0 guidelines by the developers of university websites in Turkey. In *2017 12th Iberian Conference on Information Systems and Technologies (CISTI)* (pp. 1-7). IEEE.

Akgül, Y. (2018). Accessibility evaluation of MOOCs' websites of Turkey. *Journal of Life Economics*, *5*(4), 23–36.

Akgül, Y. (2018). Banking Websites in Turkey: an Accessibility, Usability and Security Evaluation. *İşletme Araştırmaları Dergisi*, *10*(1), 782-796.

Akgül, Y. (2018a). Web accessibility of MOOCs for elderly students: The case of Turkey. *Journal of Life Economics, 5*(4), 141–150.

Akgül, Y. (2018b). An Analysis of Customers' Acceptance of Internet Banking: An Integration of E-Trust and Service Quality to the TAM–The Case of Turkey. In *E-Manufacturing and E-Service Strategies in Contemporary Organizations* (pp. 154–198). IGI Global.

Akgül, Y. (2019). The accessibility, usability, quality and readability of Turkish state and local government websites an exploratory study. *International Journal of Electronic Government Research, 15*(1), 62–81.

Akgül, Y. (2021). Accessibility, usability, quality performance, and readability evaluation of university websites of Turkey: A comparative study of state and private universities. *Universal Access in the Information Society, 20*(1), 157–170.

Akgül, Y., & Vatansever, K. (2016). Web accessibility evaluation of government websites for people with disabilities in Turkey. *Journal of Advanced Management Science, 4*(3).

Al-Khalifa, H. S. (2012). The accessibility of Saudi Arabia government Web sites: An exploratory study. *Universal Access in the Information Society, 11*(2), 201–210.

Anon. (2015). http://www.freedomscientific.com/Products/LowVision/MAGic

Bernard, E. K., & Makienko, I. (2011). The effects of information privacy and online shopping experience in e-commerce. *Academy of Marketing Studies Journal, 15*, 97.

Bose, R., & Jürgensen, H. (2014). Accessibility of e-commerce websites for vision-impaired persons. In *International Conference on Computers for Handicapped Persons* (pp. 121-128). Springer.

Cappel, J. J., & Huang, Z. (2007). A usability analysis of company websites. *Journal of Computer Information Systems, 48*(1), 117–123.

Checker. (2016). http://www.508checker.com

Cynthiasays. (2016). http://www.cynthiasays.com

Cyr, D. (2013). Website design, trust and culture: An eight-country investigation. *Electronic Commerce Research and Applications, 12*(6), 373–385.

Cyr, D., Bonanni, C., Bowes, J., & Ilsever, J. (2005). Beyond trust: Web site design preferences across cultures. *Journal of Global Information Management, 13*(4), 25–54.

Di Blas, N., Paolini, P., & Speroni, M. (2004). Usable accessibility" to the Web for blind users. *Proceedings of 8th ERCIM Workshop: User Interfaces for All.*

Elkabani, I., Hamandi, L., Zantout, R., & Mansi, S. (2015, December). Toward better web accessibility. In *2015 5th International Conference on Information & Communication Technology and Accessibility (ICTA)* (pp. 1-6). IEEE.

Éthier, J., Hadaya, P., Talbot, J., & Cadieux, J. (2008). Interface design and emotions experienced on B2C Web sites: Empirical testing of a research model. *Computers in Human Behavior, 24*(6), 2771–2791.

EvalAccess. (2016). http://sipt07.si.ehu.es/evalaccess2/

Evaluera. (2016). http://www.evaluera.co.uk

Fichten, C. S., Ferraro, V., Asuncion, J. V., Chwojka, C., Barile, M., Nguyen, M. N., ... Wolforth, J. (2009). Disabilities and e-learning problems and solutions: An exploratory study. *Journal of Educational Technology & Society, 12*(4), 241–256.

Galvez, R. A., & Youngblood, N. E. (2016). e-Government in Rhode Island: What effects do templates have on usability, accessibility, and mobile readiness? *Universal Access in the Information Society, 15*(2), 281–296.

Gilbertson, T. D., & Machin, C. H. (2012). Guidelines, icons and marketable skills: an accessibility evaluation of 100 web development company homepages. In *Proceedings of the international cross-disciplinary conference on web accessibility* (pp. 1-4). Academic Press.

Gonçalves, R., Rocha, T., Martins, J., Branco, F., & Au-Yong-Oliveira, M. (2018). Evaluation of e-commerce websites accessibility and usability: An e-commerce platform analysis with the inclusion of blind users. *Universal Access in the Information Society, 17*(3), 567–583.

Gowases, T., Bednarik, R., & Tukiainen, M. (2011). Text highlighting improves user experience for reading with magnified displays. In CHI'11 Extended Abstracts on Human Factors in Computing Systems (pp. 1891-1896). ACM.

Gutierrez, C. F., Loucopoulos, C., & Reinsch, R. W. (2005). Disability-accessibility of airlines' Web sites for US reservations online. *Journal of Air Transport Management, 11*(4), 239–247.

Harrison, C., & Petrie, H. (2007). Severity of usability and accessibility problems in eCommerce and eGovernment websites. In *People and Computers XX—Engage* (pp. 255–262). Springer.

Hasan, L., & Morris, A. (2017). Usability problem areas on key international and key Arab E-commerce websites. *Journal of Internet Commerce, 16*(1), 80–103.

Hernández, B., Jiménez, J., & Martín, M. J. (2009). Key website factors in e-business strategy. *International Journal of Information Management, 29*(5), 362–371.

Isa, W. A. R. W. M., Aziz, M. A., & Razak, M. R. B. A. (2011). Evaluating the accessibility of Small and Medium Enterprise (SME) websites in Malaysia. In *2011 International Conference on User Science and Engineering (i-USEr)* (pp. 135-140). IEEE.

Kim, W. J., Kim, I. K., Jeon, M. K., & Kim, J. (2016). UX Design guideline for health mobile application to improve accessibility for the visually impaired. In *2016 International Conference on Platform Technology and Service (PlatCon)* (pp. 1-5). IEEE.

King, A., Evans, G., & Blenkhorn, P. (2004). WebbIE: a web browser for visually impaired people. In *Proceedings of the 2nd Cambridge Workshop on Universal Access and Assistive Technology* (pp. 35-44). Academic Press.

Lazar, J., Allen, A., Kleinman, J., & Malarkey, C. (2007). What frustrates screen reader users on the web: A study of 100 blind users. *International Journal of Human-Computer Interaction, 22*(3), 247–269.

Lazar, J., Dudley-Sponaugle, A., & Greenidge, K. D. (2004). Improving web accessibility: A study of webmaster perceptions. *Computers in Human Behavior, 20*(2), 269–288.

Lazar, J., Olalere, A., & Wentz, B. (2012). Investigating the accessibility and usability of job application web sites for blind users. *Journal of Usability Studies, 7*(2), 68–87.

Lazar, J., & Sears, A. (2006). Design of E-Business Web Sites. Handbook of human factors and ergonomics, 1344-1363.

Loiacono, E. T., Romano, N. C. Jr, & McCoy, S. (2009). The state of corporate website accessibility. *Communications of the ACM, 52*(9), 128–132.

Mankoff, J., Fait, H., & Tran, T. (2005, April). Is your web page accessible? A comparative study of methods for assessing web page accessibility for the blind. In *Proceedings of the SIGCHI conference on Human factors in computing systems* (pp. 41-50). ACM.

Maswera, T., Dawson, R., & Edwards, J. (2005). Analysis of usability and accessibility errors of e-commerce websites of tourist organisations in four African countries. In ENTER (pp. 531-542). Academic Press.

Maswera, T., Edwards, J., & Dawson, R. (2009). Recommendations for e-commerce systems in the tourism industry of sub-Saharan Africa. *Telematics and Informatics*, *26*(1), 12–19.

Nielsen, J. (1999). *Designing Web Usability: The Practice of Simplicity New Riders*. Academic Press.

Olalere, A., & Lazar, J. (2011). Accessibility of US federal government home pages: Section 508 compliance and site accessibility statements. *Government Information Quarterly*, *28*(3), 303–309.

Orji, R. O. (2010). Analysis of Usability and Accessibility Problems of Financial Sectors' Website using Visitor-based Evaluation Technique. In *2nd International Conference on Information and Multimedia Technology (ICIMT 2010)* (pp. V1-252). Academic Press.

Ou, C. X., & Sia, C. L. (2010). Consumer trust and distrust: An issue of website design. *International Journal of Human-Computer Studies*, *68*(12), 913–934.

Paciello, M. (2000). *Web accessibility for people with disabilities*. CRC Press.

Park, H., & Ban, C. (2010). Implementation and evaluation of the on-line aptitude test system for people with visual impairment supporting web accessibility. *Disabil Employ*, *20*(1), 51–78.

Power, C., Freire, A., Petrie, H., & Swallow, D. (2012). Guidelines are only half of the story: accessibility problems encountered by blind users on the web. In *Proceedings of the SIGCHI conference on human factors in computing systems* (pp. 433-442). ACM.

Power, C., & Jürgensen, H. (2010). Accessible presentation of information for people with visual disabilities. *Universal Access in the Information Society*, *9*(2), 97–119.

Rababah, O. M. A., & Masoud, F. A. (2010). Key factors for developing a successful e-commerce website. *Communications of the IBIMA*.

Semaan, B., Tekli, J., Issa, Y. B., Tekli, G., & Chbeir, R. (2013, December). Toward enhancing web accessibility for blind users through the semantic web. In *2013 International Conference on Signal-Image Technology & Internet-Based Systems* (pp. 247-256). IEEE.

Sohaib, O., & Kang, K. (2012). The role of technology, human and social networks in serviceable cross-cultural B2C websites. *19th International Business Information Management Conference (IBIMA)*.

Sohaib, O., & Kang, K. (2013). The importance of web accessibility in business to-consumer (B2C) websites. In *22nd Australasian Software Engineering Conference (ASWEC 2013)* (pp. 1-11). Academic Press.

Sohaib, O., & Kang, K. (2017). E-commerce web accessibility for people with disabilities. In *Complexity in Information Systems Development* (pp. 87–100). Springer.

Sortsite. (2016). https://www.powermapper.com/products/sortsite

Takagi, H., Asakawa, C., Fukuda, K., & Maeda, J. (2003). Accessibility designer: visualizing usability for the blind. *ACM SIGACCESS Accessibility and Computing*, (77-78), 177-184.

W3C Org. (2016f). *Web Accessibility Evaluation Tools List*. http://www.w3.org/WAI/ER/tools/

W3C Org. (2016g). *Web Content Accessibility Guidelines*. http://www.w3.org/TR/WAI-WEBCONTENT

W3C.org. (2016). *Accessibility Evaluation Resources*. http://www.w3.org/WAI/eval/Overview.html

W3C.org. (2016a). *How People with Disabilities Use the Web: Overview*. http://www.w3.org/WAI/intro/people-use-web/

W3C.org. (2016b). *Style Sheets*. http://www.w3.org/TR/html4/present/styles.html

W3C.org. (2016c). *Accessibility*.http://www.w3.org/standards/webdesign/accessibility

W3C.org. (2016d). *Evaluation Tools*. http://www.w3.org/WAI/ER/existingtools.html

W3C.org. (2016e). *Evaluation, Repair, and Transformation Tools for Web Content Accessibility*. http://www.w3.org/WAI/ER/existingtools.html#Evaluation

WAVE Web accessibility evaluation tool. (2016). http://wave.webaim.org

Youngblood, N. E., & Mackiewicz, J. (2012). A usability analysis of municipal government website home pages in Alabama. *Government Information Quarterly*, *29*(4), 582–588.

Youngblood, N. E., & Youngblood, S. A. (2013). User experience and accessibility: An analysis of county web portals. *Journal of Usability Studies*, *9*(1).

Yu, D. X., & Parmanto, B. (2011). US state government websites demonstrate better in terms of accessibility compared to federal government and commercial websites. *Government Information Quarterly*, *28*(4), 484–490.

188

Chapter 8
Evaluation of the Accessibility of Elderly Individuals to Airline Company Websites:
Comparative Analysis With OWA, WASPAS, WSM, WPM

Aşkın Özdağoğlu
Dokuz Eylul University, Turkey

Murat Kemal Keleş
Keçiborlu Vocational School, Isparta University of Applied Sciences, Turkey

Barış Işıldak
Keçiborlu Vocational School, Isparta University of Applied Sciences, Turkey

ABSTRACT

Technological and social developments cause the birth and death rates to decrease. This has a direct effect on the increase in the rate of old age in the total population. In Turkey like in other countries, they face various problems in transportation in addition to education, health, justice, and social security. Therefore, the airline companies should provide some special services to elderly individuals in terms of accessibility and usability for their websites. This chapter aims to examine the accessibility of websites of airline companies for 65 and older individuals. Then, the second aim of this chapter is to determine the criteria for accessibility and alternatives. Then the next aim of this chapter is to determine the weights of these criteria and evaluate the alternatives with multi-criteria decision-making methods. The best airline company for airline website according to OWA, WASPAS, WSM, and WPM methods is Alternative 1.

DOI: 10.4018/978-1-7998-7848-3.ch008

INTRODUCTION

The transportation sector is effective in the development of activities in many fields in the world. When it is evaluated in terms of time, trust, and convenience, airway transportation is ahead of other types of transportation. (Akgüngör ve Demirel, 2004:424-427).

The aviation sector has reached an important level in the increase of intercontinental economic activities and the development and competitiveness of the countries. The aviation industry has led countries to a great change all over the world. The sector in the world has increased by 49% in terms of paid passenger-km since 2002. In Turkey, the airline industry has been evolved continuously. This development has reached important levels since 2003 and has led to the establishment of many private airline companies. In light of these developments, the civil aviation sector in Turkey has been one of the fastest-growing countries in the world in the last four years. (Turkish Airlines. Serial: XI No:29 Activity Report, 2011: 6, Access Date: 09.04.2020). As a result of these developments, the airline companies in the sector must continue to grow and follow the developments to survive in the competition.

In today's competitive world, airlines that want to gain an advantage should determine their service according to their access. Web sites of airlines are at the top of these services. Web sites have become an integral part of daily life and are used in many different areas from shopping to entertainment, communication to education.

Today, although the majority of internet users are young people, the number of older users is also considerably high. The elderly population is defined as the population aged 65 and over. The elderly population proportion in Turkey is projected to increase continuously. The proportion will be 10.2% in 2023, 16.3% in 2040, 22.6% in 2060 and 25.6% in 2080. (Disabled and Elderly Statistics Bulletin, Access Date: 22.04.2020). The majority of the elderly are interested in new technologies such as the Internet. Due to the difficulties of usage and designs made without considering the elderly population, the elderly cannot benefit from these new technologies sufficiently. This situation negatively affects the living standards and social lives of the elderly (Turper, 2008:1).

This chapter aims to examine airline firms' access to the elderly population to websites in Turkey. For this purpose, five major airline companies operating in Turkey have been analyzed with different criteria. Multicriteria Decision Making (MCDM) methods are the methods to sort and evaluate the alternatives according to the criteria after the criteria and alternatives are determined. (Özbek, 2019:178). Therefore, MCDM methods are appropriate for analyzing airline firms' web sites. OWA, WSM, WPM, and WASPAS methods have been used for analyzing web sites.

In this chapter, firstly, information about elderly web accessibility and airline web accessibility is given. Then, the OWA, WSM, WPM, and WASPAS methods, which are used in this study, are explained with mathematical notations. The literature review has been made for these methods. The evaluations of the airline companies' performances are made in the application section. The last part of this chapter shows the conclusion and recommendations.

ACCESSIBILITY

Accessibility means being easily accessible and available to any service, product, technology, or environment by anyone, including the disabled and the elderly. Internet page accessibility is defined as the mass of users that can access web pages, use them, and perceive page contents. In other words, websites should have design and content to appeal not only to a specific user group but also to different user groups such as disabled and elderly people. (KAMİS / Public Internet Sites Directory Project. Accessibility, 187, Access Date:15.04.2020).

Elderly Website Accessibility

The internet is a tool that allows people to easily access the information they want to have, as well as the communication they establish between each other. As a result of the widespread use of smartphones, nowadays, people can access the information they want to reach easily and quickly on the internet. Nowadays, companies focus on web pages. Web pages have created an environment for a store selling products more than a physical store. It is an effective network in terms of bringing a brand or person to the target audience that it cannot reach physically due to space and time constraints. In this sense, a brand, person, or business with a web page also offers the image that it is more advantageous or better in institutionalization than its competitors who do not have a web page in terms of presenting a professional image (Canöz, 2017:195).

In our age, the average human life is prolonged and the rate of the elderly population is increasing at an extraordinary rate all over the world. In contrast, despite the physical and spiritual changes they experience, the elderly continue their lives today as active and experienced individuals, not individuals disconnected from society. In this case, they are included in the segment that uses the developing internet and web pages. Although most of the internet users in the world are young people, there has been a great increase in the number of users over the age of fifty. Despite this increase, the elderly are not using the computer. The main reason for this situation is that the hardware, software, and especially the interfaces are not designed for them. However, well-designed communication and information technology systems will contribute greatly to increase the quality of life and independence of elderly people in society. (Turper, 2008:19-22). According to a study from household use of information technology in the years 2014-2018, the computer and internet usage of the elderly population aged 65-74 years in Turkey has been increasing. For example, while the computer usage rate was 5%, the internet usage rate was 5% in 2014. The computer usage rate increased to 8.5% and the internet usage rate to 17% in 2018. In the report in question, it was also stated that the computer and internet usage rates of men were higher in the 65-74 aged population compared to women. (Disabled and Elderly Statistics Bulletin, Access Date: 22.04.2020).

Due to the increasing importance of the subject, there are many studies on the internet access of the elderly in the national and international literature.

Akyazı (2018), conducted a study based on the criteria of an age-friendly website on e-commerce sites operating in Turkey for the elderly. As a result of the research, it was concluded that the deficiencies of the existing sites should be completed and designed according to them for elderly people to use them more easily.

Özer and Sarı (2018) have made a study to determine the use of information technology of the elderly. They find that the ergonomic design of the web pages will eliminate the concerns of use, expectations, and security for information technologies.

Akyazı and Kara (2017) conducted comparative analyzes of internet newspapers in terms of age-friendly website criteria. As a result of these analyzes, it was concluded that the newspapers included in the research were more careful about the access of elderly individuals and made web page designs suitable for them.

Ertürk et al. (2014), in their research on web accessibility of individuals with disabilities, concluded that awareness is critical for individuals with disabilities, and web sites should be made as much as possible for these individuals.

In the international literature; Alsaeedi (2020) conducted a study on web pages accessibility, Hassouna et al. (2020) examined web pages for individuals with disabilities and Aizpurua et al. (2016) conducted research on web accessibility based on user experience.

Airport Website Accessibility

Airway transportation has strategic importance in our country and the world. Air transportation has an important place, especially in tourism and trade. Air transportation develops countries socio-economically. Along with these developments, the number of airline companies increased in the 2000s. The usage of airline transportation has been widespread for people from all over the world. Today, the speed, comfort, and safety provided by airline transportation have an important place in people's preference for airline transportation. This is effective for people to use web pages of airline companies extensively.

The rapid development of information and internet technologies has increased the use of information technologies of airlines. Airlines benefit from the internet intensely because they can communicate directly with their customer's thanks to their websites. The intense use of airline companies' websites contributes positively to the efficiencies of airline companies, attracting more customers and increasing their business volumes. A web page that has been designed according to customer needs and evaluating the web page regularly and making improvements will provide a competitive advantage to the airline companies (Güreş, 2013:175-176).

Airlines offer a large number of services to their customers through their websites for example; check-in, online ticket sales, baggage tracking, seat preference, flight landing-departure times information, reservation, online magazine, newsletter, questionnaire, rental car, hotel, etc. additional services, flight packages, timetables, information about special passenger services, flight points, flight network (Canöz, 2017:195).

Airline companies can also provide advantages to their customers in these services through their website. For example, some airline companies can offer their customers an extra discount on ticket prices if their flight tickets are bought online. The applications such as online check-in, e-ticket can be made easier with the processes related to the boarding process, and time and energy loss is minimized. (Güreş, 2013:175). This enables airline companies to establish long-term relationships with customers and turn them into loyal customers. Services such as discounted tickets, excess baggage allowance, fast check-in for customers contribute positively to customer satisfaction (Canöz, 2017:195).

The above-mentioned services are general services provided by the airline companies through their web pages. Some of the potential customers of airlines are people over the age of 65. Internet usage rates of people over 65 are increasing. Airline companies that are aware of this, in addition to these services, also provide services that may be needed for passengers over 65 years of age through their web pages. Besides, they are working to make the web page easy to access. They try to design web page designs appropriately so that passengers over 65 can use them more effectively and easily.

When the airline companies web pages analyzed, it is seen that the menus and options for elderly passengers. For example;

- Ease of access to the home page within the website,
- Possibility to return to the top of the page,
- The home button on the website pages,
- Presenting the search engine in the same place on every page of the website,
- Enabling menus within the website to be opened with a single click,
- Using a non-condensed writing style,

- Using font size that will not make reading difficult,
- Using big font or color in the titles,
- Using a patternless background,
- Using contrasts (white background - black text),
- Using voice guidance related to texts,
- Offering alternative foreign language options on the website home page,
- Live help tab for problems,
- Features such as offering a private and video call center in response to problems are put on the airline web pages.

Besides, the requests for flight (escort, wheelchair, etc.) and other passengers above 65 years of age are also frequently used by other passengers, and the flight check-in process and services such as on the homepage are on their web pages can be seen in web sites.

The literature review from the studies on airline web access is shown in Table 1.

Table 1. Studies about airline web sites

Author (s)	Subject	Method (s)
Vatansever and Akgül (2018)	Evaluation of airline websites	Entropy and GRA
Akman et al. (2018)	Selection of flight points between airports	AHP and TOPSIS
Bayraktar (2018)	Visual-content review of the airline web page	Visual Content Analysis
Bakır and Atalık (2018)	Evaluation of airline companies' e-services	AHP and ARAS
Akgün and Soy Temür (2016)	Financial evaluation of the transportation sector	TOPSIS
Güreş et al. (2013)	Evaluation of the websites of Turkish airlines	Data Analysis
Tan (2020)	Airport strategy development study	SWOT
Adeniran and Fadare (2018)	Evaluation of passenger satisfaction and service quality	SERVQUAL
Yang et al. (2014)	Airport location selection	WLSM and TOPSIS
Heung et al. (2000)	Airport restaurant service assessment	SERVQUAL

METHODOLOGY

In this section, after the algorithms of OWA, WSM, WPM, and WASPAS methods, which are used in the study, the literature review is given with tables.

OWA Method

OWA is one of the multi-criteria decision-making methods. The calculation process is as follows (Yılmaz, 2015, 210-212).

According to the OWA method, the decision-makers evaluate the criteria in the multi-criteria decision-making problem. Then they evaluate the performances of alternatives for these criteria.

$j : criterion; j = 1, 2, 3, ..., n$

$i : alternative; i = 1, 2, 3, ..., m$

$b_j : importance\ level\ of\ criterion\ j$

$u_{ij} : performance\ level\ of\ alternative\ i\ to\ criterion\ j$

Performance levels of an alternative have been sorted from highest to lowest. Weight values have been calculated by using sorted values. Equation 1 shows the first step of this process.

$$s_{ij} = \frac{\sum_{j=1}^{j} u_{ij}}{\sum_{j=1}^{n} u_{ij}} \tag{1}$$

Weight values can be found by using Equation 2.

$w_{ij} : weight\ value\ of\ criterion\ j\ to\ alternative\ i$

$$w_{ij} = s_{ij}^{2} - s_{i(j-1)}^{2} \tag{2}$$

The overall performance value of the alternative has been found by using Equation 3.

d_i : *overall performance value of alternative i*

$$d_i = \sum_{j=1}^{n} b_j w_{ij} \qquad (3)$$

According to the OWA method, the highest overall performance value will show the best alternative in the multi-criteria decision-making problem.

Table 2 shows the studies used OWA (Ordered Weighted Averaging) method.

Table 2. Studies about OWA

Author(s)	Subject	Method(s)
Ghasemkhani et al. (2020)	Creating urban development modeling	OWA
Liu and Wang (2020)	Evaluation of expansion approach	OWA and TOPSIS
Lei et al. (2020)	Supplier selection	OWA and TOPSIS
Cena and Gagolewski (2020)	Hierarchical clustering between links	OWA and Genie
Khakzad (2020)	Alternative selection between operators	OWA
Chang and Cheng (2011)	Evaluation of the risks that may occur	OWA and DEMATEL
Chang et al. (2009)	Innovative reliability allocation	OWA
Valente ve Vettorazzi (2008)	Identification of priority areas for forest protection	OWA
Rinner ve Malczewski (2002)	Decision analysis for web pages	OWA
Cho (1995)	The fuzzy collection of modular neural networks with their operators	OWA

WSM

WSM is one of the multi-criteria decision-making methods. The calculation process is as follows (Nezhad, Zolfani, Moztarzadeh, Zavadskas, and Bahrami, 2015, 1124-1125).

The first step of WSM is to construct the decision matrix. The decision matrix can be seen in Equation 4.

i : *alternative*; $i = 1, 2, 3, \ldots, m$

j : *evaluation criterion*; $j = 1, 2, 3, \ldots, n$

x_{ij} : *performance value of alternative i to criterion j*

X : *decision matrix*

$$X = \begin{bmatrix} x_{11} & x_{12} & \cdots & x_{1n} \\ x_{21} & x_{22} & \cdots & x_{2n} \\ \cdots & \cdots & \cdots & \cdots \\ x_{1m} & x_{2m} & \cdots & x_{mn} \end{bmatrix} \tag{4}$$

The next step is to convert the decision matrix into the normalized decision matrix. Normalization is made by using Equation 5 for beneficiary criteria.

$\hat{x}_{ij}$: *normalized performance value of alternative i to criterion j*

$\hat{X}$: *normalized decision matrix*

$$\hat{x}_{ij} = \frac{x_{ij}}{\max_j x_{ij}} ; beneficiary\ criteria\ \forall i, j \tag{5}$$

Normalization is made by using Equation 6 for cost criteria.

$$\hat{x}_{ij} = \frac{\min_j x_{ij}}{x_{ij}} ; cost\ criteria\ \forall i, j \tag{6}$$

The normalized decision matrix can be seen in Equation 7.

$$\hat{X} = \begin{bmatrix} \hat{x}_{11} & \hat{x}_{12} & \cdots & \hat{x}_{1n} \\ \hat{x}_{21} & \hat{x}_{22} & \cdots & \hat{x}_{2n} \\ \cdots & \cdots & \cdots & \cdots \\ \hat{x}_{1m} & \hat{x}_{2m} & \cdots & \hat{x}_{mn} \end{bmatrix} \tag{7}$$

Then, the weighted normalized decision matrix has been constructed with Equation 8.

w_j : *weight value of criterion j*

$$w_j \hat{x}_{ij}; for \; \forall i, j \tag{8}$$

The weighted normalized decision matrix is shown in Equation 9.

$w\hat{X}$: *weighted normalized decision matrix*

$$w\hat{X} = \begin{bmatrix} w_1\hat{x}_{11} & w_2\hat{x}_{12} & \cdots & w_m\hat{x}_{1n} \\ w_1\hat{x}_{21} & w_2\hat{x}_{22} & \cdots & w_m\hat{x}_{2n} \\ \cdots & \cdots & \cdots & \cdots \\ w_1\hat{x}_{1m} & w_2\hat{x}_{2m} & \cdots & w_m\hat{x}_{mn} \end{bmatrix} \tag{9}$$

The last step of WSM is to calculate the overall performance values of the alternatives. This operation is used by using Equation 10.

WSM_i : *overall performance value of alternative i according to WSM*

$$WSM_i = \sum_{j=1}^{n} w_j \hat{x}_{ij} \tag{10}$$

The highest overall performance value will show the best alternative in the multi-criteria decision-making problem.

Table 3 shows the literature about WSM (Weighted Sum Method).

Table 3. Studies about WSM

Author(s)	Subject	Method(s)
Li et al. (2020)	Determination of internal and external quality	WSM
Sianturi (2019)	The choice of football players	WSM
Chourabi et al. (2019)	Labor force selection	WSM, AHP, and WPM
Handoko et al. (2017)	Research on fund recipients	WSM
Feng et al. (2001)	Classification of similar 2D objects	WSM

WPM

WPM process has been explained with the help of the equations (Taka et al., 2017: 1201-1202).

The first step of WPM is to construct the decision matrix like in WSM. The decision matrix can be seen in Equation 11.

$i : alternative; i = 1, 2, 3, ..., m$

$j : evaluation\ criterion; j = 1, 2, 3, ..., n$

$x_{ij} : performance\ value\ of\ alternative\ i\ to\ criterion\ j$

$X : decision\ matrix$

$$X = \begin{bmatrix} x_{11} & x_{12} & ... & x_{1n} \\ x_{21} & x_{22} & ... & x_{2n} \\ ... & ... & ... & ... \\ x_{1m} & x_{2m} & ... & x_{mn} \end{bmatrix} \tag{11}$$

The next step of WPM is to convert the decision matrix into a normalized decision matrix like in WSM. Normalization is made by using Equation 12 for beneficiary criteria.

$\hat{x}_{ij} : normalized\ performance\ value\ of\ alternative\ i\ to\ criterion\ j$

$\hat{X} : normalized\ decision\ matrix$

$$\hat{x}_{ij} = \frac{x_{ij}}{\max_{j} x_{ij}}; beneficiary\ criteria\ \forall i, j \tag{12}$$

Normalization is made by using Equation 6 for cost criteria.

$$\hat{x}_{ij} = \frac{\min_j x_{ij}}{x_{ij}}; cost\ criteria\ \forall i,j \qquad (13)$$

The normalized decision matrix can be seen in Equation 14.

$$\hat{X} = \begin{bmatrix} \hat{x}_{11} & \hat{x}_{12} & \cdots & \hat{x}_{1n} \\ \hat{x}_{21} & \hat{x}_{22} & \cdots & \hat{x}_{2n} \\ \cdots & \cdots & \cdots & \cdots \\ \hat{x}_{1m} & \hat{x}_{2m} & \cdots & \hat{x}_{mn} \end{bmatrix} \qquad (14)$$

The process of WPM is exact the same as WSM up to this point. Then, the weighted normalized decision matrix has been constructed with Equation 15.

w_j : *weight value of criterion j*

$$\bar{x}_{ij}^{w_j}; \forall i, j\ i\varsigma in \qquad (15)$$

The last step of WPM is to calculate the overall performance values of the alternatives. This operation is used by using Equation 16.

WPM_i : *overall performance value of alternative i according to WPM*

$$WPM_i = \prod_{j=1}^{n} \bar{x}_{ij}^{w_j}; for\ \forall i \qquad (16)$$

The highest overall performance value will show the best alternative in the multi-criteria decision-making problem.

Table 4 shows the studies used WPM (Weighted Product Method).

WASPAS

WASPAS is one of the multi-criteria decision-making methods. The calculation process is as follows (Nezhad, Zolfani, Moztarzadeh, Zavadskas, and Bahrami, 2015, 1124-1125).

Table 4. Studies about WPM

Author (s)	Subject	Method (s)
Senapati and Yager (2019)	Research on numbers and operations	WPM
Balusa and Singam (2018)	Selection of underground mining management	WPM and PROMETHEE
Rana and Patel (2018)	Site selection for hydroelectric power	WPM, AHP, and TOPSIS
Rao and Venkatasubbaiah (2016)	Appropriate application selection	WSM, WPM, and TOPSIS
Jain and Raj (2013)	Evaluation of flexibility in FMS	SAW and WPM

The first step of WASPAS is to construct the decision matrix like in WSM and WPM. The decision matrix can be seen in Equation 17.

$i : alternative; i = 1, 2, 3, ..., m$

$j : evaluation\ criterion; j = 1, 2, 3, ..., n$

$x_{ij} : performance\ value\ of\ alternative\ i\ to\ criterion\ j$

$X : decision\ matrix$

$$X = \begin{bmatrix} x_{11} & x_{12} & \cdots & x_{1n} \\ x_{21} & x_{22} & \cdots & x_{2n} \\ \cdots & \cdots & \cdots & \cdots \\ x_{1m} & x_{2m} & \cdots & x_{mn} \end{bmatrix} \tag{17}$$

The next step is to convert the decision matrix into the normalized decision matrix. Normalization is made by using Equation 18 for beneficiary criteria.

$\hat{x}_{ij} : normalized\ performance\ value\ of\ alternative\ i\ to\ criterion\ j$

$\hat{X} : normalized\ decision\ matrix$

$$\hat{x}_{ij} = \frac{x_{ij}}{\max\limits_{j} x_{ij}} ; beneficiary\ criteria\ \forall i, j \tag{18}$$

Normalization is made by using Equation 19 for cost criteria.

$$\hat{x}_{ij} = \frac{\min\limits_{j} x_{ij}}{x_{ij}} ; cost\ criteria\ \forall i, j \tag{19}$$

The normalized decision matrix can be seen in Equation 20.

$$\hat{X} = \begin{bmatrix} \hat{x}_{11} & \hat{x}_{12} & \cdots & \hat{x}_{1n} \\ \hat{x}_{21} & \hat{x}_{22} & \cdots & \hat{x}_{2n} \\ \cdots & \cdots & \cdots & \cdots \\ \hat{x}_{1m} & \hat{x}_{2m} & \cdots & \hat{x}_{mn} \end{bmatrix} \tag{20}$$

The process of WASPAS is exact the same as WSM and WPM up to this point. Then, the summation part weighted normalized decision matrix has been constructed with Equation 21.

w_j : *weight value of criterion j*

$\hat{x}_{ij,sum}$: *weighted normalized performance value of*
        alternative i to criterion j for summation part

$$\hat{x}_{ij,sum} = w_j \hat{x}_{ij}; for\ \forall i, j \tag{21a}$$

Then, the multiplication part weighted normalized decision matrix has been constructed with Equation 22.

w_j : *weight value of criterion j*

$\hat{x}_{ij,mult}$: *weighted normalized performance value of alternative*
        i with respect to criterion j for multiplication part

$$\hat{x}_{ij,mult} = \hat{x}_{ij}^{\ w_j}; for \ \forall i,j \tag{21b}$$

The overall performance values of the alternatives have been calculated by integrating summation and multiplication parts with Equation 22.

$\propto$: *WASPAS coefficient which effects the summation and multiplication parts*

$0 \leq \propto \leq 1$

WPS_i : *overall performance value of alternative i*

$$WPS_i = (\propto) \sum_{j=1}^{n} \hat{x}_{ij,sum} + (1-\propto) \prod_{j=1}^{n} \hat{x}_{ij,mult}; for \ \forall i \tag{22}$$

The highest overall performance value will show the best alternative in the multi-criteria decision-making problem.

Tablo 5 shows the studies used WASPAS (Weighted Aggregated Sum Product Assessment).

Table 5. Studies about WASPAS

Author(s)	Subject	Method(s)
Gavcar and Organ (2020)	Evaluation of travel agencies	WASPAS, AHP, and GRA
Gezen (2019)	Performance analysis of participation banks	WASPAS and Entropy
Bağcı and Yiğiter (2019)	Financial performance analysis in the energy sector	WASPAS and SD
Orçun (2019)	Performance analysis in the energy sector	WASPAS
Özdağoğlu et al. (2019)	Choosing the macroelisa medical device for the hospital	WASPAS and SWARA
Rençber and Avcı (2018)	Comparison of banks according to their capital	WASPAS
Mardani et al. (2017)	Evaluation of theory and current practices	WASPAS and SWARA
Baušys and Juodagalvienė (2017)	Choosing a garage for the residence	WASPAS and SVNS
Turskis et al. (2015)	Site selection in a hybrid model	WASPAS and AHP
Chakraborty and Zavadskas (2014)	Research on manufacturing applications	WASPAS

APPLICATION

Airline companies' web sites have been analyzed in this chapter. First of all the evaluation, 16 criteria have been determined. These criteria have been determined with the literature review and expert opinions. The criteria list and codes can be seen in Table 6.

Table 6. Criterion Codes and Names

Criterion Code	Criterion Name
c1	Ease of access to the home page
c2	Providing the opportunity to return to the top of the page
c3	Including the home button
c4	Present the search engine in the same place on every page
c5	Enabling menus to be opened with a single click
c6	Using a non-condensed typeface
c7	Using font size that does not complicate reading
c8	Using large points or colors in titles
c9	Using a patternless background
c10	Using contrasts (white background - black text)
c11	Using voice guidance related to texts
c12	Offering alternative foreign language options on the main page
c13	Provide live help tab for problems
c14	Providing private and video call center opportunities in response to problems
c15	Flight check-in on the main page
c16	Determination of flight demands (Accompaniment, Wheelchair, etc.)

Table 7 shows the names and meanings of the criteria.

Then the alternatives have been determined for evaluation. The alternatives can be seen in Table 8.

After determining evaluation criteria and alternatives, a questionnaire has been formed for collecting data. Evaluations have been made by the expert team. The expert team includes 1 air traffic controller, 2 passenger service officers, 2 operational officers, and 1 instructor in the transport services department and the civil aviation cabin services program.

The averages of the answers can be seen in Table 9.

Table 7. Evaluation Criteria and Meanings

Criterion Code	Criterion Name	Explanation	Source
c1	Access to the home page should be easy	Users' access to pages	Sector expert opinions
c2	Providing the opportunity to return to the top of the page	The feature that allows users to return to the top of the page	Akyazı and Kara (2017)
c3	Including the home button	The feature that allows users to return to the home page within the page	
c4	Present the search engine in the same place on every page	The mechanism used to search the content is in the same place on every page	Akyazı (2018)
c5	Enabling menus to be opened with a single click	Using the mouse while opening the menus	
c6	Using a non-condensed typeface	Selection of typography in font preferences	
c7	Using font size that does not complicate reading	Selection of typography in font preferences	Akyazı and Kara (2017)
c8	Using large points or colors in titles	Selection of typography in font preferences	
c9	Using a patternless background	The visual feature used for readability of articles	
c10	Using contrasts (white background - black text)	The visual feature used for readability of articles	
c11	Using voice guidance related to texts	Support assistance provided by voice	Sector expert opinions
c12	Offering alternative foreign language options on the main page	Language preference used	Güreş et al. (2013)
c13	Provide live help tab for problems	Support help provided by the message	Sector expert opinions
c14	Providing private and video call center opportunities in response to problems	Face-to-face support assistance	Sector expert opinions
c15	Flight check-in on the main page	Passengers' acceptance by the airline	Güreş et al. (2013)
c16	Determination of flight demands (Accompaniment, Wheelchair, etc.)	Personal requests of passengers	Sector expert opinions

Table 8. Alternative Codes and Names

Alternative Code	Alternative Name
a1	Turkish Airlines
a2	Anadolu jet
a3	Sun Expres
a4	Pegasus
a5	Onur Air

Table 9. Averages

Criterion Code	Criterion Evaluation	A1	A2	A3	A4	A5
c1	9.833333	7.500000	6.333333	5.666667	5.333333	7.000000
c2	8.666667	7.166667	5.833333	5.500000	4.833333	6.666667
c3	9.500000	7.000000	5.666667	5.500000	4.333333	5.833333
c4	8.666667	9.500000	8.166667	7.500000	7.166667	4.333333
c5	8.333333	8.666667	8.166667	8.000000	7.000000	6.833333
c6	8.333333	7.500000	6.166667	5.166667	5.500000	5.500000
c7	9.000000	7.000000	6.333333	6.000000	5.333333	4.666667
c8	7.833333	8.166667	8.333333	8.000000	8.333333	8.333333
c9	7.833333	6.000000	7.000000	6.666667	6.000000	6.166667
c10	7.000000	5.833333	6.166667	5.500000	5.500000	5.166667
c11	6.833333	2.000000	1.833333	1.500000	0.833333	0.833333
c12	7.333333	7.833333	8.000000	9.333333	9.500000	8.833333
c13	8.666667	4.333333	4.000000	2.833333	2.000000	1.666667
c14	7.666667	2.833333	2.833333	2.833333	2.333333	0.833333
c15	7.000000	8.000000	8.166667	7.500000	7.333333	6.500000
c16	10.000000	7.333333	7.000000	4.666667	6.500000	5.500000

After data collection, the multi-criteria decision-making methods have been applied to this data set. According to the OWA method, the calculations for alternative 1 can be seen in Table 10.

According to the OWA method, the calculations for alternative 2 can be seen in Table 11.

According to the OWA method, the calculations for alternative 3 can be seen in Table 12.

Table 10. OWA Calculations for Alternative 1

A1	b_j	u_{1j}	s_{1j}	w_{1j}
c4	9.500000	8.666667	0.065409	0.004278
c5	8.666667	8.333333	0.128302	0.012183
c8	8.166667	7.833333	0.187421	0.018665
c15	8.000000	7.000000	0.240252	0.022594
c12	7.833333	7.333333	0.295597	0.029657
c1	7.500000	9.833333	0.369811	0.049383
c6	7.500000	8.333333	0.432704	0.050473
c16	7.333333	10.000000	0.508176	0.071010
c2	7.166667	8.666667	0.573585	0.070757
c3	7.000000	9.500000	0.645283	0.087391
c7	7.000000	9.000000	0.713208	0.092275
c9	6.000000	7.833333	0.772327	0.087824
c10	5.833333	7.000000	0.825157	0.084395
c13	4.333333	8.666667	0.890566	0.112223
c14	2.833333	7.666667	0.948428	0.106407
c11	2.000000	6.833333	1.000000	0.100485
			d_1	5.754140

According to the OWA method, the calculations for alternative 4 can be seen in Table 13.

According to the OWA method, the calculations for alternative 5 can be seen in Table 14.

The overall performance values of the alternatives according to the OWA method can be seen in Table 15.

According to the results of the OWA method, alternative 1 is the best airline company for web site evaluation. Then different multi-criteria decision-making methods have been applied to the same data set for validating the results.

WSM procedure is explained step by step. Firstly, the criteria evaluation answers are normalized. Criteria evaluations and normalized weights can be seen in Table 16.

The decision matrix for WSM can be seen in Table 17.

The normalized decision matrix for WSM can be seen in Table 18.

The overall performance values of the alternatives according to WSM can be seen in Table 19.

Table 11. OWA Calculations for Alternative 2

A2	b_j	u_{2j}	s_{2j}	w_{2j}
c8	8.333333	7.833333	0.059119	0.003495
c4	8.166667	8.666667	0.124528	0.012012
c5	8.166667	8.333333	0.187421	0.019619
c15	8.166667	7.000000	0.240252	0.022594
c12	8.000000	7.333333	0.295597	0.029657
c9	7.000000	7.833333	0.354717	0.038446
c16	7.000000	10.000000	0.430189	0.059238
c1	6.333333	9.833333	0.504403	0.069360
c7	6.333333	9.000000	0.572327	0.073136
c6	6.166667	8.333333	0.635220	0.075946
c10	6.166667	7.000000	0.688050	0.069909
c2	5.833333	8.666667	0.753459	0.094287
c3	5.666667	9.500000	0.825157	0.113184
c13	4.000000	8.666667	0.890566	0.112223
c14	2.833333	7.666667	0.948428	0.106407
c11	1.833333	6.833333	1.000000	0.100485
			d_2	5.320918

The best airline company for airline web site according to WSM is alternative 1 like in the OWA method.

WPM calculations are as follows. Firstly, the criteria evaluation answers are normalized. Criteria evaluations and normalized weights can be seen in Table 20.

The decision matrix for WPM can be seen in Table 21.

The normalized decision matrix for WPM can be seen in Table 22.

The weighted normalized decision matrix can be seen in Table 23.

The overall performance values of the alternatives according to WPM can be seen in Table 24.

The best airline company for airline web site according to WPM is alternative 1 like in OWA and WSM.

WASPAS calculations are as follows. Firstly, the criteria evaluation answers are normalized. Criteria evaluations and normalized weights can be seen in Table 25.

The decision matrix for WASPAS can be seen in Table 26.

The normalized decision matrix for WASPAS can be seen in Table 27.

Table 12. OWA Calculations for Alternative 3

A3	b_j	u_{3j}	s_{3j}	w_{3j}
c12	9.333333	7.333333	0.055346	0.003063
c5	8.000000	8.333333	0.118239	0.010917
c8	8.000000	7.833333	0.177358	0.017476
c4	7.500000	8.666667	0.242767	0.027480
c15	7.500000	7.000000	0.295597	0.028442
c9	6.666667	7.833333	0.354717	0.038446
c7	6.000000	9.000000	0.422642	0.052802
c1	5.666667	9.833333	0.496855	0.068239
c2	5.500000	8.666667	0.562264	0.069276
c3	5.500000	9.500000	0.633962	0.085767
c10	5.500000	7.000000	0.686792	0.069776
c6	5.166667	8.333333	0.749686	0.090345
c16	4.666667	10.000000	0.825157	0.118856
c13	2.833333	8.666667	0.890566	0.112223
c14	2.833333	7.666667	0.948428	0.106407
c11	1.500000	6.833333	1.000000	0.100485
			d_3	4.663080

The summation part weighted normalized decision matrix can be constructed as in Table 28.

The multiplication part weighted normalized decision matrix can be constructed as in Table 29.

The overall performance values of the alternatives according to WASPAS can be seen in Table 30.

The best airline company for airline web site according to WASPAS is alternative 1 like in OWA, WSM, and WPM. The results have been integrated for comparison in Table 31.

Four different multi-criteria decision-making methods have been used for evaluation. The ranks are the same. A comparative analysis validated the results.

Table 13. OWA Calculations for Alternative 4

A4	b_j	u_{4j}	s_{4j}	w_{4j}
c12	9.500000	7.333333	0.055346	0.003063
c8	8.333333	7.833333	0.114465	0.010039
c15	7.333333	7.000000	0.167296	0.014885
c4	7.166667	8.666667	0.232704	0.026164
c5	7.000000	8.333333	0.295597	0.033227
c16	6.500000	10.000000	0.371069	0.050314
c9	6.000000	7.833333	0.430189	0.047370
c6	5.500000	8.333333	0.493082	0.058067
c10	5.500000	7.000000	0.545912	0.054890
c1	5.333333	9.833333	0.620126	0.086536
c7	5.333333	9.000000	0.688050	0.088857
c2	4.833333	8.666667	0.753459	0.094287
c3	4.333333	9.500000	0.825157	0.113184
c14	2.333333	7.666667	0.883019	0.098838
c13	2.000000	8.666667	0.948428	0.119793
c11	0.833333	6.833333	1.000000	0.100485
			d_4	4.310103

CONCLUSION

The aviation industry offers faster, more convenient, and safer transportation compared to other transportation networks. This sector has become a major transportation choice in Turkey and the world. The sector started to grow with the increase in airline companies. Along with the growth in the sector, competition between companies increased. This required airline companies to set different competitive strategies. The e-service quality of airline companies' web pages is also one of these important competitive strategies.

Today, although the majority of internet users are young people, the number of older users over 65 is also increasing. Airline companies should design their web sites by taking into account the elderly people.

Table 14. OWA Calculations for Alternative 5

A5	b_j	u_{5j}	s_{5j}	w_{5j}
c12	8.833333	7.333333	0.055346	0.003063
c8	8.333333	7.833333	0.114465	0.010039
c1	7.000000	9.833333	0.188679	0.022498
c5	6.833333	8.333333	0.251572	0.027689
c2	6.666667	8.666667	0.316981	0.037188
c15	6.500000	7.000000	0.369811	0.036283
c9	6.166667	7.833333	0.428931	0.047221
c3	5.833333	9.500000	0.500629	0.066648
c6	5.500000	8.333333	0.563522	0.066928
c16	5.500000	10.000000	0.638994	0.090756
c10	5.166667	7.000000	0.691824	0.070307
c7	4.666667	9.000000	0.759748	0.098597
c4	4.333333	8.666667	0.825157	0.103667
c13	1.666667	8.666667	0.890566	0.112223
c11	0.833333	6.833333	0.942138	0.094517
c14	0.833333	7.666667	1.000000	0.112375
			d_5	4.120455

Table 15. OWA Results and Ranks

Alternative	Value	Rank
A1	5.754140	1
A2	5.320918	2
A3	4.663080	3
A4	4.310103	4
A5	4.120455	5

Table 16. Criteria Evaluations and Normalizations

Criterion Code	Evaluation	w_j
c1	9.833333	0.074214
c2	8.666667	0.065409
c3	9.500000	0.071698
c4	8.666667	0.065409
c5	8.333333	0.062893
c6	8.333333	0.062893
c7	9.000000	0.067925
c8	7.833333	0.059119
c9	7.833333	0.059119
c10	7.000000	0.052830
c11	6.833333	0.051572
c12	7.333333	0.055346
c13	8.666667	0.065409
c14	7.666667	0.057862
c15	7.000000	0.052830
c16	10.000000	0.075472

Table 17. Decision Matrix for WSM

	A1	A2	A3	A4	A5
c1	7.500000	6.333333	5.666667	5.333333	7.000000
c2	7.166667	5.833333	5.500000	4.833333	6.666667
c3	7.000000	5.666667	5.500000	4.333333	5.833333
c4	9.500000	8.166667	7.500000	7.166667	4.333333
c5	8.666667	8.166667	8.000000	7.000000	6.833333
c6	7.500000	6.166667	5.166667	5.500000	5.500000
c7	7.000000	6.333333	6.000000	5.333333	4.666667
c8	8.166667	8.333333	8.000000	8.333333	8.333333
c9	6.000000	7.000000	6.666667	6.000000	6.166667
c10	5.833333	6.166667	5.500000	5.500000	5.166667
c11	2.000000	1.833333	1.500000	0.833333	0.833333
c12	7.833333	8.000000	9.333333	9.500000	8.833333
c13	4.333333	4.000000	2.833333	2.000000	1.666667
c14	2.833333	2.833333	2.833333	2.333333	0.833333
c15	8.000000	8.166667	7.500000	7.333333	6.500000
c16	7.333333	7.000000	4.666667	6.500000	5.500000

Table 18. Normalized Decision Matrix for WSM

	A1	A2	A3	A4	A5
c1	1.000000	0.844444	0.755556	0.711111	0.933333
c2	1.000000	0.813953	0.767442	0.674419	0.930233
c3	1.000000	0.809524	0.785714	0.619048	0.833333
c4	1.000000	0.859649	0.789474	0.754386	0.456140
c5	1.000000	0.942308	0.923077	0.807692	0.788462
c6	1.000000	0.822222	0.688889	0.733333	0.733333
c7	1.000000	0.904762	0.857143	0.761905	0.666667
c8	0.980000	1.000000	0.960000	1.000000	1.000000
c9	0.857143	1.000000	0.952381	0.857143	0.880952
c10	0.945946	1.000000	0.891892	0.891892	0.837838
c11	1.000000	0.916667	0.750000	0.416667	0.416667
c12	0.824561	0.842105	0.982456	1.000000	0.929825
c13	1.000000	0.923077	0.653846	0.461538	0.384615
c14	1.000000	1.000000	1.000000	0.823529	0.294118
c15	0.979592	1.000000	0.918367	0.897959	0.795918
c16	1.000000	0.954545	0.636364	0.886364	0.750000

Table 19. WSM Results and Ranks

Alternative	Value	Rank
A1	0.9767283	1
A2	0.9106726	2
A3	0.8242513	3
A4	0.7652078	4
A5	0.7299313	5

Airline companies must continue to grow and follow the developments to survive in intense competition. Airline companies that want to gain competitive advantage should act by considering the issues that elderly passengers may need. The functions that may prevent the use of the web pages of the elderly should be improved and designs should be considered in a way to facilitate the feasibility of the procedures. Airline companies will be superior to their competitors, which can effectively construct web pages, which are a means of providing direct communication with the customer, and make their designs according to customer needs, and differentiate the e-services they provide.

Table 20. Criteria Evaluations and Normalizations

Criterion Code	Evaluation	w_j
c1	9.833333	0.074214
c2	8.666667	0.065409
c3	9.500000	0.071698
c4	8.666667	0.065409
c5	8.333333	0.062893
c6	8.333333	0.062893
c7	9.000000	0.067925
c8	7.833333	0.059119
c9	7.833333	0.059119
c10	7.000000	0.052830
c11	6.833333	0.051572
c12	7.333333	0.055346
c13	8.666667	0.065409
c14	7.666667	0.057862
c15	7.000000	0.052830
c16	10.000000	0.075472

Table 21. Decision Matrix for WPM

	A1	A2	A3	A4	A5
c1	7.500000	6.333333	5.666667	5.333333	7.000000
c2	7.166667	5.833333	5.500000	4.833333	6.666667
c3	7.000000	5.666667	5.500000	4.333333	5.833333
c4	9.500000	8.166667	7.500000	7.166667	4.333333
c5	8.666667	8.166667	8.000000	7.000000	6.833333
c6	7.500000	6.166667	5.166667	5.500000	5.500000
c7	7.000000	6.333333	6.000000	5.333333	4.666667
c8	8.166667	8.333333	8.000000	8.333333	8.333333
c9	6.000000	7.000000	6.666667	6.000000	6.166667
c10	5.833333	6.166667	5.500000	5.500000	5.166667
c11	2.000000	1.833333	1.500000	0.833333	0.833333
c12	7.833333	8.000000	9.333333	9.500000	8.833333
c13	4.333333	4.000000	2.833333	2.000000	1.666667
c14	2.833333	2.833333	2.833333	2.333333	0.833333
c15	8.000000	8.166667	7.500000	7.333333	6.500000
c16	7.333333	7.000000	4.666667	6.500000	5.500000

Table 22. Normalized Decision Matrix for WPM

	A1	A2	A3	A4	A5
c1	1.000000	0.844444	0.755556	0.711111	0.933333
c2	1.000000	0.813953	0.767442	0.674419	0.930233
c3	1.000000	0.809524	0.785714	0.619048	0.833333
c4	1.000000	0.859649	0.789474	0.754386	0.456140
c5	1.000000	0.942308	0.923077	0.807692	0.788462
c6	1.000000	0.822222	0.688889	0.733333	0.733333
c7	1.000000	0.904762	0.857143	0.761905	0.666667
c8	0.980000	1.000000	0.960000	1.000000	1.000000
c9	0.857143	1.000000	0.952381	0.857143	0.880952
c10	0.945946	1.000000	0.891892	0.891892	0.837838
c11	1.000000	0.916667	0.750000	0.416667	0.416667
c12	0.824561	0.842105	0.982456	1.000000	0.929825
c13	1.000000	0.923077	0.653846	0.461538	0.384615
c14	1.000000	1.000000	1.000000	0.823529	0.294118
c15	0.979592	1.000000	0.918367	0.897959	0.795918
c16	1.000000	0.954545	0.636364	0.886364	0.750000

Table 23. Weighted Normalized Decision Matrix for WPM

	A1	A2	A3	A4	A5
c1	1.000000	0.987531	0.979413	0.975016	0.994893
c2	1.000000	0.986626	0.982836	0.974564	0.995281
c3	1.000000	0.984964	0.982858	0.966200	0.987013
c4	1.000000	0.990157	0.984657	0.981733	0.949953
c5	1.000000	0.996270	0.994979	0.986657	0.985163
c6	1.000000	0.987764	0.976834	0.980682	0.980682
c7	1.000000	0.993225	0.989584	0.981699	0.972835
c8	0.998806	1.000000	0.997590	1.000000	1.000000
c9	0.990928	1.000000	0.997120	0.990928	0.992535
c10	0.997069	1.000000	0.993974	0.993974	0.990696
c11	1.000000	0.995523	0.985273	0.955854	0.955854
c12	0.989380	0.990534	0.999021	1.000000	0.995981
c13	1.000000	0.994778	0.972592	0.950684	0.939414
c14	1.000000	1.000000	1.000000	0.988829	0.931639
c15	0.998911	1.000000	0.995511	0.994330	0.988013
c16	1.000000	0.996495	0.966463	0.990937	0.978522

Table 24. WPM Results and Ranks

Alternative	Value	Rank
A1	0.975301	1
A2	0.907877	2
A3	0.815975	3
A4	0.746618	4
A5	0.691178	5

Table 25. Criteria Evaluations and Normalizations

Criterion Code	Evaluation	w_j
c1	9.833333	0.074214
c2	8.666667	0.065409
c3	9.500000	0.071698
c4	8.666667	0.065409
c5	8.333333	0.062893
c6	8.333333	0.062893
c7	9.000000	0.067925
c8	7.833333	0.059119
c9	7.833333	0.059119
c10	7.000000	0.052830
c11	6.833333	0.051572
c12	7.333333	0.055346
c13	8.666667	0.065409
c14	7.666667	0.057862
c15	7.000000	0.052830
c16	10.000000	0.075472

In this study, the access to websites and the e-service subject provided on the websites are discussed. The criteria have been determined according to the accessibility of the elderly population to airline companies web sites. The 5 largest airline companies operating in Turkey are evaluated in terms of performance and quality of the e-services website. Comparative analysis has been made for evaluation with OWA, WASPAS, WSM, and WPM methods.

Table 26. Decision Matrix for WASPAS

	A1	A2	A3	A4	A5
c1	7.500000	6.333333	5.666667	5.333333	7.000000
c2	7.166667	5.833333	5.500000	4.833333	6.666667
c3	7.000000	5.666667	5.500000	4.333333	5.833333
c4	9.500000	8.166667	7.500000	7.166667	4.333333
c5	8.666667	8.166667	8.000000	7.000000	6.833333
c6	7.500000	6.166667	5.166667	5.500000	5.500000
c7	7.000000	6.333333	6.000000	5.333333	4.666667
c8	8.166667	8.333333	8.000000	8.333333	8.333333
c9	6.000000	7.000000	6.666667	6.000000	6.166667
c10	5.833333	6.166667	5.500000	5.500000	5.166667
c11	2.000000	1.833333	1.500000	0.833333	0.833333
c12	7.833333	8.000000	9.333333	9.500000	8.833333
c13	4.333333	4.000000	2.833333	2.000000	1.666667
c14	2.833333	2.833333	2.833333	2.333333	0.833333
c15	8.000000	8.166667	7.500000	7.333333	6.500000
c16	7.333333	7.000000	4.666667	6.500000	5.500000

Table 27. Normalized Decision Matrix for WASPAS

	A1	A2	A3	A4	A5
c1	1.000000	0.844444	0.755556	0.711111	0.933333
c2	1.000000	0.813953	0.767442	0.674419	0.930233
c3	1.000000	0.809524	0.785714	0.619048	0.833333
c4	1.000000	0.859649	0.789474	0.754386	0.456140
c5	1.000000	0.942308	0.923077	0.807692	0.788462
c6	1.000000	0.822222	0.688889	0.733333	0.733333
c7	1.000000	0.904762	0.857143	0.761905	0.666667
c8	0.980000	1.000000	0.960000	1.000000	1.000000
c9	0.857143	1.000000	0.952381	0.857143	0.880952
c10	0.945946	1.000000	0.891892	0.891892	0.837838
c11	1.000000	0.916667	0.750000	0.416667	0.416667
c12	0.824561	0.842105	0.982456	1.000000	0.929825
c13	1.000000	0.923077	0.653846	0.461538	0.384615
c14	1.000000	1.000000	1.000000	0.823529	0.294118
c15	0.979592	1.000000	0.918367	0.897959	0.795918
c16	1.000000	0.954545	0.636364	0.886364	0.750000

Table 28. Summation Part Weighted Normalized Decision Matrix for WASPAS

	A1	A2	A3	A4	A5
c1	1.000000	0.987531	0.979413	0.975016	0.994893
c2	1.000000	0.986626	0.982836	0.974564	0.995281
c3	1.000000	0.984964	0.982858	0.966200	0.987013
c4	1.000000	0.990157	0.984657	0.981733	0.949953
c5	1.000000	0.996270	0.994979	0.986657	0.985163
c6	1.000000	0.987764	0.976834	0.980682	0.980682
c7	1.000000	0.993225	0.989584	0.981699	0.972835
c8	0.998806	1.000000	0.997590	1.000000	1.000000
c9	0.990928	1.000000	0.997120	0.990928	0.992535
c10	0.997069	1.000000	0.993974	0.993974	0.990696
c11	1.000000	0.995523	0.985273	0.955854	0.955854
c12	0.989380	0.990534	0.999021	1.000000	0.995981
c13	1.000000	0.994778	0.972592	0.950684	0.939414
c14	1.000000	1.000000	1.000000	0.988829	0.931639
c15	0.998911	1.000000	0.995511	0.994330	0.988013
c16	1.000000	0.996495	0.966463	0.990937	0.978522

Table 29. Multiplication Part Weighted Normalized Decision Matrix for WASPAS

	A1	A2	A3	A4	A5
c1	1.000000	0.987531	0.979413	0.975016	0.994893
c2	1.000000	0.986626	0.982836	0.974564	0.995281
c3	1.000000	0.984964	0.982858	0.966200	0.987013
c4	1.000000	0.990157	0.984657	0.981733	0.949953
c5	1.000000	0.996270	0.994979	0.986657	0.985163
c6	1.000000	0.987764	0.976834	0.980682	0.980682
c7	1.000000	0.993225	0.989584	0.981699	0.972835
c8	0.998806	1.000000	0.997590	1.000000	1.000000
c9	0.990928	1.000000	0.997120	0.990928	0.992535
c10	0.997069	1.000000	0.993974	0.993974	0.990696
c11	1.000000	0.995523	0.985273	0.955854	0.955854
c12	0.989380	0.990534	0.999021	1.000000	0.995981
c13	1.000000	0.994778	0.972592	0.950684	0.939414
c14	1.000000	1.000000	1.000000	0.988829	0.931639
c15	0.998911	1.000000	0.995511	0.994330	0.988013
c16	1.000000	0.996495	0.966463	0.990937	0.978522

Table 30. WASPAS Results and Ranks

Alternative	Value	Rank
A1	0.976015	1
A2	0.909275	2
A3	0.820113	3
A4	0.755913	4
A5	0.710555	5

Table 31. Comparative Results and Ranks

Alternative	OWA Result	OWA Rank	WSM Result	WSM Rank	WPM Result	WPM Rank	WASPAS Result	WASPAS Rank
A1	5.754140	1	0.976728	1	0.975301	1	0.976015	1
A2	5.320918	2	0.910673	2	0.907877	2	0.909275	2
A3	4.663080	3	0.824251	3	0.815975	3	0.820113	3
A4	4.310103	4	0.765208	4	0.746618	4	0.755913	4
A5	4.120455	5	0.729931	5	0.691178	5	0.710555	5

According to the results of the analysis, the airline company named "Alternative 1" ranked first in the ranking of the airline companies in terms of design, accessibility, and e-services offered on the website, and the airline company named "Alternative 5" ranked last.

In the design of the airline companies' websites, the menu with the flight demands including the escorts, wheelchairs, etc. that will be requested by disabled passengers in addition to elderly passengers has become more important. Other important features to be considered in the design of the web page are easy to reach the main page of the airline company, existing of the home button while operating within the web page, the existence of the search engine on every page. In addition to these features, large font sizes and live help functions are critical.

When the literature is analyzed, "using voice guidance related to texts", "offering a live help tab in case of problems", "offering a private and video call center facility in response to problems" and "determining flight requests (escort, wheelchair, etc.)" criteria have been used for the first time in an MCDM problem. Also, when the Turkish literature is analyzed, there is no study in which the ranking of the airline sector web page performance is made with the MCDM methods used in this chapter. With these aspects, it is thought that this chapter contributed to the literature.

REFERENCES

Adeniran, A. O., & Fadare, S. O. (2018). Assessment of passengers' satisfaction and service quality in Murtala Muhammed Airport (MMA2), Lagos, Nigeria: Application of the SERVQUAL model. *J Hotel Bus Manage, 7*(188), 2169–0286. doi:10.4172/2169-0286.1000188

Aizpurua, A., Harper, S., & Vigo, M. (2016). Exploring the relationship between web accessibility and user experience. *International Journal of Human-Computer Studies, 91,* 13–23. doi:10.1016/j.ijhcs.2016.03.008

Akgün, M., & Soy Temür, A. (2016). BIST ulaştırma endeksine kayıtlı şirketlerin finansal performanslarının TOPSIS yöntemi ile değerlendirilmesi. *Uluslararası Yönetim İktisat ve İşletme Dergisi, 30,* 173–186.

Akgüngör, A. P., & Demirel, A. (2004). Türkiye'deki ulaştırma sistemlerinin analizi ve ulaştırma politikaları. *Mühendislik Bilimleri Dergisi, 10*(3), 423–430.

Akman, G., Özcan, B., Başlı, H., & Gündüz, E. B. (2018). Çok kriterli karar vermede AHP ve TOPSIS yöntemleriyle uçuş noktası seçimi. *Erciyes Üniversitesi Fen Bilimleri Enstitüsü Fen Bilimleri Dergisi, 34*(3), 45–57.

Akyazı, A. (2018). Dijitalleşen ticaret: Yaşlı dostu e-ticaret siteleri üzerine bir araştırma. *The Turkish Online Journal of Design Art and Communication, 8*(4), 602–614. doi:10.7456/10804100/002

Akyazı, E., & Kara, T. (2017). Bilişim çağının haber kaynağı olarak internet gazetelerinin yaşlı dostu web sitesi kriterleri açısından karşılaştırmalı analizi. *International Journal of Social Sciences and Education Research, 3*(4), 1352–1363. doi:10.24289/ijsser.309075

Alsaeedi, A. (2020). Comparing web accessibility evaluation tools and evaluating the accessibility of webpages: Proposed frameworks. *Information (Basel), 11*(1), 1–21. doi:10.3390/info11010040

Bağcı, H., & Yiğiter, Ş. Y. (2019). Bist'te yer alan enerji şirketlerinin finansal performansının SD ve WASPAS yöntemleriyle ölçülmesi. *Bingöl Üniversitesi Sosyal Bilimler Enstitüsü Dergisi, 9*(18), 877–900. doi:10.29029/busbed.559885

Bakır, M., & Atalık, Ö. (2018). *E-service quality performance measurement in airlines: An application on scheduled airlines in Turkey.* Academic Press.

Balusa, B. C., & Singam, J. (2018). Underground mining method selection using WPM and PROMETHEE. *Journal of the Institution of Engineers (India), 99*(1), 165–171. doi:10.100740033-017-0137-0

Baušys, R., & Juodagalvienė, B. (2017). Garage location selection for residential house by WASPAS-SVNS method. *Journal of Civil Engineering and Management, 23*(3), 421–429. doi:10.3846/13923730.2016.1268645

Bayraktar, S. (2018). Türk Hava Yolları web sayfasının görsel-içerik çözümlemesi. *International Journal of Tourism Economics and Business Sciences, 2*(2), 276–284.

Çalışma & Bakanlığı. (2019). *Engelli ve Yaşlı Hizmetler Genel Müdürlüğü Engelli ve Yaşlı İstatistik Bülteni.* Retrieved April 22, 2020, from, https://ailevecalisma.gov. tr/media/9085/buelten-haziran2019-son.pdf

Canöz, N. (2017). Türkiye'deki havayolu işletmelerinin hizmet anlayışlarının belirlenmesine yönelik bir araştırma. *Selçuk Üniversitesi Sosyal Bilimler Meslek Yüksekokulu Dergisi, 20*(2), 192–205. doi:10.29249elcuksbmyd.349602

Cena, A., & Gagolewski, M. (2020). Genie+OWA: Robustifying hierarchical clustering with OWA-based linkages. *Information Sciences, 520,* 324–336. doi:10.1016/j.ins.2020.02.025

Chakraborty, S., & Zavadskas, E. K. (2014). Applications of WASPAS method in manufacturing decision making. *Informatica (Vilnius), 25*(1), 1–20. doi:10.15388/ Informatica.2014.01

Chang, K. H., & Cheng, C. H. (2011). Evaluating the risk of failure using the fuzzy OWA and DEMATEL method. *Journal of Intelligent Manufacturing, 22*(2), 113–129. doi:10.100710845-009-0266-x

Chang, Y. C., Chang, K. H., & Liaw, C. S. (2009). Innovative reliability allocation using the maximal entropy ordered weighted averaging method. *Computers & Industrial Engineering, 57*(4), 1274–1281. doi:10.1016/j.cie.2009.06.007

Cho, S. B. (1995). Fuzzy aggregation of modular neural networks with ordered weighted averaging operators. *International Journal of Approximate Reasoning, 13*(4), 359–375. doi:10.1016/0888-613X(95)00059-P

Chourabi, Z., Khedher, F., Babay, A., & Cheikhrouhou, M. (2019). Multi-criteria decision making in workforce choice using AHP, WSM and WPM. *Journal of the Textile Institute, 110*(7), 1092–1101. doi:10.1080/00405000.2018.1541434

Ertürk, K. L., Şimşek, A. A., Songür, D. G., & Şengül, G. (2014). Türkiye'de engelli farkındalığı ve engelli bireylerin adalete web erişilebilirlikleri üzerine bir değerlendirme. *Information World/Bilgi Dunyasi, 15*(2), 375-395.

Feng, L., Bui, T. D., & Tang, Y. Y. (2001). Classification of similar 2-D objects by wavelet-sparse-matrix (WSM) method. *International Journal of Pattern Recognition and Artificial Intelligence, 15*(2), 329–345. doi:10.1142/S0218001401000873

Gavcar, C. T., & Organ, A. (2020). AHP-Gri İlişkisel Analiz ve AHP-WASPAS yöntemleri ile online satış yapan seyahat acentalarının değerlendirilmesi. *Business & Management Studies: An International Journal, 8*(1), 731–753.

Gezen, A. (2019). Türkiye'de faaliyet gösteren katılım bankalarının ENTROPİ ve WASPAS yöntemleri ile performans analizi. *Muhasebe ve Finansman Dergisi,* (84), 213–232. doi:10.25095/mufad.625812

Ghasemkhani, N., Vayghan, S. S., Abdollahi, A., Pradhan, B., & Alamri, A. (2020). Urban development modeling using integrated fuzzy systems, ordered weighted averaging (OWA), and geospatial techniques. *Sustainability, 12*(3), 1–26. doi:10.3390u12030809

Güreş, N., Arslan, S., & Yalçın, R. (2013). Türk havayolu işletmelerinin web sitelerinin değerlendirilmesine yönelik bir araştırma. *Niğde Üniversitesi İktisadi ve İdari Bilimler Fakültesi Dergisi, 6*(1), 173–185.

Handoko, D., Mesran, M., Nasution, S. D., Yuhandri, Y., & Nurdiyanto, H. (2017). Application of weight sum model (WSM) in determining special allocation funds recipients. *The IJICS, 1*(2), 31–35.

Hassouna, M. S., Sahari, N., & İsmail, A. (2020). University website accessibility for totally blind users. *Journal of Information and Communication Technology, 16*(1), 63–80.

Heung, V. C., Wong, M. Y., & Qu, H. (2000). Airport-restaurant service quality in Hong Kong: An application of SERVQUAL. *The Cornell Hotel and Restaurant Administration Quarterly, 41*(3), 86–96. doi:10.1177/001088040004100320

Jain, V., & Raj, T. (2013). SAW ve WPM kullanarak fms'de esnekliğin değerlendirilmesi. *Karar Bilim Mektupları, 2*(4), 223–230.

KAMİS/Kamu İnternet Siteleri Rehberi Projesi. (2012). *Erişilebilirlik.* Retrieved April 15, 2020, from, https://kamis.gov.tr/erisebilirlik-nedir/

Khakzad, H. (2020). OWA operators with different orness levels for sediment management alternative selection problem. *Water Supply, 20*(1), 173–185. doi:10.2166/ws.2019.149

Lei, F., Wei, G., Gao, H., Wu, J., & Wei, C. (2020). TOPSIS method for developing supplier selection with probabilistic linguistic information. *International Journal of Fuzzy Systems, 22*(3), 749–759. doi:10.100740815-019-00797-6

Li, L., Peng, Y., Yang, C., & Li, Y. (2020). Optical sensing system for detection of the internal and external quality attributes of apples. *Postharvest Biology and Technology, 162,* 1–10. doi:10.1016/j.postharvbio.2019.111101

Liu, X., & Wang, L. (2020). An extension approach of TOPSIS method with OWAD operator for multiple criteria decision-making. *Granular Computing, 5*(1), 135–148. doi:10.100741066-018-0131-4

Mardani, A., Nilashi, M., Zakuan, N., Loganathan, N., Soheilirad, S., Saman, M. Z. M., & Ibrahim, O. (2017). A systematic review and meta-Analysis of SWARA and WASPAS methods: Theory and applications with recent fuzzy developments. *Applied Soft Computing, 57,* 265–292. doi:10.1016/j.asoc.2017.03.045

Nezhad, M. R. G., Zolfani, S. H., Moztarzadeh, F., Zavadskas, E. K., & Bahrami, M. (2015). Planning the priority of high tech industries based on SWARA-WASPAS methodology: The case of the nanotechnology industry in Iran. *Economic Research-Ekonomska Istraživanja, 28*(1), 1111–1137. doi:10.1080/1331677X.2015.1102404

Orçun, Ç. (2019). Enerji sektöründe WASPAS yöntemiyle performans analizi. *Bolu Abant İzzet Baysal Üniversitesi Sosyal Bilimler Enstitüsü Dergisi, 19*(2), 439–453.

Özbek, A. (2019). Türkiye'deki illerin EDAS ve WASPAS yöntemleri ile yaşanabilirlik kriterlerine göre sıralanması. *Kırıkkale Üniversitesi Sosyal Bilimler Dergisi, 9*(1), 177–200.

Özdağoğlu, A., Keleş, M. K., & Yörük Eren, F. (2019). Bir üniversite hastanesinde makroelisa ekipmanı alternatiflerinin WASPAS ve SWARA yöntemleri ile değerlendirilmesi. *Süleyman Demirel Üniversitesi İktisadi ve İdari Bilimler Fakültesi Dergisi, 24*(2), 319–331.

Özer, İ., & Sarı, İ. (2018). Yaşlı bireyler için web sayfaları tasarımının ergonomik açıdan incelenmesi. *Ergonomi, 1*(3), 148–155. doi:10.33439/ergonomi.471595

Rana, S. C., & Patel, J. N. (2018). Selection of best location for small hydro power project using AHP, WPM and TOPSIS methods. *ISH Journal of Hydraulic Engineering, 173-177.* Advance online publication. doi:10.1080/09715010.2018.1468827

Rao, C. M., & Venkatasubbaiah, K. (2016). Application of WSM, WPM and TOPSIS Methods for the optimization of multiple responses. *International Journal of Hybrid Information Technology*, *9*(10), 59-72. Doi:. doi:10.14257/ijhit.2016.9.10.07

Rençber, Ö. F., & Avcı, T. (2018). BIST'te işlem gören bankaların sermaye yeterliliklerine göre karşılaştırılması: WASPAS yöntemi ile uygulama. *Anemon Muş Alparslan Üniversitesi Sosyal Bilimler Dergisi*, *6*(18), 169–175. doi:10.18506/anemon.452713

Rinner, C., & Malczewski, J. (2002). Web-enabled spatial decision analysis using ordered weighted averaging (OWA). *Journal of Geographical Systems*, *4*(4), 385–403. doi:10.1007101090300095

Senapati, T., & Yager, R. R. (2019). Some new operations over Fermatean fuzzy numbers and application of Fermatean fuzzy WPM in multiple criteria decision making. *Informatica (Vilnius)*, *30*(2), 391–412. doi:10.15388/Informatica.2019.211

Sianturi, L. T. (2019). Implementation of Weight Sum Model (WSM) in the Selection of Football Athletes. *The IJICS*, *3*(1), 24–27.

Taka, M., Raygor, S. P., Purohit, R., & Parashar, V. (2017). Selection of tool and work piece combination using multiple attribute decision making methods for computer numerical control turning operation. *Materials Today: Proceedings 4. 5th International Conference of Materials Processing and Characterization (ICMPC 2016)*, 1199–1208.

Tan, S. (2020). Study on the development strategy of airport economy in dalian. *Modern Economy*, *11*(1), 200–207. doi:10.4236/me.2020.111017

Türk Hava Yolları, A. O. (2011). *Seri:XI No:29 Sayılı Tebliğe İstinaden Hazırlanmış Yönetim Kurulu Faaliyet Raporu*. Retrieved April 09, 2020, from, https://investor.turkishairlines.com/documents/ThyInvestorRelations/download/faaliyet_raporu/faaliyet_raporu_aralik_2011.pdf

Turper, D. (2008). *Web siteleri için orta yaş ve üzeri kullanıcılara yönelik arayüz tasarımları* (Sanatta Yeterlilik Tezi). Marmara Üniversitesi Güzel Sanatlar Enstitüsü, İstanbul, Türkiye.

Turskis, Z., Zavadskas, E. K., Antucheviciene, J., & Kosareva, N. (2015). A hybrid model based on fuzzy AHP and fuzzy WASPAS for construction site selection. *International Journal of Computers, Communications & Control*, *10*(6), 113–128. doi:10.15837/ijccc.2015.6.2078

Valente, R. D. O. A., & Vettorazzi, C. A. (2008). Definition of priority areas for forest conservation through the ordered weighted averaging method. *Forest Ecology and Management, 256*(6), 1408–1417. doi:10.1016/j.foreco.2008.07.006

Vatansever, K., & Akgül, Y. (2018). Performance evaluation of websites using entropy and grey relational analysis methods: The case of airline companies. *Decision Science Letters, 7*(2), 119–130. doi:10.5267/j.dsl.2017.6.005

Yang, C. Q., Wu, T., & Liao, Y. (2014). Evaluation for the Location Selection of Airport based on WLSM-TOPSIS Method. *Applied Mechanics and Materials, 548-549*(548), 1823–1827. doi:10.4028/www.scientific.net/AMM.548-549.1823

Yılmaz, M. (2015). Okul kütüphanecisinin matematiksel yöntem ile seçimi: OWA (Sıralı Ağırlıklandırılmış Ortalama). *Millî Eğitim, 208*, 200–217.

Chapter 9
Exploring Critical Success Factors Towards Adoption of M–Government Services in Tanzania:
A Web Analytics Study

Fredrick Ishengoma
The University of Dodoma, Tanzania

ABSTRACT

For the past decade, the Tanzanian government has started implementing m-government initiatives. However, little is known about the factors surrounding m-government adoption in Tanzania. Consequently, some m-government services have been successfully adopted while others are still struggling (having a low level of adoption). In this chapter, the authors investigate critical success factors (CSFs) that favor the adoption of m-government services from a web analytics point of view. The results show that inspecting the web analytics data from multiple viewpoints and varying levels of detail, gives insights on the CSFs towards the adoption of m-government services. The findings suggest that perceived usefulness, user needs, and usability favor the adoption of one m-government service over the other. Moreover, factors like the loading time of the service, the number of requests, and bounce rate seem not to have an effect.

DOI: 10.4018/978-1-7998-7848-3.ch009

INTRODUCTION

Mobile government (m-Government) is emerging as the new frontier of public service delivery, enabling government services to be more accessible to citizens through the use of mobile technology. Governments in developing countries are gradually implementing m-Government initiatives to provide citizens, businesses, and public servants with more access to government information and services. The potential of m-Government lies in high mobile penetration, increasing low cost of mobile devices and ubiquitous feature (Gyanendra, 2007).

In Tanzania, government services that were previously provided in a manual format are now being converted into a mobile platform, allowing people to access them from anywhere and at any time. Recent studies have revealed that, despite the growing number of m-Government initiatives, the Critical Success Factors (CSFs) that underpin its successful adoption are largely untapped (Mtingwi, 2015, Ishengoma *et al.,* 2018). Furthermore, the CSFs that drive the adoption of m-Government vary by country and are affected by the social-cultural aspects (Almuraqab, 2017). Since the concept of m-Government is an add-on to e-Government that originates in the public administration systems of industrialized countries, how it operates outside that domain, such as in developing African countries, is mostly influenced by the context of that region (Sri and Mellisa, 2012).

Several researchers have studied the factors influencing citizen adoption of m-Government in the contexts of developed countries (Annie et al., 2017; Shareef M., Dwivedi Y., Laumer S., and Archer N., 2016; Love and Alssbaiheen, 2015; Al-Khamayseh and Lawrence, 2010). However, existing research has not adequately provided a better understanding of the factors that influence citizen adoption of m-Government services in Tanzania. Currently, there is a varying degree of adoption between m-Government services that belong to the same family, i.e., serve the same category of citizens. Some of these m-Government services are successfully adopted while others have been struggling for adoption. To ensure the successful adoption of m-Government services in Tanzania, CSFs needs to be known. Furthermore, little is known about the behavior of Tanzanian users of m-Government services, especially why and under what situations people prefer one m-Government service over the other. It is now the researchers' responsibility to look into the CSFs for m-Government adoption in Tanzania.

Based on the above assertions, the objective of this chapter is to investigate the CSFs for the adoption of m-Government services in Tanzania by employing web analytics approach. The chapter investigate user behavior as well as the whys and wherefores that led to different levels of adoption among m-Government services belonging to the same family.

The organization of the chapter is as follows: Section 2 presents the background of the study. The case studies that have been used in this chapter are described in Section 3. Section 4 discusses the materials and methods used in this study. Section 5 presents results and discussion. The findings and discussion are discussed in Section 5. Section 6 discusses the study's limitations, and Section 7 concludes the chapter.

BACKGROUND

Web Analytics

Web Analytics (WA) refers to the assessment, compilation, review, and reporting of web-based data with the aim of better understanding and improving web use (Sleeper, Consolvo, & Staddon, 2014). For instance, we can use WA to track the number of visitors, where they came from, what section they visited, how much time they spent on the web, how far users navigated, where their visits ended, and where they went next (Clifton, 2012). Web analytics' strength lies in its ability to deliver unbiased results, overcoming the shortage of experts, being low cost, it does not get tired, and it evades inconsistency results from experts (Dingli and Misfud, 2011). Moreover, WA collects data from the user's unobtrusiveness. By using WA, Researchers are able to gather data from users without interfering with their responses, i.e., in a non-reactive manner. As opposed to the obtrusive approach, where the participant is fully conscious that they are being observed, the participant's viewpoints and reactions will be affected (the Hawthorne effect). Studies have shown that the Hawthorne effect (HE) affects participants' responses and behavior in studies (McCarney et al., 2007). With WA, data collection happens invisibly to the users on the background, thus avoiding the Hawthorne effect (Lalmas et al., 2014).

Web Analytics and m-Government Adoption

We can understand about user behavior and the complexities surrounding the adoption of m-Government services by using web analytics. Web analytics may also expose potentially problematic areas or features that prevent users from embracing the m-Government service successfully. While several researchers have looked at m-Government adoption from the user's viewpoint, there has been very little research done explicitly on web analytics.

Using a collection of standard web diagnostic tools, (Choudrie et al., 2004) evaluates the usability, quality, and security performance of e-Government web portals in Canada, Australia, Hong Kong, Finland, and Singapore. The study strongly indicates that web designers and e-Government policymakers and stakeholders should adhere to and promote the use of recognized guidelines when designing websites. Rodriguez et al. (2010) assessed the e-Government maturity level in 16 randomly selected countries using a set of web analytics tools. The findings of the study indicate that municipal websites perform better in terms of design metrics than in terms of content metrics. Just six of the surveyed countries achieve at least 50% of the overall score for content metrics. These results illustrate the ineffective delivery of content on municipal websites, which has an impact on the adoption of the services.

Google Analytics (GA) was used in a study by (Pakkalaa et al., 2012) to monitor visitor statistics on three food composition websites (Denmark, Finland, and Switzerland). All of the websites had a large number of users, which appeared to grow as the websites matured. According to the findings of the research, GA provided valuable and flexible knowledge that can be used to better understand user behavior and compare different site usage. According to the review of the above literature, there is little research on user behavior and understanding of the success factors for the adoption of m-Government services from the perspective of WA. This chapter aims to close this gap by looking at the behaviors of users and the factors that lead m-Government services from the same family to have different levels of adoption.

CASE STUDIES

We picked three websites with different adoption rate according to traffic rank. All of the case studies fall under to the same category of carrier and education and the according to category rank traffic data of 2018 (Alexa, 2018b). The chosen case studies are tabulated in table 1. From table 1, the website refers to the name of the website under study. The two first sites (ajira.go.tz and necta.go.tz) have a higher degree of adoption compared to the third site (nacte.go.tz).

Table 1. Three case studies selected for the study according to traffic rank

SN	Website	Rank in Tanzania	Category Rank
1	Ajira.go.tz	10	709
2	Necta.go.tz	34	4,473
3	Nacte.go.tz	75	12,180

Www.ajira.go.tz

The website www.ajira.go.tz is run by the Public Service Recruitment Secretariat (PSRS), a government body created specifically to make the process of hiring public servants easier. One of its main responsibilities is to advertise open positions in the government. Moreover, the site facilitates the registration of graduates and professionals for purposes of ease of reference in the recruitment process of employees to the public service. For example, a user may visit this website in search of a new job and upload his or her cv to a database where he or she will be contacted about future job opportunities.

Www.necta.go.tz

National Examinations Council of Tanzania (NECTA) was established by the parliamentary act no. 21 of 1973. The NECTA website was launched in 2003. It mainly deals with administering secondary examinations and publication of students' results in Tanzania. The website is operated by the Information Technology (IT) section, which is part of the NECTA's department of research, evaluation and data processing. NECTA delivers secondary examination results, which are mostly used by students, teachers, parents, and guardians. Universities, colleges, government agencies, scholars, non-governmental organizations, and other education stakeholders are among the other users. The examination results can be accessed via the website (necta.go.tz) or via SMS. The user sends a coded message to the specific number 15311 via SMS. The results are sent to the sender in a response message. We chose this site as one of the case studies because it is one of Tanzania's most popular m-Government sites and fits well with our research goals.

Www.nacte.go.tz

In 1997, the National Council for Technical Education (NACTE) was formed by Act of Parliament Cap. 129 to oversee and coordinate the provision of technical education and training in Tanzania. NACTE's jurisdiction extends to all tertiary education and training institutions, excluding universities and their affiliated colleges, that offer technician, semiprofessional, and professional courses.

These websites have been chosen for this study since they bear a resemblance and are of the same nature in the following manner.

1. They all share similar demographic profiles of users, i.e., university, college and tertiary education graduates.

2. They all publish information which has a similar context to the user (education and carrier). Necta.go.tz and nacte.go.tz publish examination results, and ajira. go.tz publishes available job vacancies in the government.
3. Users on both platforms experience anxiety, with students waiting for test results to be released on necta.go.tz and nacte.go.tz, equivalent to a graduate waiting for a work vacancy to be announced on ajira.go.tz.
4. They are both related to education and employment.

MATERIALS AND METHODS

The information requirements of this chapter determined the data sources and data collection techniques used. The authors needed data that assist the understanding of the level of adoption and potential issues that could clarify the level of adoption from a web analytics standpoint. In this chapter, authors evaluate various network parameters using a collection of web analytics tools (Alexa Web Analytics, Webpage Test tool, Open Web Application Security Project Zed Attack Proxy (OWASP ZAP), and MAUVE tool), to see whether one m-Government service is more likely to be adopted than the others.

This chapter presents the findings of a one-year web traffic monitoring project (September 2017 to September 2018) where authors analyzed the following metrics: Users' demographic profiles, number of sessions, bounce rates, loading time, page size, number of requests, broken links, privacy, security, and accessibility.

Alexa Web Analytics

Alexa Web Analytics (AWA) is a front-runner in web traffic ranking providing web analytics including website traffic statistics, site comparisons, and website audience (Alexa, 2018). Its measurement is based on a diverse set of over 25,000 browser extensions and plugins used by millions of people globally (Vaughan and Yang, 2013). It is built on a vast selection of over 25,000 browser extensions and plugins that are used by millions of people around the world. We chose this as our sole source of information for this project because it is considered to be the best pick for web analytics information on the (Vaughan and Yang, 2013).

Webpagetest Tool

The Webpagetest tool was used to calculate the loading time, number of requests, and page size of the selected m-Government sites in this chapter. The authors used this tool since it is the best open source tool for measuring the three web metrics (loading time, page size and number of requests and). This method has been used by several researchers to investigate the efficiency of various web systems. The tool allows for the analysis of web traffic data for a large number of Internet users. This tool has been used by several researchers to investigate the efficiency of various web systems.

OWASP Vulnerable Assessment Tool

We use the Open Web Application Security Project, OWASP, to evaluate the security of our selected m-Government sites in this chapter (Makino and Klyuev, 2015). OWASP ZAP is a vulnerability identification tool for web applications. OWASP was adopted for this study because it is open source and studies have shown that it is the most accurate vulnerability scanner from both commercial and open-source web application penetration testing tools (Makino and Klyuev, 2015; Sagar et al., 2018).

MAUVE Tool

Multiguideline Accessibility Usability Validation Environment (MAUVE) is an environment for accessibility testing for web applications. It allows to automatically test the accessibility of web pages using the Web Content Accessibility Guidelines (WCAG) (WCAG 1.0, and WCAG 2.0). The aim of WCAG is to provide a common shared standard for web content accessibility that address the needs of individuals, organisations, and governments worldwide. It is built and maintained by a global collaboration of web users, web experts, and organizations. MAUVE is used in this analysis since it is the most commonly used method for assessing a website's accessibility.

RESULTS AND DISCUSSION

The data analysis and discussion are presented in this section of the chapter. The findings are examined and explored in terms of their potential for m-Government service adoption along three dimensions: What, Who, and How.

What Are the Keywords Used?

To understand the environment and features that support the adoption of m-Government services, we start by exploring the keyword used by users to initiate a connection to the sites. Based on the traffic data crawled, we analyzed the keywords most used on necta.go.tz, ajira.go.tz and necta.go.tz sites for the period of nine months (February

- November 2018). Table 2 shows the top 5 keywords represented according to their frequency.

Table 2. Top 10 keywords used while searching for necta.go.tz and ajira.go.tz sites

SN	Ajira.go.tz		Necta.go.tz		Nacte.go.tz Keyword	
	Keyword	Percentage	Keyword	Percentage	Keyword	Percentage
1	Ajira portal	17.57	Necta	32.66	Nacte	11
2	Ajira	15.50	Necta results 2018	5.94	Nacte online application	5.42
3	Tanzania recruitment portal pspr	8.79	Matokeo ya kidato cha sita	5.10	Saut Mwanza	4.31
4	Ajira Tanzania	8.67	Necta results	4.23	Nacte tz	3.34
5	Sekretarieti ya ajira	6.98	Necta 2017	4.20	Arusha technical college	3.12

The first observation from these keywords is that site-name plays vital role for the users in finding the site. In all sites, users used the keyword that matches the domain name. Moreover, the year is also used to describe the specific time of the information searched. This translates that, users embed the year to the keyword in trying to get specific information of that time. For instance, "necta results in 2018" translate to a user seeking information on the examination results of 2018.

This signifies that the name of the site (domain name) and the time keyword is essential towards easing user engagement with the service. Learning from these keywords, the study argues that web designers, content developers, and site maintainers should be aware of the behavior of the users in trying to access the sites. Hence, in easing access to information, the information uploaded to m-Government sites should match with the predetermined perspective of the user's searching keyword.

Who Are the Users?

Understanding the audience of m-Government services and where they access the service from can significantly assist in focusing and allowing to structure service content to meet the perceived needs of this audience. Figure 1 provides the geography of the users of the selected m-Government services in this study, observed for the period of 1 year (September 2017 to September 2018).

Figure 1. Audience geography of users of the selected m-Government services

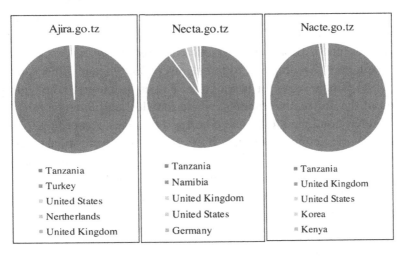

From figure 1, we observe that the majority of the users (more than 85%) are from within the country, Tanzania. Studies have shown that the potential benefits of m-Government can only be obtained if the initiatives are accepted and used by the intended users (Margetts, 2006). From figure 1, the results suggest that the intended users fully use the selected m-Government sites.

Figure 2. Gender profile of the selected m-Government services

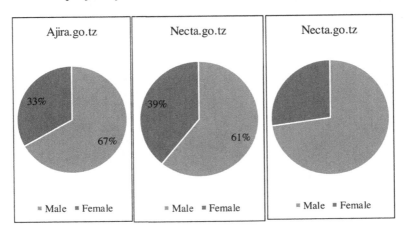

Figure 2, depicts the gender profiles of users of the selected m-Government services in Tanzania. From figure 2, we can observe that the number of male users outnumbered female users in all m-Government sites as shown in Figure 2. For necta. go.tz, male users are 61.02% compared to female users 38.98%. Also, for ajira.go.tz, male users are 66.91% compared to female users 33.09% and 72.81% male users versus 27.19% female users for necta.go.tz. This is in line with the demographic population of the Tanzanian students, where females' enrolment at tertiary levels of education has continued to be less compared to males. According to the recent report by the World Economic Forum (WEF, 2017), there were about twice as many men as women enrolled in tertiary education in 2017. The trend is the same for the last five years in the country. This translates to our study results that more male engages more with the m-Government services compared to females.

We then examine the *age distribution of users of the selected m-Government services*. Figure 3 shows that most users (more than 37%) are young people aged between 25 years and 34 years. This is a group which is composed of university students/graduates who are young and tech-savvy and looking for a job (Bommier & Lambert, 2000).

The first group is of the age of (25 - 34) years who are the most users. This group is followed by two groups of age (18 - 24) years and (30 - 44) years as shown in figure 3. These groups are also tech-savvy, searching for jobs and being of assistance to their younger ones who need service form the selected m-Government sites. In Tanzania, young people are the ones mostly observed to ICT reliant in daily life. Terms such as 'BBC - born before computer' became very popular in the social commentary which signifies elderly who are "non-tech savvy" compared to young people.

Figure 3. User's age distribution for selected m-Government sites

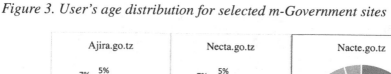

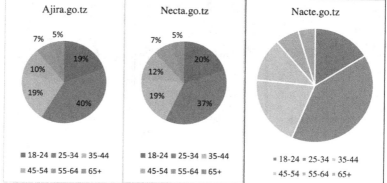

We argue that this is the targeted population of these selected m-Government sites since the demand for employment (Ajira.go.tz) and information about education and examinations (Necta.go.tz and Nacte.go.tz) match well with the age of the most users. Hence, users' needs and the usefulness of the information and services provided by these sites match well with the age group of the most users. In this context, we argue that the user's needs and Perceived Usefulness (PU) play a significant role in the adoption of m-Government services.

How Do m-Government Users and System Behave?

In this chapter section, we seek to understand users and system behavior by exploring these questions: How do users find these selected m-Government sites? What are the features of their engagement that might lead to the adoption of one m-Government site over the other? What nuances exist in m-Government sites that influences users' adoption? In answering these questions, we use the following web analytics metrics: Average number of sessions, bounce rate, deadlinks, loading time, page size, number of requests, privacy, security, and accessibility. We haven't considered other metrics such as the global "reach" because they don't fit enough for this study as local citizens are the ones who mostly use these m-Government services. These metrics were monitored and recorded for the period of 1 year (from August 2017 to August 2018).

How Do Users Find the Selected m-Government Sites?

Our study shows that most users use direct traffic followed by an organic search in attracting visitors to m-Government sites as shown in figure 4. Nearly 58% of visits from ajira.go.tz and 40% of visits from necta.go.tz come from direct traffic. Few percentages of visits originated from referrals, email, and social media. No visit was found to be arisen from a paid search.

Most of the users of ajira.go.tz (more than 57%) come through direct search. Higher percentage from organic search indicate higher awareness of the users. Most of these users are aware of the site, and they know the URL. Traditionally, we've attributed these visitors to manually entering the URL of the website or click on a bookmarked link. As for the necta.go.tz and nacte.go.tz, most of its users (48%) come from the organic channel. The next most users for ajira.go.tz is the organic searchers while for necta.go.tz, and nacte.go.tz are direct search. Referrals and email sources had the low influence of visits on all sites, whereby paid campaigns do not generate any visits.

Figure 4. How Users Find the Selected m-Government Sites

How Users Find the Selected m-Government Sites

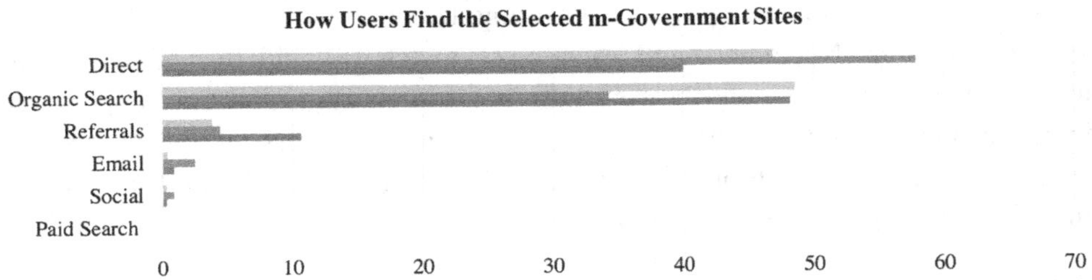

	Paid Search	Social	Email	Referrals	Organic Search	Direct
nacte.go.tz (%)	0	0.31	0.39	3.79	48.58	46.89
ajira.go.tz (%)	0	0.87	2.51	4.43	34.3	57.87
necta.go.tz (%)	0	0.28	0.85	10.7	48.17	39.98

Usability

Average Number of Sessions

The key performance indicator that shed light on m-Government adoption from a web analytics perspective is user engagement (Margetts, 2006). Studies (Unhelkar, 2003; Love S. and Alssbaiheen, 2015) have shown that the success of technology adoption is heavily dependent on how the adopters use it. As people become more engaged with the sites, hence the likelihood of adoption is increased. The higher number of sessions indicates that there is a high level of engagement between users and the services. In this section, we examine user engagement within the selected m-Government sites by using an average number of sessions for the one year (November 2017 to October 2018).

Figure 5. Average number of sessions for the period of 1 year (November 2017 – October 2018)

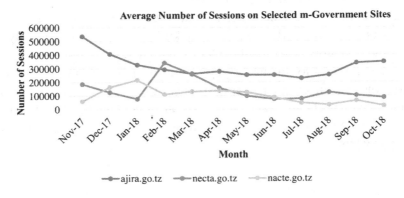

236

From figure 5 we observe that ajira.go.tz has a higher number of sessions followed by necta.go.tz and nacte.go.tz. The high number of sessions incline that users use the site more compared to a lower number of sessions. This also suggests that users find the site useful. However, it can also be argued that when a user spends much time, it might signify that the user is having difficulty in finding the information they are looking for. However, this scenario is always by the higher bounce rate (Farris et al., 2010). Moreover, since we have not observed any indicator that highlights the problem in finding information (in ajira.go.tz), then the higher number of sessions denotes that users have found the site useful. Also, the more users engage with the site; the more are likely to adopt that site. Hence, from this observation, we argue that the actual use and perceived usefulness (PU) are significant factors towards the adoption of one m-Government service over the other.

Bounce Rate

We study the bounce rate to understand whether visitors interact with the site by viewing other pages or exit after landing on the homepage. A score of 50% bounce rate is considered average while anything above 60% is deemed to be problematic (Farris et al., 2010). Figure 6 depicts the bounce rate comparison of the three m-Government sites. Nacte.go.tz was found to have a higher bounce rate compared to ajira.go.tz and necta.go.tz. The bounce rate for nacte.go.tz reaches up to 56.7 which is higher than the average bounce rate (Farris et al., 2010). This indicates that 56.7% of the people who enter nacte.got.tz, don't reach other pages on the site.

Most reasons for the higher bounce rate can be traced down to the poor page performance or poor page content. One of the reasons for the poor page performance is poor site design for instance; Unresponsive site, link error (404 or File Not Found error) and incompatible site design. Poor page content led visitors to face the material which is not useful to them. Hence, they leave the site immediately.

In trying to understand the high bounce rate in nacte.go.tz, we examine the keywords used by users to access this site. We trace the site using the second top keyword for nacte.go.tz "Saut mwanza" which leads us to a nacte page with no useful content for "Saut Mwanza" as shown in figure 7. The same occurred for the fourth top keyword "Arusha technical college." This indicates that poor content leads users to miss the needed information leading to higher bounce rate in m-Government sites. From this observation, we argue that content and usability are significant factors that favor adoption of one m-Government service over the other.

Figure 6. Screenshot of "Saut Mwanza" page on necta.go.tz *site (March, 2018)*

Deadlinks

We further explore the effect of usability by measuring the number of deadlinks on the selected m-Government sites. We used a dead link checker tool to perform a full scan and analysis for the chosen m-Government sites. The scans were performed once in a month for one year (November 2017 to October 2018). The analysis found an average of 13 broken links out of 1987 links on necta.go.tz, which equals 0.65% as shown in Figure 7. Nacte.go.tz was found to have average of 12 deadlinks out of 287 links, which is 4%. Meanwhile, ajira.go.tz had an average number of 50 dead links out of 425 links, which equals 11%.

Based on the analysis above, it indicates that anytime a user clicked on a link on the selected m-Government sites, there is a (0.65%, 4%, and 11%) probability on (necta.go.tz, nacte.go.tz, and ajira.go.tz) respectively that the user would be taken to an inaccessible page. Studies have shown that deadlinks frustrate users and reduce their chances of site-revisiting which decrease user engagement and adoption at large (Alsaghier and Hussain, 2012).

Deadlinks create a negative user experience and hamper a user's confidence that the m-Government service will perform the desired action. This eventually decreases trust in the particular m-Government service (Alsaghier and Hussain, 2012). It is, therefore, imperative for government agencies to continuously monitor their sites for broken links and repair such links immediately to reduce user frustration and motivates the adoption level of m-Government services.

Figure 7. Number of deadlinks and OK links on <u>necta.go.tz</u>

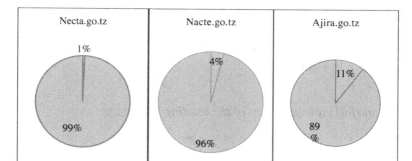

We then explore the influence of loading time, page size and number requests towards the adoption of the selected m-Government sites. Page loading time depends on several factors such as the size of the site, the number of files, and the size of the images. Loading time is measured when the browser contacts servers to download the required files. We measured the loading time, page size and a number of requests of the three selected sites on a network with the Internet download speed of 5 Mbps. The results are shown in Table 3.

Table 3. Loading Time, Page Size and Number of Requests of selected m-Government sites

SN	Metric	Site		
		Necta.go.tz	Ajira.go.tz	Nacte.go.tz
1	Loading time	4.8 seconds	8.25 seconds	4.69 seconds
2	Page size	1.3 MB	2.3 MB	2.2 MB
3	Number of requests	44	99	33

From table 3, we observe that the number of requests of ajira.go.tz is more than twice the number of necta.go.tz and thrice the number of nacte.go.tz. This indicates that ajira.go.tz has got a much larger number of files to be loaded compared to nacte.go.tz and necta.go.tz.

We then try to understand what makes a number of requests and loading time on ajira.go.tz so high compared to other m-Government sites. We take a look at a waterfall chart of ajira.go.tz web structure using Webpagetest tool. We capture the site HAR file and analyze the kind of requests that are made while the site is loading as shown in Figure 8.

Figure 8. Waterfall view structure of the loading ajira.go.tz

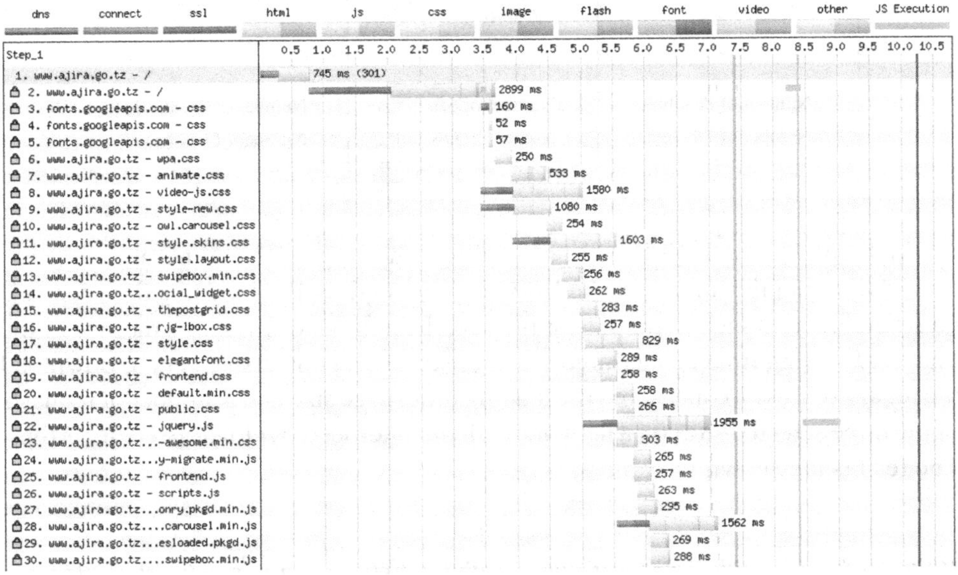

We found out that most of the requests made to the server load multiple Javascript and CSS files (as shown in Figure 9) compared to a low number of Javascript and CSS files on nacte.go.tz and necta.go.tz.

While most of these files are mere kilobytes in size, the user can only download a few of them at a time; browsers limit users to a maximum number of parallel connections. Browsers limit the number of HTTP connections with the same domain name. Most modern browsers allow six connections per domain. Most older browsers allow only two connections per domain (Grigorik, 2013). As a result, the majority of these request times are spent waiting for a connection to become available. This adds seconds of wasted time to page's load. This problem can be fixed by consolidating JavaScript and CSS files or by limiting the number of files that load. Fewer files mean fewer requests and therefore a faster website

Despite ajira.go.tz having a higher number of sessions (Fig. 5) and reasonable bounce rate (Fig. 6), it has a higher loading time and a number of requests. Studies have shown that, when people have to wait a longer time for a site to load for too long, they tend to abandon what they were browsing on altogether (Gann,1999). The study by (Loiacono and Lin 2003) confirmed that long waiting times experienced by users to download or open websites impact negatively on website users' experience. A recent report by Google argues that "As page load time goes from one second to five seconds, the probability of bounce increases by 90%" (Google, 2017).

However, in this study, despite the higher loading time of ajira.go.tz, the site still had a lower bounce rate and a high number of sessions. This suggests that loading time is not a predominant factor that influences the user to engage or disengage with the m-Government sites. Based on these observations, we argue that perceived usefulness (PU) and users' needs of the site are the predominant factors that led users to wait for higher loading time.

The need for the user to access the information is the strong factor. In this study context, the need for young people to get information about available job vacancies and the perceived usefulness of this information outperform the sluggish loading time factor in engaging with the m-Government service. Under this section, we conclude that loading time, page size and number of requests are not significant towards the adoption of m-Government services. We suggest that perceived usefulness (PU), users' needs and contents of the site are the predominant factors towards the adoption of m-Government services.

Privacy and Security

Security is one of the most significant factors for the adoption of m-Government services (Ishengoma, Mselle, and Mongi, 2018). Thereupon, emphasizing on improving security and privacy environment is essential for enhancing the adoption of m-Government services.

Privacy

From observation of the three selected m-Government sites (ajira.go.tz, necta.go.tz, and nacte.go.tz), we couldn't find any privacy policy. Placement of privacy policy on m-Government sites is an essential aspect of legitimacy because privacy has been known to influence user trust in and influence adoption (Bwalya & Healy, 2010; Khanyako & Maiga, 2013).

This is an issue that needs to be addressed as Roach and Cayer (2010) argued that users needed to see privacy statements throughout the website, in order to be assured that their privacy needs were met. Given the fact that privacy concerns act as a success factor to m-Government users (Ishengoma et al., 2018), it becomes imperative for policymakers to ensure that privacy statements become an integral part of m-Government sites to encourage citizens' adoption. While privacy policy can affect the adoption of m-Government sites, in the context of this study, we argue that it is not significant. This is because all of the selected m-Government services had no privacy policy. Hence, it could not have an effect leading to one m-Government service being adopted more than the other.

Security

In our study context, security issue refers to any nuances that created security vulnerability for an m-Government service. We analyzed the security of our selected m-Government sites using Open Web Application Security Project, OWASP ZAP (Makino and Klyuev, 2015). The results of OWASP ZAP analysis indicated all sites had no high-level risk vulnerabilities. The site ajira.go.tz was found to be more vulnerable compared to necta.go.tz and nacte.go.tz. Ajira.go.tz was found to have 89 medium risk level compared to necta.go.tz and nacte.go.tz which had no medium level alerts. Low-risk alerts were found to be 303 for ajira.go.tz, 175 for necta.go.tz and 4 for nacte.go.tz as shown in table 4.

In this study, we will focus on the medium-level alerts founds which are "application error disclosure," "buffer overflow" and "x-frame options header not set." We explore more on the medium level risks discovered to understand the nuances that led to these security risks. For instance, if the fault causes it in designing or it is a technology bug that has not been patched yet.

Table 4. OWASP Vulnerability Assessment on Selected m-Government Sites

SN	Name of Vulnerability	Risk Level	Number of Vulnerabilities		
			Ajira.go.tz	Necta.go.tz	Nacte.go.tz
1	Application error disclosure	Medium	1	0	0
2	Buffer Overflow	Medium	1	0	0
3	X-Frame Options Header Not Set	Medium	87	0	0
4	Cross-Domain JavaScript Source File Inclusion	Low	27	4	16
5	Incomplete or No-Cache Control and Pragma HTTP Header Set	Low	1	80	0
6	Secure Pages includes mixed content	Low	1	0	0
7	Web browser XSS Protection Not Enabled	Low	92	95	3
8	X-Content-Type-Options Header Missing	Low	209	0	1

i. X-Frame Options Header Not Set

This medium-level vulnerability had a high number of occurrences on ajira.go.tz. The X-Frame-Options HTTP response header can be used to indicate whether or not a browser should be allowed to render a page in a <frame>, <iframe> or <object>. If not configured correctly, the site could be a victim of clickjacking attacks. Proper configuration should be used by ensuring that site content is not embedded into other sites.

There are three possible configurations for X-Frame-Options: "Deny" which will deny loading a page from both within and from other sites. "Same origin," which page can still be used in a frame as long as the site includes it in a frame is the same as the one serving the page. "Allow-from https://example.com/" will display the page from specified origin. From the above three options, depending on the server locations of the m-Government services, "same origin" and "allow from https://example.com/" could be used. ii.

i. Application Error Disclosure

This vulnerability appears when pages contain an error/warning message that may disclose sensitive information like the location of the file that produced the unhandled exception. This information can be used to launch further attacks against the web application. Solution to this vulnerability is to implement a mechanism that provides a unique error reference/identifier to the client (browser) while logging the details on the server side and not exposing them to the user.

iii. Buffer Overflow

A buffer overflow condition exists when a program attempts to put more data in a buffer than it can hold or when an application tries to put data in a memory area past a buffer. At the code level, buffer overflow vulnerabilities usually involve the violation of a programmer's assumptions. Buffer overrun to some extent can be mitigated by ensuring development in an environment that encourages a high-quality code that requires developers to participate in code review and testing. Reviewing and rewriting the background program is needed to solve this vulnerability.

Security issues are crucial because together with privacy issues they form the basis of trust in e-government systems (Alzahrani et al., 2016; Karkin & Janssen, 2014). A sense that the website is secure is a significant factor for users to adopt the site. This is important since most m-Government services; users use their personal information. However, security efforts remain an on-going process as new security threats emerge continually, as new technologies evolve.

It has been argued in the literature that, privacy and security must be protected to increase user's trust while using e-government services (Liu and Carter, 2018; Ishengoma, Mselle and Mongi, 2018). As the technologies advance, the number of sophisticated attacks increases and simultaneously, cyber-criminals are coming up with new attack methods every day. Hence, for improving the adoption of m-Government services, security and privacy of systems and users are vital.

Accessibility

Accessibility of m-Government services by everyone is an essential aspect towards m-Government adoption. In this study, we analyzed accessibility of the selected m-Government services in the context of accessibility on multiple channels, disability access, and foreign language access. World Wide Web Consortium's (W3C) Web Accessibility Initiative (WAI) has established standards for web developers about the accessibility these are named as Web Content Accessibility Guidelines (WCAG).

In this study, the MAUVE tool analyzes how satisfactorily the selected guidelines are applied to the selected m-Government sites. Currently, there are two versions of WCAG (WCAG version 1 and WCAG version 2). This study focuses on the latest version WCAG 2.0. WCAG 2.0 is divided into three guideline priorities (A-AA-AAA). Level A deals with the basic web accessibility features. Level AA deals with advanced barriers for disabled users and level AAA deals with the highest level of web accessibility.

Table 5. WCAG Guidelines Priority on Web Accessibility

Priority	Description	Conformance Level
Priority 1	The developer must follow these guidelines to make all the information on a website accessible for all users including persons with disabilities.	A
Priority 2	The developer should follow these guidelines to remove the important accessibility barriers in accessing the information on a website.	AA
Priority 3	The developer may follow these guidelines as these are not so important but make the website more comfortable for the use of disabled person.	AAA

For ajira.go.tz the analysis found 32 errors under level A-WCAG 2.0 and 135 errors under level AA-WCAG 2.0. Total warnings were 19. For necta.go.tz, the analysis found 49 errors under level A-WCAG and 24 errors under level AA-WCAG 2.0.

Figure 9. Web accessibility compliance on selected m-Government sites

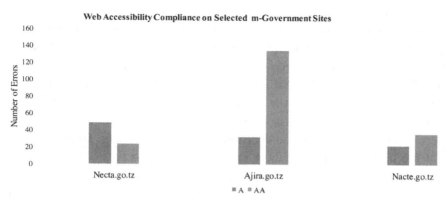

As shown in Figure 11, necta.go.tz and nacte.go.tz proved to have higher accessibility than ajira.go.tz. However, both sites failed to meet the minimum accessibility conformance level, i.e., having zero errors for level A. Since the results show that all sites do not pass A or AA compliance level, then the test for AAA compliance was not performed. Resolving the existing errors in ajira.go.tz could increase accessibility hence the number of users which will influence more adoption.

Cost and Infrastructure

The factors of cost and infrastructure were ignored on this study since: The cost of accessing information on all three selected m-Government sites is the same. In this case, cost will not be a factor for one site to be adopted more than the other. Similarly, to infrastructure, all the m-Government sites operate under the same infrastructure. Hence, infrastructure cannot favor one m-Government service over the other.

LIMITATIONS

As with any methodology, web analytics methodology has some limitations. We point out some limitations associated with this study. In web analytics, an IP address symbolize a user. Since more than one person can use the same computer for m-Government services, an IP address seems to be limited as a representation of the user. However, web analytics are currently improving this limitation by using cookies.

When cookies are used, a text file is placed on a visitor's computer while browsing a website which identifies the visitor on returning to the site. Hence, cookies must be enabled on individual computers for JavaScript to detect unique visitors and track their behavior. If an individual uses multiple computers, works at a company with strict IT regulations that do not allow cookies, their behavior will not be tracked reliably.

Another limitation is that WATs cannot give answers to the why questions. For instance, why did the users behave the way they did? Why didn't users complete the task they started? Web analytics cannot offer any information about the motivations of the users or shed any light on the decision process of the users. To explore the motives of the users, attitudinal data is required, such as surveys, interviews or direct in-context observations. However, the web analytics data can be the starting point for the gathering of the attitudinal data. Unclear behaviors discovered through the web analytics data can be the basis for attitudinal data gathering and research.

CONCLUSION

In this chapter, we presented an analysis of a large-scale traffic data from selected m-Government sites (ajira.go.tz, necta.go.tz, and nacte.go.tz) with the aim of understanding the underlying factors favoring the successful adoption of one site compared to the other. The findings prove that web analytics methodology is suitable in exploring the system and the user's behavior of m-Government sites.

The study found that both sites have similar demographic profiles of users mainly who are males between age 25 and 34 years. Majority of these are in college and those who have just finished colleges and universities. They visit the sites mainly from direct search and organic search. The study also noted that the keywords used by the users include the primary information name along with the time, for instance "necta results 2018".

All of the sites have shown poor accessibility quality, issues in usability and security. The study encourages the need for awareness among the developers and designers that websites should comply with international accessibility and usability standards. Further findings have shown that Perceived Usefulness (PU), user's needs and the content are significant factors towards the adoption of one m-Government service over the other.

The results from this chapter need to be interpreted more by linking it to additional research using other evaluation methods like qualitative and quantitative methods. For instance, the study shows what pages are visited and the frequency and duration of visits, but they do not reveal why visitors behave as such. Further study will augment these by involving actual users of m-Government services.

ACKNOWLEDGMENT

This research received no specific grant from any funding agency in the public, commercial, or not-for-profit sectors.

REFERENCES

Accenture. (2005). *Leadership in Customer Service: New Expectations, New Experiences*. Author.

Agarwal, R., & Prasad, J. (1997). The Role of Innovation Characteristics and Perceived Voluntariness in the Acceptance of Information Technologies. *Decision Sciences*, *28*(3), 557–582. doi:10.1111/j.1540-5915.1997.tb01322.x

Akamai. (2017). *The state of online retail performance*. https://www.soasta.com/wp-content/uploads/2017/04/Stateof-Online-Retail-Performance-Spring-2017.pdf

Al-Khamayseh, S., & Lawrence, E. (2010). *Towards Citizen Centric Mobile Government Services: A Roadmap*. Faculty of Information Technology, University of Technology.

Alexa. (2018a). *Alexa: Keyword Research, Competitive Analysis, & Website Ranking*. http://www.alexa.com

Alexa. (2018b). *Top Sites in Tanzania*. https://www.alexa.com/topsites/countries/TZ

Alsaghier, H., & Hussain, R. (2012). Conceptualization of trust in the e-government context: a Qualitative analysis. In A. Manohran & M. Holzer (Eds.), *Active citizen participation in e-government: A global perspective* (pp. 528–557). Information Science. doi:10.4018/978-1-4666-0116-1.ch027

Alshahwan, N., & Harman, M. (2012). State Aware Test Case Regeneration for Improving Web Application Test Suite Coverage and Fault Detection. *Proceedings of the 2012 International Symposium on Software Testing and Analysis*, 45-55. 10.1145/2338965.2336759

Annie, C. S., Choy, J. Y., Krishna, M., & Alex, L. (2017). Intention to Use m-Government Services: Age, Gender and Education Matter? International Journal of e-Business and e-Government Studies, 9(2).

Aubert, B. A., & Hamel, G. (2001). Adoption of Smart Cards in the Medical Sector: The Canadian Experience. *Social Science & Medicine*, *53*(7), 879–894. doi:10.1016/S0277-9536(00)00388-9 PMID:11522135

Axelsson, K., & Melin, U. (2012). Citizens' Attitudes towards Electronic Identification in a Public E-Service Context – An Essential Perspective in the eID Development Process. In. Lecture Notes in Computer Science: Vol. 7443. *Electronic Government. EGOV 2012*. Springer.

Barker, T. (2012). *Pro JavaScript Performance: Monitoring and Visualization.* Apress. doi:10.1007/978-1-4302-4750-0

Bommier, A., & Lambert, S. (2000). Education Demand and Age at School Enrollment in Tanzania. *The Journal of Human Resources, 35*(1), 177–203. doi:10.2307/146360

Bwalya, K. J., & Healy, M. (2010). Harnessing e-Government Adoption in the SADC Region: A Conceptual Underpinning. *Electronic. Journal of E-Government, 8*(1), 23–32.

CDT & infoDev. (2007). *E-Government Handbook: Accessibility.* Retrieved June 19, 2007, from https://www.cdt.org/egov/handbook/accessibility.shtml

Criado, J. I., & Ramilo, M. C. (2003). E-Government in practice: An analysis of website orientation to citizens in Spanish municipalities. *International Journal of Public Sector Management, 18*(3), 191–218. doi:10.1108/09513550310472320

Deepika, S., Kukreja, S., Brahma, J., Tyagi, S., & Jain, P. (2018). Studying Open Source Vulnerability Scanner for Vulnerabilities in Web Applications. *Computer Science, 9*(2), 43–49.

Dingli, A., & Mifsud, J. (2011). USEFul: A Framework to Mainstream Web Site Usability through Automated Evaluation. *International Journal of Human-Computer Interaction, 2*(1).

Doupé, A., Cui, W., Jakubowski, M. H., Peinado, M., Kruegel, C., & Vigna, D. (2013). deDacota: Toward Preventing Server-side XSS via Automatic Code and Data Separation. *Proceedings of the 2013 ACM SIGSAC Conference on Computer & Communications Security.*

Farris, P. W., Bendle, N. T., Pfeifer, P. E., & Reibstein, D. J. (2010). *Marketing metrics; The definitive guide to measuring marketing performance* (2nd ed.). Prentice Hall.

Fichman, R. G., & Kemerer, C. F. (1997). The Assimilation of Software Process Innovations. An Organizational Learning Perspective. *Management Science, 43*(10), 1345–1363. doi:10.1287/mnsc.43.10.1345

Fong, E. M., & Chung, W. Y. (2013). Mobile Cloud-Computing-Based Healthcare Service by Noncontact ECG Monitoring. *Sensors (Basel), 13*(12), 16451–16473. doi:10.3390131216451 PMID:24316562

Gann, R. (1999). *Every second count*. Competing.

Grigorik, I. (2013). Making the Web Faster with HTTP 2.0. *Communications of the ACM, 56*(12), 42–49. doi:10.1145/2534706.2534721

Gyanendra, P. (2007). Addressing the Digital Divide: E-Governance and M-Governance in A Hub and Spoke Model. *The Electronic Journal on Information Systems in Developing Countries, 31*(1), 1–14. doi:10.1002/j.1681-4835.2007. tb00210.x

Hasan, L. (2009). *Usability Evaluation Framework for E-commerce Websites in Developing Countries* (Doctoral Thesis). Loughborough University

HESLB. (2006). *Annual Report, 2005 – 2006*. Dar es Salaam: Higher Education Students' Loans Board.

Karkin, N., & Janssen, M. (2014). Evaluating websites from a public value perspective: A Review of Turkish Local Government Websites. *International Journal of Information Management, 34*(3), 351–363. doi:10.1016/j.ijinfomgt.2013.11.004

Khanyako, E., & Maiga, G. (2013). *An information security model for e-government services adoption in Uganda*. IST-Africa Conference.

Lalmas, M., O'Brien, H., & Yom-Tov, E. (2014). Measuring User Engagement. *Synthesis Lectures on Information Concepts, Retrieval, and Services, 6*(4), 1–132. doi:10.2200/S00605ED1V01Y201410ICR038

Liu & Carter. (2018). Impact of citizens' privacy concerns on e-government adoption. In *Proceedings of the 19th Annual International Conference on Digital Government Research: Governance in the Data Age*. ACM.

Loiacono, E., & Lin, H. (2005). Website Quality: Cross-cultural Comparison of U.S. and China. *The Journal of International Information Technology Management, 14*(1), 53–69.

Love, S., & Alssbaiheen, A. (2015). Exploring the Challenges of m-Government Adoption in Saudi Arabia. *The Electronic. Journal of E-Government, 13*(1), 1, 18–27.

Margetts, H. (2006). E-Government in Britain—A Decade On. *Parliamentary Affairs, 59*(2), 250–265. doi:10.1093/pa/gsl003

Mateos, Mera, González, & González López. (2001). A New Web Assessment Index: Spanish Universities Analysis. *Internet Research, 11*(3), 226–234.

Merrill, W., Gefen, D., Pavlou, P. A., & Rose, G. M. (2002). Encouraging Citizen Adoption of e-Government by Building Trust. *Electronic Markets, 12*(3), 157–162. doi:10.1080/101967802320245929

Moore, G. C., & Benbasat, I. (1991). Development of an Instrument to Measure the Perceptions of Adopting an Information Technology Innovation. *Information Systems Research, 2*(3), 192–222. doi:10.1287/isre.2.3.192

Mtingwi, J. E. (2015). Mobile Government in African Least Developed Countries (LDCs): Proposed Implementing Framework. *Proceedings of IST-Africa*, 1-14.

Nejati, J., & Balasubramanian, A. (2016). An In-depth Study of Mobile Browser Performance. *Proceedings of the 25th International Conference on World Wide Web (WWW '16)*, 1305-1315. 10.1145/2872427.2883014

Pakkala, H., Presser, K., & Christensenc, T. (2012). Using Google Analytics to Measure Visitor Statistics: The Case of Food Composition Websites. *International Journal of Information Management, 32*(6), 504–512. doi:10.1016/j.ijinfomgt.2012.04.008

Roach, C., & Cayer, J. (2010). Bridging the other divide: An assessment of the usability of Trinidad and Tobago government ministry website. In C. Reddick (Ed.), *Comparative E-government* (pp. 483–504). Springer Science Business Media. doi:10.1007/978-1-4419-6536-3_25

Rodriguez, R., Estevez, E., Giulianelli, D., & Vera, P. (2010). Assessing e-Governance Maturity through Municipal Websites - Measurement Framework and Survey Results. *Selected Papers in XV Argentine Congress of Computer Science*, 175 – 212.

Romero-Frías, E. (2009). Googling Companies - a Webometric Approach to Business Studies. *Electronic Journal of Business Research Methods, 7*(1), 93–106.

Sæbø, Ø. (2012). E-government in Tanzania: Current Status and Future Challenges. In J. S. Hans, J. Marijn, A. W. Maria, E. Carl, L. Moe, & F. Skiftenes (Eds.), *Electronic Government* (pp. 198–209). Springer. doi:10.1007/978-3-642-33489-4_17

Scowen, G., & Regenbrecht, H. (2009). Increased Popularity through Compliance with Usability Guidelines in E-Learning Web Sites. *International Journal of Information Technology and Web Engineering, 4*(3), 38–57. doi:10.4018/jitwe.2009100603

Shareef, M., Dwivedi, Y., Laumer, S., & Archer, N. (2016). Citizens' Adoption Behavior of Mobile Government (mGov): A Cross-Cultural Study. *Information Systems Management, 33*(3), 268–283. doi:10.1080/10580530.2016.1188573

Sleeper, M., Consolvo, S., & Staddon, J. (2014). Exploring the Benefits and Uses of Web Analytics Tools for Non-transactional Websites. *Proceedings of the Conference on Designing Interactive Systems: Processes, Practices, Methods, and Techniques.* 10.1145/2598510.2598555

Sri & Ezmieralda (2012). *Investigating the Potential of Mobile Phones for E-Governance in Indonesia.* CPRafrica 2012/CPRsouth7 Conference, Port Louis, Mauritius.

Fagan. (2014). The Suitability of Web Analytics Key Performance Indicators in the Academic Library Environment. *Journal of Academic Librarianship*, 40(1).

The United Republic of Tanzania. (2004). *Higher Education Students Loans Board (HELBS) Act, 2004.* Dar es Salaam: URT.

Unhelkar, B. (2003). Understanding the Impact of Cultural Issues in Global e-Business Alliances. *4th International We-B Conference.*

Vaughan, L., & Yang, R. (2013). Web Traffic and Organization Performance Measures: Relationships and Data Sources Examined. *Journal of Informetrics*, 7(3), 699–711. doi:10.1016/j.joi.2013.04.005

Venkatesh, V., & David, F. R. (2000). A Theoretical Extension of the Technology Acceptance Model: Four Longitudinal Field Studies. *Management Science*, 46(2), 186–204. doi:10.1287/mnsc.46.2.186.11926

West, D. (2002). *Global E-Government.* Retrieved from http://www.insidepolitics. org/egovt02int.html

World Economic Forum. (2017). Global Gender Gap Report. WEF.

Yuma, M., & Vitaly, K. (2015). Evaluation of Web Vulnerability Scanners. *The 8th IEEE International Conference on Intelligent Data Acquisition and Advanced Computing Systems: Technology and Applications.*

Zhang, Z., Shu, L., Zhu, C., & Mukherjee, M. (2018). A Short Review on Sleep Scheduling Mechanism in Wireless Sensor Networks. In Quality, Reliability, Security and Robustness in Heterogeneous Systems. QShine 2017. Lecture Notes of the Institute for Computer Sciences, Social Informatics and Telecommunications Engineering, vol 234. Springer. doi:10.1007/978-3-319-78078-8_7

ADDITIONAL READING

Balusamy, B., Venkata Krishna, P., & Sridhar, J. (2016). Web Analytics: Assessing the Quality of Websites Using Web Analytics Metrics. In G. Sreedhar (Ed.), *Design Solutions for Improving Website Quality and Effectiveness* (pp. 253–275). IGI Global. doi:10.4018/978-1-4666-9764-5.ch010

Kaur, S., Kaur, K., Singh, H., & Kaur, P. (2016). An Empirical study of Usability Metric for Websites. In G. Sreedhar (Ed.), *Design Solutions for Improving Website Quality and Effectiveness* (pp. 162–186). IGI Global. doi:10.4018/978-1-4666-9764-5.ch007

Rao, A. P. (2016). Quality Measures for Semantic Web Application. In G. Sreedhar (Ed.), *Design Solutions for Improving Website Quality and Effectiveness* (pp. 130–139). IGI Global. doi:10.4018/978-1-4666-9764-5.ch005

Redkina, N. S. (2017). The development tendencies of web analytics tools. *Automatic Documentation and Mathematical Linguistics*, *51*(3), 112–116. doi:10.3103/S0005105517030050

Sreedhar, G. (2016). Identifying and Evaluating Web Metrics for Assuring the Quality of Web Designing. In G. Sreedhar (Ed.), *Design Solutions for Improving Website Quality and Effectiveness* (pp. 1–23). IGI Global. doi:10.4018/978-1-4666-9764-5.ch001

Xun, J. (2015). Return on web site visit duration: Applying web analytics data. *Journal of Direct, Data and Digital Marketing Practice*, *17*(1), 54–70. doi:10.1057/dddmp.2015.33

KEY TERMS AND DEFINITIONS

Accessibility: The ease of attaining information and services offered through an e-government channel.

Bounce Rate: The effectiveness of a website in keeping visitors engaged and is often used as an indicator of a site's relevance and ability to generate interest.

Direct Traffic: Traffic generated from users who are familiar with the site name, and they go directly to the website by typing the site URL.

Loading Time: The amount of time needed by the browser to load and display the web page.

Number of Requests: The total number of requests that needed to be executed to retrieve a complete web page.

Organic Search Results: The natural listings that are suggested by search algorithms for example from Google.com.

Page Size: The size (in bytes) of the web page rendered by the browser.

Chapter 10
Evaluating Accessibility and Usability of Airline Websites:
The Case of Airline Companies in Turkey

Yakup Akgül

ⓘD https://orcid.org/0000-0001-5344-4359
Alanya Alaaddin Keykubat University, Turkey

ABSTRACT

The website has become a crucial part of digitalization. In recent years, the airline sector has shifted to online platforms in order to expand its client base and provide consumers with timely information and services. Usability and accessibility are essential aspects of web quality that influence consumer acquisition and retention. As a result, the purpose of this study is to assess the quality of Turkish airline websites. The website is assessed based on its accessibility, usability, and readability utilizing online automated techniques. Finally, internet tools are used to assess the mobile-friendliness of websites. According to the findings, none of the Turkish airline websites meet the WCAG 2.0 accessibility criteria and have severe usability problems.

INTRODUCTION

In today's digital age, the growing number of internet users has made site quality a critical component in gaining access to online services and expanding a company's client base. The internet and developments in information technology have given the e-commerce sector new dimensions. The traditional approach of doing offline business has changed to the internet platform, and the success mantra for every sector is to manage an excellent e-commerce website for attracting clients and

DOI: 10.4018/978-1-7998-7848-3.ch010

company promotion. Hootsuite and We Are Social report of 2020 has claimed that total global internet user has reached to 4.66 billion in 2020 which has 59,5% of the global population (Hootsuite and We Are Social, 2020).

According to the International Telecommunication Union (ITU, 2017), the total number of global Internet users reached 3.5 billion in 2016, which accounts for a 47% penetration rate of the global population. The ITU expected this number to increase to 3.9 billion with a 54% penetration rate by the end of 2017. By January 2017, the number of people who purchased goods or services via electronic (e) commerce reached 1.6 billion, which corresponds to an e-commerce penetration rate of 22% of the global population.

These figures show the significance and rapid and continuous growth of e-commerce in the current business environment. These numbers also confirm that maintaining effective websites is crucial for the survival of every industry, such as tourism and hospitality, in the competitive market by attracting additional customers and retaining their loyalty.

The airline industry is no exception. According to the International Air Transport Association (IATA, 2016), the share of online ticket sales via airline websites reached 33% and that of airline mobile applications was 2%, as of the second quarter of 2016. These numbers are expected to increase to 37% and 7% respectively, by 2021. One of the successful low-cost carriers (LCCs) in the world, namely easyJet, reported selling 90% of tickets online since 2003 and 20% of total tickets via mobile application in 2016 (easyJet plc, 2016). These figures show that successful LCCs mainly depend on online ticket sales, and their sales via mobile applications are increasing. Thus, to achieve market sustainability, airline industry participants should transform their websites from marketing tools to fully fledged online sales channels that provide additional necessary functions for customers, such as close communication and relationship building with clients, on top of basic functions, such as searching, booking, ticketing, and check-in services.

The International Civil Aviation Organization (ICAO, 2017) reported that the network of global airlines transported 3.5 billion passengers on 34 million scheduled departures in 2015. ICAO expects these numbers to nearly double by 2030. LCCs played a significant role in the substantial expansion of airline business over the past 30 years and are expected to continue doing so. In 2016, LCCs transported over one billion passengers, which accounted for 28% of the total number of scheduled passengers worldwide. This number has been increasing continually at an average rate of 10% per annum since 2014. A growth that is 1.5 times faster than the average growth rate of the total number of scheduled passengers worldwide that has been recorded (ICAO, 2017). Even with such an expansion in the airline business, the situation of the research on airline website evaluation is poor.

The airline business has also been severely influenced by the IT revolution; the airline industry's use of the internet has resulted in a significant rise in profit. Almost every airline has its own website where clients may communicate directly with them and receive timely information. According to a report by the International Air Transport Association, airline websites accounted for nearly 33% of airline ticket bookings in 2016, and 2% of ticket bookings were made using a mobile app or mobile-optimized websites, with website and mobile bookings expected to reach 45 percent by 2021. According to IATA, there will be more elderly passengers on planes by 2021 than there are now (IATA, 2016). In light of these facts, Turkish airline participants should have a fully functional, high-quality website that serves to the needs of individuals of all ages, and any aging or physical handicap should not be a barrier to online accessibility. Users will be dissatisfied with the service offered by a badly designed website, resulting in a loss of revenue. Consumers are more inclined to utilize websites that are easy to use, and they are also more likely to attract new customers. As suggested by Spencer Ivey (2016) usability and accessibility of the website are the two important website design metric.

In 1998 usability is defined by International standard organization ISO9241 as "usability is the extent to which a product can be used by a specified user to achieve specified goals with effectiveness and efficiency".

According to a WHO study on disability, 15% of the world's population suffers from impairments (WHO, 2011), and social and economic inclusion of these individuals is a major problem for developing countries like Turkey. To meet the needs of these individuals with disabilities, Turkey passed the Right of Persons with Disabilities Act on December 27, 2016, which guarantees that people with disabilities have equal access to the physical environment, information and communication technologies, and web-based services.

W3C has published Web Content accessibility guideline(WCAG) to make the web accessible to all (Caldwell et al., 2008). The first version of these guidelines known as WCAG 1.0 was published in 1999, the second version WCAG 2.0 was published in 2008 which has been adopted by most of the countries as the accessibility guidelines. Recently WCAG 2.1 has been released which is based on WCAG 2.0 with some additional checkpoints.

The purpose of this study is to assess the usability and accessibility of the Turkish airline industry's website, since numerous studies in the literature show that usability and accessibility are important elements to consider when developing a website. The remaining paper is structured out as follows: Sect. 2 contains a literature review, Sect. 3 has a list of research questions, Sect. 4 contains an overview of the methodology, automated tools, and parameters utilized in the study, Sect. 5 contains the overall results, and Sect. 6 contains the conclusion.

LITERATURE REVIEW

Worldwide much research has been done to evaluate the quality of the airline website. Aktaş and Mutlu (2015) performed the usability analysis of the airline websites operating in turkey on seven functional characteristics namely information provision, networking, participation, campaigning, online processes, mobile application, and social media application and six delivery characteristics of the website. The results revealed that websites have improved from 2012 to 2014.

In another study of Turkey airline Vatansever and Akgül (2017), the authors proposed the website performance framework using hybrid multi-criteria decision-making techniques and evaluated the performance of 11 airlines on seven parameters using online diagnostics tools.

Murillo et al. (2017) performed the usability evaluation of the airline website on three important airline website's functionalities namely airline ticket purchase, airline package purchase, and airline check-in service using heuristic evaluation. The results showed that the majority of websites have three major usability issues namely presence of broken links, absence of help menu and has consistency errors. Elberkawi et al. (2016) proposed a method to evaluate web usability of Emirates airline website based on five user's task evaluated on three usability metrics namely time to complete the task, total mistakes done and mistake time. Results showed that out of five tasks, the task of ticket purchase fails on all three parameters and the best result is obtained for the task of flight search. In the study of Malaysian airline website Dominic et al. (2011) measured the performance of airline websites using fuzzy and non-fuzzy MCDM techniques. Websites were evaluated considering load time, page size, broken link, markup validation, page rank, traffic as the web quality parameters, using online tools to collect the data. The authors also proposed a hybrid multi-criteria decision-making model approach to rank the website. The results showed that four Asian airline websites did not meet the website quality criteria and needed improvement.

A framework (ASEF) focusing on the airline industry on the Web was proposed by Apostolou et al. (2008) to be used as a guide in order to improve the online services of the airline industry and also, evaluated the sites of thirty major airlines across all over the world based on the Index. The model was based on five dimensions namely interface design, site navigability, information content, the reliability of embedded software functions and appropriateness of technical implementation. This framework not only ensures the delivery of service to the customer but was also useful for developer of the airline website.

Ekşioğlu et al. (2013) analyzed the website quality of airlines in Turkey through usability testing and heuristic evaluation. In recent studies, Ishaq et al. (2018) evaluated the usability and accessibility of websites of Nigerian airline. The heuristic method was used to evaluate the usability and four different automated online tools for checking the compliance of the website with WCAG 2.0 accessibility guidelines. The result showed that the website under study had many functional usability and accessibility error and most of the Nigerian airline website needs improvement.

Alwahaishi et al. proposed the framework for evaluating the quality of airline website based on four parameters namely website design, Informational content, transactional content and customer support and evaluated the seven airlines of the Arabian Gulf. Statistical correlation among various parameters was identified and finally, the author proposed an Airline Website Assessment Index (AWAI) (Alwahaishi et al., 2009).

Another similar study conducted on Indian healthcare websites evaluated the accessibility, usability and security aspects found that the hospital websites are not mature enough and they are neglecting the usability and accessibility parameters in their website design and need lots of improvement in order to meet the expectation of people and motivate them to use the digital media for health-related information (Kaur et al., 2014).

Studies have repeatedly found accessibility issues in a range of fields, including education sites (Akgül, 2017; Akgül, 2021; Fichten et al., 2009), corporate sites (Cappel and Huang, 2007; Gilbertson and Machin, 2012; Loiacono et al., 2009), e-commerce sites (Isa et al., 2011; Lazar et al., 2012; Sohaib and Kang, 2017), the airline industry (Abbasi et al., 2018; Bakır and Atalık, 2021; Chong and Law, 2019; Dominic and Khan, 2014; Gutierrez et al., 2005; Hernandez et al., 2020; Pant and Sinha, 2020; Pontus, 2019; Shchiglik and Barnes, 2004), MOOCs (Akgül, 2018; Akgül, 2018a), banking websites (Akgül, 2018; Akgül, 2018b) and, of course, e-government sites at the national, state, and local levels (Akgül and Vatansever, 2016; Akgül, 2019; Akgül, 2016; Akgül, 2016a; Akgül, 2015; Galvez and Youngblood, 2016; Olalere and Lazar, 2011; Youngblood and Mackiewicz, 2012; Youngblood and Youngblood, 2013; Yu and Parmanto, 2011).

RESEARCH QUESTIONS

In order to investigate the quality of airline websites, the following research questions were formulated.

1. What is the status of accessibility of airline websites according to WCAG 2.0 accessibility guidelines?
2. What is the status of usability of Turkish airline website based on the various parameters?

3. What is the readability score of the airline websites using Flesch Kincaid readability ease score?

METHODOLOGY

In this paper, home pages of websites of airlines based in Turkish were investigated for usability and accessibility criteria. As shown in Table 1, a total of 12 Turkish airline websites were investigated. Accessibility evaluation of website under study is based on Web Content Accessibility Guideline (WCAG). The World Wide Web consortium publishes the web content accessibility guidelines, following these guidelines makes the web accessible beyond the limitations of disabilities. Thus forming a global web quality standard. The first version WCAG 1.0 was published in the year 1999 (Caldwell et al., 2008).

WCAG 1.0 consists of 65 checkpoints divided under fourteen guidelines and has three conformance level A, AA, AAA. Later in the year 2008, the second version of accessibility guideline WCAG 2.0 was published (W3, 2021). WCAG 2.0 consists of twelve guidelines included under four principles namely perceivable, operable, understandable and robust. The first principle perceivable ensures that information present on the web should be easily perceived by the user irrespective of any physical disability, Operable ensures that the web interface provided is operable and provide easy navigation on the web, Understandable principle ensures that the web content and the operation should be understandable by all, Robust principle ensures that the assistive technology can be easily embedded in the web page so that web is accessible to all and any future technological advancement can be easily adapted, to implement and test these principles these guidelines consist of sixty-one testable success criteria.

Turkish Airline websites under study are evaluated against WCAG 2.0 guidelines. There are many automated online tools available to check the conformance of WCAG 1.0 and 2.0. The tool employed for evaluating website accessibility in this study is Taw. Taw is a set of tools for analysis of the accessibility in websites. It is an online service to check the accessibility of websites using the URL and generate a summary of an error on the analyzed page.

To evaluate the usability status of the website under study, page load time and page size are evaluated using Pingdom online tool, broken links of the website were evaluated through websitepulse tool, online version of WAVEAIM tool is used to evaluate the color contrast error on the webpage, readability score of the websites are evaluated using the Webpagefx tool, Mobile friendliness and mobile page test is evaluated using the tool illustrated in Table 2.

Table 1. List of Airlines websites evaluated

Sr. No.	Website Name
1	https://www.anadolujet.com/tr
2	https://www.corendonairlines.com/tr
3	https://www.freebirdairlines.com/tr
4	https://www.mngairlines.com/
5	http://www.actairlines.com/
6	https://www.onurair.com/tr/
7	https://www.flypgs.com/
8	http://www.sagava.net/
9	https://www.sunexpress.com/tr/
10	https://www.tailwind.com.tr/
11	https://www.turkishairlines.com/tr-int/
12	https://ulsairlines.com/

Expert manual evaluation of the website under study is done to evaluate the presence of search option on the website, presence of Multilanguage option of the webpage, which increases the usability, presence of sitemap and presence of screen reader on the webpage.

Table 2. Tools used

Parameter	Website
Mobile friendly	Google mobile-friendly test
Desktop web accessibility test	Taw
Response time	Websitepulse
Broken links	drlinkcheck
Color contrast errors	Wave
Load time	Pingdom
Page size	Pingdom
Readability	Webpagefx

RESULTS

The result of the study for accessibility, usability, and readability are presented in the following section.

Accessibility Analysis

Accessibility errors reported by TAW tool is shown in Table 3. A total of 1642 errors, averaging 136,83 errors were found in the websites under study. The result shows that the minimum number of accessibility errors was 1 for the website of Turkishairlines and the website of pegasusairlines reported maximum accessibility errors (331 in number). 50% of websites had accessibility errors greater than the average number of errors of the websites under study.

Table 3. Accessibility issues reported by TAW of Perceivable (P), Operable (O), Understandable (U), Robust (R) category

Websites	P	O	U	R	Total
https://www.anadolujet.com/tr	47	25	12	24	108
https://www.corendonairlines.com/tr	122	22	42	90	276
https://www.freebirdairlines.com/tr	91	7	21	27	146
https://www.mngairlines.com/	34	21	9	17	81
http://www.actairlines.com/	3	1	1	18	23
https://www.onurair.com/tr/	77	7	33	85	202
https://www.flypgs.com/	143	32	43	113	331
http://www.sagava.net/	111	12	9	127	259
https://www.sunexpress.com/tr/	85	18	12	52	167
https://www.tailwind.com.tr/	15	9	2	2	28
https://www.turkishairlines.com/tr-int/	0	0	1	0	1
https://ulsairlines.com/	9	6	0	5	20

22% of errors reported were of the perceivable type, showing that the information presented on the webpages of the airline websites are perceived with difficulty. 50% errors were of robust type i.e., assistive technology can't interpret the information presented on the page. 17% errors were of the understandable type, resulting in content or operation on webpage beyond the understating of the end user. 0,05% of errors lie in the operable category, resulting in the non-operable interface. The most frequently violated WCAG2.0 success criteria are listed in Table 4. Criteria 1.1.1 Non-text content ensures that all the non-text content of the webpage should have an equivalent text alternative. Criteria 1.3.1 ensure that information and relationship of content should be preserved while presenting the content through assistive technology tools to a disabled person. Criteria 2.4.4 ensures that the text of the hyperlink on the webpage should define the purpose of the link. Criteria 3.3.2 ensures the proper organization of web page by dividing the webpage into different sections and each section have a proper heading. It also ensures that the page should have the proper information that can guide the people with a disability while navigating and providing input through a web page. Criteria 4.1.1 and 4.1.2 ensures the compatibility of the web content with future assistive technology. Failure of these success criteria will hinder the use of the assistive technological tool on the website by the disabled people thus making it inaccessible to them.

Another important factor that affects the people's ability to perceive the information presented on the web is the color contrast between the background of the web page and the text written on it. The color contrast error on the webpage will hinder the accessibility of the vision impaired person as he will not be able to recognize and distinguish between text, links and other web component present on the web page, thus decreasing the usability of website as the vision impaired person will not be able to perform simple task on airline website such as flight booking, route identification and even navigation on web page (Ennis, 2015). WCAG 2.0 accessibility guideline caters the need of these visually impaired people by including Success Criterion 1.4.1 and 1.4.3. The objective of former Success Criterion is to ensure that people with color vision disability should easily perceive the difference in color on the web page and later ensures the use of minimum contrast between text and background so that it can be perceivable and understandable by the people with low vision. Only the actairlines of website had no contarast error. All the websites under study had very low contrast shading with contrast errors ranging from 2 (Turkish Airlines) to 322 (Sunexpress). Results of contrast error are shown in Table 5.

Website should provide the option for changing the language of the web page which increases its usability so the Language of the webpage is an important criterion for increasing the accessibility of the webpage. WCAG Criteria 3.1.1. (Language of Page) ensures that user agent and assistive technology like screen reader can identify the syntax and semantics of the language used on the page so that the text of the page can be correctly rendered by them. On analyzing the website for language, it was found that almost all the websites were in English and had other language options.

Another web accessibility feature important for differently abled people is the presence of a screen reader. Screen readers are audio interfaces that allow visually impaired users to use computers by reading the text on the computer screen. Only one website had a screen reader option. Results are shown in Table 5.

Table 4. Frequently occurring WCAG 2.0 violation found in airline websites

Guideline	Total Errors	No. of Websites
1.1.1 Non-text content (A)	484	11
1.3.1. Info and Relationship (A)	253	10
2.4.4. Link Purpose (In Context) (A)	160	11
3.1.1 - Language of Page (A)	5	5
3.2.2 - On Input (A)	9	5
3.3.2. Labels or Instructions (A)	171	9
4.1.1. Parsing (A)	359	11
4.1.2. Name, Role, Value (A)	201	8

Usability Analysis

The usability of a website tells us how easily effectively, efficiently, and satisfactorily users use the websites and get the information they require. Apart from the content, user experience in using the website contributes greatly to increase the usability of the website and increases its user base. If the website is difficult to use, users are more likely to leave it.

The factors that affect the usability of the website include response time, loading time, broken links, search option, sitemap, and how a website is rendered on mobile devices.

Sitemaps are a visual representation of the entire website for users to understand the website's areas in a single glance. Sitemaps help users navigate the website quickly and easily. Sitemaps help a visually impaired user to jump to a specific section on the website. Only 2 websites under study had a sitemap. Average load time of websites under study was 2.9 s and the average response time was 7.79 s. The average page size was found to be 4.78 MB. Larger pages take more time to load and consequently divert user's attention away from the page. Another factor impacting the usability of the website is the broken links. Broken links decrease the usability quality of the website.

Broken links stop the tracking of search engine crawlers. This damages ranking by preventing search engines from indexing the pages. It has negative impact on user experience as it redirect visitors to error pages. There are many broken links in the websites under study. All the websites were found to be mobile friendly except Freebird, Sagava, and Tailwind airline websites.

Table 5. Usability and Accessibility parameters data for airline websites

Website	Search	Multilanguage	Sitemap	Load Time	Page Size (mb)	Broken Links	Response Time	Screen Reader	Contrast Errors
https://www.anadolujet.com/tr	Y	Y	N	3,96	13,8	10	3,066	0	205
https://www.corendonairlines.com/tr	N	Y	N	3,53	3,4	2	0,921	0	28
https://www.freebirdairlines.com/tr	N	Y	N	2,83	4,9	1	65.252	0	53
https://www.mngairlines.com/	N	Y	N	5,96	2,5	3	1.583	0	25
http://www.actairlines.com/	N	N	N	1,77	1,4	0	2.004	0	0
https://www.onurair.com/tr/	N	Y	Y	2,13	4,3	49	0.770	0	56
https://www.flypgs.com/	Y	Y	Y	3,61	2,9	2	1.194	0	71
http://www.sagava.net/	N	N	N	2,3	8,4	155	0.478	0	21
https://www.sunexpress.com/tr/	N	Y	N	1,1	2,5	9	0.766	0	322
https://www.tailwind.com.tr/	Y	Y	N	3,6	4,4	30	1.276	0	29
https://www.turkishairlines.com/tr-int/	Y	Y	N	1,3	4,9	116	0.758	1	2
https://ulsairlines.com/	N	Y	N	2,61	3,9	9	1.286	0	15

Readability Analysis

Readability is the measure of how easy it is to read and understand the written text. It measures the complexity of the text in the content. The Internet is dynamic and fast changing. There is a very little window of opportunity to convey the message across to the users. If the content of the website is not easy to understand, the users will move on.

The more readable content will also result in search engines favoring the site and help it rank higher. Therefore, it is very important that the information conveyed on the websites is easy to understand for larger masses. In order to determine the ease of readability, there are many algorithms. Flesch Kincaid Reading Ease (FKRE) is one such algorithm that is used to test the readability-ease of the website content. The scores usually range between 0 and 100. A high FKRE score indicates that the written text is easier to understand and the low value of Score symbolizes a complicated and difficult to understand text. FKRE uses the following formula to calculate the reading score:

$$FKRE = 206.835 - 1015*(words/sentences) - 84.6*(syllables/words) \qquad (1)$$

For investigating the readability score of the websites under study, an online tool is used which test readability in three ways: test by URL, test by direct input and test by reference. In this study test by URL, was used to collect the readability score of websites. Result obtained is shown in Table 6.

The average readability score was found to be 20.85, which is interpreted as fairly difficult to read. While calculating the average, the readability score of ULS Airlines whose score was reported by the tool as 0.73 as the lowest readability score could be zero.

The result shows that most of the websites under study (nearly 5%) contains fairly easily understandable English text being understood by students in the age of 12 to 15 years. While 92% of the websites have a readability score that is interpreted as very difficult to read and best understood by university graduates.

Table 6. Flesch Kincaid Reading Ease (FKRE) score of airline website

Website	FKRE
https://www.anadolujet.com/tr	3,94
https://www.corendonairlines.com/tr	6,8
https://www.freebirdairlines.com/tr	21,9
https://www.mngairlines.com/	44,3
http://www.actairlines.com/	33,7
https://www.onurair.com/tr/	23,4
https://www.flypgs.com/	24,8
http://www.sagava.net/	73,8
https://www.sunexpress.com/tr/	6
https://www.tailwind.com.tr/	9,9
https://www.turkishairlines.com/tr-int/	0,92
https://ulsairlines.com/	0,73

CONCLUSION

This paper evaluates the accessibility, usability, and readability of Turkish airline websites. The results show that none of the websites under study satisfies the WCAG 2.0 accessibility guidelines thus making them less accessible to differently able people. These airline websites suffer from various usability issues such as broken links, lack of sitemap, larger page size resulting in poor usability and accessibility of airline website. The readability score shows that the majority of the website under study has easily understandable text. The result of the study shows that awareness regarding usability and accessibility standards are required among website designers and developers so that they can cater the needs of disabled people in terms of physical disability and language disability making a universally accessible online environment. In June 2018 the third version of web content accessibility guideline known as WCAG 2.1 was released. WCAG 2.1 is built on WCAG 2.0 and has added seventeen new success criteria to improve the web accessibility for the user with a cognitive disability, low vision disability and disabilities of people on mobile devices, so in near future, we intend to take the evaluation of accessibility by WCAG2.1 guideline.

REFERENCES

Abbasi, R., Rezaei, N., Esmaili, S., & Abbasi, Z. (2018). Website quality and evaluation: A perspective of Iranian airline industry. *International Journal of Electronic Business*, *14*(2), 103–127. doi:10.1504/IJEB.2018.094868

Agrawal, G., Kumar, D., Singh, M., & Dani, D. (2019, April). Evaluating accessibility and usability of airline websites. In *International Conference on Advances in Computing and Data Sciences* (pp. 392-402). Springer. 10.1007/978-981-13-9939-8_35

Akgül, Y. (2015). Web content accessibility of municipal web sites in Turkey. In *European Conference on Digital Government* (p. 1). Academic Conferences International Limited.

Akgül, Y. (2016). Quality evaluation of E-government websites of Turkey. In *2016 11th Iberian conference on information systems and technologies (CISTI)* (pp. 1-7). IEEE. 10.1109/CISTI.2016.7521567

Akgül, Y. (2016a). Web site accessibility, quality and vulnerability assessment: A survey of government web sites in the Turkish republic. *Journal of Information Systems Engineering & Management*, *1*(4), 50. doi:10.20897/lectito.201650

Akgül, Y. (2017). The most violated WCAG 1.0 guidelines by the developers of university websites in Turkey. In *2017 12th Iberian Conference on Information Systems and Technologies (CISTI)* (pp. 1-7). IEEE.

Akgül, Y. (2018). Accessibility evaluation of MOOCs' websites of Turkey. *Journal of Life Economics*, *5*(4), 23–36. doi:10.15637/jlecon.259

Akgül, Y. (2018). Banking Websites in Turkey: an Accessibility, Usability and Security Evaluation. *İşletme Araştırmaları Dergisi, 10*(1), 782-796.

Akgül, Y. (2018a). Web accessibility of MOOCs for elderly students: The case of Turkey. *Journal of Life Economics*, *5*(4), 141–150. doi:10.15637/jlecon.266

Akgül, Y. (2018b). An Analysis of Customers' Acceptance of Internet Banking: An Integration of E-Trust and Service Quality to the TAM–The Case of Turkey. In *E-Manufacturing and E-Service Strategies in Contemporary Organizations* (pp. 154–198). IGI Global. doi:10.4018/978-1-5225-3628-4.ch007

Akgül, Y. (2019). The accessibility, usability, quality and readability of Turkish state and local government websites an exploratory study. *International Journal of Electronic Government Research*, *15*(1), 62–81. doi:10.4018/IJEGR.2019010105

Akgül, Y. (2021). Accessibility, usability, quality performance, and readability evaluation of university websites of Turkey: A comparative study of state and private universities. *Universal Access in the Information Society*, *20*(1), 157–170. doi:10.100710209-020-00715-w

Akgül, Y., & Vatansever, K. (2016). Web accessibility evaluation of government websites for people with disabilities in Turkey. *Journal of Advanced Management Science*, *4*(3), 201–210. doi:10.12720/joams.4.3.201-210

Aktaş, E. B., & Mutlu, Ö. (2015). Website usability in marketing communications: The case of airline companies in Turkey. *American Journal of Educational Research*, *3*(10A), 7–16. doi:10.12691/education-3-10A-2

Alwahaishi, S., Snášel, V., & Nehari-Talet, A. (2009). Website evaluation an empirical study of arabian gulf airlines. *International Journal of Information*, *1*(3), 213.

Apostolou, G., & Economides, A. A. (2008). Airlines websites evaluation around the world. In *World Summit on Knowledge Society* (pp. 611–617). Springer.

Bakır, M., & Atalık, Ö. (2021). Application of fuzzy AHP and fuzzy MARCOS approach for the evaluation of e-service quality in the airline industry. *Decision Making: Applications in Management and Engineering*, *4*(1), 127–152.

Caldwell, B., Cooper, M., Reid, L. G., Vanderheiden, G., Chisholm, W., Slatin, J., & White, J. (2008). Web content accessibility guidelines (WCAG) 2.0. *WWW Consortium (W3C), 290.*

Cappel, J. J., & Huang, Z. (2007). A usability analysis of company websites. *Journal of Computer Information Systems, 48*(1), 117–123.

Chong, S., & Law, R. (2019). Review of studies on airline website evaluation. *Journal of Travel & Tourism Marketing, 36*(1), 60–75. doi:10.1080/10548408.2018.1494084

Dominic, P. D. D., Jati, H., Sellappan, P., & Nee, G. K. (2011). A comparison of Asian e-government websites quality: Using a non-parametric test. *International Journal of Business Information Systems, 7*(2), 220–246. doi:10.1504/IJBIS.2011.038513

Dominic, P. D. D., & Khan, H. (2014). Performance measure of airline websites using analytical hierarchy process & fuzzy analytical hierarchy process. In *2014 IEEE International Conference on Control System, Computing and Engineering (ICCSCE)* (pp. 530–535). IEEE. 10.1109/ICCSCE.2014.7072775

easyJet plc. (2016). *Annual report and accounts 2016.* Retrieved from https://corporate.easyjet.com/~/media/Files/E/Easyjet/pdf/investors/result-center-investor/annual-report-2016.pdf

Ekşioğlu, M., Kiriş, E., Çakir, T., Güvendik, M., Koyutürk, E. D., & Yilmaz, M. (2013). A user experience study of airline websites. *Lecture Notes in Computer Science, 8015 LNCS*(PART 4), 173–182. doi:10.1007/978-3-642-39253-5_19

Elberkawi, E. K., El-Firjani, N. F., Maatuk, A. M., & Aljawarneh, S. A. (2016, September). Usability evaluation of web-based systems: A new method and results. In *2016 International Conference on Engineering & MIS (ICEMIS)* (pp. 1-5). IEEE.

Ennis, A. (2015). *Testing airline web sites for accessibility compliance: use of colour.* https://www.accessibilityoz.com/2015/11/testing-airline-web-sites-for-accessibility-compliance/

Fichten, C. S., Ferraro, V., Asuncion, J. V., Chwojka, C., Barile, M., Nguyen, M. N., ... Wolforth, J. (2009). Disabilities and e-learning problems and solutions: An exploratory study. *Journal of Educational Technology & Society, 12*(4), 241–256.

Galvez, R. A., & Youngblood, N. E. (2016). e-Government in Rhode Island: What effects do templates have on usability, accessibility, and mobile readiness? *Universal Access in the Information Society, 15*(2), 281–296.

Gilbertson, T. D., & Machin, C. H. (2012, April). Guidelines, icons and marketable skills: an accessibility evaluation of 100 web development company homepages. In *Proceedings of the international cross-disciplinary conference on web accessibility* (pp. 1-4). Academic Press.

Gutierrez, C. F., Loucopoulos, C., & Reinsch, R. W. (2005). Disability-accessibility of airlines' Web sites for US reservations online. *Journal of Air Transport Management, 11*(4), 239–247.

Harteveldt, H. H. (2016). *The Future Of Airline Distribution A Look Ahead To 2017.* Atmosphere Research Group.

Hernandez, C. C., Palos-Sánchez, P., & Rios, M. A. (2020). Website quality assessment: A case study of chinese airlines. *Indian Journal of Marketing, 50*(1), 42–64.

Hootsuite and We Are Social. (2020). https://www.hootsuite.com/pages/digital-trends-2021

International Air Transport Association. (2016). *IATA airline distribution online study. The Future of Airline Distribution, 2016-2021.* Retrieved from http://www.iata.org/whatwedo/airline-distribution/ndc/Documents/ndc-future-airline-distribution-report.pdf

International Civil Aviation Organization. (2017). *Economic development of air transport - low cost carriers (LCCs).* Retrieved from https://www.icao.int/sustainability/Pages/Low-Cost-Carriers.aspx

International Telecommunication Union. (2017). *ICT facts and figures 2017.* Retrieved from https://www.itu.int/en/ITU-D/Statistics/Documents/facts/ICTFactsFigures2017.pdf

Isa, W. A. R. W. M., Aziz, M. A., & Razak, M. R. B. A. (2011). Evaluating the accessibility of Small and Medium Enterprise (SME) websites in Malaysia. In *2011 International Conference on User Science and Engineering (i-USEr)* (pp. 135-140). IEEE.

Ishaq, O. O., Onuja, A. M., & Zubairu, H. A. (2018). An Analytical Approach to Accessibility and Usability Evaluation of Nigerian Airlines Websites. *Am. J. Comput. Sci. Inf. Technol., 6*(2), 21.

Kaur, A., Dani, D., & Agrawal, G. (2017). Evaluating the accessibility, usability and security of Hospitals websites: An exploratory study. In *2017 7th international conference on cloud computing, data science & engineering-confluence* (pp. 674-680). IEEE.

Kirchner, M. (2002, October). Evaluation, repair, and transformation of Web pages for Web content accessibility. Review of some available tools. In *Proceedings. Fourth International Workshop on Web Site Evolution* (pp. 65-72). IEEE.

Lazar, J., Olalere, A., & Wentz, B. (2012). Investigating the accessibility and usability of job application web sites for blind users. *Journal of Usability Studies, 7*(2), 68–87.

Loiacono, E. T., Romano, N. C. Jr, & McCoy, S. (2009). The state of corporate website accessibility. *Communications of the ACM, 52*(9), 128–132.

Murillo, B., Vargas, S., Moquillaza, A., Fernández, L., & Paz, F. (2017). Usability testing as a complement of heuristic evaluation: A case study. In *International conference of design, user experience, and usability* (pp. 434-444). Springer.

Olalere, A., & Lazar, J. (2011). Accessibility of US federal government home pages: Section 508 compliance and site accessibility statements. *Government Information Quarterly, 28*(3), 303–309.

Pant, M., & Sinha, A. (2020). Evaluating State of Web Accessibility Standards in Top Airline Websites. In *2020 IEEE International IOT, Electronics and Mechatronics Conference (IEMTRONICS)* (pp. 1-5). IEEE.

Pingdom website speed test. (n.d.). https://tools.pingdom.com/

Pontus, V. (2019). *Evaluating the Accessibility of Localised Websites: The Case of the Airline Industry in Switzerland* (Doctoral dissertation). University of Geneva.

Shchiglik, C., & Barnes, S. J. (2004). Evaluating website quality in the airline industry. *Journal of Computer Information Systems, 44*(3), 17–25.

Sohaib, O., & Kang, K. (2017). E-commerce web accessibility for people with disabilities. In *Complexity in Information Systems Development* (pp. 87–100). Springer.

Spencer, I. (2016). *The Importance of Usability and Accessibility in Design.* Career Foundry.

TAW. (n.d.). https://www.tawdis.net/

Vatansever, K., & Akgŭl, Y. (2018). Performance evaluation of websites using entropy and grey relational analysis methods: The case of airline companies. *Decision Science Letters*, *7*(2), 119–130.

W3. (2021). https://www.w3.org/WAI/standards-guidelines/wcag/

Web content accessibility guidelines (WCAG) 2.0. (n.d.). https://www.w3.org/TR/2008/RECWCAG20-20081211/

Web Readability test tool. (n.d.). https://www.webfx.com/tools/read-able/ContentAccessibilityGuidelines

Websitepulse. (n.d.). https://www.websitepulse.com/tools/

World Health Organization. (2011). *World report on disability 2011*. World Health Organization.

Youngblood, N. E., & Mackiewicz, J. (2012). A usability analysis of municipal government website home pages in Alabama. *Government Information Quarterly*, *29*(4), 582–588.

Youngblood, N. E., & Youngblood, S. A. (2013). User experience and accessibility: An analysis of county web portals. *Journal of Usability Studies*, *9*(1).

Yu, D. X., & Parmanto, B. (2011). US state government websites demonstrate better in terms of accessibility compared to federal government and commercial websites. *Government Information Quarterly*, *28*(4), 484–490.

Compilation of References

Checker. (2016). http://www.508checker.com

Abanumy, A., Al-Badi, A., & Mayhew, P. (2005). e-Government Website accessibility: In-depth evaluation of Saudi Arabia and Oman. *The Electronic. Journal of E-Government*, *3*(3), 99–106.

Abascal, J., Arrue, M., Fajardo, I., Garay, N., & Tomás, J. (2004). The use of guidelines to automatically verify Web accessibility. *Universal Access in the Information Society*, *3*(1), 71–79. doi:10.100710209-003-0069-3

Abascal, J., Arrue, M., & Valencia, X. (2019). Tools for web accessibility evaluation. In *Web Accessibility* (pp. 479–503). Springer. doi:10.1007/978-1-4471-7440-0_26

Abbasi, R., Rezaei, N., Esmaili, S., & Abbasi, Z. (2018). Website quality and evaluation: A perspective of Iranian airline industry. *International Journal of Electronic Business*, *14*(2), 103–127. doi:10.1504/IJEB.2018.094868

Abu-Addous, H. Y. M., Jali, W. A. W. A. B. S. M., & Basir, N. (2015). WABS: Web Accessibility Barrier Severity Metric. *Proceedings of the 5 Th International Conference on Computing and Informatics, ICOCI 2015*, 481–487.

Abu-Addous, H. Y., Jali, M. Z., & Basir, N. (2017). Quantitative metric for ranking web accessibility barriers based on their severity. *Journal of Information and Communication Technology*, *16*(1), 81–102.

Acart Communications. (2017). *WCAG Contrast Checker*. https://contrastchecker.com/

Accenture. (2005). *Leadership in Customer Service: New Expectations, New Experiences*. Author.

Access Monitor. (2016). https://www.acessibilidade.gov.pt/accessmonitor/

Accesslint. (2016). http://accesslint.com

AccessN. V. (2020). *NV Access*. https://www.nvaccess.org/

AChecker web accessibility checker. (2016). http://achecker.ca

Achecker. (2011). *IDI Web Accessibility Checker: Web Accessibility Checker*. https://achecker.ca/checker/index.php

AChecker. (2021). *IDI Web Accessibility Checker: Web Accessibility Checker.* https://achecker.ca/checker/index.php

Acosta-Vargas, P., Acosta, T., & Luján-Mora, S. (2018a). Challenges to assess accessibility in Higher Education websites: A Comparative study of Latin America Universities. *IEEE Access: Practical Innovations, Open Solutions, 6,* 36500–36508. doi:10.1109/ACCESS.2018.2848978

Acosta-Vargas, P., Hidalgo, P., Acosta-Vargas, G., Gonzalez, M., Guaña-Moya, J., & Salvador-Acosta, B. (2020). Challenges and improvements in website accessibility for health services. *International Conference on Intelligent Human Systems Integration,* 875-881. 10.1007/978-3-030-39512-4_134

Acosta-Vargas, P., Luján-Mora, S., Acosta, T., & Salvador-Ullauri, L. (2018b). Toward a combined method for evaluation of web accessibility. *International Conference on Information Theoretic Security,* 602-613. 10.1007/978-3-319-73450-7_57

Acosta-Vargas, P., Luján-Mora, S., & Salvador-Ullauri, L. (2016). Evaluation of the web accessibility of higher-education websites. *15th International Conference on Information Technology Based Higher Education and Training (ITHET),* 1-6. 10.1109/ITHET.2016.7760703

Adeniran, A. O., & Fadare, S. O. (2018). Assessment of passengers' satisfaction and service quality in Murtala Muhammed Airport (MMA2), Lagos, Nigeria: Application of the SERVQUAL model. *J Hotel Bus Manage, 7*(188), 2169–0286. doi:10.4172/2169-0286.1000188

Adepoju, S. A., & Shehu, I. S. (2014b). Usability evaluation of academic websites using automated tools. *2014 3rd International Conference on User Science and Engineering (i-USEr),* 186-191. 10.1109/IUSER.2014.7002700

AFB.org. (2015). *Screen Magnification Systems—Browse by Category—American Foundation.* Author.

AFB.org. (2015a). *The Visually Impaired Web User's Technology—American Foundation for the Blind.* https://www.afb.org/info/accessibility/creating-accessible-websites/the-users-technology/235

Agarwal, N., & Shiju, P. S. (2018). A Study on Content Generation for Internet Usage. *International Journal of Advanced Research and Development, 3*(2), 1380–1382. doi:10.5281/zenodo.3764806

Agarwal, R., & Prasad, J. (1997). The Role of Innovation Characteristics and Perceived Voluntariness in the Acceptance of Information Technologies. *Decision Sciences, 28*(3), 557–582. doi:10.1111/j.1540-5915.1997.tb01322.x

Agrawal, G., Kumar, D., Singh, M., & Dani, D. (2019, April). Evaluating accessibility and usability of airline websites. In *International Conference on Advances in Computing and Data Sciences* (pp. 392-402). Springer. 10.1007/978-981-13-9939-8_35

Ahmi, A., & Mohamad, R. (2015). Web accessibility of the Malaysian public university websites. *International Conference on E-Commerce (ICoEC) 2015.*

Aizpurua, A., Arrue, M., Vigo, M., & Abascal, J. (2011). Validating the effectiveness of EvalAccess when deploying WCAG 2.0 tests. *Universal Access in the Information Society, 10*(4), 425–441.

Aizpurua, A., Harper, S., & Vigo, M. (2016). Exploring the relationship between web accessibility and user experience. *International Journal of Human-Computer Studies, 91,* 13–23. doi:10.1016/j.ijhcs.2016.03.008

Akamai. (2017). *The state of online retail performance.* https://www.soasta.com/wp-content/uploads/2017/04/Stateof-Online-Retail-Performance-Spring-2017.pdf

Akgül, Y. (2015). Web content accessibility of municipal web sites in Turkey. In *European Conference on Digital Government* (p. 1). Academic Conferences International Limited.

Akgül, Y. (2016). Quality evaluation of E-government websites of Turkey. *11th Iberian Conference on Information Systems and Technologies (CISTI) Proceedings,* 1-7. 10.1109/CISTI.2016.7521567

Akgül, Y. (2016). Quality evaluation of E-government websites of Turkey. In *2016 11th Iberian conference on information systems and technologies (CISTI)* (pp. 1-7). IEEE.

Akgül, Y. (2017). The most violated WCAG 1.0 guidelines by the developers of university websites in Turkey. *2017 12th Iberian Conference on Information Systems and Technologies (CISTI),* 1-7.

Akgül, Y. (2017). The most violated WCAG 1.0 guidelines by the developers of university websites in Turkey. In *2017 12th Iberian Conference on Information Systems and Technologies (CISTI)* (pp. 1-7). IEEE.

Akgül, Y. (2018). Banking Websites in Turkey: an Accessibility, Usability and Security Evaluation. *İşletme Araştırmaları Dergisi, 10*(1), 782-796.

Akgül, Y. (2016a). Web site accessibility, quality and vulnerability assessment: A survey of government web sites in the Turkish republic. *Journal of Information Systems Engineering & Management, 1*(4), 50.

Akgül, Y. (2018). Accessibility evaluation of MOOCs' websites of Turkey. *Journal of Life Economics, 5*(4), 23–36.

Akgül, Y. (2018a). Web accessibility of MOOCs for elderly students: The case of Turkey. *Journal of Life Economics, 5*(4), 141–150.

Akgül, Y. (2018b). An Analysis of Customers' Acceptance of Internet Banking: An Integration of E-Trust and Service Quality to the TAM–The Case of Turkey. In *E-Manufacturing and E-Service Strategies in Contemporary Organizations* (pp. 154–198). IGI Global.

Akgül, Y. (2019). The accessibility, usability, quality and readability of Turkish state and local government websites an exploratory study. *International Journal of Electronic Government Research, 15*(1), 62–81. doi:10.4018/IJEGR.2019010105

Akgül, Y. (2021). Accessibility, usability, quality performance, and readability evaluation of university websites of Turkey: A comparative study of state and private universities. *Universal Access in the Information Society, 20*(1), 157–170. doi:10.100710209-020-00715-w

Akgül, Y., & Vatansever, K. (2016). Web Accessibility Evaluation of Government Websites for People with Disabilities in Turkey. *Journal of Advanced Management Science, 4*(3), 201–210. doi:10.12720/joams.4.3.201-210

Akgül, Y., & Vatansever, K. (2016). Web accessibility evaluation of government websites for people with disabilities in Turkey. *Journal of Advanced Management Science, 4*(3).

Akgüngör, A. P., & Demirel, A. (2004). Türkiye'deki ulaştırma sistemlerinin analizi ve ulaştırma politikaları. *Mühendislik Bilimleri Dergisi, 10*(3), 423–430.

Akgün, M., & Soy Temür, A. (2016). BIST ulaştırma endeksine kayıtlı şirketlerin finansal performanslarının TOPSIS yöntemi ile değerlendirilmesi. *Uluslararası Yönetim İktisat ve İşletme Dergisi, 30*, 173–186.

Akman, G., Özcan, B., Başlı, H., & Gündüz, E. B. (2018). Çok kriterli karar vermede AHP ve TOPSIS yöntemleriyle uçuş noktası seçimi. *Erciyes Üniversitesi Fen Bilimleri Enstitüsü Fen Bilimleri Dergisi, 34*(3), 45–57.

Akram, M., & Sulaiman, R. B. (2017). A systematic literature review to determine the web accessibility issues in Saudi Arabian university and government websites for disable people. *International Journal of Advanced Computer Science and Applications, 8*(6). Advance online publication. doi:10.14569/IJACSA.2017.080642

Aktaş, E. B., & Mutlu, Ö. (2015). Website usability in marketing communications: The case of airline companies in Turkey. *American Journal of Educational Research, 3*(10A), 7–16. doi:10.12691/education-3-10A-2

Akyazı, A. (2018). Dijitalleşen ticaret: Yaşlı dostu e-ticaret siteleri üzerine bir araştırma. *The Turkish Online Journal of Design Art and Communication, 8*(4), 602–614. doi:10.7456/10804100/002

Akyazı, E., & Kara, T. (2017). Bilişim çağının haber kaynağı olarak internet gazetelerinin yaşlı dostu web sitesi kriterleri açısından karşılaştırmalı analizi. *International Journal of Social Sciences and Education Research, 3*(4), 1352–1363. doi:10.24289/ijsser.309075

Alahmadi, T., & Drew, S. (2016). An evaluation of the accessibility of top-ranking university websites: Accessibility rates from 2005 to 2015. *DEANZ Biennial Conference*, 224-233.

Alahmadi, T., & Drew, S. (2017). An evaluation of the accessibility of top-ranking university websites: Accessibility rates from 2005 to 2015. *Journal of Open, Flexible, and Distance Learning, 21*(1), 7–24.

Alajarmeh, N. (2021). Evaluating the accessibility of public health websites: An exploratory cross-country study. *Universal Access in the Information Society*, 1–19. PMID:33526996

Alexa. (2018a). *Alexa: Keyword Research, Competitive Analysis, & Website Ranking*. http://www.alexa.com

Alexa. (2018b). *Top Sites in Tanzania*. https://www.alexa.com/topsites/countries/TZ

Alexender, D. (2006). Usability and accessibility: Best friends or worst enemies. *Proceedings of the 13th VALA Biennial Conference and Exhibition.*

Alır, G., Soydal, İ., & Öztürk, Ö. (2007). Türkiye'de E-devlet Uygulamaları Kapsamında Kamu Kurumlarına Ait Web Sayfalarının Değerlendirilmesi. In S. Kurbanoğlu, Y. Tonta, & U. Al (Eds.), Değişen Dünyada Bilgi Yönetimi Sempozyumu Proceedings. Academic Press.

Al-Khalifa, H. S. (2012a). *WCAG 2.0 Semi-automatic Accessibility Evaluation System: Design.* Academic Press.

Al-Khalifa, H. S. (2012). The accessibility of Saudi Arabia government Web sites: An exploratory study. *Universal Access in the Information Society, 11*(2), 201–210.

Al-Khamayseh, S., & Lawrence, E. (2010). *Towards Citizen Centric Mobile Government Services: A Roadmap*. Faculty of Information Technology, University of Technology.

Al-Kilidar, H., Cox, K., & Kitchenham, B. (2005). The use and usefulness of the ISO/IEC 9126 quality standard. *Proceedings of the 2005 International Symposium on Empirical Software Engineering*, 1-7. 10.1109/ISESE.2005.1541821

Almahamid, S. M., Tweiqat, A. F., & Almanaseer, M. S. (2016). University website quality characteristics and success: Lecturers' perspective. *International Journal of Business Information Systems, 22*(1), 41–61. doi:10.1504/IJBIS.2016.075717

Almeida, F., & Monteiro, J. A. (2017). Approaches and Principles for UX Web Experiences. *International Journal of Information Technology and Web Engineering, 12*(2), 49–65. doi:10.4018/IJITWE.2017040103

Alonso-Ríos, D., Vázquez-García, A., Mosqueira-Rey, E., & Moret-Bonillo, V. (2009). Usability: A critical analysis and a taxonomy. *International Journal of Human-Computer Interaction, 26*(1), 53–74. doi:10.1080/10447310903025552

Alonso-Virgós, L., Espada, J. P., & Crespo, R. G. (2019). Analyzing compliance and application of usability guidelines and recommendations by web developers. *Computer Standards & Interfaces, 64*, 117–132. doi:10.1016/j.csi.2019.01.004

Alsaeedi, A. (2020). Comparing web accessibility evaluation tools and evaluating the accessibility of webpages: Proposed frameworks. *Information (Basel), 11*(1), 1–21. doi:10.3390/info11010040

Alsaghier, H., & Hussain, R. (2012). Conceptualization of trust in the e-government context: a Qualitative analysis. In A. Manohran & M. Holzer (Eds.), *Active citizen participation in e-government: A global perspective* (pp. 528–557). Information Science. doi:10.4018/978-1-4666-0116-1.ch027

Alshahwan, N., & Harman, M. (2012). State Aware Test Case Regeneration for Improving Web Application Test Suite Coverage and Fault Detection. *Proceedings of the 2012 International Symposium on Software Testing and Analysis*, 45-55. 10.1145/2338965.2336759

Alwahaishi, S., Snášel, V., & Nehari-Talet, A. (2009). Website evaluation an empirical study of arabian gulf airlines. *International Journal of Information*, *1*(3), 213.

Ananjeva, A., Persson, J. S., & Bruun, A. (2020). Integrating UX work with agile development through user stories: An action research study in a small software company. *Journal of Systems and Software*, *170*, 1–10. doi:10.1016/j.jss.2020.110785

Annie, C. S., Choy, J. Y., Krishna, M., & Alex, L. (2017). Intention to Use m-Government Services: Age, Gender and Education Matter? International Journal of e-Business and e-Government Studies, 9(2).

Anon. (2015). http://www.freedomscientific.com/Products/LowVision/MAGic

Apostolou, G., & Economides, A. A. (2008). Airlines websites evaluation around the world. In *World Summit on Knowledge Society* (pp. 611–617). Springer.

Apuke, O. D., & Iyendo, T. O. (2018). University students' usage of the internet resources for research and learning: Forms of access and perceptions of utility. *Heliyon*, *4*(12), e01052. doi:10.1016/j.heliyon.2018.e01052 PMID:30582057

Arch, A. (2009). Web accessibility for older users: Successes and opportunities (keynote). *Proceedings of the 2009 International Cross-Disciplinary Conference on Web Accessibility (W4A)*, 1–6. 10.1145/1535654.1535655

Arı, Y. (2021). Engle-Granger Cointegration Analysis Between GARCH-Type Volatilities of Gold and Silver Returns. *Alanya Akademik Bakış*, *5*(2), 589-618. Retrieved from https://dergipark.org.tr/tr/pub/alanyaakademik/issue/62638/838284

Armstrong, M. (2019). How Many Websites Are There? *Statistica*. https://www.statista.com/chart/19058/how-many-websites-are-there/

Astani, M. (2013). A decade of changes in university website design. *Issues in Information Systems*, *14*(1), 189–196.

Aubert, B. A., & Hamel, G. (2001). Adoption of Smart Cards in the Medical Sector: The Canadian Experience. *Social Science & Medicine*, *53*(7), 879–894. doi:10.1016/S0277-9536(00)00388-9 PMID:11522135

Axelsson, K., & Melin, U. (2012). Citizens' Attitudes towards Electronic Identification in a Public E-Service Context – An Essential Perspective in the eID Development Process. In. Lecture Notes in Computer Science: Vol. 7443. *Electronic Government. EGOV 2012*. Springer.

Aziz, M. A., Isa, W. A. R. W. M., & Nordin, N. (2010). Assessing the accessibility and usability of Malaysia Higher Education Website. *International Conference on User Science and Engineering (i-USEr)*, 203-208. 10.1109/IUSER.2010.5716752

Babich, N. (2016). *Mobile Form Usability*. Retrieved from https://uxplanet.org/mobile-form-usability-2279f672917d

Badran, O., & Al-Haddad, S. (2018). The impact of software user experience on customer satisfaction. *Journal of Management Information and Decision Sciences, 21*(1), 1–20.

Baeza-Yates, R. (2020). Bias on the web and beyond: an accessibility point of view. In *Proceedings of the 17th International Web for All Conference* (pp. 1-1). Academic Press.

Bağcı, H., & Yiğiter, Ş. Y. (2019). Bist'te yer alan enerji şirketlerinin finansal performansının SD ve WASPAS yöntemleriyle ölçülmesi. *Bingöl Üniversitesi Sosyal Bilimler Enstitüsü Dergisi, 9*(18), 877–900. doi:10.29029/busbed.559885

Bailey, J., & Burd, E. (2007). Towards more mature web maintenance practices for accessibility. *2007 9th IEEE International Workshop on Web Site Evolution*, 81–87.

Bailey, J., & Burd, E. (2005). Tree-map visualisation for web accessibility. *29th Annual International Computer Software and Applications Conference (COMPSAC'05), 1*, 275–280. 10.1109/COMPSAC.2005.161

Baiocchi, G., & Distaso, W. (2003). *GRETL: Econometric software for the GNU generation.* JSTOR.

Bakır, M., & Atalık, Ö. (2018). *E-service quality performance measurement in airlines: An application on scheduled airlines in Turkey*. Academic Press.

Bakır, M., & Atalık, Ö. (2021). Application of fuzzy AHP and fuzzy MARCOS approach for the evaluation of e-service quality in the airline industry. *Decision Making: Applications in Management and Engineering, 4*(1), 127–152.

Balusa, B. C., & Singam, J. (2018). Underground mining method selection using WPM and PROMETHEE. *Journal of the Institution of Engineers (India), 99*(1), 165–171. doi:10.100740033-017-0137-0

Banati, H., Bedi, P., & Grover, P. S. (2006). Evaluating web usability from the user's perspective. *Journal of Computational Science, 2*(4), 314–317. doi:10.3844/jcssp.2006.314.317

Barker, T. (2012). *Pro JavaScript Performance: Monitoring and Visualization*. Apress. doi:10.1007/978-1-4302-4750-0

Batty, M. (2009). Accessibility: In search of a unified theory. *Environment and Planning. B, Planning & Design, 36*(2), 191–194. doi:10.1068/b3602ed

Baušys, R., & Juodagalvienė, B. (2017). Garage location selection for residential house by WASPAS-SVNS method. *Journal of Civil Engineering and Management, 23*(3), 421–429. doi:10.3846/13923730.2016.1268645

Baylé, M. (2018). *Experience Design: a new discipline?* Retrieved from https://uxdesign.cc/experience-design-a-new-discipline-e62db76d5ed1

Bayraktar, D. M., & Bayram, S. (2018). Teachers' Website Design Experiences and Usability Test: The Case of Weebly. Com. *World Journal on Educational Technology: Current Issues, 10*(4), 37–51. doi:10.18844/wjet.v10i4.3783

Bayraktar, S. (2018). Türk Hava Yolları web sayfasının görsel-içerik çözümlemesi. *International Journal of Tourism Economics and Business Sciences, 2*(2), 276–284.

Benbunan-Fich, R. (2001). Using protocol analysis to evaluate the usability of a commercial web site. *Information & Management, 39*(2), 151–163. doi:10.1016/S0378-7206(01)00085-4

Bernard, M. (2003). *Criteria for optimal web design (designing for usability).* Academic Press.

Bernard, E. K., & Makienko, I. (2011). The effects of information privacy and online shopping experience in e-commerce. *Academy of Marketing Studies Journal, 15*, 97.

Bertot, J. C., Snead, J. T., Jaeger, P. T., & McClure, C. R. (2006). *Functionality, usability, and accessibility: Iterative user-centered evaluation strategies for digital libraries.* Performance Measurement and Metrics. doi:10.1108/14678040610654828

Bocchi, E., De Cicco, L., Mellia, M., & Rossi, D. (2017). The web, the users, and the mos: Influence of http/2 on user experience. In *International Conference on Passive and Active Network Measurement* (pp. 47-59). Springer. 10.1007/978-3-319-54328-4_4

Bommier, A., & Lambert, S. (2000). Education Demand and Age at School Enrollment in Tanzania. *The Journal of Human Resources, 35*(1), 177–203. doi:10.2307/146360

Borg, J., Lantz, A., & Gulliksen, J. (2015). Accessibility to electronic communication for people with cognitive disabilities: A systematic search and review of empirical evidence. *Universal Access in the Information Society, 14*(4), 547–562. doi:10.100710209-014-0351-6

Borgman, C. L. (1999). What are digital libraries? Competing visions. *Information Processing & Management.* Advance online publication. doi:10.1016/S0306-4573(98)00059-4

Bose, R., & Jürgensen, H. (2014). Accessibility of e-commerce websites for vision-impaired persons. In *International Conference on Computers for Handicapped Persons* (pp. 121-128). Springer.

Bourne, R. R. A., Flaxman, S. R., Braithwaite, T., Cicinelli, M. V., Das, A., Jonas, J. B., Keeffe, J., Kempen, J. H., Leasher, J., Limburg, H., Naidoo, K., Pesudovs, K., Resnikoff, S., Silvester, A., Stevens, G. A., Tahhan, N., Wong, T. Y., Taylor, H. R., Bourne, R., ... Zheng, Y. (2017). Magnitude, temporal trends, and projections of the global prevalence of blindness and distance and near vision impairment: A systematic review and meta-analysis. *The Lancet. Global Health, 5*(9), e888–e897. doi:10.1016/S2214-109X(17)30293-0 PMID:28779882

Braga, H., Pereira, L. S., Ferreira, S. B. L., & Da Silveira, D. S. (2014). Applying the barrier walkthrough method: Going beyond the automatic evaluation of accessibility. *Procedia Computer Science, 27*, 471–480. doi:10.1016/j.procs.2014.02.051

Brajnik, G. (2011). *Barrier walkthrough.* https://users.dimi.uniud.it/~giorgio.brajnik/projects/bw/bw.html

Brajnik, G., & Vigo, M. (2019). *Automatic Web Accessibility Metrics-Where We Were and Where We Went.* Academic Press.

Brajnik, G. (2004). Comparing accessibility evaluation tools: A method for tool effectiveness. *Universal Access in the Information Society, 3*(3), 252–263. doi:10.100710209-004-0105-y

Brajnik, G. (2008a). A comparative test of web accessibility evaluation methods. *Proceedings of the 10th International ACM SIGACCESS Conference on Computers and Accessibility,* 113–120. 10.1145/1414471.1414494

Brajnik, G. (2008b). Beyond conformance: The role of accessibility evaluation methods. *International Conference on Web Information Systems Engineering,* 63–80. 10.1007/978-3-540-85200-1_9

Brajnik, G., & Lomuscio, R. (2007). SAMBA: A semi-automatic method for measuring barriers of accessibility. *Proceedings of the 9th International ACM SIGACCESS Conference on Computers and Accessibility,* 43–50. 10.1145/1296843.1296853

Brajnik, G., Mulas, A., & Pitton, C. (2007). Effects of sampling methods on web accessibility evaluations. *Proceedings of the 9th International ACM SIGACCESS Conference on Computers and Accessibility,* 59–66. 10.1145/1296843.1296855

Brajnik, G., Yesilada, Y., & Harper, S. (2009). Guideline aggregation: Web accessibility evaluation for older users. *Proceedings of the 2009 International Cross-Disciplinary Conference on Web Accessibility (W4A),* 127-135. 10.1145/1535654.1535686

Brajnik, G., Yesilada, Y., & Harper, S. (2011). Web accessibility guideline aggregation for older users and its validation. *Universal Access in the Information Society, 10*(4), 403–423. doi:10.100710209-011-0220-5

Brankovic, J., Ringel, L., & Werron, T. (2018). How rankings produce competition: The case of global university rankings. *Zeitschrift für Soziologie, 47*(4), 270–288. doi:10.1515/zfsoz-2018-0118

Brügger, N. (2009). Website history and the website as an object of study. *New Media & Society, 11*(1-2), 115–132. doi:10.1177/1461444808099574

BTK Internet. (2021). https://internet.btk.gov.tr/istatistikler

Bühler, C., Heck, H., Perlick, O., Nietzio, A., & Ulltveit-Moe, N. (2006). Interpreting results from large scale automatic evaluation of web accessibility. *International Conference on Computers for Handicapped Persons,* 184–191. 10.1007/11788713_28

Buley, L. (2013). *The User Experience Team of One: A Research and Design Survival Guide.* Rosenfeld Media.

Burki, T. K. (2020). COVID-19: Consequences for higher education. *The Lancet. Oncology, 21*(6), 758. doi:10.1016/S1470-2045(20)30287-4 PMID:32446322

Buscher, G., Cutrell, E., & Morris, M. R. (2009). What do you see when you're surfing? Using eye tracking to predict salient regions of web pages. *Conference on Human Factors in Computing Systems - Proceedings.* 10.1145/1518701.1518705

Bwalya, K. J., & Healy, M. (2010). Harnessing e-Government Adoption in the SADC Region: A Conceptual Underpinning. *Electronic. Journal of E-Government, 8*(1), 23–32.

Caglar, E., & Mentes, S. A. (2012). The usability of university websites–a study on European University of Lefke. *International Journal of Business Information Systems, 11*(1), 22–40. doi:10.1504/IJBIS.2012.048340

Caldwell, B., Cooper, M., Reid, L. G., Vanderheiden, G., Chisholm, W., Slatin, J., & White, J. (2008). Web content accessibility guidelines (WCAG) 2.0. *WWW Consortium (W3C), 290.*

Çalışma & Bakanlığı. (2019). *Engelli ve Yaşlı Hizmetler Genel Müdürlüğü Engelli ve Yaşlı İstatistik Bülteni.* Retrieved April 22, 2020, from, https://ailevecalisma.gov.tr/media/9085/buelten-haziran2019-son.pdf

Camburn, B., Viswanathan, V., Linsey, J., Anderson, D., Jensen, D., Crawford, R., Otto, K., & Wood, K. (2017). Design prototyping methods: State of the art in strategies, techniques, and guidelines. *Design Science, 3*, e13. doi:10.1017/dsj.2017.10

Canöz, N. (2017). Türkiye'deki havayolu işletmelerinin hizmet anlayışlarının belirlenmesine yönelik bir araştırma. *Selçuk Üniversitesi Sosyal Bilimler Meslek Yüksekokulu Dergisi, 20*(2), 192–205. doi:10.29249elcuksbmyd.349602

Cappel, J. J., & Huang, Z. (2007). A usability analysis of company websites. *Journal of Computer Information Systems, 48*(1), 117–123.

Cattaneo, M., Malighetti, P., Meoli, M., & Paleari, S. (2017). University spatial competition for students: The Italian case. *Regional Studies, 51*(5), 750–764. doi:10.1080/00343404.2015.1135240

CDT & infoDev. (2007). *E-Government Handbook: Accessibility.* Retrieved June 19, 2007, from https://www.cdt.org/egov/handbook/accessibility.shtml

Cena, A., & Gagolewski, M. (2020). Genie+OWA: Robustifying hierarchical clustering with OWA-based linkages. *Information Sciences, 520*, 324–336. doi:10.1016/j.ins.2020.02.025

Chakraborty, S., & Zavadskas, E. K. (2014). Applications of WASPAS method in manufacturing decision making. *Informatica (Vilnius), 25*(1), 1–20. doi:10.15388/Informatica.2014.01

Chan, M., & Zoellick, R. B. (2011). *World report on disability.* WHO. https://www.who.int/disabilities/world_report/2011/report/en/

Chandra, T., Hafni, L., Chandra, S., Purwati, A. A., & Chandra, J. (2019). The influence of service quality, university image on student satisfaction and student loyalty. *Benchmarking, 26*(5), 1533–1549. doi:10.1108/BIJ-07-2018-0212

Chang, K. H., & Cheng, C. H. (2011). Evaluating the risk of failure using the fuzzy OWA and DEMATEL method. *Journal of Intelligent Manufacturing*, *22*(2), 113–129. doi:10.100710845-009-0266-x

Chang, Y. C., Chang, K. H., & Liaw, C. S. (2009). Innovative reliability allocation using the maximal entropy ordered weighted averaging method. *Computers & Industrial Engineering*, *57*(4), 1274–1281. doi:10.1016/j.cie.2009.06.007

Chareonwongsak, K. (2002). Globalization and technology: How will they change society? *Technology in Society*, *24*(3), 191–206. doi:10.1016/S0160-791X(02)00004-0

Chauhan, S., Gupta, P., Palvia, S., & Jaiswal, M. (2020). Information technology transforming higher education: A meta-analytic review. *Journal of Information Technology Case and Application Research*, 1-33.

Chiew, T. K., & Salim, S. S. (2003). Webuse: Website usability evaluation tool. *Malaysian Journal of Computer Science*, *16*(1), 47–57.

Chong, S., & Law, R. (2019). Review of studies on airline website evaluation. *Journal of Travel & Tourism Marketing*, *36*(1), 60–75. doi:10.1080/10548408.2018.1494084

Cho, S. B. (1995). Fuzzy aggregation of modular neural networks with ordered weighted averaging operators. *International Journal of Approximate Reasoning*, *13*(4), 359–375. doi:10.1016/0888-613X(95)00059-P

Chourabi, Z., Khedher, F., Babay, A., & Cheikhrouhou, M. (2019). Multi-criteria decision making in workforce choice using AHP, WSM and WPM. *Journal of the Textile Institute*, *110*(7), 1092–1101. doi:10.1080/00405000.2018.1541434

Cluster, W. A. B. (2006). *UWEM 1.0 released (Unified Web-Accessibility Evaluation Methodology)* [Text]. Shaping Europe's Digital Future - European Commission. https://ec.europa.eu/digital-single-market/en/news/uwem10-released-unified-web-accessibility-evaluation-methodology

Cojocar, G. S., & Guran, A. M. (2013). Evaluation of Romanian Academic Websites Accessibility: A Case Study. *Studia Universitatis Babes-Bolyai. Informatica*, *58*(4).

Constantine, L. L., & Lockwood, L. A. (1999). *Software for use: a practical guide to the models and methods of usage-centered design*. Pearson Education.

Contrast Checker. (2017). *WCAG Contrast Checker*. Contrast Checker. https://contrastchecker.com/

Costa, D., Carriço, L., & Duarte, C. (2015). The differences in accessibility of tv and desktop web applications from the perspective of automated evaluation. *Procedia Computer Science*, *67*, 388–396. doi:10.1016/j.procs.2015.09.283

Criado, J. I., & Ramilo, M. C. (2003). E-Government in practice: An analysis of website orientation to citizens in Spanish municipalities. *International Journal of Public Sector Management*, *18*(3), 191–218. doi:10.1108/09513550310472320

Crutzen, R., Peters, G. J., & Mondschein, C. (2019). Why and how we should care about the General Data Protection Regulation. *Psychology & Health, 34*(11), 1347–1357. doi:10.1080/08 870446.2019.1606222 PMID:31111730

Curran, J., Fenton, N., & Freedman, D. (2016). *Misunderstanding the internet.* Routledge. doi:10.4324/9781315695624

Cynthiasays. (2016). http://www.cynthiasays.com

Cyr, D. (2013). Website design, trust and culture: An eight-country investigation. *Electronic Commerce Research and Applications, 12*(6), 373–385.

Cyr, D., Bonanni, C., Bowes, J., & Ilsever, J. (2005). Beyond trust: Web site design preferences across cultures. *Journal of Global Information Management, 13*(4), 25–54.

Daniela, L., Visvizi, A., Gutiérrez-Braojos, C., & Lytras, M. D. (2018). Sustainable higher education and technology-enhanced learning (TEL). *Sustainability, 10*(11), 3883. doi:10.3390u10113883

Daoust, F. (2020). Update from the World Wide Web Consortium (WC3). *SMPTE Motion Imaging Journal, 129*(8), 80–83. doi:10.5594/JMI.2020.3001776

Daskalantonakis, M. K. (1992). A practical view of software measurement and implementation experiences within Motorola. *IEEE Transactions on Software Engineering, 18*(11), 998–1010. doi:10.1109/32.177369

De Kock, E., Van Biljon, J., & Pretorius, M. (2009). Usability evaluation methods: Mind the gaps. *Proceedings of the 2009 Annual Conference of the South African Institute of Computer Scientists and Information Technologists,* 122-131. 10.1145/1632149.1632166

Deepika, S., Kukreja, S., Brahma, J., Tyagi, S., & Jain, P. (2018). Studying Open Source Vulnerability Scanner for Vulnerabilities in Web Applications. *Computer Science, 9*(2), 43–49.

Deshmukh, M., Phatak, D., & Save, B. (2018). User Experience for Person with Disabilities. *International Journal of Computers and Applications, 180*(44), 6–11. doi:10.5120/ijca2018917141

Di Blas, N., Paolini, P., & Speroni, M. (2004). Usable accessibility" to the Web for blind users. *Proceedings of 8th ERCIM Workshop: User Interfaces for All.*

Dias, A. L., de Mattos Fortes, R. P., & Masiero, P. C. (2014). HEUA: A Heuristic Evaluation with Usability and Accessibility requirements to assess Web systems. *Proceedings of the 11th Web for All Conference,* 1–4. 10.1145/2596695.2596706

Digital 2019: Global Internet Use Accelerates. (2019). *We Are Social.* https://wearesocial.com/blog/2019/01/digital-2019-global-internet-use-accelerates

Dingli, A., & Mifsud, J. (2011). USEFul: A Framework to Mainstream Web Site Usability through Automated Evaluation. *International Journal of Human-Computer Interaction, 2*(1).

Dominic, P. D. D., Jati, H., Sellappan, P., & Nee, G. K. (2011). A comparison of Asian e-government websites quality: Using a non-parametric test. *International Journal of Business Information Systems, 7*(2), 220–246. doi:10.1504/IJBIS.2011.038513

Dominic, P. D. D., & Khan, H. (2014). Performance measure of airline websites using analytical hierarchy process & fuzzy analytical hierarchy process. In *2014 IEEE International Conference on Control System, Computing and Engineering (ICCSCE)* (pp. 530–535). IEEE. 10.1109/ICCSCE.2014.7072775

Doupé, A., Cui, W., Jakubowski, M. H., Peinado, M., Kruegel, C., & Vigna, D. (2013). deDacota: Toward Preventing Server-side XSS via Automatic Code and Data Separation. *Proceedings of the 2013 ACM SIGSAC Conference on Computer & Communications Security.*

Doush, I. A., Alkhateeb, F., Al Maghayreh, E., & Al-Betar, M. A. (2013). The design of RIA accessibility evaluation tool. *Advances in Engineering Software, 57*, 1–7. doi:10.1016/j.advengsoft.2012.11.004

Dreheeb, A. E., & Fabil, N. B. (2016). Impact of System Quality on Users' Satisfaction in Continuation of the Use of e-Learning System. *International Journal of e-Education, e-Business, e- Management Learning, 6*(1), 13–20.

Dunn, T. J., & Kennedy, M. (2019). Technology Enhanced Learning in higher education; motivations, engagement and academic achievement. *Computers & Education, 137*, 104–113. doi:10.1016/j.compedu.2019.04.004

Durmus, S., & Cagiltay, K. (2012). Kamu Kurumu Web Siteleri ve Kullanılabilirlik. In M. Z. Sobacı & M. Yıldız (Eds.), *E-Devlet Kamu Yönetimi ve Teknoloji İlişkisinde Güncel Gelişmeler* (pp. 293–322). Nobel Akademik Yayıncılık.

Dzulfiqar, M. D., Khairani, D., & Wardhani, L. K. (2018). The Development of University Website using User Centered Design Method with ISO 9126 Standard. In *2018 6th International Conference on Cyber and IT Service Management (CITSM)* (pp. 1-4). IEEE.

easyJet plc. (2016). *Annual report and accounts 2016.* Retrieved from https://corporate.easyjet.com/~/media/Files/E/Easyjet/pdf/investors/result-center-investor/annual-report-2016.pdf

Ehmke, C., & Wilson, S. (2007). Identifying web usability problems from eye-tracking data. *People and Computers XXI HCI.But Not as We Know It - Proceedings of HCI 2007: The 21st British HCI Group Annual Conference.* 10.14236/ewic/HCI2007.12

Ekman, B. (2004). Community-based health insurance in low-income countries: A systematic review of the evidence. *Health Policy and Planning, 19*(5), 249–270. doi:10.1093/heapol/czh031 PMID:15310661

Ekşioğlu, M., Kiriş, E., Çakir, T., Güvendik, M., Koyutürk, E. D., & Yilmaz, M. (2013). A user experience study of airline websites. *Lecture Notes in Computer Science, 8015 LNCS*(PART 4), 173–182. doi:10.1007/978-3-642-39253-5_19

Elberkawi, E. K., El-Firjani, N. F., Maatuk, A. M., & Aljawarneh, S. A. (2016, September). Usability evaluation of web-based systems: A new method and results. In *2016 International Conference on Engineering & MIS (ICEMIS)* (pp. 1-5). IEEE.

El-Firjani, N. F., Elberkawi, E. K., & Maatuk, A. M. (2017). *Method For Website Usability Evaluation* (Doctoral dissertation). University of Benghazi.

Elkabani, I., Hamandi, L., Zantout, R., & Mansi, S. (2015, December). Toward better web accessibility. In *2015 5th International Conference on Information & Communication Technology and Accessibility (ICTA)* (pp. 1-6). IEEE.

Elsantil, Y. (2020). User Perceptions of the Security of Mobile Applications. *International Journal of E-Services and Mobile Applications, 12*(4), 24–41. doi:10.4018/IJESMA.2020100102

Engle, R., & Granger, J. (1987). Co-Integration and Error Correction: Representation. Estimation. and Testing. *Econometrica, 55*(2), 251–276. doi:10.2307/1913236

Ennis, A. (2015). *Testing airline web sites for accessibility compliance: use of colour.* https://www.accessibilityoz.com/2015/11/testing-airline-web-sites-for-accessibility-compliance/

Ertürk, K. L., Şimşek, A. A., Songür, D. G., & Şengül, G. (2014). Türkiye'de engelli farkındalığı ve engelli bireylerin adalete web erişilebilirlikleri üzerine bir değerlendirme. *Information World/ Bilgi Dunyasi, 15*(2), 375-395.

Éthier, J., Hadaya, P., Talbot, J., & Cadieux, J. (2008). Interface design and emotions experienced on B2C Web sites: Empirical testing of a research model. *Computers in Human Behavior, 24*(6), 2771–2791.

Eusébio, C., Silveiro, A., & Teixeira, L. (2020). Website accessibility of travel agents: An evaluation using web diagnostic tools. *Journal of Accessibility and Design for All, 10*(2), 180–208.

EvalAccess. (2016). http://sipt07.si.ehu.es/evalaccess2/

Evaluera. (2016). http://www.evaluera.co.uk

EVDS. (2020). All Series in Electronic Data Delivery System. *TCMB EVDS.* Retrieved from https://evds2.tcmb.gov.tr/index.php?/evds/serieMarket

Fabricant, R. (2013). *Scaling Your UX Strategy.* Retrieved from https://hbr.org/2013/01/scaling-your-ux-strategy

Fagan. (2014). The Suitability of Web Analytics Key Performance Indicators in the Academic Library Environment. *Journal of Academic Librarianship, 40*(1).

Fang, X., & Holsapple, C. W. (2007). An empirical study of web site navigation structures' impacts on web site usability. *Decision Support Systems, 43*(2), 476–491. doi:10.1016/j.dss.2006.11.004

Farris, P. W., Bendle, N. T., Pfeifer, P. E., & Reibstein, D. J. (2010). *Marketing metrics; The definitive guide to measuring marketing performance* (2nd ed.). Prentice Hall.

Feng, L., Bui, T. D., & Tang, Y. Y. (2001). Classification of similar 2-D objects by wavelet-sparse-matrix (WSM) method. *International Journal of Pattern Recognition and Artificial Intelligence, 15*(2), 329–345. doi:10.1142/S0218001401000873

Fenton, N., & Bieman, J. (2014). *Software metrics: A rigorous and practical approach.* CRC press. doi:10.1201/b17461

Fernandes, J., & Benavidez, C. (2011). A zero in echecker equals a 10 in examinator: A comparison between two metrics by their scores. *W3C Symposium on Website Accessibility Metrics, 8.*

Fernandes, N., Batista, A. S., Costa, D., Duarte, C., & Carriço, L. (2013). Three web accessibility evaluation perspectives for RIA. *Proceedings of the 10th International Cross-Disciplinary Conference on Web Accessibility,* 1–9. 10.1145/2461121.2461122

Fernandes, N., & Carriço, L. (2012). A macroscopic Web accessibility evaluation at different processing phases. *Proceedings of the International Cross-Disciplinary Conference on Web Accessibility,* 1–4. 10.1145/2207016.2207025

Fernandes, N., Kaklanis, N., Votis, K., Tzovaras, D., & Carriço, L. (2014). An analysis of personalized web accessibility. *Proceedings of the 11th Web for All Conference,* 1–10.

Fernandes, N., Lopes, R., & Carriço, L. (2011). An architecture for multiple web accessibility evaluation environments. *International Conference on Universal Access in Human-Computer Interaction,* 206-214. 10.1007/978-3-642-21672-5_23

Fernández, D. P. (2020). Will the Internet fragment? Sovereignty, globalization and cyberspace. *Revista española de ciencia política,* (53), 195-200.

Ferris, C., & Farrell, J. (2003). What are web services? *Communications of the ACM, 46*(6), 31. doi:10.1145/777313.777335

Fichman, R. G., & Kemerer, C. F. (1997). The Assimilation of Software Process Innovations. An Organizational Learning Perspective. *Management Science, 43*(10), 1345–1363. doi:10.1287/mnsc.43.10.1345

Fichten, C. S., Ferraro, V., Asuncion, J. V., Chwojka, C., Barile, M., Nguyen, M. N., ... Wolforth, J. (2009). Disabilities and e-learning problems and solutions: An exploratory study. *Journal of Educational Technology & Society, 12*(4), 241–256.

Firth, A. (2019). *Practical Web Inclusion and Accessibility: A Comprehensive Guide to Access Needs.* Apress. doi:10.1007/978-1-4842-5452-3

Flom, P. (2018, December 11). *Stopping stepwise: Why stepwise selection is bad and what you should use instead.* Medium. Retrieved from https://towardsdatascience.com/stopping-stepwise-why-stepwise-selection-is-bad-and-what-you-should-use-instead-90818b3f52df

Fong, E. M., & Chung, W. Y. (2013). Mobile Cloud-Computing-Based Healthcare Service by Noncontact ECG Monitoring. *Sensors (Basel), 13*(12), 16451–16473. doi:10.3390131216451 PMID:24316562

Fox, J., & Weisberg, S. (2020). *car: Companion to Applied Regression* [R package]. Retrieved from https://cran.r-project.org/package=car

Freire, A. P., Fortes, R. P., Turine, M. A., & Paiva, D. M. (2008). An evaluation of web accessibility metrics based on their attributes. *Proceedings of the 26th Annual ACM International Conference on Design of Communication*, 73–80. 10.1145/1456536.1456551

Fuhr, N., Tsakonas, G., Aalberg, T., Agosti, M., Hansen, P., Kapidakis, S., Klas, C.-P., Kovács, L., Landoni, M., Micsik, A., Papatheodorou, C., Peters, C., & Sølvberg, I. (2007). Evaluation of digital libraries. *International Journal on Digital Libraries*, *8*(1), 21–38. Advance online publication. doi:10.100700799-007-0011-z

Fukuda, K., Saito, S., Takagi, H., & Asakawa, C. (2005). Proposing new metrics to evaluate web usability for the blind. *CHI'05 Extended Abstracts on Human Factors in Computing Systems*, 1387–1390.

Galvez, R. A., & Youngblood, N. E. (2016). e-Government in Rhode Island: What effects do templates have on usability, accessibility, and mobile readiness? *Universal Access in the Information Society*, *15*(2), 281–296.

Ganiyu, A. A., Mishra, A., Elijah, J., & Gana, U. M. (2017). The Importance of Usability of a Website. *IUP Journal of Information Technology, 13*(3).

Gann, R. (1999). *Every second count.* Competing.

Gavcar, C. T., & Organ, A. (2020). AHP-Gri İlişkisel Analiz ve AHP-WASPAS yöntemleri ile online satış yapan seyahat acentalarının değerlendirilmesi. *Business & Management Studies: An International Journal*, *8*(1), 731–753.

Gay, G., & Li, C. Q. (2010). AChecker: Open, interactive, customizable, web accessibility checking. *W4A 2010 - International Cross Disciplinary Conference on Web Accessibility Raleigh 2010.* 10.1145/1805986.1806019

Gezen, A. (2019). Türkiye'de faaliyet gösteren katılım bankalarının ENTROPİ ve WASPAS yöntemleri ile performans analizi. *Muhasebe ve Finansman Dergisi*, (84), 213–232. doi:10.25095/mufad.625812

Ghandour, A. (2015). Ecommerce website value model for SMEs. *International Journal of Electronic Commerce Studies*, *6*(2), 203–222. doi:10.7903/ijecs.1403

Ghasemkhani, N., Vayghan, S. S., Abdollahi, A., Pradhan, B., & Alamri, A. (2020). Urban development modeling using integrated fuzzy systems, ordered weighted averaging (OWA), and geospatial techniques. *Sustainability*, *12*(3), 1–26. doi:10.3390u12030809

Gibson, B. (2007). Enabling an accessible web 2.0. *Proceedings of the 2007 International Cross-Disciplinary Conference on Web Accessibility (W4A)*, 1–6.

Gilbert, R. M. (2019). *Inclusive Design for a Digital World: Designing with Accessibility in Mind.* Apress. doi:10.1007/978-1-4842-5016-7

Gilbertson, T. D., & Machin, C. H. (2012). Guidelines, icons and marketable skills: an accessibility evaluation of 100 web development company homepages. In *Proceedings of the international cross-disciplinary conference on web accessibility* (pp. 1-4). Academic Press.

Gilbertson, T. D., & Machin, C. H. (2012, April). Guidelines, icons and marketable skills: an accessibility evaluation of 100 web development company homepages. In *Proceedings of the international cross-disciplinary conference on web accessibility* (pp. 1-4). Academic Press.

Godoi, T. X., & Valentim, N. M. (2019). Towards an Integrated Evaluation of Usability, User Experience and Accessibility in Assistive Technologies. *Proceedings of the XVIII Brazilian Symposium on Software Quality*, 234-239. 10.1145/3364641.3364669

Gohin, B., & Vinod, V. (2014). AAEM: Accessibility assistance evaluation metric. *Int. Rev. Comput. Softw*, 9(5), 872–882.

Gold, M. (2003). *Making your website work-for your user.* Stanford Videos.

Goldsborough, R. (2005). Gauging the Success of Your Web Site. *Black Issues in Higher Education*, 21(24), 37.

Gonçalves, R., Rocha, T., Martins, J., Branco, F., & Au-Yong-Oliveira, M. (2018). Evaluation of e-commerce websites accessibility and usability: An e-commerce platform analysis with the inclusion of blind users. *Universal Access in the Information Society*, 17(3), 567–583.

Gonzalez-Holland, E., Whitmer, D., Moralez, L., & Mouloua, M. (2017). Examination of the Use of Nielsen's 10 Usability Heuristics & Outlooks for the Future. *Proceedings of the Human Factors and Ergonomics Society Annual Meeting*, 61(1), 1472–1475. doi:10.1177/1541931213601853

González, J., Macías, M., Rodríguez, R., & Sánchez, F. (2003). Accessibility metrics of web pages for blind end-users. *International Conference on Web Engineering*, 374–383. 10.1007/3-540-45068-8_68

Gowases, T., Bednarik, R., & Tukiainen, M. (2011). Text highlighting improves user experience for reading with magnified displays. In CHI'11 Extended Abstracts on Human Factors in Computing Systems (pp. 1891-1896). ACM.

Grigorik, I. (2013). Making the Web Faster with HTTP 2.0. *Communications of the ACM*, 56(12), 42–49. doi:10.1145/2534706.2534721

Gulsecen, S. (2020). İnsan ve Bilgisayar. In S. Gülseçen, K. Rızvanoğlu, N. Tosun, & E. Akadal (Eds.), *İnsan Bilgisayar Etkileşimi: Araştırma ve Uygulamalar*. Istanbul University Press., doi:10.26650/B/ET07.2020.012.01

Güreş, N., Arslan, S., & Yalçın, R. (2013). Türk havayolu işletmelerinin web sitelerinin değerlendirilmesine yönelik bir araştırma. *Niğde Üniversitesi İktisadi ve İdari Bilimler Fakültesi Dergisi*, 6(1), 173–185.

Gutierrez, C. F., Loucopoulos, C., & Reinsch, R. W. (2005). Disability-accessibility of airlines' Web sites for US reservations online. *Journal of Air Transport Management*, 11(4), 239–247.

Gyanendra, P. (2007). Addressing the Digital Divide: E-Governance and M-Governance in A Hub and Spoke Model. *The Electronic Journal on Information Systems in Developing Countries*, *31*(1), 1–14. doi:10.1002/j.1681-4835.2007.tb00210.x

Hackett, S., Parmanto, B., & Zeng, X. (2003). Accessibility of Internet websites through time. *ACM SIGACCESS Accessibility and Computing*, *77–78*(77-78), 32–39. doi:10.1145/1029014.1028638

Handoko, D., Mesran, M., Nasution, S. D., Yuhandri, Y., & Nurdiyanto, H. (2017). Application of weight sum model (WSM) in determining special allocation funds recipients. *The IJICS*, *1*(2), 31–35.

Harper, K. A., & DeWaters, J. (2008). A quest for website accessibility in higher education institutions. *The Internet and Higher Education*, *11*(3-4), 160–164. doi:10.1016/j.iheduc.2008.06.007

Harper, S., & Yesilada, Y. (2008). *Web accessibility: A foundation for research.* Springer. doi:10.1007/978-1-84800-050-6

Harrison, C., & Petrie, H. (2007). Severity of usability and accessibility problems in eCommerce and eGovernment websites. In *People and Computers XX—Engage* (pp. 255–262). Springer.

Harteveldt, H. H. (2016). *The Future Of Airline Distribution A Look Ahead To 2017.* Atmosphere Research Group.

Hasan, L. (2009). *Usability Evaluation Framework for E-commerce Websites in Developing Countries* (Doctoral Thesis). Loughborough University

Hasan, L., & Morris, A. (2017). Usability problem areas on key international and key Arab E-commerce websites. *Journal of Internet Commerce*, *16*(1), 80–103.

Hashemian, B. J. (2011). Analyzing web accessibility in Finnish higher education. *ACM SIGACCESS Accessibility and Computing*, *101*(101), 8–16. doi:10.1145/2047473.2047475

Hassan, S., Din, I. U., Habbal, A., & Zakaria, N. H. (2016). A popularity based caching strategy for the future Internet. In 2016 ITU Kaleidoscope: ICTs for a Sustainable World (ITU WT) (pp. 1-8). IEEE. doi:10.1109/ITU-WT.2016.7805723

Hassouna, M. S., Sahari, N., & İsmail, A. (2020). University website accessibility for totally blind users. *Journal of Information and Communication Technology*, *16*(1), 63–80.

Henry, S. L. (2002). Another–ability: Accessibility primer for usability specialists. *UPA 2002, the Usability Professionals' Association Annual Conference.*

Henry, S. L., Abou-Zahra, S., & Brewer, J. (2014). The role of accessibility in a universal web. *Proceedings of the 11th Web for all Conference*, 1-4. 10.1145/2596695.2596719

Henzinger, M. R., Heydon, A., Mitzenmacher, M., & Najork, M. (2000). On near-uniform URL sampling. *Computer Networks*, *33*(1–6), 295–308. doi:10.1016/S1389-1286(00)00055-4

He, R. Y. (2015). Design and implementation of web based on Laravel framework. In *2014 International Conference on Computer Science and Electronic Technology (ICCSET 2014)* (pp. 301-304). Atlantis Press. 10.2991/iccset-14.2015.66

Herhausen, D., Miočević, D., Morgan, R. E., & Kleijnen, M. H. (2020). The digital marketing capabilities gap. *Industrial Marketing Management, 90*, 276–290. doi:10.1016/j. indmarman.2020.07.022

Hernández, B., Jiménez, J., & Martín, M. J. (2009). Key website factors in e-business strategy. *International Journal of Information Management, 29*(5), 362–371.

Hernandez, C. C., Palos-Sánchez, P., & Rios, M. A. (2020). Website quality assessment: A case study of chinese airlines. *Indian Journal of Marketing, 50*(1), 42–64.

HESLB. (2006). *Annual Report, 2005 – 2006*. Dar es Salaam: Higher Education Students' Loans Board.

Heung, V. C., Wong, M. Y., & Qu, H. (2000). Airport-restaurant service quality in Hong Kong: An application of SERVQUAL. *The Cornell Hotel and Restaurant Administration Quarterly, 41*(3), 86–96. doi:10.1177/001088040004100320

Hix, D., & Hartson, H. R. (1993). *Developing user interfaces: ensuring usability through product & process*. John Wiley & Sons, Inc.

Hoober, S. (2017). *Design for Fingers, Touch, and People, Part 1*. Retrieved from https://www. uxmatters.com/mt/archives/2017/03/design-for-fingers-touch-and-people-part-1.php

Hootsuite and We Are Social. (2020). https://www.hootsuite.com/pages/digital-trends-2021

Hossain, M. N., & Ahmed, S. Z. (2020). *Use of scholarly communication and citation-based metrics as a basis for university ranking in developing country perspective*. Global Knowledge, Memory and Communication. doi:10.1108/GKMC-09-2019-0112

International Air Transport Association. (2016). *IATA airline distribution online study. The Future of Airline Distribution, 2016-2021*. Retrieved from http://www.iata.org/whatwedo/airline-distribution/ndc/Documents/ndc-future-airline-distribution-report.pdf

International Civil Aviation Organization. (2017). *Economic development of air transport - low cost carriers (LCCs)*. Retrieved from https://www.icao.int/sustainability/Pages/Low-Cost-Carriers.aspx

International Organization for Standardization. (1998). *ISO 9241-11: Ergonomic requirements for office work with visual display terminals (VDTs) - part 11: guidance on usability*. International Organization for Standardization. doi:10.1038j.mp.4001776

International Telecommunication Union. (2017). *ICT facts and figures 2017*. Retrieved from https://www.itu.int/en/ITU-D/Statistics/Documents/facts/ICTFactsFigures2017.pdf

Isa, W. A. R. W. M., Aziz, M. A., & Razak, M. R. B. A. (2011). Evaluating the accessibility of Small and Medium Enterprise (SME) websites in Malaysia. In *2011 International Conference on User Science and Engineering (i-USEr)* (pp. 135-140). IEEE.

Ishaq, O. O., Onuja, A. M., & Zubairu, H. A. (2018). An Analytical Approach to Accessibility and Usability Evaluation of Nigerian Airlines Websites. *Am. J. Comput. Sci. Inf. Technol.*, 6(2), 21.

Ismail, A., & Kuppusamy, K. S. (2018a). Accessibility of Indian universities' homepages: An exploratory study. *Journal of King Saud University-Computer and Information Sciences*, 30(2), 268–278. doi:10.1016/j.jksuci.2016.06.006

Ismail, A., Kuppusamy, K. S., & Paiva, S. (2019). Accessibility analysis of higher education institution websites of Portugal. *Universal Access in the Information Society*, ●●●, 1–16. doi:10.100710209-019-00653-2

Ismailova, R., & Inal, Y. (2016). Web Site Accessibility and Quality in Use: A Comparative Study of Government Web Sites in Kyrgyzstan, Azerbaijan, Kazakhstan and Turkey. *Universal Access in the Information Society*, 1–10.

Ismailova, R., & Inal, Y. (2018). Accessibility evaluation of top university websites: A comparative study of Kyrgyzstan, Azerbaijan, Kazakhstan, and Turkey. *Universal Access in the Information Society*, 17(2), 437–445. doi:10.100710209-017-0541-0

Ismailova, R., & Kimsanova, G. (2017). Universities of the Kyrgyz Republic on the Web: Accessibility and usability. *Universal Access in the Information Society*, 16(4), 1017–1025. doi:10.100710209-016-0481-0

Isman, A., & Isbulan, O. (2010). Usability level of distance education website (sakarya university sample). *Turkish Online Journal of Educational Technology-TOJET*, 9(1), 243–258.

ISO. (1991). *ISO/IEC 9126:1991 Software engineering - Product quality.* Retrieved from https://www.iso.org/standard/16722.html

ISO. (2008). Ergonomics of human-system interaction — Part 171 : Guidance on software accessibility. *International Organization.*

ISO. (2008). *ISO 9241-20. (2008), Ergonomics of human-system interaction—Part 20: Accessibility guidelines for information/communication technology (ICT) equipment and services.* https://www.iso.org/obp/ui/#iso:std:iso:9241:-20:ed-1:v1:en:en/

ISO. (2008). *ISO 9241-20:2008(en), Ergonomics of human-system interaction—Part 20: Accessibility guidelines for information/communication technology (ICT) equipment and services.* ISO 9241-20:2008(En), Ergonomics of Human-System Interaction — Part 20: Accessibility Guidelines for Information/Communication Technology (ICT) Equipment and Services. https://www.iso.org/obp/ui/#iso:std:iso:9241:-20:ed-1:v1:en:en/

ISO. (2011). *ISO/IEC 25010:2011 Systems and software engineering — Systems and software Quality Requirements and Evaluation (SQuaRE) - System and software quality models.* Retrieved from https://www.iso.org/standard/35733.html

ISO. (2019). *ISO 9241-210. (2019). Ergonomics of Human-System Interaction — Part 210: Human-Centred Design for Interactive Systems.* https://www.iso.org/cms/render/live/en/sites/isoorg/contents/data/standard/07/75/77520.html

ISO. (2021). *ISO/DIS 9241-20(en), Ergonomics of human-system interaction—Part 20: An ergonomic approach to accessibility within the ISO 9241 series.* https://www.iso.org/obp/ui#iso:std:iso:9241:-20:dis:ed-2:v1:en

Issa, T., & Isaias, P. (2015). Usability and human computer interaction (HCI). In *Sustainable design* (pp. 19–36). Springer. doi:10.1007/978-1-4471-6753-2_2

Ivory, M. Y., Sinha, R. R., & Hearst, M. A. (2001). Empirically validated web page design metrics. In *Proceedings of the SIGCHI conference on Human factors in computing systems* (pp. 53-60). 10.1145/365024.365035

Iwarsson, S., & Staahl, A. (2003). Accessibility, usability, and universal design—Positioning and definition of concepts describing person-environment relationships. *Disability and Rehabilitation,* 25(2), 57–66. doi:10.1080/dre.25.2.57.66 PMID:12554380

Jabeen, M., Qinjian, Y., Yihan, Z., Jabeen, M., & Imran, M. (2017). *Usability study of digital libraries: An analysis of user perception, satisfaction, challenges, and opportunities at university libraries of Nanjing.* Library Collections, Acquisition and Technical Services. doi:10.1080/14 649055.2017.1331654

Jain, V., & Raj, T. (2013). SAW ve WPM kullanarak fms'de esnekliğin değerlendirilmesi. *Karar Bilim Mektupları,* 2(4), 223–230.

Jeng, J. (2006). Usability of the digital library: An evaluation model. *College & Research Libraries News.*

Jennings, A. S. (2004). Son of Web Pages That Suck: Learn Good Design by Looking at Bad Design. *Technical Communication (Washington),* 51(3), 421–423.

Ji, H., Yun, Y., Lee, S., Kim, K., & Lim, H. (2018). An adaptable UI/UX considering user's cognitive and behavior information in distributed environment. *Cluster Computing,* 21(1), 1045–1058. doi:10.100710586-017-0999-9

Johnson, J. (2000). GUI Bloopers: Don'ts and Do's for Software Developers and Web Designers. San Francisco, CA: Morgan Kaufmann Publishers.

Johnson, J. (2021). Number of internet users worldwide from 2005 to 2019. *Statistica.* https://www.statista.com/statistics/273018/number-of-internet-users-worldwide/

Joo, H. (2017). A Study on Understanding of UI and UX, and Understanding of Design According to User Interface Change. *International Journal of Applied Engineering Research: IJAER,* 12(20), 9931–9935.

Joo, S., & Lee, J. Y. (2011). Measuring the usability of academic digital libraries: Instrument development and validation. *The Electronic Library*, *29*(4), 523–537. Advance online publication. doi:10.1108/02640471111156777

Jungherr, A. (2019). Book Review: Social Theory after the Internet: Media, Technology and Globalization.SAGE Publications.

Kamal, I. W., Alsmadi, I. M., Wahsheh, H. A., & Al-Kabi, M. N. (2016a). Evaluating web accessibility metrics for Jordanian universities. *International Journal of Advanced Computer Science and Applications*, *7*(7), 113–122.

KAMİS. (2021, February 12). *Dijital Akademi*. https://dijitalakademi.bilgem.tubitak.gov.tr/kamis

KAMİS. (n.d.). *Erişilebilirlik nedir?* https://kamis.gov.tr/erisebilirlik-nedir/

KAMİS/Kamu İnternet Siteleri Rehberi Projesi. (2012). *Erişilebilirlik*. Retrieved April 15, 2020, from, https://kamis.gov.tr/erisebilirlik-nedir/

Kamoun, F., & Almourad, M. B. (2014). Accessibility as an integral factor in e-government web site evaluation: The case of Dubai e-government. *Information Technology & People*, *27*(2), 208–228. doi:10.1108/ITP-07-2013-0130

Kane, S. K., Shulman, J. A., Shockley, T. J., & Ladner, R. E. (2007). A web accessibility report card for top international university web sites. *Proceedings of the 2007 international cross-disciplinary conference on Web accessibility (W4A)*, 148-156. 10.1145/1243441.1243472

Kantner, L., & Rosenbaum, S. (1997). Usability studies of WWW sites: Heuristic evaluation vs. laboratory testing. In *Proceedings of the 15th annual international conference on Computer documentation* (pp. 153-160). 10.1145/263367.263388

Karkin, N., & Janssen, M. (2014). Evaluating websites from a public value perspective: A Review of Turkish Local Government Websites. *International Journal of Information Management*, *34*(3), 351–363. doi:10.1016/j.ijinfomgt.2013.11.004

Karmokar, S., Singh, H., & Tan, F. B. (2016). Using Multidisciplinary Design Principles to Improve the Website Design Process. *Pacific Asia Journal of the Association for Information Systems*, *8*(3), 17–28. doi:10.17705/1pais.08302

Kasday, L. R. (2000). A tool to evaluate universal web accessibility. *Proceedings of the Conference on Universal Usability*. 10.1145/355460.355559

Kashfi, P., Feldt, R., & Nilsson, A. (2019). Integrating UX principles and practices into software development organizations: A case study of influencing events. *Journal of Systems and Software*, *154*, 37–58. doi:10.1016/j.jss.2019.03.066

Kaur, A., Dani, D., & Agrawal, G. (2017). Evaluating the accessibility, usability and security of Hospitals websites: An exploratory study. In *2017 7th international conference on cloud computing, data science & engineering-confluence* (pp. 674-680). IEEE.

Kayaalp, G., Çelik Güney, M., & Cebeci, Z. (2015). Çoklu Doğrusal Regresyon Modelinde Değişken Seçiminin Zootekniye Uygulanışı. *Çukurova Üniversitesi Ziraat Fakültesi Dergisi, 30*(1), 1-8. Retrieved from https://dergipark.org.tr/tr/pub/cuzfd/issue/23798/253617

Keevil, B. (1998). Measuring the usability index of your web site. In *Proceedings of the 16th annual international conference on Computer documentation* (pp. 271-277). 10.1145/296336.296394

Keller, G., Warrack, B., & Bartel, H. (1990). *Statistics for Management and Economics. A System Approach* (2nd ed.). Wadsworth Publishing Company.

Kesswani, N., & Kumar, S. (2016). Accessibility analysis of websites of educational institutions. *Perspectives in Science, 8*, 210–212. doi:10.1016/j.pisc.2016.04.031

Khakzad, H. (2020). OWA operators with different orness levels for sediment management alternative selection problem. *Water Supply, 20*(1), 173–185. doi:10.2166/ws.2019.149

Khanyako, E., & Maiga, G. (2013). *An information security model for e-government services adoption in Uganda.* IST-Africa Conference.

Kim, D., & Lee, S. (2020). Study of identifying and managing the potential evidence for effective Android forensics. *Forensic Science International: Digital Investigation, 33*, 1–18.

Kim, W. J., Kim, I. K., Jeon, M. K., & Kim, J. (2016). UX Design guideline for health mobile application to improve accessibility for the visually impaired. In *2016 International Conference on Platform Technology and Service (PlatCon)* (pp. 1-5). IEEE.

King, A., Evans, G., & Blenkhorn, P. (2004). WebbIE: a web browser for visually impaired people. In *Proceedings of the 2nd Cambridge Workshop on Universal Access and Assistive Technology* (pp. 35-44). Academic Press.

King, M., Thatcher, J. W., Bronstad, P. M., & Easton, R. (2005). Managing usability for people with disabilities in a large web presence. *IBM Systems Journal, 44*(3), 519–535. doi:10.1147j.443.0519

Kirchner, M. (2002, October). Evaluation, repair, and transformation of Web pages for Web content accessibility. Review of some available tools. In *Proceedings. Fourth International Workshop on Web Site Evolution* (pp. 65-72). IEEE.

Kitchenham, B. A., & Charters, S. (2007). *Guidelines for performing Systematic Literature Reviews in Software Engineering (EBSE 2007-001)* [Keele University and Durham University Joint Report]. Keele University and Durham University. https://www.bibsonomy.org/bibtex/aed0229656ada843d3e3f24e5e5c9eb9

Kitchenham, B. A., Dyba, T., & Jorgensen, M. (2004). Evidence-based software engineering. *Proceedings. 26th International Conference on Software Engineering*, 273–281.

Kitchenham, B., Brereton, O. P., Budgen, D., Turner, M., Bailey, J., & Linkman, S. (2009). Systematic literature reviews in software engineering–a systematic literature review. *Information and Software Technology, 51*(1), 7–15. doi:10.1016/j.infsof.2008.09.009

Koman, R. (1998). The scent of information: Helping users find their way by making your site "smelly.". *Dr. Dobb's Journal, 5*(15), 1.

Król, K., & Zdonek, D. (2020). Local Government Website Accessibility—Evidence from Poland. *Administrative Sciences, 10*(2), 22. doi:10.3390/admsci10020022

Kumar, A. (2018). *The World Wide Web. Web Technology*. Chapman and Hall/CRC.

Kurt, S. (2017a). Accessibility of Turkish university Web sites. *Universal Access in the Information Society, 16*(2), 505–515. doi:10.100710209-016-0468-x

Kusek, M. (2018). Internet of things: Today and tomorrow. In *2018 41st International Convention on Information and Communication Technology, Electronics and Microelectronics (MIPRO)* (pp. 335-338). IEEE.

Kushniruk, A. W., & Patel, V. L. (2004). Cognitive and usability engineering methods for the evaluation of clinical information systems. *Journal of Biomedical Informatics, 37*(1), 56–76. doi:10.1016/j.jbi.2004.01.003 PMID:15016386

Lalmas, M., O'Brien, H., & Yom-Tov, E. (2014). Measuring User Engagement. *Synthesis Lectures on Information Concepts, Retrieval, and Services, 6*(4), 1–132. doi:10.2200/S00605ED1V01Y201410ICR038

Langley, D. J., van Doorn, J., Ng, I. C., Stieglitz, S., Lazovik, A., & Boonstra, A. (2021). The Internet of Everything: Smart things and their impact on business models. *Journal of Business Research, 122*, 853–863. doi:10.1016/j.jbusres.2019.12.035

Laux, L. (1998). Designing Web pages and applications for people with disabilities. Human Factors and Web Development, 87-95.

Lazar, J., & Sears, A. (2006). Design of E-Business Web Sites. Handbook of human factors and ergonomics, 1344-1363.

Lazar, J., Allen, A., Kleinman, J., & Malarkey, C. (2007). What frustrates screen reader users on the web: A study of 100 blind users. *International Journal of Human-Computer Interaction, 22*(3), 247–269.

Lazar, J., Dudley-Sponaugle, A., & Greenidge, K. D. (2004). Improving web accessibility: A study of webmaster perceptions. *Computers in Human Behavior, 20*(2), 269–288.

Lazar, J., Goldstein, D. F., & Taylor, A. (2015). *Ensuring Digital Accessibility through Process and Policy*. Morgan Kaufmann.

Lazar, J., Olalere, A., & Wentz, B. (2012). Investigating the accessibility and usability of job application web sites for blind users. *Journal of Usability Studies, 7*(2), 68–87.

Leavitt, M. O., & Shneiderman, B. (2006). *Based web design & usability guidelines*. Health and Human Services Department.

Lee, Y., & Chen, A. N. (2011). Usability design and psychological ownership of a virtual world. *Journal of Management Information Systems, 28*(3), 269–308. doi:10.2753/MIS0742-1222280308

Lei, F., Wei, G., Gao, H., Wu, J., & Wei, C. (2020). TOPSIS method for developing supplier selection with probabilistic linguistic information. *International Journal of Fuzzy Systems, 22*(3), 749–759. doi:10.100740815-019-00797-6

Le, T. D., & Vo, H. (2017). Consumer attitude towards website advertising formats: A comparative study of banner, pop-up and in-line display advertisements. *International Journal of Internet Marketing and Advertising, 11*(3), 202–217. doi:10.1504/IJIMA.2017.085654

Li, L., Peng, Y., Yang, C., & Li, Y. (2020). Optical sensing system for detection of the internal and external quality attributes of apples. *Postharvest Biology and Technology, 162*, 1–10. doi:10.1016/j.postharvbio.2019.111101

Lima, J. F., Caran, G. M., Molinaro, L. F., & Garrossini, D. F. (2012). Analysis of Accessibility Initiatives Applied to the Web. *Procedia Technology, 5*, 319–326. doi:10.1016/j.protcy.2012.09.035

Liu & Carter. (2018). Impact of citizens' privacy concerns on e-government adoption. In *Proceedings of the 19th Annual International Conference on Digital Government Research: Governance in the Data Age.* ACM.

Liu, C. Y. A., & Jones, K. J. (2018). Determining the Student Services which Align with Undergraduate Student Expectations A Study of Student Perceptions and University Service Delivery. *Journal of Leadership and Management, 2*(12).

Liu, X., & Wang, L. (2020). An extension approach of TOPSIS method with OWAD operator for multiple criteria decision-making. *Granular Computing, 5*(1), 135–148. doi:10.100741066-018-0131-4

Loiacono, E. T., Romano, N. C. Jr., & McCoy, S. (2009). The state of corporate website accessibility. *Communications of the ACM, 52*(9), 128–132.

Loiacono, E., & Lin, H. (2005). Website Quality: Cross-cultural Comparison of U.S. and China. *The Journal of International Information Technology Management, 14*(1), 53–69.

Longdon, P. M., Lazar, J., & Heylighen, A. (2014). *Inclusive Designing: Joining Usability, Accessibility, and Inclusion.* Springer. doi:10.1007/978-3-319-05095-9

Lopes, A., Valentim, N., Moraes, B., Zilse, R., & Conte, T. (2018). Applying user-centered techniques to analyze and design a mobile application. *Journal of Software Engineering Research and Development, 6*(5), 1–23. doi:10.118640411-018-0049-1

Lopes, R., & Carriço, L. (2008). The impact of accessibility assessment in macro scale universal usability studies of the web. *Proceedings of the 2008 International Cross-Disciplinary Conference on Web Accessibility (W4A)*, 5–14. 10.1145/1368044.1368048

Lopes, R., Gomes, D., & Carriço, L. (2010). Web not for all: A large scale study of web accessibility. *Proceedings of the 2010 International Cross Disciplinary Conference on Web Accessibility (W4A)*, 1–4. 10.1145/1805986.1806001

Lorca, P., De Andrés, J., & Martínez, A. B. (2016). Does Web accessibility differ among banks? *World Wide Web (Bussum)*, *19*(3), 351–373. doi:10.100711280-014-0314-0

Love, S., & Alssbaiheen, A. (2015). Exploring the Challenges of m-Government Adoption in Saudi Arabia. *The Electronic. Journal of E-Government*, *13*(1), 1, 18–27.

Luna-Nevarez, C., & Hyman, M. R. (2012). Common practices in destination website design. *Journal of Destination Marketing & Management*, *1*(1-2), 94–106. doi:10.1016/j.jdmm.2012.08.002

Lynch, P. J., & Horton, S. (2016). *Web style guide: Foundations of user experience design*. Yale University Press.

Ma, H.-Y. T., & Zaphiris, P. (2003). *The usability and content accessibility of the e-government in the UK*. Lawrence Erlbaum.

Mack, R. L. (1994). *Executive Summary*. Usability Inspection Methods.

Mankoff, J., Fait, H., & Tran, T. (2005, April). Is your web page accessible? A comparative study of methods for assessing web page accessibility for the blind. In *Proceedings of the SIGCHI conference on Human factors in computing systems* (pp. 41-50). ACM.

Manning, H., McCarthy, J., & Souza, R. (1998). *Why Most Web Sites Fail Interactive Technology Series, 3.7*. Forrester Research.

Manzoor, M., Hussain, W., Sohaib, O., Hussain, F. K., & Alkhalaf, S. (2019). Methodological investigation for enhancing the usability of university websites. *Journal of Ambient Intelligence and Humanized Computing*, *10*(2), 531–549. doi:10.100712652-018-0686-6

Mardani, A., Nilashi, M., Zakuan, N., Loganathan, N., Soheilirad, S., Saman, M. Z. M., & Ibrahim, O. (2017). A systematic review and meta-Analysis of SWARA and WASPAS methods: Theory and applications with recent fuzzy developments. *Applied Soft Computing*, *57*, 265–292. doi:10.1016/j.asoc.2017.03.045

Marelli, S., Castelnuovo, A., Somma, A., Castronovo, V., Mombelli, S., Bottoni, D., Leitner, C., Fossati, A., & Ferini-Strambi, L. (2021). Impact of COVID-19 lockdown on sleep quality in university students and administration staff. *Journal of Neurology*, *268*(1), 8–15. doi:10.100700415-020-10056-6 PMID:32654065

Margetts, H. (2006). E-Government in Britain—A Decade On. *Parliamentary Affairs*, *59*(2), 250–265. doi:10.1093/pa/gsl003

Martínez, A. B., De Andrés, J., & García, J. (2014). Determinants of the Web accessibility of European banks. *Information Processing & Management*, *50*(1), 69–86. doi:10.1016/j.ipm.2013.08.001

Martínez, A. B., Juan, A. A., Álvarez, D., & del Carmen, S. M. (2009). WAB*: A quantitative metric based on WAB. *International Conference on Web Engineering*, 485–488. 10.1007/978-3-642-02818-2_44

Masha, S. (2019). *UX Guide: Password Reset User Flow*. Retrieved from https://blog.prototypr.io/ux-guide-password-reset-user-flow-bfa35a16e527

Masri, F., & Luján-Mora, S. (2011). A combined agile methodology for the evaluation of web accessibility. *IADIS International Conference Interfaces and Human Computer Interaction (IHCI 2011)*, 423–428.

Maswera, T., Dawson, R., & Edwards, J. (2005). Analysis of usability and accessibility errors of e-commerce websites of tourist organisations in four African countries. In ENTER (pp. 531-542). Academic Press.

Maswera, T., Edwards, J., & Dawson, R. (2009). Recommendations for e-commerce systems in the tourism industry of sub-Saharan Africa. *Telematics and Informatics*, *26*(1), 12–19.

Mateos, Mera, González, & González López. (2001). A New Web Assessment Index: Spanish Universities Analysis. *Internet Research*, *11*(3), 226–234.

Matera, M., Rizzo, F., & Carughi, G. T. (2006). Web usability: Principles and evaluation methods. Web Engineering. doi:10.1007/3-540-28218-1_5

McGrew, S., Smith, M., Breakstone, J., Ortega, T., & Wineburg, S. (2019). Improving university students' web savvy: An intervention study. *The British Journal of Educational Psychology*, *89*(3), 485–500. doi:10.1111/bjep.12279 PMID:30993684

Mcguire, J. M., Scott, S. S., & Shaw, S. F. (2006). Universal design and its applications in educational environments. *Remedial and Special Education*, *27*(3), 166–175. doi:10.1177/07419325060270030501

McKenna, B. (2018). *Data overload is not about human limitations; it's about design failure*. Retrieved from https://uxdesign.cc/data-overload-is-a-design-problem-bcdb76e3cd6c

Medina, J. L., Cagnin, M. I., & Paiva, D. M. B. (2015). Evaluation of web accessibility on the maps domain. *Proceedings of the 30th Annual ACM Symposium on Applied Computing*, 157–162. 10.1145/2695664.2695771

Mendenhall, W., & Sincich, T. (1996) A Second Course in Statistics: Regression Analysis (5th ed.). Simon and Schuster.

Merrill, W., Gefen, D., Pavlou, P. A., & Rose, G. M. (2002). Encouraging Citizen Adoption of e-Government by Building Trust. *Electronic Markets*, *12*(3), 157–162. doi:10.1080/101967802320245929

Minge, M., & Thüring, M. (2018). Hedonic and pragmatic halo effects at early stages of User Experience. *International Journal of Human-Computer Studies*, *109*, 13–25. doi:10.1016/j.ijhcs.2017.07.007

Minhas, S. (2019). *How to Design a Perfect Date Picker Control?* Retrieved from https://uxplanet. org/how-to-design-a-perfect-date-picker-control-7f47d1290c3a

Mogaji, E. (2016). *University website design in international student recruitment: Some reflections. International marketing of higher education.* Palgrave Macmillan.

Molero Jurado, M., Martos Martínez, Á., Cardila Fernández, F., Barragán Martín, A. B., Pérez-Fuentes, M., Gázquez Linares, J. J., & Roales-Nieto, J. G. (2021). *Use of Internet and social networks by university students.* European Journal of Child Development, Education and Psychopathology., doi:10.30552/ejpad.v2i3.20

Montgomery, D. C., Peck, E. A., & Vining, G. G. (2001). *Introduction to Linear Regression Analysis* (3rd ed.). John Wiley & Sons.

Moore, G. C., & Benbasat, I. (1991). Development of an Instrument to Measure the Perceptions of Adopting an Information Technology Innovation. *Information Systems Research, 2*(3), 192–222. doi:10.1287/isre.2.3.192

Morse, A. (2017). *The higher education market.* National Audit Office.

Morville, P. (2004). *User Experience Design.* Retrieved from http://semanticstudios.com/ user_experience_design/

Mtingwi, J. E. (2015). Mobile Government in African Least Developed Countries (LDCs): Proposed Implementing Framework. *Proceedings of IST-Africa*, 1-14.

Muller, M. J., Matheson, L., Page, C., & Gallup, R. (1998). Methods & tools: participatory heuristic evaluation. *Interactions, 5*(5), 13-18.

Murillo, B., Vargas, S., Moquillaza, A., Fernández, L., & Paz, F. (2017). Usability testing as a complement of heuristic evaluation: A case study. In *International conference of design, user experience, and usability* (pp. 434-444). Springer.

Mustafa, S. H., & Al-Zoua'bi, L. F. (2008). Usability of the academic websites of Jordan's universities an evaluation study. In *Proceedings of the 9th International Arab Conference for Information Technology* (pp. 31-40). Academic Press.

Myers, R. H. (1990). *Classical and Modern Regression with Applications* (2nd ed.). PWS-Kent Publishers.

Nagpal, R., Mehrotra, D., & Bhatia, P. K. (2017). *The state of art in website usability evaluation methods. In Design Solutions for User-Centric Information Systems.* IGI Global.

Nejati, J., & Balasubramanian, A. (2016). An In-depth Study of Mobile Browser Performance. *Proceedings of the 25th International Conference on World Wide Web (WWW '16)*, 1305-1315. 10.1145/2872427.2883014

Nezhad, M. R. G., Zolfani, S. H., Moztarzadeh, F., Zavadskas, E. K., & Bahrami, M. (2015). Planning the priority of high tech industries based on SWARA-WASPAS methodology: The case of the nanotechnology industry in Iran. *Economic Research-Ekonomska Istraživanja*, *28*(1), 1111–1137. doi:10.1080/1331677X.2015.1102404

Niederst, J., & Robbins, J. N. (2001). *Web design in a nutshell: A desktop quick reference* (Vol. 2). O'Reilly Media, Inc.

Nielsen, J. (1999). *Designing Web Usability: The Practice of Simplicity New Riders*. Academic Press.

Nielsen, J. (2000). Designing Web Usability: The Practice of Simplicity. Indianapolis, IN: New Riders Publishing.

Nielsen, J. (2003). *Persuasive Design: New Captology Book*. Jakob Nielsen's Alertbox.

Nielsen, J. (1993). *Usability Engineering*. Academic Press. doi:10.1016/B978-0-08-052029-2.50007-3

Nielsen, J. (1994). *Usability engineering*. Morgan Kaufmann.

Nielsen, J. (1999). User interface directions for the web. *Communications of the ACM*, *42*(1), 65–72. doi:10.1145/291469.291470

Nielsen, J., & Loranger, H. (2006). *Prioritizing Web Usability: the practice of simplicity*. New Riders Publishing.

Nietzio, A., Strobbe, C., & Velleman, E. (2008). The unified Web evaluation methodology (UWEM) 1.2 for WCAG 1.0. *International Conference on Computers for Handicapped Persons*, 394-401. 10.1007/978-3-540-70540-6_57

Nikulchev, E., Ilin, D., Silaeva, A., Kolyasnikov, P., Belov, V., Runtov, A., Pushkin, P., Laptev, N., Alexeenko, A., Magomedov, S., Kosenkov, A., Zakharov, I., Ismatullina, V., & Malykh, S. (2020). Digital Psychological Platform for Mass Web-Surveys. *Data*, *5*(4), 95. doi:10.3390/data5040095

Nong, Z., & Gainsbury, S. (2020). Website design features: Exploring how social cues present in the online environment may impact risk taking. *Human Behavior and Emerging Technologies*, *2*(1), 39–49. doi:10.1002/hbe2.136

Norman, K. L., & Panizzi, E. (2006). Levels of automation and user participation in usability testing. *Interacting with Computers*, *18*(2), 246–264. doi:10.1016/j.intcom.2005.06.002

Nowak, M. (2020). *Why Usability and Accessibility Matter in App Development*. Retrieved from https://www.nomtek.com/blog/usability-accessibility

O'Regan, G. (2018). *World Wide Web. In The Innovation in Computing Companion*. Springer. doi:10.1007/978-3-030-02619-6

Ochoa, R. L., & Crovi, D. M. (2019). Evaluation of accessibility in Mexican cybermedia. *Universal Access in the Information Society*, *18*(2), 413–422. doi:10.100710209-018-0613-9

Olalere, A., & Lazar, J. (2011). Accessibility of US federal government home pages: Section 508 compliance and site accessibility statements. *Government Information Quarterly, 28*(3), 303–309.

Olsina, L., & Rossi, G. (2002). Measuring Web application quality with WebQEM. *IEEE MultiMedia, 9*(4), 20–29. doi:10.1109/MMUL.2002.1041945

Orçun, Ç. (2019). Enerji sektöründe WASPAS yöntemiyle performans analizi. *Bolu Abant İzzet Baysal Üniversitesi Sosyal Bilimler Enstitüsü Dergisi, 19*(2), 439–453.

Orji, R. O. (2010). Analysis of Usability and Accessibility Problems of Financial Sectors' Website using Visitor-based Evaluation Technique. In *2nd International Conference on Information and Multimedia Technology (ICIMT 2010)* (pp. V1-252). Academic Press.

Ou, C. X., & Sia, C. L. (2010). Consumer trust and distrust: An issue of website design. *International Journal of Human-Computer Studies, 68*(12), 913–934.

Owoyele, S. (2017). *Website as a marketing communication tool.* Theseus.

Özbek, A. (2019). Türkiye'deki illerin EDAS ve WASPAS yöntemleri ile yaşanabilirlik kriterlerine göre sıralanması. *Kırıkkale Üniversitesi Sosyal Bilimler Dergisi, 9*(1), 177–200.

Özdağoğlu, A., Keleş, M. K., & Yörük Eren, F. (2019). Bir üniversite hastanesinde makroelisa ekipmanı alternatiflerinin WASPAS ve SWARA yöntemleri ile değerlendirilmesi. *Süleyman Demirel Üniversitesi İktisadi ve İdari Bilimler Fakültesi Dergisi, 24*(2), 319–331.

Özer, İ., & Sarı, İ. (2018). Yaşlı bireyler için web sayfaları tasarımının ergonomik açıdan incelenmesi. *Ergonomi, 1*(3), 148–155. doi:10.33439/ergonomi.471595

Paciello, M. (2000). *Web accessibility for people with disabilities.* CRC Press.

Pakkala, H., Presser, K., & Christensenc, T. (2012). Using Google Analytics to Measure Visitor Statistics: The Case of Food Composition Websites. *International Journal of Information Management, 32*(6), 504–512. doi:10.1016/j.ijinfomgt.2012.04.008

Pant, M., & Sinha, A. (2020). Evaluating State of Web Accessibility Standards in Top Airline Websites. In *2020 IEEE International IOT, Electronics and Mechatronics Conference (IEMTRONICS)* (pp. 1-5). IEEE.

Park, H., & Ban, C. (2010). Implementation and evaluation of the on-line aptitude test system for people with visual impairment supporting web accessibility. *Disabil Employ, 20*(1), 51–78.

Parmanto, B., & Zeng, X. (2005). Metric for web accessibility evaluation. *Journal of the American Society for Information Science and Technology, 56*(13), 1394–1404. doi:10.1002/asi.20233

Patro, C. S. (2021). *Internet-Enabled Business Models and Marketing Strategies. In Impact of Globalization and Advanced Technologies on Online Business Models.* IGI Global.

Peacock, M. (2011). *Why its more important to have an Effective Website than an Efficient Website.* Retrieved from https://wp-agency.co.uk/why-its-more-important-to-be-effective-than-efficient/

Pengnate, S. F., & Sarathy, R. (2017). An experimental investigation of the influence of website emotional design features on trust in unfamiliar online vendors. *Computers in Human Behavior, 67*, 49–60. doi:10.1016/j.chb.2016.10.018

Perdomo, E. G., Cardozo, M. T., Perdomo, C. C., & Serrezuela, R. R. (2017). A Review of the User Based Web Design: Usability and Information Architecture. *International Journal of Applied Engineering Research: IJAER, 12*(21), 11685–11690.

Perlman, G. (1998). *Web-based user interface evaluation with questionnaires.* Academic Press.

Perna, L. W. (2020). Higher Education: Handbook of Theory and Research. Springer.

Persada, A. (2018). Emotional Design on User Experience-based Development System. *Proceedings of the 2018 International Conference on Electrical Engineering and Computer Science (ICECOS)*, 1-6. 10.1109/ICECOS.2018.8605199

Pesce, M. (2017, April). The Web-Wide World. *Proceedings of the 26th International Conference on World Wide Web.* 10.1145/3038912.3050770

Petrie, H. L., Savva, A., & Power, C. (2015). Towards a unified definition of web accessibility. *Proceedings of the 12th Web for All Conference*, 1-13. 10.1145/2745555.2746653

Pingdom website speed test. (n.d.). https://tools.pingdom.com/

Polson, P. G., Lewis, C., Rieman, J., & Wharton, C. (1992). Cognitive walkthroughs: A method for theory-based evaluation of user interfaces. *International Journal of Man-Machine Studies, 36*(5), 741–773. doi:10.1016/0020-7373(92)90039-N

Pontus, V. (2019). *Evaluating the Accessibility of Localised Websites: The Case of the Airline Industry in Switzerland* (Doctoral dissertation). University of Geneva.

Powell, T. A. (2000). *The complete reference: Web design.* Osborne, McGraw-Hill.

Power, C., Freire, A., Petrie, H., & Swallow, D. (2012). Guidelines are only half of the story: accessibility problems encountered by blind users on the web. In *Proceedings of the SIGCHI conference on human factors in computing systems* (pp. 433-442). ACM.

Power, C., & Jürgensen, H. (2010). Accessible presentation of information for people with visual disabilities. *Universal Access in the Information Society, 9*(2), 97–119.

PowerMapper. (2015). *Website Error Checker: Accessibility & Link Checker—SortSite.* https://www.powermapper.com/products/sortsite/

Qadri, B., & Bhat, M. (2018). Interface between globalization and technology. *Asian J. Manag. Sci, 7*(3), 1–6.

Quijano-Solís, Á., & Novelo-Peña, R. (2005). Evaluating a monolingual multinational digital library by using usability: An exploratory approach from a developing country. *The International Information & Library Review, 37*(4), 329–336. Advance online publication. doi:10.1080/10572317.2005.10762690

Quintero, L. J. C., & Selwyn, N. (2018). More than tools? Making sense of the ongoing digitizations of higher education. *International Journal of Educational Technology in Higher Education*, (15), 26.

R Core Team. (2021). *R: A Language and environment for statistical computing (Version 4.0)* [Computer software]. Retrieved from https://cran.r-project.org

Rababah, O. M. A., & Masoud, F. A. (2010). Key factors for developing a successful e-commerce website. *Communications of the IBIMA*.

Rachwani, J., Tamis-LeMonda, C. S., Lockman, J. J., Karasik, L. B., & Adolph, K. E. (2020). Learning the designed actions of everyday objects. *Journal of Experimental Psychology. General*, *149*(1), 67–78. doi:10.1037/xge0000631 PMID:31219298

Rana, S. C., & Patel, J. N. (2018). Selection of best location for small hydro power project using AHP, WPM and TOPSIS methods. *ISH Journal of Hydraulic Engineering*, *173-177*. Advance online publication. doi:10.1080/09715010.2018.1468827

Rao, C. M., & Venkatasubbaiah, K. (2016). Application of WSM, WPM and TOPSIS Methods for the optimization of multiple responses. *International Journal of Hybrid Information Technology*, *9*(10), 59-72. Doi:. doi:10.14257/ijhit.2016.9.10.07

Rençber, Ö. F., & Avcı, T. (2018). BIST'te işlem gören bankaların sermaye yeterliliklerine göre karşılaştırılması: WASPAS yöntemi ile uygulama. *Anemon Muş Alparslan Üniversitesi Sosyal Bilimler Dergisi*, *6*(18), 169–175. doi:10.18506/anemon.452713

Rezaeean, A., Bairamzadeh, S., & Bolhari, A. (2012). The importance of Website Innovation on Students' Satisfaction of University Websites. *World Applied Sciences Journal*, *18*(8), 1023–1029.

Riihiaho, S. (2017). *Usability testing. The Wiley Handbook of Human Computer Interaction Set*.

Rinner, C., & Malczewski, J. (2002). Web-enabled spatial decision analysis using ordered weighted averaging (OWA). *Journal of Geographical Systems*, *4*(4), 385–403. doi:10.1007101090300095

Roach, C., & Cayer, J. (2010). Bridging the other divide: An assessment of the usability of Trinidad and Tobago government ministry website. In C. Reddick (Ed.), *Comparative E-government* (pp. 483–504). Springer Science Business Media. doi:10.1007/978-1-4419-6536-3_25

Rodriguez, R., Estevez, E., Giulianelli, D., & Vera, P. (2010). Assessing e-Governance Maturity through Municipal Websites - Measurement Framework and Survey Results. *Selected Papers in XV Argentine Congress of Computer Science*, 175 – 212.

Rogers, Y., Sharp, H., & Preece, J. (2011). *Interaction design: Beyond human-computer interaction*. John Wiley & Sons.

Romero-Frías, E. (2009). Googling Companies - a Webometric Approach to Business Studies. *Electronic Journal of Business Research Methods*, *7*(1), 93–106.

Rose, A. F., Schnipper, J. L., Park, E. R., Poon, E. G., Li, Q., & Middleton, B. (2005). Using qualitative studies to improve the usability of an EMR. *Journal of Biomedical Informatics*, *38*(1), 51–60. doi:10.1016/j.jbi.2004.11.006 PMID:15694885

Ruiz, N. V. (2021). How to Use the Internet for University Work. *Aularia: Revista Digital de Comunicación*, *10*(1), 131–136.

Rusdi, R., Sahari, N., & Noor, S. (2017). Usability guidelines for elderly website interface. *Asia-Pacific Journal of Information Technology and Multimedia*, *6*(2), 109–122. doi:10.17576/apjitm-2017-0602-10

Rzeszewski, M., & Kotus, J. (2019). Usability and usefulness of internet mapping platforms in participatory spatial planning. *Applied Geography (Sevenoaks, England)*, *103*, 56–69. doi:10.1016/j.apgeog.2019.01.001

Sæbø, Ø. (2012). E-government in Tanzania: Current Status and Future Challenges. In J. S. Hans, J. Marijn, A. W. Maria, E. Carl, L. Moe, & F. Skiftenes (Eds.), *Electronic Government* (pp. 198–209). Springer. doi:10.1007/978-3-642-33489-4_17

Sanchez-Gordon, S., & Luján-Mora, S. (2018). Research challenges in accessible MOOCs: A systematic literature review 2008–2016. *Universal Access in the Information Society*, *17*(4), 775–789. doi:10.100710209-017-0531-2

Santiworarak, L., & Choochaiwattana, W. (2018). A Case Study of Usability Design Principle in Responsive e-Commerce Web Application. *International Journal of e-Education, e-Business, e-Management Learning*, *8*(3).

Saracevic, T. (2004). How were digital libraries evaluated? *DELOS WP7 Workshop on the Evaluation of Digital Libraries*.

Schaeffer, R. K. (2003). Globalization and technology. *Phi Kappa Phi Forum*, *83*(4), 30-34.

Schmutz, S., Sonderegger, A., & Sauer, J. (2017). Implementing Recommendations From Web Accessibility Guidelines: A Comparative Study of Nondisabled Users and Users With Visual Impairments. *Human Factors*, *49*(6), 956–972. doi:10.1177/0018720817708397 PMID:28467134

Schnall, R., Rojas, M., Bakken, S., Brown, W., Carballo-Dieguez, A., Carry, M., Gelaude, D., Mosley, J. P., & Travers, J. (2016). A user-centered model for designing consumer mobile health (mHealth) applications (apps). *Journal of Biomedical Informatics*, *60*, 243–251. doi:10.1016/j.jbi.2016.02.002 PMID:26903153

Schroeder, R. (2018). *Social theory after the internet: Media, technology and globalization*. UCL Press. doi:10.2307/j.ctt20krxdr

Scowen, G., & Regenbrecht, H. (2009). Increased Popularity through Compliance with Usability Guidelines in E-Learning Web Sites. *International Journal of Information Technology and Web Engineering*, *4*(3), 38–57. doi:10.4018/jitwe.2009100603

Seckler, M., Heinz, S., Forde, S., Tuch, A. N., & Opwis, K. (2015). Trust and distrust on the web: User experiences and website characteristics. *Computers in Human Behavior, 45*, 39–50. doi:10.1016/j.chb.2014.11.064

Semaan, B., Tekli, J., Issa, Y. B., Tekli, G., & Chbeir, R. (2013, December). Toward enhancing web accessibility for blind users through the semantic web. In *2013 International Conference on Signal-Image Technology & Internet-Based Systems* (pp. 247-256). IEEE.

Senapati, T., & Yager, R. R. (2019). Some new operations over Fermatean fuzzy numbers and application of Fermatean fuzzy WPM in multiple criteria decision making. *Informatica (Vilnius), 30*(2), 391–412. doi:10.15388/Informatica.2019.211

Shackel, B. (2009). Usability–Context, framework, definition, design and evaluation. *Interacting with Computers, 21*(5-6), 339–346. doi:10.1016/j.intcom.2009.04.007

Shareef, M., Dwivedi, Y., Laumer, S., & Archer, N. (2016). Citizens' Adoption Behavior of Mobile Government (mGov): A Cross-Cultural Study. *Information Systems Management, 33*(3), 268–283. doi:10.1080/10580530.2016.1188573

Shchiglik, C., & Barnes, S. J. (2004). Evaluating website quality in the airline industry. *Journal of Computer Information Systems, 44*(3), 17–25.

Shneiderman, B. (2000). Universal Usability. *Communications of the ACM, 43*(5), 84–91. doi:10.1145/332833.332843

Shneiderman, B., & Plaisant, C. (2010). *Designing the user interface: Strategies for effective human-computer interaction*. Pearson Education India.

Shum, S. B., & McKnight, C. (1997). World Wide Web usability: Introduction to this special issue. *International Journal of Human-Computer Studies, 47*(1), 1–4. doi:10.1006/ijhc.1997.0132

Sianturi, L. T. (2019). Implementation of Weight Sum Model (WSM) in the Selection of Football Athletes. *The IJICS, 3*(1), 24–27.

Sinha, M., & Fukey, L. N. (2020). Web user Experience and Consumer behaviour: The Influence of Colour, Usability and Aesthetics on the Consumer Buying behaviour. *Test Engineering and Management, 82*, 16592–16600.

Sirithumgul, P., Suchato, A., & Punyabukkana, P. (2009). Quantitative evaluation for web accessibility with respect to disabled groups. *Proceedings of the 2009 International Cross-Disciplinary Conference on Web Accessibililty (W4A)*, 136–141. 10.1145/1535654.1535687

Slatin, J. M., & Rush, S. (2003). *Maximum accessibility: Making your web site more usable for everyone*. Addison-Wesley Professional.

Sleeper, M., Consolvo, S., & Staddon, J. (2014). Exploring the Benefits and Uses of Web Analytics Tools for Non-transactional Websites. *Proceedings of the Conference on Designing Interactive Systems: Processes, Practices, Methods, and Techniques*. 10.1145/2598510.2598555

Smith, G. (2018). Step away from stepwise. *Journal of Big Data*, *5*(1), 32. doi:10.118640537-018-0143-6

Soegoto, E. S., & Rafi, M. S. F. (2018). Internet role in improving business transaction. *IOP Conference Series. Materials Science and Engineering*, *407*(1), 012059. doi:10.1088/1757-899X/407/1/012059

Sohaib, O., & Kang, K. (2013). The importance of web accessibility in business to-consumer (B2C) websites. In *22nd Australasian Software Engineering Conference (ASWEC 2013)* (pp. 1-11). Academic Press.

Sohaib, O., & Kang, K. (2012). The role of technology, human and social networks in serviceable cross-cultural B2C websites. *19th International Business Information Management Conference (IBIMA)*.

Sohaib, O., & Kang, K. (2017). E-commerce web accessibility for people with disabilities. In *Complexity in Information Systems Development* (pp. 87–100). Springer.

Song, S., Bu, J., Shen, C., Artmeier, A., Yu, Z., & Zhou, Q. (2018a). Reliability aware web accessibility experience metric. In *Proceedings of the Internet of Accessible Things* (pp. 1–4). Academic Press.

Song, S., Bu, J., Wang, Y., Yu, Z., Artmeier, A., Dai, L., & Wang, C. (2018b). Web accessibility evaluation in a crowdsourcing-based system with expertise-based decision strategy. In *Proceedings of the Internet of Accessible Things* (pp. 1–4). 10.1145/3192714.3192827

Song, S., Bu, J., Artmeier, A., Shi, K., Wang, Y., Yu, Z., & Wang, C. (2018c). Crowdsourcing-based web accessibility evaluation with golden maximum likelihood inference. *Proceedings of the ACM on Human-Computer Interaction, 2*(CSCW), 1–21. 10.1145/3274432

Song, S., Wang, C., Li, L., Yu, Z., Lin, X., & Bu, J. (2017). WAEM: A web accessibility evaluation metric based on partial user experience order. *Proceedings of the 14th Web for All Conference on The Future of Accessible Work*, 1–4. 10.1145/3058555.3058576

Sortsite. (2016). https://www.powermapper.com/products/sortsite

SortSite. (2021). *Website Error Checker: Accessibility & Link Checker—SortSite*. https://www.powermapper.com/products/sortsite/

Speedtest. (2020). *Monthly comparisons of internet speeds from around the world*. Speedtest Global Index. Retrieved from https://www.speedtest.net/global-index

Spencer, I. (2016). *The Importance of Usability and Accessibility in Design*. Career Foundry.

Sri & Ezmieralda (2012). *Investigating the Potential of Mobile Phones for E-Governance in Indonesia*. CPRafrica 2012/CPRsouth7 Conference, Port Louis, Mauritius.

Ssemugabi, S., & de Villiers, M. R. (2010). Effectiveness of heuristic evaluation in usability evaluation of e-learning applications in higher education. *South African Computer Journal, 45*, 26–39. doi:10.18489acj.v45i0.37

Student, R., Kendall, K., & Day, L. (2017). Being a refugee university student: A collaborative auto-ethnography. *Journal of Refugee Studies, 30*(4), 580–604.

Sullivan, T., & Matson, R. (2000). Barriers to use: Usability and content accessibility on the Web's most popular sites. *Proceedings on the 2000 Conference on Universal Usability*, 139–144. 10.1145/355460.355549

Sun, X., & May, A. J. (2014). Design of the User Experience for Personalized Mobile Services. *International Journal of Human-Computer Interaction, 5*(2), 21–39.

Taka, M., Raygor, S. P., Purohit, R., & Parashar, V. (2017). Selection of tool and work piece combination using multiple attribute decision making methods for computer numerical control turning operation. *Materials Today: Proceedings 4. 5th International Conference of Materials Processing and Characterization (ICMPC 2016)*, 1199–1208.

Takagi, H., Asakawa, C., Fukuda, K., & Maeda, J. (2003). Accessibility designer: visualizing usability for the blind. *ACM SIGACCESS Accessibility and Computing*, (77-78), 177-184.

Tan, S. (2020). Study on the development strategy of airport economy in dalian. *Modern Economy, 11*(1), 200–207. doi:10.4236/me.2020.111017

Tanvir, S., Safdar, M., Tufail, H., & Qamar, U. (2017). Merging Prototyping with Agile Software Development Methodology. *Proceedings of the International Conference on Engineering, Computing & Information Technology*, 50-54.

TAW. (n.d.). https://www.tawdis.net/

Teixeira, P., Eusébio, C., & Teixeira, L. (2021). How diverse is hotel website accessibility? A study in the central region of Portugal using web diagnostic tools. *Tourism and Hospitality Research*, 14673584211022796.

Thatcher, J., Lauke, P. H., Waddell, C., Henry, S. L., Lawson, B., Lawson, B., Heilmann, C., Burks, M. R., Regan, B., & Rutter, R. (2006). *Web accessibility: Web standards and regulatory compliance*. Apress.

The jamovi project (2021). *jamovi (Version 1.8)* [Computer Software]. Retrieved from https://www.jamovi.org

The United Republic of Tanzania. (2004). *Higher Education Students Loans Board (HELBS) Act, 2004*. Dar es Salaam: URT.

Thompson, T., Burgstahler, S., & Comden, D. (2003). Research on web accessibility in higher education. *Journal of Information Technology and Disabilities, 9*(2).

Tio, E., Torkildson, M., Su, D., Toussaint, H., Bhargava, A., & Shaikh, D. (2019). Measuring Holistic User Experience: Keeping an Eye on What Matters Most to Users. *Proceedings of the 21st International Conference on Human-Computer Interaction with Mobile Devices and Services (MobileHCI '19)*, 1-4. 10.1145/3338286.3344425

Tran, T. H. (2019). *What does mobile-first design mean for digital designers?* Retrieved from https://www.invisionapp.com/inside-design/mobile-first-design/

Tsakonas, G., & Papatheodorou, C. (2008). Exploring usefulness and usability in the evaluation of open access digital libraries. *Information Processing & Management, 44*(3), 1234–1250. Advance online publication. doi:10.1016/j.ipm.2007.07.008

Tuchkov, I. (2018). *Color blindness: how to design an accessible user interface.* Retrieved from https://uxdesign.cc/color-blindness-in-user-interfaces-66c27331b858

Türk Hava Yolları, A. O. (2011). *Seri:XI No:29 Sayılı Tebliğe İstinaden Hazırlanmış Yönetim Kurulu Faaliyet Raporu.* Retrieved April 09, 2020, from, https://investor.turkishairlines.com/documents/ThyInvestorRelations/download/faaliyet_raporu/faaliyet_raporu_aralik_2011.pdf

Turper, D. (2008). *Web siteleri için orta yaş ve üzeri kullanıcılara yönelik arayüz tasarımları* (Sanatta Yeterlilik Tezi). Marmara Üniversitesi Güzel Sanatlar Enstitüsü, İstanbul, Türkiye.

Turskis, Z., Zavadskas, E. K., Antucheviciene, J., & Kosareva, N. (2015). A hybrid model based on fuzzy AHP and fuzzy WASPAS for construction site selection. *International Journal of Computers, Communications & Control, 10*(6), 113–128. doi:10.15837/ijccc.2015.6.2078

Unhelkar, B. (2003). Understanding the Impact of Cultural Issues in Global e-Business Alliances. *4th International We-B Conference.*

US Access Board. (2000). *Section 508 Standards—United States Access Board.* Section 508 Standards for Electronic and Information Technology. https://www.access-board.gov/guidelines-and-standards/communications-and-it/about-the-section-508-standards/section-508-standards

US Access Board. (2000). *U.S. Access Board—Revised 508 Standards and 255 Guidelines.* https://www.access-board.gov/ict/

US EPA. O. (2013, September 26). *What is Section 508?* [Overviews and Factsheets]. US EPA. https://www.epa.gov/accessibility/what-section-508

Uslu, B. (2018). Dünya Üniversiteler Sıralaması: Genişletilen Gösterge Setine Göre Sıralamada Oluşan Farklılıklar. *Journal of Higher Education & Science/Yükseköğretim ve Bilim Dergisi, 12*(3).

Valente, R. D. O. A., & Vettorazzi, C. A. (2008). Definition of priority areas for forest conservation through the ordered weighted averaging method. *Forest Ecology and Management, 256*(6), 1408–1417. doi:10.1016/j.foreco.2008.07.006

Valero, A., & Van Reenen, J. (2019). The economic impact of universities: Evidence from across the globe. *Economics of Education Review, 68*, 53–67. doi:10.1016/j.econedurev.2018.09.001

Valle, J. W., & Connor, D. J. (2019). *Rethinking Disability: A Disability Studies Approach to Inclusive Practices*. Routledge. doi:10.4324/9781315111209

van der Vaart, R., van Driel, D., Pronk, K., Paulussen, S., Te Boekhorst, S., Rosmalen, J. G., & Evers, A. W. (2019). The role of age, education, and digital health literacy in the usability of Internet-based cognitive behavioral therapy for chronic pain: Mixed methods study. *JMIR Formative Research*, *3*(4), e12883. doi:10.2196/12883 PMID:31750839

Van Duyne, D. K., Landay, J. A., & Hong, J. I. (2003). The Design of Sites: Patterns, Principles and Processes for Crafting a Customer-Centered Web Experience. Boston, MA: Addison-Wesley.

Van Duyne, D. K., Landay, J. A., & Hong, J. I. (2007). *The design of sites: Patterns for creating winning web sites*. Prentice Hall Professional.

Vatansever, K., & Akgül, Y. (2018). Performance evaluation of websites using entropy and grey relational analysis methods: The case of airline companies. *Decision Science Letters*, *7*(2), 119–130. doi:10.5267/j.dsl.2017.6.005

Vaughan, L., & Yang, R. (2013). Web Traffic and Organization Performance Measures: Relationships and Data Sources Examined. *Journal of Informetrics*, *7*(3), 699–711. doi:10.1016/j.joi.2013.04.005

Venkatesh, V., & David, F. R. (2000). A Theoretical Extension of the Technology Acceptance Model: Four Longitudinal Field Studies. *Management Science*, *46*(2), 186–204. doi:10.1287/mnsc.46.2.186.11926

Vigo, M., Arrue, M., Brajnik, G., Lomuscio, R., & Abascal, J. (2007). Quantitative metrics for measuring web accessibility. *Proceedings of the 2007 International Cross-Disciplinary Conference on Web Accessibility (W4A)*, 99–107. 10.1145/1243441.1243465

Vigo, M., & Brajnik, G. (2011). Automatic web accessibility metrics: Where we are and where we can go. *Interacting with Computers*, *23*(2), 137–155. doi:10.1016/j.intcom.2011.01.001

W3. (2016). *Web Accessibility Evaluation Tools List*. https://www.w3.org/WAI/ER/tools/

W3. (2021). https://www.w3.org/WAI/standards-guidelines/wcag/

W3.org. (1999). *Web Content Accessibility Guidelines 1.0.* https://www.w3.org/TR/WAI-WEBCONTENT/

W3.org. (2008). *Web Content Accessibility Guidelines (WCAG) 2.0.* https://www.w3.org/TR/WCAG20/

W3C Org. (2016f). *Web Accessibility Evaluation Tools List*. http://www.w3.org/WAI/ER/tools/

W3C Org. (2016g). *Web Content Accessibility Guidelines*. http://www.w3.org/TR/WAI-WEBCONTENT

W3C. (1999). *Web Content Accessibility Guidelines 1.0.* https://www.w3.org/TR/WCAG10/

W3C. (2008). *Web Content Accessibility Guidelines (WCAG) 2.0.* https://www.w3.org/TR/WCAG20/

W3C. (2017). *Diverse Abilities and Barriers.* Retrieved from https://www.w3.org/WAI/people-use-web/abilities-barriers/

W3C. (2018). *Web Content Accessibility Guidelines (WCAG) 2.1.* https://www.w3.org/TR/WCAG21/

W3C. (2020). *Internet Live Stats—Internet Usage & Social Media Statistics.* https://www.internetlivestats.com/

W3C. (2020). *WAI-ARIA Overview.* Web Accessibility Initiative (WAI). https://www.w3.org/WAI/standards-guidelines/aria/

W3C. (2021, January 21). *Web Content Accessibility Guidelines (WCAG) 3.0.* https://www.w3.org/TR/wcag-3.0/

W3C. (n.d.). *World Wide Web Consortium (W3C).* https://www.w3.org/

W3C. (n.d.a). *Web Accessibility Initaitive.* Web Accessibility Initiative (WAI). Retrieved May 8, 2021, from https://www.w3.org/WAI/

W3C. (n.d.b). *World Wide Web Consortium (W3C).* https://www.w3.org/

W3C.org. (2016). *Accessibility Evaluation Resources.* http://www.w3.org/WAI/eval/Overview.html

W3C.org. (2016a). *How People with Disabilities Use the Web: Overview.* http://www.w3.org/WAI/intro/people-use-web/

W3C.org. (2016b). *Style Sheets.* http://www.w3.org/TR/html4/present/styles.html

W3C.org. (2016c). *Accessibility.* http://www.w3.org/standards/webdesign/accessibility

W3C.org. (2016d). *Evaluation Tools.* http://www.w3.org/WAI/ER/existingtools.html

W3C.org. (2016e). *Evaluation, Repair, and Transformation Tools for Web Content Accessibility.* http://www.w3.org/WAI/ER/existingtools.html#Evaluation

W3C_WAI. (2005a). *Authoring Tool Accessibility Guidelines (ATAG) Overview.* Web Accessibility Initiative (WAI). https://www.w3.org/WAI/standards-guidelines/atag/

W3C_WAI. (2005b). *User Agent Accessibility Guidelines (UAAG) Overview.* Web Accessibility Initiative (WAI). https://www.w3.org/WAI/standards-guidelines/uaag/

W3C_WAI. (2016). *Accessibility, Usability, and Inclusion. Accessibility, Usability, and Inclusion, Web Accessibility Initiative (WAI).* https://www.w3.org/WAI/fundamentals/accessibility-usability-inclusion/

W3C_WAI. (2019a). *Introduction to Web Accessibility.* https://www.w3.org/WAI/fundamentals/accessibility-intro/

WAI. (n.d.). *Web Accessibility Initiative (WAI)*. https://www.w3.org/WAI/

WAI. W. (2005). *Introduction to Web Accessibility*. Web Accessibility Initiative (WAI). https://www.w3.org/WAI/fundamentals/accessibility-intro/

Watanabe, W. M., Dias, A. L., & Fortes, R. P. D. M. (2015). Fona: Quantitative metric to measure focus navigation on rich internet applications. *ACM Transactions on the Web*, *9*(4), 1–28. doi:10.1145/2812812

WAVE Web accessibility evaluation tool. (2016). http://wave.webaim.org

WCAG. (2015). *Mobile Accessibility: How WCAG 2.0 and Other W3C/WAI Guidelines Apply to Mobile*. Retrieved from https://www.w3.org/TR/mobile-accessibility-mapping/

WCAG. (2020). *Web Content Accessibility Guidelines (WCAG) Overview*. Retrieved from https://www.w3.org/WAI/standards-guidelines/wcag/

Web content accessibility guidelines (WCAG) 2.0. (n.d.). https://www.w3.org/TR/2008/RECWCAG20-20081211/

Web Readability test tool. (n.d.). https://www.webfx.com/tools/read-able/ContentAccessibilityGuidelines

Websitepulse. (n.d.). https://www.websitepulse.com/tools/

Wedel, M., & Pieters, R. (2008). Eye Tracking for Visual Marketing. *Foundations and Trends® in Marketing, 1*(4), 231–320. doi:10.1561/1700000011

West, D. (2002). *Global E-Government*. Retrieved from http://www.insidepolitics.org/egovt02int.html

Whitehead, C. C. (2006). Evaluating web page and web site usability. *Proceedings of the 44th annual Southeast regional conference*, 788-789. 10.1145/1185448.1185637

Whittaker, S. (2013). *Interaction Design: What we know and what we need to know*. Retrieved from https://interactions.acm.org/archive/view/july-august-2013/interaction-design

Wibowo, A., Aryotejo, G., & Mufadhol, M. (2018). Accelerated Mobile Pages from JavaScript as Accelerator Tool for Web Service on E-Commerce in the E-Business. *Iranian Journal of Electrical and Computer Engineering, 8*(4), 2399–2405. doi:10.11591/ijece.v8i4.pp2399-2405

Williams, P. (2020). *Methods to test website usability. In Learning Disabilities and e-Information*. Emerald Publishing Limited. doi:10.1108/9781789731514

Windriyani, P., Ferdiana, R., & Najib, W. (2014). Accessibility evaluation using WCAG 2.0 guidelines webometrics-based assessment criteria (case study: Sebelas Maret University). *2014 International Conference on ICT for Smart Society (ICISS)*, 305-311. 10.1109/ICTSS.2014.7013192

Wixon, D., & Wilson, C. (1997). The usability engineering framework for product design and evaluation. In Handbook of human-computer interaction (pp. 653-688). North-Holland. doi:10.1016/B978-044481862-1.50093-5

Wohlin, C. (2014). Guidelines for snowballing in systematic literature studies and a replication in software engineering. *Proceedings of the 18th International Conference on Evaluation and Assessment in Software Engineering*, 1–10. 10.1145/2601248.2601268

World Bank. (2020). Individuals using the Internet (%of Population). In *World Development Indicators*. The World Bank Group. Retrieved from: https://data.worldbank.org/indicator/IT.NET. USER.ZS

World Economic Forum. (2017). Global Gender Gap Report. WEF.

World Health Organization. (2011). *World report on disability 2011*. World Health Organization.

Xia, V. (2017). *What is Mobile First Design? Why It's Important & How To Make It?* Retrieved from https://medium.com/@Vincentxia77/what-is-mobile-first-design-why-its-important-how-to-make-it-7d3cf2e29d00

Xiao, L. (2019). *What designers need to know about mobile accessibility*. Retrieved from https://uxplanet.org/what-designers-need-to-know-about-mobile-accessibility-9f6360f53f38

Xie, H. I. (2008). Users' evaluation of digital libraries (DLs): Their uses, their criteria, and their assessment. *Information Processing & Management, 44*(3), 1346–1373. Advance online publication. doi:10.1016/j.ipm.2007.10.003

Yamada, T. (2021). On the Spectrum of Communication: Locating the Use of New Media in the 2020 COVID-19 Emergency Response. In Handbook of Research on New Media Applications in Public Relations and Advertising (pp. 422-432). IGI Global.

Yan, P., & Guo, J. (2010). The research of web usability design. *2010 The 2nd International Conference on Computer and Automation Engineering, ICCAE 2010*. 10.1109/ICCAE.2010.5451619

Yang, C. Q., Wu, T., & Liao, Y. (2014). Evaluation for the Location Selection of Airport based on WLSM-TOPSIS Method. *Applied Mechanics and Materials, 548-549*(548), 1823–1827. doi:10.4028/www.scientific.net/AMM.548-549.1823

Yerlikaya, Z., & Onay Durdu, P. (2017). Evaluation of Accessibility of University Websites: A Case from Turkey. *International Conference on Human-Computer Interaction*, 663-668. 10.1007/978-3-319-58753-0_94

Yesilada, Y., Brajnik, G., & Harper, S. (2009). How much does expertise matter? A barrier walkthrough study with experts and non-experts. *Proceedings of the 11th International ACM SIGACCESS Conference on computers and accessibility*, 203-210.

Yesilada, Y., Brajnik, G., Vigo, M., & Harper, S. (2012). Understanding web accessibility and its drivers. *Proceedings of the international cross-disciplinary conference on web accessibility*, 1-9.

Yesilada, Y., Chuter, A., & Henry, S. L. (2013). *Shared web experiences: Barriers common to mobile device users and people with disabilities.* http://www. w3. org/WAI

Yesilada, Y., Chuter, A., & Henry, S. L. (2013). Shared web experiences: Barriers common to mobile device users and people with disabilities. *W3C Web Accessibility Initiative.* Http://Www. W3. Org/WAI

Yesilada, Y., Brajnik, G., Vigo, M., & Harper, S. (2012). Understanding web accessibility and its drivers. *Proceedings of the International Cross-Disciplinary Conference on Web Accessibility,* 1–9.

Yılmaz, M. (2015). Okul kütüphanecisinin matematiksel yöntem ile seçimi: OWA (Sıralı Ağırlıklandırılmış Ortalama). *Millî Eğitim, 208,* 200–217.

Youngblood, N. E., & Mackiewicz, J. (2012). A usability analysis of municipal government website home pages in Alabama. *Government Information Quarterly, 29*(4), 582–588.

Youngblood, N. E., & Youngblood, S. A. (2013). User experience and accessibility: An analysis of county web portals. *Journal of Usability Studies, 9*(1).

Yu, D. X., & Parmanto, B. (2011). US state government websites demonstrate better in terms of accessibility compared to federal government and commercial websites. *Government Information Quarterly, 28*(4), 484–490.

Yuma, M., & Vitaly, K. (2015). Evaluation of Web Vulnerability Scanners. *The 8th IEEE International Conference on Intelligent Data Acquisition and Advanced Computing Systems: Technology and Applications.*

Yu, N., & Huang, Y. T. (2020). Important Factors Affecting User Experience Design and Satisfaction of a Mobile Health App - A Case Study of Daily Yoga App. *International Journal of Environmental Research and Public Health, 17*(19), 1–16. doi:10.3390/ijerph17196967 PMID:32977635

Zaphiris, P., & Ellis, R. D. (2001). *Website usability and content accessibility of the top USA universities.* WebNet 2001 Conference, Orlando, FL. https://ktisis.cut.ac.cy/handle/10488/5263

Zaphiris, P., & Ellis, R. D. (2001). Website usability and content accessibility of the top USA universities. *Proceedings of WebNet 2001 Conference.*

Zaphiris, P., & Ellis, R. D. (2001). Website usability and content accessibility of the top USA universities. *Proceedings of WebNet 2001 World Conference on the WWW and Internet (WebNet),* 1380-1385.

Zeng, X. (2004). Evaluation and enhancement of web content accessibility for persons with disabilities (Doctoral Dissertation, University of Pittsburgh, 2004). *Dissertation Abstracts International, 65*(8), 8.

Zhang, Z., Shu, L., Zhu, C., & Mukherjee, M. (2018). A Short Review on Sleep Scheduling Mechanism in Wireless Sensor Networks. In Quality, Reliability, Security and Robustness in Heterogeneous Systems. QShine 2017. Lecture Notes of the Institute for Computer Sciences, Social Informatics and Telecommunications Engineering, vol 234. Springer. doi:10.1007/978-3-319-78078-8_7

Zhang, M., Wang, C., Bu, J., Li, L., & Yu, Z. (2017). An optimal sampling method for web accessibility quantitative metric and its online extension. *Internet Research*, 27(5), 1190–1208. doi:10.1108/IntR-07-2016-0205

Zhang, M., Wang, C., Bu, J., Yu, Z., Lu, Y., Zhang, R., & Chen, C. (2015). An optimal sampling method for web accessibility quantitative metric. *Proceedings of the 12th Web for All Conference*, 1–4. 10.1145/2745555.2746663

Zhang, Y. (2010). Developing a holistic model for digital library evaluation. *Journal of the American Society for Information Science and Technology*, 61(1), 88–110. Advance online publication. doi:10.1002/asi.21220

About the Contributors

Yakup Akgül Ph.D., Associate Professor of Management Information Systems. He studied the Department of Information Management at the University of Hacettepe, Ankara (Turkey), from which he graduated in 2001. He received a Master's (2010) and Ph.D. (2015) in Business Administration at Süleyman Demirel University, Isparta, Turkey. He works as an Assoc. Prof. at the Alanya Alaaddin Keykubat University, Alanya/ANTALYA, Turkey. He currently working on research projects on web accessibility, usability, technology acceptance, human-computer interaction, artificial intelligence, neural networks, deep learning.

* * *

Fernando Luís Almeida has a Ph.D. in Computer Science Engineering from the Faculty of Engineering of University of Porto (FEUP). He also holds an MSc in Innovation and Entrepreneurship and in Informatics Engineering from FEUP. He has around 10 years of teaching experience at higher education levels in the field of computer science and management. He has also worked for 15 years in several positions as a software engineer and project manager for large organizations and research centers like Critical Software, CICA/SEF, INESC TEC, and ISR Porto. He is a founder member of the International Association of Innovation Professionals and he is involved in the development of the US TAG group for ISO 56000 (Innovation Management). His current research areas include innovation policies, entrepreneurship, software development, and decision support systems.

Zehra Altuntaş graduated from Kocaeli University, Department of Computer Engineering with a bachelor's degree. She received her master's degree in 2020 from Kocaeli University Department of Computer Engineering program. She worked as a programmer at Kocaeli University department of Information Technology between 2011-2019. Since 2019, she has been working in Turkish Higher Education Quality Council as a computer engineer. Her research focuses on User Experience, website usability, website accessibility.

Yakup Arı is an Assistant Professor in the Department of Economics at Alanya Alaaddin Keykubat University. Having graduated with a bachelor's degree in Mathematics, he pursued an MBA degree in Finance and a PhD degree in Financial Economics – all of which at Yeditepe University with full scholarships. He worked as a statistical consultant at several private consultancy firms in Istanbul. He teaches courses in time series analysis, mathematical economics, technical analysis, probability and statistics, biostatistics and econometrics. His primary research interest lies in the area of time series analysis, Lévy driven stochastic processes, the Bayesian approach in statistics and econometrics, in addition to statistical methods in engineering and social sciences.

Sihem Ben Saad is an assistant professor in Marketing at Carthage Business School, the University of Tunis Carthage, Tunisia. She holds a Ph.D. diploma from the Institute of Higher Business Studies of Carthage (IHEC Carthage). Her teaching areas are introduction to marketing, consumer behavior, project management, entrepreneurship and corporate culture. She also taught at Higher School of Communications of Tunis (Supcom Tunis), Higher Institute of Computer Science (ISI Tunis), and Higher Institute of Technological Studies of Communications of Tunis (ISET'COM). She presented papers at national and international conferences, such as the Tunisian Association of Marketing (ATM), the French Association of Marketing (AFM). Her current research activities include digital marketing and child behavior.

Nuno Bernardo has a BSc. in Computer Science Engineering from Higher Polytechnic Institute of Gaya (ISPGaya). He works in the computer industry field, where he is responsible for the development of new applications for Web and mobile platforms. His current research areas include software engineering, human interaction, and Web applications.

Ersin Caglar is currently a senior lecturer at the European University of Lefke. He holds a PhD in Management Information Systems (MIS) from Girne American University. He also obtained his MBA in Business from the European University of Lefke (EUL). He teaches network, computing and information systems courses. His research interest is in the areas of information systems, social media, network security, cloud computing, cryptocurrency and IoT.

Silvia Fajardo-Flores is a Master of Information Technology by Monash University (Australia), PhD of Computer Science by Université Paris 8 Vincennes-Saint-Denis (France). Associate Professor at the School of Telematics in Universidad de Colima, Mexico.

Fredrick Ishengoma is a PhD candidate at the University of Dodoma, College of Informatics, in the department of Information Systems. He holds a Master's degree in Computer and Information Engineering (CIE) from Daegu University, South Korea, and a Bachelor degree in Information and Communication Technology Management (ICTM) from Mzumbe University, Tanzania. His research interests include e-Government, m-Government, social dimensions of ICT, and ICT4D.

Barış Işıldak graduated from Süleyman Demirel University, Faculty of Economics and Administrative Sciences, Department of Business Administration in 2014. He worked as a passenger services agent in the civil aviation sector until 2017. He graduated from the master's degree in Business Administration from Süleyman Demirel Univercity in 2017. He started to work as lecturer at Süleyman Demirel University, Keçiborlu Vocational School in 2017. He is still working as a lecturer in the Department of Transportation Services at Keçiborlu Vocational School of Isparta University of Applied Sciences. His research fields are social-humanities and administrative sciences, production and management of operation, and civil aviation.

Murat Kemal Keleş gained his B.S. degree from Wood Affairs Industrial Engineering Department at Hacettepe University in 1994 with honorary degree. Until 2002, he worked as a production and planning engineer in the private sector. In 2002, he became a lecturer at Suleyman Demirel University in Isparta. He received his M.S. and Ph.D. degrees from the Department of Business Administration of Süleyman Demirel University in 2007 and 2014, respectively. He is currently working at Department of Transportation Service Keçiborlu Vocational School of Isparta University of Applied Sciences as an Assist Prof. Dr. His research areas are multi criteria decision making, production management, civil aviation, marketing, planning, entrepreneurship, Technoparks, Technology Transfer Offices, R &D, and Innovation.

Rúben Lacerda has a BSc. in Computer Science Engineering from Higher Polytechnic Institute of Gaya (ISPGaya). He works in the computer industry field, where he is responsible for the development of new applications for Web and mobile platforms. His current research areas include software engineering and requirements analysis.

Gonca Gokce Menekse Dalveren is currently an assistant professor at the Department of Software Engineering at the Atılım University, Ankara. She holds a Ph.D. degree in Software Engineering from Atılım University in Turkey.

Pınar Onay Durdu graduated from Middle East Technical University (METU), Department of Computer Education and Instructional Technology (CEIT) with a bachelor's degree. She received her master's degree in 2003 from METU CEIT program, and her PhD in Information Systems from METU Informatics Institute. She worked as a research assistant at METU Informatics Institute between 2003-2007. Since 2008, she has been working in Kocaeli University Department of Computer Engineering as a faculty member. Her research focuses on Human-Computer Interaction, User Experience, user interaction, website accessibility, brain-computer interaction, and software engineering.

Aşkın Özdağoğlu, Associate Professor at Dokuz Eylul University, Faculty of Business, Dept. of Business Administration, Division of Production Management and Marketing. In 1999, he graduated from Dokuz Eylul University Faculty of Economics and Administrative Sciences, Department of Business Administration. He gained MSc. in Production Management in 2003 and PhD degree in 2008. Askin Ozdagoglu is still working as Associate Professor at Dokuz Eylul University Faculty of Business, Division of Production Management and Marketing. He is also the member of Systems Thinking Society in Turkey and Production Researches Society in Turkey. His research interests are multi criteria decision making, fuzzy logic, and system dynamics.

Serhat Peker is currently an assistant professor at Department of Management Information Systems in the İzmir Bakircay University, Turkey. He holds a Ph.D. degree in Information Systems from Middle East Technical University in Turkey. His research interests are mainly business intelligence, data science, machine learning and human-computer-interaction. He has been author and reviewer of number of publications in journals and international conference proceedings.

Miguel A. Rodríguez-Ortiz is currently the producer manager of the General Officer of Educational Resources, a lecturer at School of Telematics, and a member of the IHCLab Research Group of the University of Colima, México.

Pedro C. Santana-Mancilla is an Assistant Professor at the School of Telematics at the Universidad de Colima in Mexico. His research interests focus on HCI, ICT for elderly people and Software Engineering. Professor Santana currently serves on the board of the Mexican Association on Human-Computer Interaction (AMexIHC) and has served as an Officer of the Mexican ACM SIGCHI Chapter (CHI-Mexico) for several years.

Ömer Naci Soydemir is studying at Kocaeli University, Department of Computer Engineering. His work is mainly focused on web accessibility evaluations and metrics.

Index

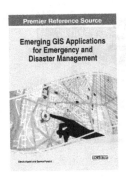

IGI Global Author Services

Providing a high-quality, affordable, and expeditious service, IGI Global's Author Services enable authors to streamline their publishing process, increase chance of acceptance, and adhere to IGI Global's publication standards.

Benefits of Author Services:

- **Professional Service:** All our editors, designers, and translators are experts in their field with years of experience and professional certifications.
- **Quality Guarantee & Certificate:** Each order is returned with a quality guarantee and certificate of professional completion.
- **Timeliness:** All editorial orders have a guaranteed return timeframe of 3-5 business days and translation orders are guaranteed in 7-10 business days.
- **Affordable Pricing:** IGI Global Author Services are competitively priced compared to other industry service providers.
- **APC Reimbursement:** IGI Global authors publishing Open Access (OA) will be able to deduct the cost of editing and other IGI Global author services from their OA APC publishing fee.

Author Services Offered:

English Language Copy Editing
Professional, native English language copy editors improve your manuscript's grammar, spelling, punctuation, terminology, semantics, consistency, flow, formatting, and more.

Scientific & Scholarly Editing
A Ph.D. level review for qualities such as originality and significance, interest to researchers, level of methodology and analysis, coverage of literature, organization, quality of writing, and strengths and weaknesses.

Figure, Table, Chart & Equation Conversions
Work with IGI Global's graphic designers before submission to enhance and design all figures and charts to IGI Global's specific standards for clarity.

Translation
Providing 70 language options, including Simplified and Traditional Chinese, Spanish, Arabic, German, French, and more.

Hear What the Experts Are Saying About IGI Global's Author Services

"Publishing with IGI Global has been *an amazing experience* for me for sharing my research. The *strong academic production* support ensures quality and timely completion." – **Prof. Margaret Niess, Oregon State University, USA**

"The service was *very fast, very thorough, and very helpful* in ensuring our chapter meets the criteria and requirements of the book's editors. I was *quite impressed and happy* with your service." – **Prof. Tom Brinthaupt, Middle Tennessee State University, USA**

Learn More or Get Started Here: For Questions, Contact IGI Global's Customer Service Team at cust@igi-global.com or 717-533-8845

IGI Global
PUBLISHER of TIMELY KNOWLEDGE
www.igi-global.com

Printed in the United States
by Baker & Taylor Publisher Services